LIFE IN THE SPIRIT

THRESHOLDS IN PHILOSOPHY AND THEOLOGY

Jeffrey Bloechl and Kevin Hart, series editors

Philosophy is provoked and enriched by the claims of faith in a revealed God. Theology is stimulated by its contact with the philosophy that proposes to investigate the full range of human experience. At the threshold where they meet, there inevitably arises a discipline of reciprocal interrogation and the promise of mutual enhancement. The works in this series contribute to that discipline and that promise.

LIFE *in the* SPIRIT

TRINITARIAN GRAMMAR

AND PNEUMATIC COMMUNITY

IN HEGEL AND AUGUSTINE

DOUGLAS FINN

University of Notre Dame Press
Notre Dame, Indiana

University of Notre Dame Press
Notre Dame, Indiana 46556
undpress.nd.edu

All Rights Reserved

Copyright © 2016 by University of Notre Dame
Published in the United States of America

Library of Congress Cataloging-in-Publication Data

Finn, Douglas Edward.
 Life in the spirit : Trinitarian grammar and pneumatic community in Hegel and Augustine / Douglas Finn.
   pages cm. — (Thresholds in philosophy and theology)
 Includes bibliographical references and index.
 ISBN 978-0-268-02895-4 (pbk. : alk. paper) — ISBN 0-268-02895-8 (pbk. : alk. paper)
 1. Trinity—History of doctrines. 2. Augustine, Saint, Bishop of Hippo.
 3. Hegel, Georg Wilhelm Friedrich, 1770–1831. 4. Holy Spirit. I. Title.
   BT111.3.F535   2015
   231'.0440922—dc23
                       2015031815

∞ *The paper in this book meets the guidelines for permanence and durability of the Committee on Production Guidelines for Book Longevity of the Council on Library Resources.*

CONTENTS

Abbreviations	vii
Acknowledgments	xi
Introduction	1

PART I. WORD AND SPIRIT

Chapter 1.	The Logic of Christ: Hegel's Christology	21
Chapter 2.	The Rhetoric of Christ: Augustine's Christology	52

PART II. PENTECOST

Chapter 3.	Hegel's Language of Spirit and Its Social Realization	97
Chapter 4.	Augustine: The Holy Spirit and the Transformation of Language	129

PART III. CHURCH

Chapter 5.	Hegel's Spiritual Community	175
Chapter 6.	Augustine and a Catholic Church with Soul?	238
Conclusion		297
Notes		307
Bibliography		365
Index		389

ABBREVIATIONS

Because of the comparative nature and broad intended audience of this work, I have as a rule cited only English translations of Hegel's and Augustine's texts. Where the German or Latin made a difference to my exposition, I have included a reference to the original-language edition used.

In the text and notes I have abbreviated the titles of Augustine's works according to the standards set forth in Allan Fitzgerald, ed., *Augustine through the Ages: An Encyclopedia* (Grand Rapids, MI: Eerdmans, 1999), xxxv–xlii.ABBREVIATIONs of the series' titles from which I draw Augustine's works in either the original language or English translation are as follows:

BA   Bibliothèque augustinienne. Oeuvres de Saint Augustin. Paris: Desclée de Brouwer, 1949–.

CCL   Corpus Christianorum. Series Latina. Turnhout: Brepols, 1953–.

CSEL   Corpus Scriptorum Ecclesiasticorum Latinorum. Vienna: Tempsky, 1865–.

FC   The Fathers of the Church. Edited by R. J. Deferrari. Washington, DC: Catholic University Press, 1947–.

PL   Patrologia Cursus Completus. Series Latina. Edited by J.-P. Migne. Paris: 1844–64.

WSA   The Works of St. Augustine: A Translation for the 21st Century. Edited by J. E. Rotelle. New York: New City Press, 1990–.

Abbreviations of Hegel's works and the English translations used are as follows:

Aes.	*Aesthetics: Lectures on Fine Art.* Translated by T. M. Knox. Oxford: Clarendon Press, 1975.
Enc.	*Logic* (Part I of the *Encyclopedia of the Philosophical Sciences*). Translated by William Wallace. Oxford: Clarendon Press, 1975. = *Logic*
	The Philosophy of Nature (Part II of the *Encyclopedia of the Philosophical Sciences*). Translated by A. V. Miller. Oxford: Clarendon Press, 1970. = *Nature*
	Philosophy of Mind (Part III of the *Encyclopedia of the Philosophical Sciences*). Translated by William Wallace. Zusätze from Boumann's 1845 edition translated by A. V. Miller. Oxford: Clarendon, 1971. = *Mind*
ETW	*Early Theological Writings.* Translated by T. M. Knox. With an Introduction and Fragments translated by Richard Kroner. Chicago: University of Chicago Press, 1948. Includes *The Spirit of Christianity and Its Fate*, 182–301.
LHP	*Lectures on the History of Philosophy: The Lectures of 1825–26.* Edited by Robert F. Brown. Translated by R. F. Brown and J. M. Stewart. Berkeley: University of California Press, 1990.
LPH	*The Philosophy of History.* Translated by J. Sibree. New York: Dover Publications, 1956.
LPR	*Lectures on the Philosophy of Religion.* Edited by Peter C. Hodgson. Translated by R. F. Brown, P. C. Hodgson, and J. M. Stewart. 3 vols. Berkeley: University of California Press, 1984–87.
PR	*Elements of the Philosophy of Right.* Edited by Allen W. Wood. Translated by H. B. Nisbet. Cambridge: Cambridge University Press, 1991.
PS	*Phenomenology of Spirit.* Translated by A. V. Miller. Oxford: Clarendon Press, 1977.

Reason *Lectures on the Philosophy of World History: Introduction.* Translated by H. B. Nisbet. Cambridge: Cambridge University Press, 1975.

Science of Logic *Hegel's Science of Logic.* Translated by A. V. Miller. London: Allen & Unwin, 1969.

ACKNOWLEDGMENTS

My family tells me that this project has taken much too long. It certainly would have taken much longer without the help of many people along the way. I owe immense gratitude to my teachers at Notre Dame: Cyril O'Regan, who first suggested the topic and offered invaluable critique and encouragement throughout the work's composition; John Cavadini, whose influence upon my reading of Augustine should be unmistakable; and Lawrence Cunningham, who always asked helpful questions and reminded those of us who spoke perhaps too boldly that Augustine himself died praying the psalms of lament.

The Kaneb Institute for Teaching and Learning at the University of Notre Dame provided funding and institutional support for my stay at Brown University during the 2010–11 academic year. I am grateful to the Religious Studies Department at Brown and the students in the Religion and Critical Thought area for graciously welcoming me. Special thanks are due my host and mentor at Brown, Thomas Lewis, for all he taught me about Hegel and about teaching.

My friend Andrew Hofer, O.P., has been amazingly helpful with his suggestions for improvement. More significantly, my life would have been greatly impoverished were it not for his friendship. Niki Clements, Jon Sozek, Fannie Bialek, David Lê, and Jessica Wrobleski read early drafts of several chapters, and I am grateful for their feedback. The two anonymous readers at the University of Notre Dame Press offered great encouragement and very useful suggestions for improvement. Finally, Stephen Little and Jeff Bloechl were instrumental in ushering the manuscript through the publishing process. I offer many thanks to all the above. Any flaws that remain in this work are my own.

A few personal notes are also in order. I am glad that my silly dog Clement insisted, quite tenaciously at times, on breaking up the writing with walks and games of fetch. My other dear friend, Augustine Marie Reisenauer, O.P., has offered constant counsel and a listening ear over the years, and I am thankful for his presence in my life. Last and most importantly, I want to express in some meager way my virtually inexpressible feelings of gratitude to my parents, Gary and Joan Finn, for all their love, wisdom, and support. My father is the most generous and loving person I know, and I am ever thankful for the wise lessons he has imparted to me. My mother is loving, patient, sensitive, and wise. Her talents as a mother and grandmother are awe-inspiring. It is to my parents that I dedicate this work.

INTRODUCTION

Stories told about the Holy Spirit are not always happy ones. For some it is a story of loss. They lament the vanishing of a prelapsarian pneumatological tradition, of the richness of spiritual experience that the early Christians had and that found expression in the biblical texts of Luke, Paul, and John. But precisely because the teaching on the Holy Spirit, unlike that of the Father or Son, proved so exclusively reliant upon biblical language and hence resistant to philosophical translation, it was, contends the influential church historian Adolf von Harnack, an "embarrassing" doctrine for an early church bent on making its theology comprehensible to the Greek mind.[1] Consequently, in von Harnack's view, the doctrine of the Holy Spirit never really found a home, variously subsumed as it was into Christology, ecclesiology, and sacramental theology.[2]

A common villain in such accounts of pneumatic decline is Saint Augustine. Of all the church fathers, he is viewed as having most effectively integrated the Holy Spirit into a philosophical doctrine of the Trinity to calamitous effect. His claim that the Holy Spirit proceeds from the Father *and* the Son (*filioque*) and his search for insight into God's triune nature through an inward investigation into the human mind—an investigation in which Augustine describes the Holy Spirit as the bond of love between the Father and the Son—have led interpreters to pin blame upon him for an overly intellectualizing, quasi-modalistic tendency in subsequent Western Trinitarian theology. This tendency, it is claimed, subordinates the

Holy Spirit to Christ, resulting in pneumatic depersonalization and functionalization. Doctrinal domestication then enabled the church to increasingly usurp control of the Spirit by confining the Spirit's operation to the sacraments and a narrowly construed understanding of tradition. Neglect of the Holy Spirit in theology thus meant a real loss to Christian life. The Spirit's wings had been clipped, and Christians were thereby robbed of their freedom.

Another narrative of Spirit is animated not by nostalgia for some lost golden age, but by growth toward a more glorious end. This story has its telos in Hegel's philosophy, where *Geist*, or Spirit, is the governing concept.[3] To be sure, the Hegelian narrative is also, in a way, one of retrieval. In the fragmentary wake of the Enlightenment critique of religion, when the Christian doctrine of the Trinity was put under the knife for its lack of rational coherence and Pietist Lutherans were retreating from doctrinal substance to the safe harbor of Jesus' immediate presence in the heart, Hegel set for himself the grand task of unification and reconciliation. This he attempted to do by reconstructing the Trinity according to his concept of Spirit. Spirit for Hegel is all-encompassing, uniting God and the world, divinity and humanity in a dynamic rational movement of becoming. It is a movement of broad ethical and social import that seeks to take account of the autonomy of reason, the inclinations of the heart, and their changing historical, social, and religious contexts. Spirit is the movement of reason through history toward the achievement of self-conscious freedom in the world.

Consequently, while Hegel viewed his project as a critical retrieval of the truth of Trinitarian doctrine, it was not a retrieval of that truth in either its biblical or traditional doctrinal formulations. In their finite representational form, these Trinitarian articulations remained inadequate to their infinite content. Rather, Hegel assigned those insufficient forms a penultimate historical position in his narrative of divine becoming, an assignment he could make only, of course, from a historical standpoint in which the earlier forms had been sublated and the truth was now manifest in a form commensurate to itself: absolute Spirit.

Against the background of these divergent narratives, this work will tell a different story about the Holy Spirit, one that brings Augustine and Hegel together in a mutually illuminating way. In this story, Augustine contributes not to pneumatology's decline, but rather to its enrichment. At the same time, in this story the expository enrichment Augustine offers is not continuous with, much less progressing toward, a later pneumatic fulfillment in Hegel's philosophy of Spirit. Whereas Hegel, in accordance with his logical pneumatic paradigm, judges the biblical and theological tradition to be inadequate, Augustine will step forward as a voice from the tradition whose biblically grounded pneumatology emerges not in terms of logic and rational necessity, but rather in terms of a rhetorical paradigm that operates according to the standards of fittingness and harmony. The Augustinian paradigm is in fact more adequate to the Christian belief that God has revealed his love for the world through Jesus Christ. And it is more existentially persuasive in individual and communal human experience.

The greatest impediment to this comparative project, however, is that, in his historical treatment of the tradition, Hegel never addresses Augustine directly. In fact, he hardly ever mentions Augustine at all.[4] All the same, there is historical warrant for bringing the two thinkers together around the theme of the Holy Spirit, for what history did not bring together directly, the writing of history immediately after Hegel soon would.

Between 1841 and 1843, the German theologian, scripture scholar, and historian of doctrine Ferdinand Christian Baur published a three-volume work entitled *Die christliche Lehre von der Dreieinigkeit und Menschwerdung Gottes in ihrer geschichtlichen Entwicklung*.[5] Baur there devotes some sixty pages to Augustine's *De Trinitate* and its significance in the development of Trinitarian doctrine. At this point in his career, Baur's work was undeniably governed by the conceptual dynamics of Hegelian *Geist*. He sought to trace the dialectical movement of reason through history. To think historically, according to Baur, is to think through and along with eternal Spirit, whose work is history.[6] More specifically, to trace the historical development of the doctrines of the Trinity and the incarnation is to think through the essential developmental moments of the uniquely Christian concept of God.[7]

In Baur's work, Augustine occupies an intermediate position within a historical movement culminating in Hegel's reformulation of Trinitarian doctrine. Within this developmental scheme, Baur thinks that Augustine makes two advances over earlier Trinitarian theology. First, in response to the potentially subordinationist implications of earlier Trinitarian doctrine, Augustine finds a more adequate conception of the equality between the three persons than any Greek father besides Athanasius.[8] Second, in an effort to avoid a dualism of infinite and finite, which Baur thinks lies at the heart of Arian subordinationism, Augustine attempts to come closer to the objective Trinity by means of analogies derived from observation of the human subject.[9]

Praise of Augustine's contribution to the development of Trinitarian doctrine, however, does not prevent Baur from detecting more fundamental difficulties. First, Baur claims to uncover logical problems inherent to Augustine's Trinitarian grammar. To ward off Arianism, Baur thinks, Augustine denies any substantial difference between the Trinitarian persons and attempts instead to explain the distinction between persons according to the "mediating" concept of relative distinction.[10] However, the relative distinctions Augustine cites appear arbitrary and inessential to Baur and are in his view accompanied by too much emphasis upon the unity of the divine persons. Because Augustine takes the notion of person as given, rather than deducing it necessarily from the concept of God,[11] Augustine cannot explain the distinction between divine persons who are nevertheless equal in substance. Consequently, personal distinction remains, alongside the substantial unity of the divine—a logical contradiction for human *Verstand*. Baur implies a Hegelian solution to the dilemma. Both the Father and the Son ought to be understood as subjects of a necessary movement of double *kenosis* issuing in the self-conscious unity of Spirit. In that way the distinctions between Father, Son, and Spirit are essential and yet formative of one divine person.[12] Through a Hegelian reformulation, Augustine's Trinitarian grammar becomes rational and personal.

Second, Baur finds that Augustine's subjective turn as the means to objective knowledge of the divine betrays a similar mix of progress and stasis. On the one hand, Baur thinks that, by identifying the image of God with the mind remembering, understanding, and loving itself remembering, understanding, and loving God, Augustine has found the divine content adequate to the form of thought.[13] On the other hand, Baur argues that Augustine impedes his own speculative progress by insisting upon a difference between the human and divine minds. There is thus no way for Augustine to proceed from the analogy of the human mind to the doctrine of the triune God. Yet if reason is one and the essence of the human being is rational, then the deepest core of the human being ought to reveal the very essence of God. In this way, Baur claims, the human person as *imago Dei* would become one with that which he or she images, with God himself.[14] But Augustine never identifies the essence of the human being with *Geist*. He does not determine the moments of the mind in a speculative way, as moments of self-actualizing absolute Spirit. Rather, Baur claims, he simply borrows them from empirical psychology.[15]

Baur's assessment of Augustine's Trinitarian theology as well as his suggestion that the latter be reformulated according to a logical paradigm à la Hegel would appear to foreclose any conversation between the two thinkers. Hegel's teleological Trinitarian grammar simply functions too imperiously. Yet if we focus the discussion in terms of spirit, perhaps a space for dialogue starts to open. Because the apparent inadequacy of Augustine's Trinitarian grammar and its image in the human mind originates, in Baur's view, from his inability to conceive a rational, spiritual unity between the finite and infinite, the entire problem could be cast as fundamentally pneumatological.[16] Through an analysis of the Holy Spirit, the contrast between Augustine's rhetorical and Hegel's logical paradigms can emerge and point toward their broader Trinitarian implications.

This possibility for pneumatological dialogue and its broader Trinitarian significance is evident even in explicitly christological texts. From his Hegelian perspective, Baur finds Augustine's Christology problematic, inasmuch as Christ's birth by the Holy Spirit

(Mt 1.18; Lk 1.35) manifests for Augustine the operation of grace in the assumption of Christ's human nature into personal unity with the divine Logos. On Baur's view, the introduction of grace into incarnational doctrine puts an end to all christological speculation,[17] because it impedes a rational, and hence truly spiritual, explanation for the identity of the divine and human in Christ. Yet, as we will see below, the pneumatic operation of grace, when considered in terms of Augustine's image of oral discourse for the incarnation, could also be viewed as witnessing to God's free expression of love toward humankind in Jesus Christ.

A specifically pneumatological plane upon which Baur offers a means of framing a dialogue between Hegel and Augustine comes to the fore in one of his footnotes,[18] where he examines Augustine's *De civitate Dei* 11.24. In that passage Augustine asks whether the Holy Spirit can be considered the goodness of both the Father and the Son. By establishing that the Holy Spirit is the holiness of both the Father and the Son, and that divine holiness is identical to divine goodness, Augustine discovers a warrant for calling the Holy Spirit God's goodness and for finding a trace of the Trinity in creation. The created world derives from the Father, is made through the Word, and in the Holy Spirit is declared to conform to the goodness according to which it was created. Baur thinks that Augustine here stumbles upon a genuinely spiritual truth, that God, in himself absolute goodness, creates the world in the Son, and recognizes his unity with that world in the Spirit.[19]

Augustine then relates the community of believers, the Holy City, to the Trinitarian properties he has just detected in God's creative work: God is that City's origin, enlightenment, and joy (*frui Deo*); God is its existence, its vision, its love.[20] Here Baur's reading is telling: in Augustine's pneumatic *frui Deo* he sees the truth content of *Geist*: God self-consciously and concretely realized in the pneumatic community.[21] Nonetheless, for Augustine this truth content remains at odds with the form in which it is expressed. Love cannot be attributed arbitrarily to the Holy Spirit, but must be derived necessarily from the concept of God.[22] And Baur insists that the concept of God as triune is known through the investigation of thought on the condition that one not sunder the unity of reason, the radical identity of the human and divine minds qua rational. Ultimately, according to Baur, the separation of finite and infinite Spirit leaves Augustine standing still.[23]

Baur's Hegelian reading of Augustine helps set the stage for our project in several ways. It offers not only historical warrant for a Trinitarian comparison between Hegel and Augustine, but also gets that conversation going. However, the way Baur frames the conversation in terms of a teleological narrative assesses Augustine's strengths and weaknesses according to Hegel's logico-historical paradigm of Spirit. From Augustine's end the conversation is closed insofar as his Trinitarian theology is ultimately sublated in Hegel's philosophy. Yet, in spite of the closure intrinsic to Baur's critique, we have also seen an opening for discussion, one that points us in a pneumatological direction. We can now orient that conversation further around the theme of language.

Baur suggests that Augustine's theological language is incompatible with the truth it contains. By continuing to use biblical language for God, language simply given through divine revelation, Augustine is not conscious of the spiritual truth that the post-Hegelian Baur finds latent in Augustine's Trinitarian thought. Absent from Augustine's mind was the category and logical grammar of Spirit, which in uniting form and content, subject and object, thought and being in a dynamic process of divine self-actualization would have enabled him to grasp and explain, rather than merely assert, God's Trinitarian essence.[24] In so doing Augustine would have become conscious of himself as part of the dynamic divine process. Theological language would be one with its object, and the human being, as *imago Dei*, would be one with the God he or she images.

But there is another way to look at the situation. In the face of this Hegelian critique, Augustine's use of biblical language might actually offer a rich and dynamic theology of the Holy Spirit and the Trinity. Hegel claims that his Trinitarian articulation contains biblical and biblically grounded doctrinal language as rationally sublated. But a comparison between his pneumatology and that of Augustine highlights such a lack of narrative correspondence between them and such a general neglect of biblical and traditional Trinitarian language on Hegel's part that it becomes hard to see Hegel as in theological continuity with the biblical and doctrinal tradition. Moreover, Hegel's contraction of pneumatological and Trinitarian language to a dynamic of philosophical rationality issues ultimately in an eschatological closure that, in aiming to secure a freedom from all external authorities, can be interpreted as thereby constricting Christian freedom, defined here as the freedom from idolatrous masters, including oneself, in order to have the freedom for the love of God and neighbor.

The nature of such a critique of Hegel raises the question of what type of comparison will follow. Perhaps it is easiest to state first what this work is not. It is neither a purely philosophical comparison adjudicated by the criteria of reason alone, nor a merely descriptive historical inquiry into the transmission and reception of ideas. Where the latter is concerned we will, to be sure, pay attention to historical influences upon both thinkers for the purposes of ensuring a precise interpretation of their thought and a fair evaluation of their claims. The best reading of Hegel, in fact, may be a religious and theological one.[25] The issue turns on what kind of religious thinker Hegel is. Some Christian thinkers have tried to appropriate Hegelian categories in whole or in part as a means of re-articulating Trinitarian theology,[26] but such appropriation may be founded upon an uncritical acceptance of Hegel's claim to stand in line with and to complete the longer theological tradition. Indeed, the appropriation of Hegel may in fact set one in a completely different line of theological thought and entail, implicitly or explicitly, a critique and possible rejection of the very doctrinal tradition to which one is attempting to contribute.

IF THIS THEOLOGICAL assessment of Hegel's Trinitarian paradigm is to succeed, however, Hegel cannot be permitted to set the terms of the discussion. Otherwise we end up with a teleological narrative like Baur's that assimilates and supersedes Augustine in Hegel's philosophy of Spirit. This is in many ways the problem posed by contemporary Trinitarian theologies that have adopted Hegelian conceptual dynamics. Their attendant reading of the preceding tradition becomes so conditioned by Hegel's appropriation and reconstruction of traditional Christian doctrines and his all-consuming teleological thrust that they are unable to gain an outside perspective from which to assess Hegel's theological adequacy vis-à-vis that same tradition.

Consequently, our analysis of Hegel will be organized thematically around more traditional christological, pneumatological, and ecclesiological categories, such that we can better assess how the teleological force of Hegel's spiritual paradigm subverts and transforms those categories into something completely different. For our purposes this is a necessary means of analysis, yet one not unfair to Hegel. Hegel takes up these various doctrines at one place or another in his mature system, and where we supplement our investigation with material from his earlier texts, in particular from *The Spirit of Christianity and Its Fate*, we will do so only if that material is consistent with his mature position. And, in fact, as we have begun to see in Baur's Hegelian reading of Augustine, to frame the discussion in theological terms makes possible a very rich comparison by offering a more comprehensive sense of Augustine's Trinitarian narrative and its integral relation to his practical concerns with soteriology, ethics, ecclesiology, and history. These are themes which Hegel, in his effort to unite the theoretical and the practical, also treats at length. Our purpose, then, is to assess Hegel's theological adequacy vis-à-vis the longer tradition of Trinitarian theology, and how Augustine, as one representative of the tradition, might respond to the critique of it that is intrinsic to Hegel's Trinitarian thought.

It is conceivable, then, that other figures like Thomas Aquinas or Martin Luther could just as well have been used as theological interlocutors. Nonetheless, in addition to Augustine's foundational influence on the Western theological tradition, including Aquinas and Luther, several other reasons recommend him as Hegel's conversation partner. Not the least of these is Hegel's own general avoidance of Augustine in his works, especially when viewed in light of the fact that such avoidance has not stopped scholars after Hegel from bringing them together in a variety of ways, typically around (1) the question of the self and self-consciousness, especially as a means of knowing the triune God, and (2) the meaning of history and human institutions, as the context in which humans seek to know God.[27]

If in our comparison Augustine's doctrine of the Holy Spirit is to be permitted to emerge in its true richness, however, he must be freed of the interpretive shackles that have led to his villainization by twentieth-century theological commentators. That negative assessment can be understood only against the backdrop of Hegelianism and the reaction of neo-scholasticism against it. Our effort to liberate Augustine from oppressive hermeneutic lenses thus gives further impetus to the project, inasmuch as Hegelian dynamics have colored the way Augustine's Trinitarian theology has been read. Hence this comparison is of value to historically oriented Augustinian studies as well. Indeed, the patristic scholar Lewis Ayres, in the conclusion to his 2004 work on fourth-century Trinitarian theology, gestures toward Hegel's influence upon twentieth-century theology and its interpretation of early Christian Trinitarian theology.[28]

The question Ayres raises proves apt when one considers the history of Augustinian scholarship from Baur onward.[29] Baur and the Augsburg Benedictine abbot Theodor Gangauf, who published the first major monograph on Augustine's *De Trinitate* in 1865, were major exponents of what one could call the Idealist interpretation of Augustine's Trinitarian theology.[30] In general, the Idealist interpretation argued that Augustine's *De Trinitate* conceives of the Trinity as divine self-consciousness. This reading—which in Gangauf's case moves necessarily from the structure of finite human self-consciousness to that of absolute divine self-consciousness—subsequently informed a narrative of the history of philosophy told by such scholars as Dilthey, Windelband, and Charles Taylor.[31] In one form or another, they all recount a story—still prevalent today—of Augustine's influence upon modern theories of subjectivity set forth by the likes of Descartes and Hegel.[32]

Hegel continued to influence interpretation of Augustine negatively through the neoscholastic reaction against modern thought, especially against the integration of German Idealism into theology.[33] Neoscholastics viewed Augustine and his *De Trinitate* as the precursor not to Descartes and Hegel, but rather to Thomas Aquinas and the theological treatise *De Deo trino*.[34] In this line of interpretation, Michael Schmaus was especially influential. Schmaus assumed that Augustine begins with the unity of God rather than with the revelation of the Trinitarian persons in salvation history. Like the Idealists, then, he focused on Augustine's investigation into the human mind. But unlike the Idealists, he adhered to the neoscholastic limitation of human reason, with the result that Augustine's description of the human mind becomes merely a set of psychological observations that serve as an analogy for the Trinity. On both the Idealist and neoscholastic readings, Augustine's Trinity is interpreted as divine self-consciousness. For the neoscholastics, though, this insight is achieved analogically rather than by rational necessity.[35]

The Augustine cast from a neoscholastic mold seems to have been the object of much of the critique leveled at him by twentieth-century systematic theologians. In this regard Colin Gunton is typical. He contends that the disjunct in Augustine's Trinitarian thought between discussion of God *in se* and divine action outward in world history can be attributed in part to Augustine's neglect of the Holy Spirit's role in salvation history. The result, Gunton thinks, is the sundering of the dogmatic treatise *De Deo uno* from *De Deo trino*,[36] a separation likewise decried by Rahner as contributing to the loss of any sense of the Trinity's significance in Christian life.[37] Gunton fears the erosion of a distinctively Trinitarian-shaped Christian life on account of Augustine's model of love for the Holy Spirit. The characterization of the Holy Spirit as the bond of love between the Father and Son is, in Gunton's view, too intellectual and, because conceived primarily as self-love, individualistic. Any operation the Holy Spirit has in the world is reduced to the immanent epistemological level. So, Gunton thinks, the biblical witness to the Spirit's unique eschatological work—transcendent, liberating, community forming—is lost.[38]

Yet, precisely by liberating Augustine from his Hegelian and neoscholastic fetters, we can show the richness of his biblically grounded pneumatology in all its critical, emancipatory, and social import, and in that way help put Guntonesque criticisms to rest. That goal therefore affects our selection of primary Augustinian texts. I will use several of Augustine's well-known works of theology: *De Trinitate*, *De doctrina Christiana*, and *De civitate Dei*. With regard to the *De Trinitate*, I will treat both the ontological-immanent and economic aspects of Augustine's Trinitarian theology, insofar as they mutually inform each other—that is, insofar as he thinks human beings come to know and love the triune God through God's self-revelation in the world.

For this reason, it is imperative that we draw also from *De doctrina Christiana* and *De civitate Dei*. In these works Augustine reflects extensively not only on what God has done in history, but also on the degree to which one can say how and why he has spoken and acted thus. The former text is important because there Augustine sets forth his theory of signs and how it relates to revelation—God's speaking in the world through the incarnation and the words of scripture—and to the way in which humans then speak about divine self-manifestation. In other words, Augustine there explores the creative tension between divine and human language. Moreover, he concludes in *doc. Chr.* that it is love of God and neighbor that imbues that tension with its creativity, a creativity aimed at building up the Christian community.

The ethical-social dynamic of language points us toward *civ. Dei*, where we gain insight into Augustine's thinking on the role of the Christian church in history and society. Because for Augustine it is through the very reading and teaching of scripture that the church is conformed to God's Word and called to be a sacramental witness to the world, we need to consider not only what Augustine theorizes about the character of divine revelation in scripture, but also some of the texts in which he himself interprets scripture and thereby seeks to bring it to bear upon the life of the Christian community. Accordingly, we will also draw from his *In Johannis evangelium tractatus, Enarrationes in Psalmos,* and various pneumatologically relevant homilies.

Our selection of Hegelian texts is guided by similar pneumatological topics, in particular those of language and love. This decision is not, I think, a brute imposition of Augustinian themes onto Hegel, but rather a helpful lens through which to view development within Hegel's thought and how it differs from Augustine's Trinitarian theology. We will look at Hegel's early theological works, in particular *The Spirit of Christianity and Its Fate*, where he attempts to discover the ground of freedom, the unity of God and the world, in a concept of love. In that early work the love proclaimed by Jesus proves inadequate because it leads Jesus and his followers to withdraw from the world in order to maintain their purity. Freedom in the world proves elusive. Nevertheless, Hegel's pursuit of unity and freedom through love is not fruitless, insofar as the dialectical movement of his mature system is already adumbrated in the painful juxtaposition of opposites that love entails. When we turn our attention to the christologically and pneumatologically relevant sections of Hegel's mature works, including *The Phenomenology of Spirit*, the *Encyclopedia of the Philosophical Sciences*, *Aesthetics*, and the *Lectures on the Philosophy of Religion*, we can observe how, although he does not discard the Christian *theologoumenon* of love altogether, he does subordinate it to the dialectical movement of reason (*Vernunft*), which he thinks possesses an explanatory capacity that love does not, and which thus makes rational sense of the otherwise arbitrary divine acts of creation and incarnation.

In this way the movement of reason relates to language. Hegel readily employs the image of oral language and the ephemeral nature of the spoken word to illustrate the dynamism he attributes to Spirit. He uses the dynamics of oral speech to establish the grammar of an all-inclusive Trinitarian narrative containing the intradivine sphere and the world. For him language is not simply a metaphor. Hegelian thought could thus justifiably be interpreted as logos philosophy, as a quest to uncover the reason unifying all of reality.[39] But Hegel exploits the multifarious meanings of *logos*—variously word, speech, or reason—to indicate, on the one hand, the essential ephemerality of the Trinitarian moment of the Son, in which he includes God's creation of and reconciliation with the world, and, on the other, the sublation of the Son in the fullness of Spirit. In this respect, Hegel's Trinitarian understandings of language and love have practical ramifications. Just as the transient word, the kenotic love manifest on the cross, issues in the fullness of spiritual presence in the world, so too for Hegel does the church eventually pass away into society. Accordingly, we will explore the ethical, social, and historical implications of this condition of pneumatic fulfillment—and how they differ from Augustine—in Hegel's mature works mentioned above as well as in his *The Philosophy of History* and the *Elements of the Philosophy of Right*.

The expressive and communal dynamics of the pneumatological themes informing the selection of primary sources also help us structure our investigation. Part I explores how each thinker understands God to speak through the incarnation of the eternal Word. In that regard it contrasts Hegel's logic of Christ to Augustine's rhetoric of Christ. Part II falls under the heading of "Pentecost" broadly conceived. It explores how each thinker understands the human response to the divine Word through the agency of the Holy Spirit. The major question is whether the Spirit, in Hegel's and Augustine's respective Trinitarian narratives, carries forth the message of humility and love spoken in the incarnation, and if so, how. Finally, Part III turns to the types of human community made possible, according to each thinker, by God's entry into language. We will ask after the broader sacramental function of the church in each thinker's work, that is, how through itself and the concrete modes of communication by which it is built up the church witnesses to divine love.

In this way this comparison can contribute to (a) a better understanding of the religious commitments and implications of the Hegelian philosophy of Spirit and (b) a better grasp and stronger appreciation of Augustine's Trinitarian theology, especially the richness of his pneumatology; and in so doing, (c) it can help awaken among those Christian thinkers who would criticize or overlook the Trinitarian thought of the patristic period an awareness of the latter's potential strengths. The premodern, perhaps rather obscure doctrine of the Holy Spirit is vital to comprehending not only Augustine's concept of God, but also his vision of the Christian community and its relationship to broader human society. That vision is one that, in perhaps surprising contrast to Hegel's modern paradigm of *Geist*, strongly affirms the depth and breadth of ensouled and embodied human experience by giving voice to people in their joy and suffering. What is more, it is a vision whereby those experiences of joy and lamentation are not only affirmed but transfigured through the gift of the Holy Spirit, the love of God and neighbor.

PART I

WORD AND SPIRIT

Following the Gospel of John, both Hegel and Augustine develop theologies of Christ as the divine Logos, or Word of God. Both, moreover, exposit their theology of the Word by employing an image of the spoken word. However, variance in the extent to which each thinks the image is applicable across the broader narrative of the Logos results in very different christological paradigms, paradigms which I label Hegel's logic of Christ, on the one hand, and Augustine's rhetoric of Christ, on the other. These paradigms entail different understandings of the relationship between God and the world and between Christ and the Holy Spirit as each Trinitarian person reveals the character of divine love in the world. They bear upon how each thinker conceives of God's speaking and acting in the world and the way in which human beings are called to respond to God's Word, to model themselves individually and communally upon Christ through the inspiration of the Spirit.

By logic I mean that Hegel's Logos speculation links the two basic meanings of the Greek word—reason and speech—in an attempt to discover and explain the meaning of the whole of reality. Hegel employs the image of the transient oral word—spoken only to fade away instantly—to illustrate the mediating and mediated character of the incarnate Word of God, that is, to show on the cross the reality of the opposition between God and the world but also how that opposition has been definitively overcome. Indeed, to show just how seriously God takes the world, Hegel applies the image of oral speech not only to God's operations *ad extra*, but to the inner Trinitarian sphere as well. In this way there is structural continuity and rational transparency between the divine essence and God's work in the world. On Hegel's account, these dynamics of orality are developmental and oriented upward; hence God's action in history is not merely consistent with his divine essence, but in fact defines who he is as God, the God who is love.

Both historically in Hegel's development and systematically in his philosophy, however, the dynamism of his Logos speculation moves beyond love in a way that possibly vitiates the seriousness with which he had tried to infuse it. In his historical development, Hegel gradually supplants an early, yet formative concept of love with that of reason.[1] By the time he arrives at his mature system, he has come to view love as limited by its residual sensuousness and inability to explain the connections between its ostensibly contradictory moments. Systematically too, then, Hegel's dynamic logic strives to sublate the representational form of the Christian religion and advance toward a conceptual mode of expression commensurate to its truth content. Religion, accordingly, gives way to absolute knowledge or philosophy, where form and content, subject and object, God and the world are united in self-conscious freedom. Trinitarianly speaking, the objective Logos of Christ, including the creation and salvation of the world, knows itself as but a passing moment in the rational process or history of divine becoming, of the triune God as absolute Logos, that is, as absolute Spirit.

These features of Hegel's Christology—namely, its teleologically philosophical and pneumatological inflection—affect the manner in which we can compare it to Augustine's understanding of Christ. The latter I label a rhetorical Christology, inasmuch as Augustine also uses oral linguistic imagery, but only for the incarnation. Thus, in contrast to Hegel, there is in Augustine's use of Logos imagery a distinction between the eternal, inner-Trinitarian Word and the incarnate Word spoken in the world. Whereas Hegel seeks to bridge that gap by integrating the dynamism of the spoken word into an all-encompassing concept of reason, Augustine's use of the rhetorical motif is intended to underscore the difference between God and the world, not their rational identity. Augustine frames the incarnation of the eternal Word in terms of fittingness—God speaks fittingly to the problem of sin and death that humans have caused. In this way God's incarnate Word is for Augustine a Word of freedom and love.

Thus, Part I attempts to illustrate this difference between Hegel's logical and Augustine's rhetorical christological paradigms by tracing how they play out across the span of Christ's life and death. The use of such a method, however, brings with it a difficulty that must be explained on material and formal levels. There is a material disparity between the two thinkers' treatments of the historical events in Jesus' life. Hegel, in spite of his attempt to take history seriously through his dynamic logic of becoming, is driven by that same logic, where the historical Christ is concerned, to focus primarily, if not exclusively, upon the definitive moment of negativity within the history of God—Christ's crucifixion—and, moreover, to find in that negativity a dynamism that necessarily moves beyond Christ to the spiritual community. Contrariwise, Augustine, who has been accused of a Platonizing devaluation of humanity's historical existence because of his distinction between divine eternity and the flux of temporality—epitomized in his theology by the restricted utility of oral linguistic imagery—devotes more attention to various events of Christ's life beyond just his death and resurrection. Augustine's Christology, in terms of form, then, is much more biblically based than Hegel's. In Hegelian terminology, Augustine remains on the level of religious representation.

Nevertheless, this incongruity proves important for our comparison because it allows us to discern already on the christological plane (1) differences between the two thinkers at the more fundamental level of Trinitarian theology, in particular where the relationship between Christ and the Holy Spirit is concerned, and (2) some of the practical effects these differences in Trinitarian theology have on the life of the Christian individually and in the church. On the one hand, Hegel's focus on Christ's death leads also to the displacement of Christ by the community. There results less of a sense of Christ as the way for the Christian life, because his individual person has been sublated in the eschatological advent of Spirit and surpassed by believers who appropriate his death and resurrection into their lives. In Augustine, on the other hand, we find a greater emphasis upon the Christian's need to conform him- or herself to Christ within his ecclesial body—a process for which the various events of Christ's life remain definitive in both an exemplary and transformative way. The result, in Augustine's case, is a very different relationship between Christ and the Spirit in the journey of the Christian toward an eschatological end not yet realized.

Chapter 1

THE LOGIC OF CHRIST
Hegel's Christology

LOGOS OF THE FATHER: THE IMMANENT TRINITY

"Immanent Trinity" is not a term Hegel uses. Its hermeneutic utility with regard to Hegel arises not from the traditional contrast drawn between it and the economic Trinity—God's triune operation outward in the temporal world as opposed to the immanent triune relations of the eternal divine nature—but rather from Hegel's principled rejection of the immanent-economic divide and his philosophical reformulation of the relationship between God and the world. As with any part of Hegel's mature philosophical system, talk of the "immanent Trinity" is intelligible only in relation to the whole. Cyril O'Regan, accordingly, contrasts the "immanent Trinity" in Hegel with the "inclusive Trinity"—inclusive insofar as Hegel includes along with the logical inner-Trinitarian foundation the outward acts of creation, redemption, sanctification, and eschatological fulfillment in a single all-encompassing narrative of divine becoming.[1]

With this dynamic theology of growth or development, Hegel strives to conceive of God as at once rational and personal. Toward that end, Hegel understands personality as a result, the fruit of obedience to the Delphic injunction γνῶθι σεαυτόν (Know yourself), and, as such, as the end of an agonic and developmental process.[2] As in the *Bildungsromane* of the late eighteenth century, Hegel conceives of personality as self-conscious subjectivity realized through the struggle with alienation, difference, and death. It is no wonder, then, that Hegel cannot make any sense of the orthodox Trinitarian conception of three persons, or hypostases, in one divine nature. To his mind, there is no escaping tritheism in such a formulation. In the various natural relations applied to it, such as the Father's begetting of the Son, it is the product of sensuously informed picture thinking (*Vorstellung*). For discursive understanding (*Verstand*), which operates according to the principle of noncontradiction, there is no way of conceiving three discrete personalities as one personal God. Additionally, Hegel finds problematic the static nature according to which such personalities are conceptualized. A personality in its immediacy, one that does not go beyond itself toward an other, can never come to know itself, can never attain the full personality of subjectivity; in sum, such immediate personhood remains self-centered and even evil.[3]

To avert such pitfalls, Hegel argues that it is better to consider the Father, Son, and Spirit as moments in the development of the divine to full self-conscious personality. In more philosophical terms, reason (*Vernunft*), as the highest mode of thought, reconciles the contradictions of *Verstand* in the self-actualizing process of the absolute concept (*Begriff*). No longer are Father, Son, and Spirit static personalities placed arbitrarily alongside each other in the eternal godhead. They are, rather, moments whose connection to each other and to the whole can be explained according to the necessary logic of the absolute concept that develops itself out of itself. As absolute and operative according to the logic that it itself is, the divine concept is not merely an aggregate of parts. The whole is contained to varying degrees of explicitness in each of its moments along an ultimately upward developmental trajectory. Accordingly, the moment of the Father, the abstract idea of God, immediate divine subjectivity considered apart from the world, is the most undeveloped and nonetheless contains within it the implicit Trinitarian logic according to which the concept will realize itself. In other words, Hegel situates the entire immanent sphere within the first moment of the "inclusive Trinity," that of the Father.[4]

This shift of the entire immanent Trinity to the moment of the Father, however, does not signal a loss of christological relevance, albeit for a Christology of a very different sort than that of traditional orthodoxy.[5] The "logic of the Father," as it were, sets forth the structural paradigm of Hegel's entire system. The immanent positing and sublating of the second "moment" within the moment of the Father are the dialectical signposts according to which Hegel makes rational sense of the second (inclusive Trinitarian) moment of the Son. Consequently, we must look to the logic of the Father if we are to discern the logic of Christ. Already there, at the level of the immanent divine, Hegel illustrates his Trinitarian logic with the image of the spoken word.

In the abstract medium of immediate thought, the divine concept posits an other over against itself and then immediately sublates this distinction. This purely abstract dynamism takes the form of God's speaking and hearing himself in solitude in the *Phenomenology of Spirit*:

> Essence beholds only its own self in its being-for-self; in this externalization of itself it stays only with itself: the being-for-self that shuts itself out from essence is *essence's knowledge of its own self*. It is the word which, when uttered, leaves behind, externalized and emptied, him who uttered it, but which is as immediately heard, and only this hearing of its own self is the existence of the Word. Thus the distinctions made are immediately resolved as soon as they are made, and are made as soon as they are resolved, and what is true and actual is precisely this immanent circular movement.[6]

Integrating the logic of the spoken word into the immanent divine has a number of important consequences. The logic not only of the immanent divine concept, but also of Hegel's entire system, takes on an intrinsic structure of kenotic dynamism, of self-emptying and pleromatic return.[7] Because the immanent utterance of the

Logos entails the (abstract) emptying into an other and the immediate sublation of that distinction, the two subsequent moments of the Son and Spirit are anticipated in the moment of the Father. The second moment is marked by the transience of an audible word:

> The logical Idea is the Idea itself in its pure essence, the Idea enclosed in simple identity within its Notion prior to its *immediate reflection* [*Scheinen*] in a form-determinateness. Hence logic exhibits the self-movement of the absolute Idea only as the original *word*, which is an *outwardizing* or *utterance* [*Äusserung*], but an utterance that in being has immediately vanished again as something outer [*Äusseres*]; the Idea is, therefore, only in this self-determination of *apprehending itself*; it is in *pure thought*, in which difference is not yet *otherness*.[8]

Against the suspicion that such transitoriness threatens the existence of the Son, Daniel Cook points out that, for Hegel, the divine Logos exists precisely in its expression and immediate evaporation.[9] This point is valid to the extent that spoken language is taken as paradigmatic for the generation of the eternal Logos. But we ought to look closely at the above quotation from *PS*: "It is the word which, when uttered, leaves behind . . . him who uttered it, but which is as immediately heard, and *only this hearing of its own self is the existence of the Word*."[10] The existence of the Logos as a fleeting expression of the divine idea necessarily gives way to a third moment: it is heard and known as its own self by the one who uttered it. The immanent logic of the divine concept suggests, then, that the Word *is* precisely in its self-conscious transcendence in Spirit.

The pneumatic upshot of "linguistic" logic, the sublation, in the concept's immediate self-knowledge, of the distinction posited by the utterance of the Word, also finds expression in *LPR* 3 in terms of love:

> Not only is this distinction implicitly sublated, and not only do we know that, but also it is established that the two distinguished

moments are the same, that this distinction is sublated insofar as it is precisely what posits itself as no distinction at all; hence the one remains present to itself in the other.

That this is so is the Holy Spirit itself, or, expressed in the mode of sensibility, it is eternal love: *the Holy Spirit is eternal love*.[11]

This could be viewed as grounding a perichoretic community of love in the immanent divine and in fact might avoid the Augustinian dilemma of how to call the triune God love and at the same time to appropriate unitive love to the person of the Holy Spirit, since for Hegel the Spirit is identified with the totality of the developmental process.[12] But other passages suggest that the transitoriness of the second moment leads to a circular identity of the first and the last moments at the level of the pure concept, since the second moment, the "Logos[,] has already itself the characteristic of return within itself."[13] It follows that

Insofar as love is present, its *utterance* . . . whereby it is simultaneously brought forth and supported, merely confirm[s] it. What is brought forth is already there: the confirmation of love is a confirmation whereby nothing comes forth save what is already there. . . . The differentiation that the divine life goes through is not an external [process] but must be defined solely as internal, so that the first, the Father, is to be grasped just like the last [the Spirit]. Thus the process is nothing but . . . a play of self-confirmation.[14]

Hegel here seeks the form of love, since as love itself, God must also include its universal form.[15] But by absorbing the logic of the spoken word into the immanent Trinity, into love's universal form, Hegel possibly undermines the genuinely relational foundation of God as love. The immanent Trinity has been reduced to the play of love with itself. It then becomes difficult to accept the seriousness of love in its temporal manifestation on the cross, because of its logical character as particularity giving definitive content to a playful universal form, or to see how any genuine relationality of love is ever established between the infinite and the finite, when the logic according to which it operates is God merely playing.

Indeed, play, by implying a dearth of seriousness and actuality, could be considered the defining aspect of Hegel's immanent Trinity, one which helps clarify the immanent Trinity's distinction over against the economic or inclusive Trinity, that is, the Trinity as it is enacted in salvation history. At the same time, though, play relativizes that distinction inasmuch as, first, the immanent Trinity's character of lack establishes it as the beginning of the inclusive Trinitarian process of divine self-actualization and, second, that logical play anticipates and sets that process in motion. The immanent process of differentiation and self-recognition occurs within the abstract sphere of the divine idea; no real distinction has been drawn, no real other yet produced. But from the perspective of the inclusive Trinity, the expressive movement of distinction and reconciliation contained in the moment of the Father anticipates the moments of the Son and the Spirit. The immanent moments of the Father lay the implicit logical groundwork for the genuine othering of God in finite creation and the self-conscious eschatological reconciliation of infinite and finite in the pneumatic community—the final two moments of the inclusive Trinity.

Creation and the Expression of the Word

As Father, according to Hegel, God utters his Logos and immediately hears himself in abstract self-knowledge; he is love at play with itself. The twofold meaning of Logos, however, as both reason and word, undergirds the all-encompassing dynamism of the divine concept. God is the alpha and the omega, not just the beginning but also the end.[16] These moments are necessarily linked by the self-expressive, self-transcending movement of the Word. The interplay between the two meanings of Logos, then, grounds Hegel's claim that God, as Trinitarian, is the whole eternal process. Furthermore, the expressive logic of the immanent Trinity enables Hegel to define the divine nature—or, rather, enables God to define himself—as inherently revelatory. A God dwelling unchangingly beyond the world cannot, in Hegel's view, be the living God revealed in Christianity. An immobile, otherworldly God cannot be known as the truth because he cannot enter into relationship with others or himself:

> Spirit, if it is thought immediately, simply, and at rest, is not spirit; for spirit's essential [character] is *to be altogether active*. More exactly, it is the activity of *self-manifesting*. Spirit that does not manifest or reveal itself is something dead. "Manifesting" signifies "becoming for an other."[17]

Hegel conceives of God as fully active not in a sense exclusive of all potentiality, but as a necessary developmental process of self-manifestation and actualization, of movement from abstraction and implicitness to the determinate reality and explicit knowledge of who God is as personality. While God as Father is already implicitly active in that revelatory dynamic—an implicit activity whereby Hegel can establish the identity of beginning and end in the process of divine becoming[18]—that immanent movement remains abstract, a universal sans content that has not yet entered into relationship with a genuine other.

Hence God "creates" the world. Hegel's dialectical Trinitarian logic enables him to offer a reason for creation, its rational necessity, inasmuch as the abstract universal posits its other in the finite particularity of the spatio-temporal world. With creation, then, we move to the second Trinitarian moment, that of the Son. As such, creation, too, assumes the character of the spoken word. To be sure, in seeking to avoid a simplistic pantheism, Hegel stresses in *LPR* 3 that the creation of the world as separate from God is not coterminous with the moment of the Son, that is, the moment of divine distinction in general. Rather the self-differentiation of the divine idea lays the logical foundation for the positing of actual difference in the creation of finite reality.[19] Nevertheless, both differentiations are marked by the ephemerality of the audible word, and therefore each has its being precisely in its return, in its pneumatic link of identity with its origin:

> For the world, to be means to have being *only for an instant*, so to speak, but also to sublate this its separation or estrangement from God. It means to return to its origin, to enter into the relationship of spirit, of love—to *be* this relationship of spirit, of love, which is the third element. The second element is, therefore, the process of the world in love by which it *passes over* from fall and separation into reconciliation.[20]

The truth of creation rests, Hegel says immediately beforehand, solely in "its *ideality*."[21] This is not the ideal immanent realm that we have just examined, as if the task were to shun the trappings of the physical world altogether for some spiritual beyond. Rather it is in Spirit, the unity of the ideal universal and the finite particular, for only Spirit as all-encompassing process, as inclusive Trinity—not the abstract ideal or the abstract particular in itself—possesses "genuine actuality."[22]

Implicit in the quotation above is the spoken linguistic character of the created world. For Hegel, the world is revelatory of the divine. But given God's intrinsically revelatory nature, creation is simultaneously definitive of who God is. As revelatory by nature, God is also intrinsically incarnational, and Hegel extends the incarnational rubric to the whole of finite created reality. In this way, Hegel is able to establish a rational continuity between creation and the incarnation. The rational necessity of this link is then made more explicit as Hegel assimilates the fall into the act of creation and hence into the Son's descending incarnational trajectory. Hegel can thereby show the intrinsic rationality of the incarnation's redemptive telos. The rebranding of the fall as a defining moment in the life of the divine is evidenced by the dual implications of the term *Urteil*, which Hegel uses to describe God's act of self-differentiation. It means both primordial division and judgment.[23] Hegel insists that God, while creating the world out of himself—as opposed to ex nihilo—nevertheless gives the world its own independent being.²⁴ Precisely therein consists its evil, its separation from God: in its immediate being for self. However, the evil of creation reaches its peak not in physical nature, but in the other aspect of creation, finite spirit, which can voluntarily deny God as its origin and truth, which can say no to God and yes to itself alone.²⁵

Here we ought to keep in mind that, although our investigation into Hegel's Christology is proceeding according to the logic of Christ, Hegel's philosophy aims at truth and freedom. Accordingly, with respect to creation, Hegel claims that only a free being can release and acknowledge another as free. The creation of a free and independent world is God's own free self-determination.²⁶ Yet for Hegel this cannot be a purely formal freedom devoid of objective content; such a freedom is immediate, subjectivistic, and at bottom selfish. Lacking in objective shape, moreover, such a freedom eludes rational conception. As such it remains sundered from the truth and excludes any genuinely free relationship grounded therein. For Hegel the true freedom of creation, as both subjective and objective genitive, is an end, eschatologically achieved and hence initially only implicit. It is no surprise, then, that immediately after stressing God's free creation, Hegel asserts that the "truth of the world is only its *ideality*."²⁷ Hegel locates this ideal truth in love, in the third moment of the Spirit, where the distinction between the first two moments, God and the world, God and humanity, has been sublated and the world is now elevated, that is, known in its identity with its origin. This means that freedom and truth obtain in the world only through self-sacrifice, through the kenotic movement beyond oneself toward another in love.

Like the freedom in which God creates the world, so the goodness of creation is realized eschatologically. This is for our purposes most usefully seen in Hegel's treatment of that element of creation capable of knowing God and hence also of rejecting him most evilly: finite spirit. Humanity's goodness, like that of all creation, is eschatological. When scripture speaks of human beings as made in the image of God, Hegel interprets this to indicate their implicit goodness, which becomes explicit only through sacrifice of self and self-conscious return in truth and freedom.[28] That is, Hegel speaks of an implicit goodness that is actualized only in humanity's explicit recognition of its fundamental identity with the divine. Consequently, this developmental logic issues in an *imago Dei* that could just as well be relabeled an *imago Spiritus*. Only to the extent that the third moment of Hegel's Trinitarian grammar recollects the first two moments as the presupposition of its realization could Hegel's *imago Dei* be said to be an image of the whole Trinity. In this regard he differs from Augustine, for whom the image of God in the human being is an image of the eternally triune God, not just Christ or the Holy Spirit.[29]

The eschatological "postponement" of human goodness enables Hegel to make sense of human evil. He levels critique at his contemporaries who, he thinks, naively claim that human beings are good by nature.[30] Such a view fails to see the pedagogical fact that knowledge—in this case, knowledge of self as made in the image of God—arises only by passing through difference, the negative, death.[31] The correlate, then, to the claim of implicit human goodness is Hegel's assertion that humanity is by nature evil. This view emerges in his interpretation of the fall narrative in Gn 3. Whereas Augustine, as well as Hegel's more proximate predecessor Kant, diagnoses radical human evil in a corruption of the will, Hegel's analysis proceeds according to the dynamics of knowledge.[32] Just as the Trinitarian moment of the Father, so humankind's initial innocence is viewed by Hegel as a deficiency akin to ignorance.[33] Humanity, as self-conscious spirit, is something one must become.[34] But knowledge of oneself requires the positing of distinction: I am this, not that. For Hegel it is this necessary drawing of distinctions that constitutes humanity's fall. Yet it is this lapsarian division that also makes reconciliation with God possible. Distinction is necessary to come to know one's self, but also in order to know oneself as identical to the divine. For this reason, Hegel claims that knowledge is at once a wound and its own cure.[35] He can thereby argue for the rational necessity of the fall, rather than considering it a contingent occurrence of the human will that calls divine providence into question. Fallen humanity can be located in the second moment of Hegel's Trinitarian logic, that of the Logos spoken, posited as distinct from the God who utters it. But for Hegel this word—here finite spirit as the expression of infinite Spirit—is comprehended only when it is heard and taken up into the mind (*Geist*), when it returns to its origin in Spirit (*Geist*). It is, moreover, comprehended in its truth only when it is recognized in the unity of spirit, when Spirit comes to know itself through its other.

THE BIRTH OF THE WORD—THE BIRTH OF THE SPIRIT

Thus, as Hegel renders the Christian narrative, God speaks to human beings through his incarnate Word, to call them to be in union with him. Because this divine-human unity is dialectical or spiritual, an identity in nonidentity—or, put in terms of love, a finding of oneself in the other—God must himself enter into that otherness to the fullest extent. Hegel's logic consequently necessitates the singular historical appearance of the God-human savior, with all the contingent historical trappings that would attach to such an appearance. But because it is a manifestation of divine love, in which the finite world is to be known preeminently in its rational truth, this appearance likewise dictates the renunciation of an errant attention to the contingent and hence unimportant historical details of that appearance. That is not to say that Hegel overlooks or avoids events from the life of Christ. But his treatment of them is intended to show that their very form drives toward rational sublation in Spirit.

Consider the virgin birth of Christ. The objective event itself does not really attract Hegel's attention. This stems in part from the fact that he rejects a concept of miracle as a supernatural intervention into the world. What is miraculous for Hegel is the rational intelligibility of nature and history.[36] However, inquiry into the external details of Christ's birth, or any other contingent historical facts for that matter, distracts from what is central to the revelation of Christ: "So regarded, the question is asked, What are we to make of his birth, his Father and Mother, his early domestic relations, his miracles, etc.?—*i.e.* What is he *unspiritually* regarded? . . . Make of Christ what you will, exegetically, critically, historically . . . the only concerning question is: What is the Idea or the Truth in and for itself?"[37] In this passage Hegel explicitly attempts to insulate the divine revelation in Christ from rationalist historical-critical exegesis of the Gospels, whose errant focus on external details, at best, reduces Christ to a good moral teacher and role model like Socrates or, at worst, endeavors to destroy Christian faith through the excavation of unsavory motives and acts. Either way one illicitly attempts to cross Lessing's ditch from contingent historical fact to rational truth, as if the moral exemplarity or degeneracy of a teacher could prove or disprove the truthfulness of what he or she teaches. Such a position, by ascribing an eternal, rational value to the contingent qua contingent, effectively maintains the distinction between God and the world by blinding itself to the fact that the finite has value only insofar as it is a moment in the self-revelation of the infinite divine concept. That is, the only licit crossing of Lessing's ditch is for Hegel the one that Spirit itself enacts. The corollary of this spiritual revelation, however, is that the finite is but a moment of infinite Spirit. With regard to Christ, then, it is in Hegel's view equally mistaken to ascribe spiritual value to the external aspects of his historical existence, because the truth of divine-human identity revealed objectively in Christ becomes actually infinite only when it is appropriated subjectively by the members of the spiritual community, when human beings know not only Christ but also themselves as identical with the divine.[38]

According to Hegel, then, Spirit freely determines itself according to a double negativity that necessitates, on the one hand, the singular historical incarnation of God and, on the other, that the singularity of the incarnate savior be sublated in the concrete universality of the spiritual community. The former incarnational trajectory is aimed at ensuring that God is truly infinite and does not remain in pure thought alone. God must appear as an individual who can be seen and felt. But this sensuous immediacy must ultimately be grounded in rational truth, lest it fall into the abyss of arbitrary subjectivity or mechanistic dependence upon external objects. Hence feeling must be transfigured into the universality of Spirit.

Yet Hegel, in integrating this incarnational moment into his logic of Spirit, recognizes that human beings learn about the world around them through their senses. In his *Aesthetics*, he thus finds a necessary incarnational warrant for the use of art in Christianity.[39] Art speaks to the human heart and can arouse the feeling of reconciliation with God.[40] Consequently, it is especially well suited to revealing that "God is love."[41] At the same time, though, because art operates on the level of feeling, Hegel senses its limitation: "The absolute Spirit is, as spirit, not an immediate topic for art."[42] It is within this context of Christian art, with all its revelatory potential and limitation, that we find a christologically and pneumatologically telling passage on the significance of Jesus' mother Mary and her maternal love.

Hegel considers romantic art to be the properly Christian art. The content that it seeks to depict in its religious milieu is love. However, it assumes the "truly ideal configuration" of that love only when it "expresses the *affirmative* immediate reconciliation of the spirit."[43] Because that reconciliation is achieved only by passing through the negative, through suffering and death, the first object of romantic art is, accordingly, the salutary Christ-event, the unity of God and humankind in a single individual.[44] The artist faces a challenge, though, in depicting Christ in the various events of his life, because "Christ should have on the one hand subjective personality and *individuality*, and, on the other, inwardness and pure *universal* spirituality."[45] As the manifestation of divine love, moreover, Christ must be depicted not only as individual subjectivity, for whom love might take only the restricted form of a romantic relationship or friendship, but even more so as the manifestation of universal love present in the form of feeling.[46] It requires great skill to combine these two extremes of divine love artistically.[47]

The challenge of depicting the love of God in the form of the individual Christ leads Hegel to conclude that "the most accessible topic for art is Mary's love, *maternal love*, the most successful object of the religious imagination of romantic art."[48] In Mary's maternal love Hegel finds an image of Spirit appropriate to the sphere of art.[49] It is both human and spiritual, marked not by sensuous desire, but by the unity of an organic connection. This natural connection between mother and son is at the same time a spiritual transcendence, a feeling of union with God:

> In the child which she conceived and then bore in travail, Mary has the complete knowledge and feeling of herself; and the same child, blood of her blood, stands all the same high above her, and nevertheless this higher being belongs to her and is the object in which she forgets and maintains herself. The natural depth of feeling in the mother's love is altogether spiritualized; it has the divine as its proper content, but this spirituality remains lowly and unaware, marvellously penetrated by natural oneness and human feeling.[50]

Faced with the death of her son, Mary too suffers grief in her love. But hers is not a grief issuing from having truly moved outside oneself and faced the negativity of one's existence on one's own.[51] There is therefore something immediate and innocent about Mary's love on Hegel's reading.[52] The reconciliation it manifests is undeveloped and hence not really good either.

In the sphere of art, Mary's maternal love is most adequate to Spirit in that it shows God as love. But this depiction of divine love appeals to the heart, where "this subjective existence as feeling . . . is not compelled to explain itself to the length of complete clarity."[53] Love must ultimately give way to reason, to Spirit, which can explain, can "reveal its content, bringing it into consciousness in its determinacy and universality . . . unfolding . . . all the ramifications which its wealth contains."[54] For a period of Christian history, Hegel argues, Mary's love was "worshipped and represented" as one of the sacred objects of faith. But religion must advance beyond sensuous immediacy and representational thought. The religious community must come to know the movement of Spirit through the negativity of death as its own kenotic movement. Otherwise, it remains divided, feeling its reconciliation with God in the heart, but not in actuality. Until then, the living, universal Spirit has not yet been born. The Virgin Mary and the virgin birth do not represent real unity with God, but persisting division standing in the way of rational freedom:

> Just as the *individual* divine Man has a father *in principle* and only an *actual* mother, so too the universal divine man, the community, has for its father its own doing and knowing, but for its mother, eternal love which it only *feels*, but does not behold in its consciousness as an actual, immediate *object*. Its reconciliation, therefore, is in its heart, but its consciousness is still divided against itself and its actual world is still disrupted.[55]

Only when Spirit comes to know itself in the conceptual language of philosophy, shorn of the vestiges of sensuousness, is the truth freely attained. However, a step in this direction, Hegel thinks, had already been taken historically with the Reformation and the sublation of virgin love that has not yet faced the negativity of the world and been reconciled to it in Spirit: "and so, after all, in Protestantism, in contrast to mariolatry in art and in faith, the Holy Spirit and the inner mediation of the Spirit has become the higher truth."[56] Hegel's hermeneutic is essentially shaped by a distinctive pneumatic interpretation of Lutheran Protestantism, one that sees in Catholicism an obsession with sensuous immediacy devoid of subjective appropriation and a tendency to sunder the world into sacred and profane realms.

Baptism in the Jordan

These inadequate elements diagnosed by Hegel in the biblical and Marian traditions and their transcendence in Spirit emerge in greater detail in a passage from *The Spirit of Christianity and Its Fate* where Hegel discusses Jesus' baptism in the Jordan. Despite its early location in the Hegelian corpus, Hegel's account merits our attention because it is linked with several christological and pneumatological features that remain significant throughout his mature system.

In *The Spirit of Christianity* Hegel connects Christ's baptism with his exhortation to the disciples in Mt 28.19 to teach all nations and baptize them in the name of the Father, the Son, and the Holy Spirit. With regard to Mt 28.19, he argues that neither "baptize into" nor "teach" (μαθητεύειν) is limited here to its basic meaning related to ritual purification or the imparting of information. Rather, their connection with the term "name" (ὄνομα), which he interprets as "spirit" or "spiritual relation,"⁵⁷ suggests to him a very real and radical integration of the baptized into the Trinitarian divine life. Βάπτισμα, Hegel argues, essentially "means the entire consecration of spirit and character." The spiritual experience of this consecration is necessary if one is to know God, because, Hegel contends, "God cannot be taught or learned, since he is life and can be apprehended only with life." To be baptized into the name of the Father, Son, and Holy Spirit, to know the triune God, then, is to be filled "with the spiritual relation . . . which connects the One, the modification (separation), and the developed reunification in life and spirit."⁵⁸

It is the Holy Spirit who imparts knowledge of God as triune and who is likewise the relation between Father and Son and between God and the baptized believer. Pneumatic knowledge of and unity with the divine life comes at the end of a dialectical Trinitarian development, in the "developed reunification" of the Spirit. The achievement of this unity, the divinizing link between baptism and Pentecost, is affirmed when Hegel argues, in a gloss on Mt 12.28, that "in the spirit" is equivalent to "as one with God" and then adds: "[Christ] will press upon you with fire and the holy spirit and will fill you with these because when he who is himself filled with the spirit consecrates ἐν πνεύματι (Mk 1.8), he consecrates them also εἰσ πνεῦμα, εἰς ὄνομα (Mt 28.19). What they receive, what comes into them, is nothing other than what is in him."⁵⁹

Following his baptism, the spirit drives Christ into the desert for forty days. This retreat completes his detachment from the world, such that afterwards "he enters the world with confidence but in firm opposition to it."[60] In his later *Lectures on the Philosophy of World History*, Hegel asserts that there has never been a more revolutionary teaching than what one hears in the Gospels.[61] The core of this teaching is the advent of the kingdom of God, which is, as Brito describes, "certainement, à son niveau plus élevé, explication de la nature de Dieu."[62] Hegel offers an eloquent description of it in *The Spirit of Christianity*:

> What Jesus calls the "Kingdom of God" is the living harmony of men, their fellowship in God, it is the development of the divine among men, the relationship with God which they enter through being filled with the Holy Spirit, i.e., that of becoming his sons and living in the harmony of their developed many-sidedness and their entire being and character. In this harmony their many sided consciousness chimes in with one spirit and their many different lives with one life, but, more than this, by its means the partitions against other godlike beings are abolished, and the same living spirit animates the different beings, who therefore are no longer merely similar but one; they make up not a collection but a communion, since they are unified not in a universal ... but through life and through love.[63]

Here it is important to observe the kingdom's thoroughly pneumatic inflection and its attenuating effect upon Hegel's Christology. Hegel underscores the urgency with which Christ proclaims the need to enter into the coming kingdom of God. This urgency results from the newness of the kingdom over against the Roman and Jewish environs, in which humanity remained sundered from God and the world, as well as from the need to attract believers to the new religion.[64] In the earlier *Spirit of Christianity and Its Fate*, this opposition between Christ and the surrounding world had led Hegel to an impasse. There Hegel argues that, once Christ realized that the Jews were obstinately devoted to their distant God and his objective commandments, and thus that they were incapable of receiving the Spirit and grasping the living unity of all humans with

God, he withdrew from the world and could actualize the kingdom of God only in his heart.[65] Christ's inability to reconcile himself with the world, his passivity vis-à-vis the state, affects the fate of his followers as well. After his death, the disciples consolidate their belief in an undeveloped, exclusive love oriented around the individual personality of the resurrected Christ. In so doing, they separate themselves from the world and prevent the full receipt of the Holy Spirit and the realization of God's kingdom on earth.[66] In his later works, however, Hegel is able to reach a solution to this problem in part through a greater understanding of history, in both its eternal divine and temporal registers. Accordingly, in *LPH* he maintains that, in preaching the kingdom, Christ provides the goal or end, but not the form which is commensurate to it and by which it is to be actualized in the world.[67]

In this way Hegel deems Christ's teachings, at least in their shocking revolutionary form, as unsustainable over the long haul.[68] In a move adumbrating the necessary acculturation and domestication of the gospel's radicalness, Hegel argues that Christ's teaching is not and cannot be that of the church.[69] This stems in part from the fact that his preaching appeals to his hearers' sentiments and from the unspiritual character of his followers' minds. But it also derives from the abstract and one-sided universality of Jesus' teaching on the kingdom. Language, for Hegel, is the preeminent sign, because it possesses the ability to break the restrictive shackles of its objects' *Dasein* and make possible a spiritual communication between minds.[70] Language is therefore a universal medium, and teaching, as a linguistic phenomenon, shares in that universality. Accordingly, in Jesus' teaching, the kingdom operates in a universal milieu. Yet because religious language takes the form of representation and is not yet conceptual, its universality has not taken on actual individuality. Even the content of Christ's teaching is at this point still lacking, inasmuch as it gains determinacy only with his death on the cross and is actualized as the concrete reign of God only after Pentecost, indeed, after Spirit has effected a real self-conscious freedom in which the kingdom is reconciled with, rather than opposed to, the world.[71]

The proclamation of the kingdom of God is the universal aspect of God's self-revelation in Christianity. The second aspect is the particular: Christ's life and destiny on the cross, where the content of the kingdom is manifest concretely. Yet only the rational Spirit, first realized in the Christian community through its representational doctrine and cultic practice, and then fully in the conceptual language of philosophy, can grasp the unity of these two moments. Thus, Hegel's pneumaticism implies more than just the need for finding a more spiritual doctrinal form for transmission of Christian truth. At its extreme, it requires the necessary transcendence not only of Christ's historically contingent words, but also of the incarnate Word, Christ's singular personality, as a reality continually informing the life of the believer and the church. For Hegel, the person of Christ is definitive of Christian truth and the communal life to which it gives rise only insofar as he is surpassed in the fullness of Spirit. In *The Spirit of Christianity*, this is the upshot of Christ's baptism and the command to baptize in the name of the Father, Son, and Holy Spirit—into the name, the spiritual relation, into the Spirit who as that relation subsumes the Father and the Son:

> At this moment when Jesus is represented as freed from all worldliness and personality [when he, glorified, instructs his disciples to teach and baptize all nations in the name of the Father, Son, and Holy Spirit], there can less than ever be any thought that his essence is an individuality, a personality. He is among those whose essence is permeated by the Holy Spirit, who are initiated into the divine, whose essence lives in the divine which is now consummated and living in Jesus.[72]

THE CROSS

According to Hegel, the kenosis manifest in Christ's life is not yet complete, because his immediate external singularity remains an "*inwardly reflected* self of *singularity, inwardly* present *subjective* universality,"[73] wherein that abstract universality has not given itself over entirely to its opposite. In Christ's life one sees not only the distinction between the finite and the infinite, but also their implicit unity, a mere possibility for humankind at this point. But for the truth of that unity to be known, God must give up his immediate external particularity in the death of Christ.[74] Thus, the cross makes explicit the double movement of self-emptying (*Entäußerung*) signaled already in Hegel's interpretations of the events in Christ's life: (1) the divine idea's abandonment of abstract infinity in its externalization to the utter limit of finitude in death, and (2) Christ's abandonment of sensible particularity in the transition to spiritual presence.[75]

On the one hand, Christ's death undergirds the incarnation of God as a genuine human being, for this death bears "the sense that Christ was God, the God who had human nature implicit in him. He had it in full, even unto death—and he had it therefore in absolute finitude. . . . This death is the testimony that humanity is in Christ even to the most extreme point."[76] Christ's corpse, now lifeless, is no longer an end in itself, no longer finite spirit able to reject God in its abstract subjectivity. In Hegel's logical terms, death is the negativity of qualitative being, the moment that marks the finitude and mutability of *etwas*. As such it is a limit.[77] But it is, furthermore, a limit in the sphere of reality, not just logic; it is natural negation, a lack of life that is life's limit. The corpse is, it is something, but something determined negatively. It appears immediately as something past. The negativity of being is here temporal and, as such, the explicit manifestation of the incarnation, that God has entered into time, his other, to the fullest.[78] The fact that human finitude was an implicit part of God—in the eternal birth of the Word, in the play of love with itself—means that, in the explicitness of the paradoxical union of divine and human on the cross, "God himself is dead—despair as to any higher truth."[79]

Here the seriousness with which Hegel takes suffering and death reaches its peak. In this way the essential identification of God with death is also revelation of the highest love. Love entails self-renunciation, being for another at the expense of exclusive being for self. It means giving up isolation for relationship and community and only then coming to the truth of one's being. The expression of the highest love, then, occurs at the point of greatest *Entäußerung*, in death. Death, for Hegel, is the negative means by which the shackles of immediacy are broken and subjectivity attains to its truth.[80] As language liberates the thing (*Sache*) from its external immediacy, so in death natural exteriority is transfigured into interior spirituality. Thus, "the meaning attached to death is that through death the human element is stripped away and the divine glory comes into view once more—death is a stripping away of the human, the negative."[81]

In this stripping away, the second movement of divine kenosis is evident: Christ's renunciation of finite particularity. The first movement of self-emptying, God's renunciation of abstract being for self and entry into his other, the world, is determined negatively by God's nonidentity with himself. The second *Entäußerung* reestablishes dialectically the dynamic unity of the infinite and the finite, of God and humankind: "Humanity, the finite, is posited in death itself as a moment of God. . . . The identity of the divine and the human means that God is at home with himself in humanity, in the finite, and in its death this finitude is itself a determination of God."[82] On the cross, then, God does not just act in accord with the love that he already is; rather, that death defines God as love: "Death is love itself; in it absolute love is envisaged."[83] Only through death is the claim "God is love" (1 Jn 4.8) actually true. Yet precisely in the seriousness of love, in its definition of the divine, Christ's death is relativized as a necessary, albeit passing, moment: "The death of God is *infinite* negation, and God maintains himself in death, so that this process is rather a putting to death of death, a resurrection into life."[84] In this way Hegel can situate the cross at the heart of the Trinity.[85] The God whose inner life is a mere play of love with itself is known as actual love; the Father and the Son are known in their dialectical unity as absolute Spirit.[86]

Suffering and death define who God is for Hegel. Far from devaluing suffering and death as mere appearance or accident, Hegel views the negative as an essential moment of reality, one that gives shape to love and, even more importantly, makes possible the discernment of the Logos in all things. Croce thus argues against the assessment of Hegel's philosophy as naively optimistic: "Hegel cancels neither the evil nor the ugly . . . *nothing could be more alien to his conception of reality, so dramatic, and in a certain sense so tragic*. What he sets himself to do is to understand the function of evil and of error; and to understand it as evil and as error is surely not to deny it as such, but rather to strengthen it."[87] To be sure, Hegel has a point when he argues that to gesture toward God's providential plan in history and then to deny that humans can know that plan ultimately leaves one empty handed. And it is easy to see how a vain word like "providence" could be insulting especially to those in the midst of suffering. But Hegel is not concerned with such personal suffering.[88] The cross, in Hegel's account, explains a universal, rational end, God's reconciliation with himself through the achievement of freedom in modern history, and thus there is a way in which Hegel simply cannot account for the magnitude of suffering history has witnessed on its way to that goal. By making the self-legitimating pneumatic perspective normative and rejecting the moral appeals of the particular human being as contingent and arbitrary, Hegel's theodicy ultimately relinquishes its explanatory character as theodicy.[89] Hegel undermines the centrality of the cross in his own system.[90]

It is here that Augustine's account of evil's unintelligibility might in fact offer a stronger account of evil in its radicalness. Augustine, too, entertains no illusions about the misery and suffering of the world. One need only consult the latter chapters of *De civitate Dei* to witness his acute sense of the brute ugliness and misery besetting the human condition.[91] However, in contradistinction to Hegel, Augustine underscores evil's inexplicable emergence as distinct from God. He is clear that no words can penetrate and thereby neutralize the primal obscurity of death, which he sees as the paradigmatic consequence of human sin. Death is evil and never good for anyone.[92] The meaning Hegel finds in death for the autonomous rational subject falters in the face of the countless many who find themselves helpless and hopeless in their suffering.

The Logic of Christ: Hegel's Christology 43

For Augustine, by contrast, the cross shows that God can overcome evil, can transform suffering and death, and hence through faith in God's gift and promise of salvation, one can have hope even in the midst of a suffering that is undeniably real.

Because the cross is marked for Hegel by its double negativity, at once the moment of death and life, some commentators have noted similarities to Luther's *theologia crucis*.[93] But stark differences remain. Although we cannot equate Augustine's account of the cross to Luther's *theologia crucis*, a brief comparison of Hegel with Luther on this point would be helpful in working out some of the defining characteristics of Hegel's Christology, which will, in turn, be very different from that of Augustine.

The cross, for Luther, highlights the thoroughly negative character of suffering and death, the nothingness of sinful humanity over against God. Christ hangs there dying in utter humiliation, abandoned by God. Such weakness seems to be the last place God would show himself. Yet there God shows himself in his hiddenness, not in accordance with human expectations, but to faith that, in negating human claims to wisdom and power, opens itself to God's gift of grace. The *theologia crucis* thus depends upon a clear distinction between God and the world. Precisely this distinction undergirds the grace manifest on the cross. It is integral for Luther that the paradox of the cross is not mediated away. The simultaneity of life and death remains. Suffering remains suffering, and God is known to faith only as hidden in suffering. As a paradox and scandal, the cross continually undermines human efforts to save oneself. It marks the precarious position the human being occupies in this life and the constant need to open oneself to God's grace in faith, hope, and love.[94]

Several different features emerge in Hegel's treatment of the cross. He takes death seriously by integrating it into the rational essence of reality. The result is a theology of radical divine pathos that turns on a monophysite Christology. Hegel fears that a distinction between Christ's divine and human natures falls back into a reflective mode of thought that cannot think God and the world together and that, in shielding God from suffering and death, robs the cross of its ability to give suffering any real meaning.[95] Accordingly, the reconciliation that the cross effects does not merely set humanity in a new relationship to an unchanging God, but rather radically unites the human with the divine and in so doing reconciles God with himself.

The human narrative, in Hegel's account, has been situated into the broader development of Spirit, which determines itself out of itself. As a consequence, one might point to the gift character of Hegel's doctrine of reconciliation.[96] However, that same narrative is one that moves beyond the cross of Christ, beyond God's radical absence, to spiritual presence in the kingdom of God.[97] This unity of divine and human spirit, known through the death of external particularity on the cross, results in fact in a subversion of an Augustinian-Lutheran concept of grace. Hegel's theocentric soteriology tends toward a rational, pneumatic telos in which humans come to know the process of reconciliation as their own, inasmuch as they know themselves to be a moment of the divine, a moment in the process of the reconciliation of the divine with itself. In this way Christ's cross fades; his reconciling action belongs in fact to his followers.

Resurrection and Ascension

Because the negativity of the cross in Hegel's narrative is marked by a twofold movement of *Entäußerung*, radical kenosis unto death as well as death's own death unto life, it has been related to Luther's *theologia crucis*. However, in addition to the differences just observed, the mediatory aspect of Hegel's interpretation of the cross suggests what O'Regan calls a sort of paschal "narrative punctuation," a sequence of death, then life. At first glance this might not seem so surprising. Even when taking into consideration the Johannine paschal narrative, in which the cross and resurrection are all part of Christ's glorification, most traditional accounts treat Christ's death, resurrection, and ascension as distinct events. Nonetheless, they are all events attributed to Christ. It is in that regard that Hegel differs. He does not treat the cross and resurrection as an objective christological whole to be appropriated with the help of the Holy Spirit. Rather, Hegel's Trinitarian grammar separates the resurrection from the cross and identifies it with the movement of appropriation itself.[98] In this way Hegel transfers the resurrection from Christ to the Spirit, more precisely, to the appropriating spiritual community. Furthermore, he makes the resurrection immanent among Christ's followers. While still an eschatological good, it is no longer characterized by eschatological distention.

Hegel identifies the resurrection and ascension with the descent of the Holy Spirit upon Christ's followers. However, the Holy Spirit does not just give the faith whereby one grasps the meaning of Christ's death, resurrection, and ascension, but rather actualizes that meaning in the interpretive appropriation itself as a Pentecostal "perspective" on Christ's death:[99] "The history of the resurrection and ascension of Christ to the right hand of God begins at the point where this history receives a spiritual interpretation. That is when it came about that the little community achieved the certainty that God has appeared as a human being."[100] From an empirical, historical standpoint, Hegel identifies the departure announced in Jn 16.7 with Christ's death rather than with a sensible ascension.[101] The resurrection and ascension, as interpretations, are attached to the crucifixion, but as actual obtain only in and through the pneumatically founded Christian community.

It is instructive to observe the way in which Hegel thinks Christ's followers perceive and speak of his death and resurrection. The historian can write about Christ's death. She can then try to document the resurrection in the same way. The former is acceptable, in Hegel's view, but the latter misses the spiritual truth of the resurrection and hence ultimately of Christ's and, indeed, of all suffering and death. Perception of the glorified Christ entails conversion (*Umkehrung*),[102] a conversion from the external Christ to the Holy Spirit. In this respect Brito aptly points out that whereas Hegel's depiction of the death of Christ starts with intuition and moves to *Gedächtnis* by way of *Erinnerung*, his treatment of the resurrection and ascension goes no further than immediate intuition.

For something to become part of history, *Geschichte*, it must have reached the form of *Vorstellung*, which is retained in memory. In Hegel's system, it is at the kenotic extreme of *Vorstellung* that what is real becomes spiritual.[103] From memory it enters into the universal and more spiritual medium of language. Thus, while one can say something about Christ's death, those words falter when one tries to remember and describe the exalted Christ.[104]

Christ's human nature, although it vanishes from immediate sensibility, is not completely destroyed. In Hegel's polyvalent terminology, it is *aufgehoben*—both ended and preserved. Christ's finite human nature comes to an end, is negated, but is, at the limit of that negation, the end of that end, the making in-finite of the finite in absolute love, the exaltation, raising up (*Aufhebung*), of Christ in Spirit. It is thus in the dialectical process of Spirit that the unity of the divine and human natures is affirmed, that the nothingness of the finite in itself is raised up and known in its infinite and universal value.[105]

Faith begins, for Hegel, with the external history of Christ. But that externality is transfigured and glorified in the universality of Spirit.[106] The Spirit testifies to the universal objective content, the eternal divine history into which the particular history of Christ is now understood to fit as a moment in its development. Such is the objective facet of Hegel's spiritualizing interpretation of the ascension: "Essentially the Son is recognized by the community as the one who has been raised to the right hand of God (i.e., that he is essentially a determination for the nature of God itself), not as he who was here in sense experience."[107] To identify Christ as God through the witness of the Spirit, then, is to grasp the fact that the moments implicit in the abstract divine idea, the infinite love at play with itself, have been externalized in Christ's life and death. It is to recognize that divine love, by its very nature, a nature which is intrinsically a process of development, has thus necessarily emptied itself unto its uttermost opposite on the cross. On the cross God has reconciled himself with his other, the world, which constitutes evil most especially in its extreme of natural self-centeredness as finite spirit. In affirming that Christ is God, and conversely that

God is human, the Spirit testifies that God's love is greater than evil, indeed, that, as infinite, divine love encompasses and thereby overcomes evil.

This divine history, the radical union of divine and human, is made objective in the death of Christ and grasped as such through the witness of the Spirit. But inasmuch as it is an object, it is an object for others, for finite spirit. And inasmuch as this divine history is grasped as a universal history in which reconciliation has already been accomplished eternally,[108] it is now known to include each and every individual subject. At Pentecost finite subjectivity knows itself as part of the eternal divine history. The Spirit at Pentecost makes known that reconciliation is already accomplished and thereby enables the subject to undertake an *imitatio Christi*.[109] Hegel's twofold characterization of death as both the limit of finitude and the overcoming of that limit issues in the religious moment of love. Love is the moment of Spirit's self-conscious realization of its universality, wherein the finite, natural will is sacrificed for spiritual inwardness. The finite subject claims the merit of Christ, then, not inasmuch as he or she appeals to an external sacrifice, but rather as the subject puts to death in him- or herself the particular natural will by becoming spirit.[110] To this extent, the *imitatio Christi* lies in individual renunciation, in the realization, mediated by Christ's death, that external, contingent distinctions have no ultimate value, that in one's naturalness one is intrinsically evil. By this inward turn, moreover, the individual overcomes the distinction between him- or herself and others—as Hegel puts it, God looks only at the heart, at the universal aspect of humanity—and can enter into the self-conscious community of faith.[111]

Hegel's pneumatically, communally grounded mimesis, however, eludes the typical debate between an anthropology in which Christ functions as moral exemplar whom humans can freely follow and one in which fallen humanity needs the grace of Christ to be able to follow his example of self-giving love. This mimesis rests on an image theology of radical identity rather than the Augustinian tradition of resemblance or analogy.[112] Given its dynamic teleological thrust, it is an identity possible only because Christ's discrete personality gives way to the Spirit in Hegel's all-encompassing Trinitarian narrative. Christ sacrifices his sensible presence in order that he might be spiritually present in the community. Hegel therefore interprets Mt 18.20 and 28.20, which contain Christ's promises of continued presence with his disciples, by noting, "Christ [is] objective, but in the expressions 'with you,' 'in you,' he is the Holy Spirit."[113] It is the Spirit who realizes this identity in the community conscious of itself in union with God. With the advent of the Holy Spirit, the infinite divine idea becomes actual and takes the shape of the community: "Thus the community itself is the existing Spirit, the Spirit in its existence [*Existenz*], God existing as community."[114]

God's presence in human shape is no longer the particular sensible individual of Christ, but the totality of the community. For Hegel, there is no personal, objective resurrection of Christ. Christ has died sensibly forever.[115] Accordingly there is no future bodily resurrection of the believer guaranteed by Christ's resurrection and promised by the Holy Spirit. Hegel's affirmation of the sensible, finite world does not go to the length of a future bodily resurrection, because in his view such a belief operates in finite imagistic modes of thought that fail to achieve true infinity and presence of Spirit. Hegel thinks that such views devalue the actual world in the hope of transforming it later. Such self-renunciation demands that even the most particularizing aspect of life, my death—the particularity of which leads to the desire for my resurrection, and a future one at that—also be given up. A quotation from *PS* suggests that the transfiguration [*Verklärung*], traditionally conceived as a proleptic vision of the glorified Christ, is hereby also shifted to the auspices of the Spirit present in the community: "Death loses this natural meaning in spiritual self-consciousness ... Death becomes transfigured [*verklärt*] from its immediate meaning, viz. the non-being of this *particular* individual, into the *universality* of the Spirit who dwells in his community, dies in it every day, and is daily resurrected."[116] For Hegel natural death is not done away with. It cannot be. But it is transfigured, as is the particular individual it specifies, by the knowledge of one's rational essence shared and hence realized as infinite by the community, the totality of rational spirits constituting the one universal Spirit. Indeed, just as evil is for Hegel the result of knowledge, so is its transfiguration: "Eternity is not mere duration, as mountains endure. On the contrary, it is *knowing*, and thus understood, it is what spirit is in itself."[117]

Hegel's transfigurative vision consists in the fullness of self-knowledge, of oneself as an autonomous, rational subject able to realize one's essence in the world. The transfiguration is no longer subjectively transformative in its anticipatory orientation toward Christ as both way and goal, but rather in its very appropriation by the spiritual community. Hegel has conflated the transfiguration with the resurrection and the ascension and made it into an intra-historical reality.

The realization of the self-conscious identity of God and humanity enables Hegel to speak of the equality of all human beings in the Spirit, since Christ's death and withdrawal have rendered all external finite distinction valueless. The true and infinite value of the individual is mediated, is known as real only when known objectively, as achieved outside the individual, but precisely through appropriation of this infinite content as achieved in and through that individual and in fact all individuals.[118] In this sense, the renunciation of individual particularity, in imitation of Christ, is for Hegel also the individual's real affirmation as universal and divine. With the transvaluation of values initiated by Christ's death[119]—the dishonor attached to the death of a criminal becomes the means whereby humans come to know the honor of human nature in its unity with divine Spirit—Hegel can, in contrast to Augustine, gesture toward the historical realization of universal justice and knowledge of freedom,[120] a freedom consonant with the necessary logical development of the concept, inasmuch as finite spirit comes to know itself essentially as truth and precisely in this identity with the divine to bring forth this content from itself. Of course, Hegel thinks that knowledge of human equality and freedom remains merely implicit in the early historical development of Christianity. In the historical context of the Roman Empire, Christianity could realize these principles only in the heart, not yet in the world. Such would be the later historical task of the German nations.

HEGEL'S CHRISTOLOGY, AS Logos speculation, is characterized by the conflation of two dynamic processes that fall within the semantic range of the Greek term: (1) the self-transcending character of oral speech, which Hegel sees not only as illustrative of, but also animating (2) an all-encompassing, logically necessary movement of divine self-manifestation. Hegel's particular way of speaking about Christ is intended to make possible the comprehension and explanation of the whole of the finite world and its history through the realization of it as God's own Word, thus as dialectically identical with the infinite.

Against the backdrop of the Trinity as a whole, the effects of this "oral linguistic logic" may be seen across the span of Christ's life and death. Hegel's reconfiguration of the Trinity and Christology according to the dynamics of knowledge brings with it (1) the historical displacement of Christ by the Spirit and a parallel displacement of representative religious accounts of Christ by conceptual language, as well as (2) an attendant pneumatic immanence of the divine in the world and history—not, to be sure, with the advent of Christ or the early Christian church, but, as we shall see in the next few chapters, at a later, post-Reformation and post-Enlightenment Pentecostal moment in the German world. It is in that way and at that moment that Hegel sees real human freedom achieved in the world, a freedom that knows itself as free in accord with its essence, in accord with truth. An external, individual Christ and representative accounts of him must give way if humans are to know themselves and to act in the freedom of unity with God.

This conclusion, however, raises a question that will guide us as we turn now to Augustine. Could it be the case that Augustine's "representational" account of Christ—particularly his account of the Holy Spirit's role in ensuring the grace of Christ's incarnation—in fact guarantees a broader understanding of Christian freedom? Does not Augustine's understanding of freedom avert arbitrariness, inasmuch as it operates in accord with divine love? And does not Augustine's Christology avoid making the divine immanent to such an extent that God is barred from speaking his Word in every time and place, and to such an extent that humans lose the freedom to respond, to witness through their own words and deeds inspired by the love of the Holy Spirit?

Chapter 2

THE RHETORIC OF CHRIST
Augustine's Christology

We have seen how the semantic logic that Hegel employs to link the immanent and inclusive Trinities plays out historically in the various episodes of the christological narrative. In interpreting that narrative, Hegel does more than develop views on the virgin birth or Christ's baptism; he systematically deviates from the traditional representational account by rejecting an insuperable distinction between God and the world and emphasizing pneumatology throughout his own account of Christ. Now by patterning the following analysis of Augustine's Christology upon the previous chapter, we are able to ascertain not only the extent to which Hegel deviates from Augustine's representational account at a theological level, but also the way in which Augustine, by maintaining the distinction between God and the world, is able to develop a stronger Trinitarian relationship between Christ and the Holy Spirit, and in turn to make possible a more comprehensive relationship of love and freedom between the triune God and humankind.

We will examine several Augustinian texts. *De Trinitate* will remain prominent throughout as a resource for determining the relationship between the eternal Word and the incarnate Christ as well as the relationship between Christ and the Holy Spirit. Because we investigate Augustine's use of linguistic imagery for Christ, it is also important to analyze what Augustine says about the relationship of language to the fall and to the building up of human societies. In this regard, we will consult *De Genesi adversus Manicheos*, *Confessiones*, *De civitate Dei*, and *De doctrina Christiana*. Finally, pneumatologically significant descriptions of the events in Christ's life are to be found in his *In Johannis evangelium tractatus* and the *Enchiridion*, in addition to those in *Trin*. In using these different texts, we are able to take account of developments in Augustine's thought that coincide with the Donatist and Pelagian controversies.

Seeking the Face of the Lord

Like Hegel, Augustine employs the language of word and utterance at both the level of the eternal Trinitarian relations and their temporal manifestations. In Augustine's case, though, talk of God's utterance of his Word does not indicate an inherently revelatory divine nature. Nor does the dynamism with which Augustine describes the *imago Dei* in human beings form in any way a definitive moment in his Trinitarian narrative. Augustine seeks to elucidate the Trinity by way of an investigation into an *imago Dei* whose dynamism, animated and qualified throughout by its difference from God, aims at restoration of a genuinely Trinitarian image.

It is not surprising, then, that the prime locus for Augustine's comparison of the divine Word and the mind's inner word, book 15 of *De Trinitate*, is marked at once by its emphasis on the distinction between God and his image as well as by its relentless pursuit of insight into the Trinity. Augustine appeals at the outset of book 15 to the guiding precept of the entire work: *Seek his face always* (Ps 105.4).[1] Against those who would deride as futile the effort to understand the incomprehensible, Augustine answers that, in the case of God, there is in fact a dialectical relation of seeking and finding in the Christian life:

> Why then look for something when you have comprehended the incomprehensibility of what you are looking for, if not

because you should not give up the search as long as you are making progress in your inquiry into things incomprehensible, and because you become better and better by looking for so great a good which is both sought in order to be found and found in order to be sought? It is sought in order to be found all the more delightfully, and it is found in order to be sought all the more avidly.²

Augustine's search has brought him in the course of *Trin.* to an image of the Trinity in the human mind—memory, understanding, and will—and more precisely to the mind as it remembers, understands, and loves itself remembering, understanding, and loving God. Yet Augustine qualifies this achievement:

> So those who see their mind insofar as it can be seen, and in it this trinity which I have discussed ... but do not believe or understand it to be the image of God, see indeed a mirror, but are so far from seeing by the mirror the one who now can only be seen by a mirror, that they do not even know the mirror they see *is* a mirror, that is to say an image.³

Augustine is referring here to 1 Cor 13.12: "We see now through a mirror in an enigma, but then it will be face to face."⁴ This verse, in tandem with Mt 5.8, "Blessed are the pure of heart, for they shall see God,"⁵ constitutes, along with Ps 105.4, perhaps the most influential scripture in *Trin.* and infuses Augustine's portrayal of Christian life with its dynamism.

For Augustine, the basic problem is pride (*superbia*), the ontologically disordered, deep-seated, and often subconscious elevation of the self over God, who as creator and savior ought to be the center of one's existence.⁶ Accordingly, progress in the Christian life gets its start with the humility of faith in and love of God. That is, only by looking at oneself and others through the eyes of faith and by listening with a humble ear to scripture as God's word is one able to know that he or she has been made in the image of God and that through sin this image has been vitiated and needs to be restored. Thus, even the most perceptive philosophical insight into the structure of the human mind is of no salutary benefit if it merely gives reason for self-inflation rather than for submission to the God who said, "Let us make man to our image and likeness" (Gn 1.26).[7] What is more, the fallen state of this image makes it, in Augustine's view, a mirror that reveals only an enigma, as Paul says, an obscure image of God. Only eschatologically will one be able to see God face-to-face, and only, on Augustine's reading of Mt 5.8, if one's heart has been purified in the humility of faith.

Like Hegel, then, Augustine does not separate his Trinitarian theology from soteriological concerns. Similarly, at the anthropological level, the gnoseological and ethical do not make any sense if thought apart from each other. These form interrelated facets of a dynamic and agonic understanding of human being, one that is always conditioned by God's prior movement toward humankind. However, in Augustine's case, the dynamism of agonic anthropology finds its ground and impetus, most decisively, in the thoroughgoing and insuperable distinction between an eternal, unchanging God and finite humanity, but also in fallen humankind's unending struggle in this life to conform itself to God's image, to follow Christ, who is the truth and the way.[8] Gnoseologically, purgative faith—preeminently faith in the historical incarnation, death, and resurrection of Christ—remains, in Augustine's view, determinative throughout this life.[9] Ethically, those justified by faith in Christ's death still struggle in this life against selfish flesh, in the effort to increase and perfect their love according to Christ's example of selflessness.

What is significant is that (1) Augustine never loses sight of the personal Christ at the temporal or the eternal level, since indeed both natures form one person, that (2) this continued focus on the personal existence of Christ is structurally definitive for the Christian life, gnoseologically, ethically, and ecclesially, hence that (3) in his two *formae, servi* and *Dei,* Christ forms the temporal way and the eschatological goal, but that (4) the eschatological postponement of the latter *forma*'s manifestation opens the space in which the Holy Spirit operates, thereby (5) establishing perhaps a more authentically Trinitarian foundation for individual and communal Christian life in the world.

In addition to the purgative role of faith and the eschatological postponement of vision, Augustine offers a more determinative focus on the function of love in the process of restoring the image of God. For Hegel the logical dynamism of knowledge is determinative of love in both its theological and anthropological registers. Augustine, by contrast, holds that the salutary value of knowledge, and of its more restricted form in faith, derives from the orientation of the will, from the love of God and neighbor as opposed to love of self. He consistently follows Paul in maintaining that knowledge without love is without benefit, for, as scripture recounts, even the demons had knowledge of Christ's divinity.[10] This inversion and its soteriological implications shape the way Augustine describes how God has spoken and acted out of love for humankind. Significantly, if the personality of God's Word who has come into the world remains so structurally definitive for Christian life, that is, if Augustine's spirituality, ethics, and ecclesiology are so christologically conditioned, and yet if love determines the salutary value of Christian knowledge, then how do these conditions affect the way the faithful communicate with each other and build up their community around those words and deeds? How are the word and spirit of the Christian community related to God's Word and Holy Spirit? And how can one inquire into the eternal Trinity when its created image is itself so thoroughly enigmatic? Hence Augustine's prayer:

> From myself indeed I understand how wonderful and incomprehensible is your knowledge with which you have made me, seeing that I am not even able to comprehend myself whom you have made; and yet a *fire burns up in my meditation* (Ps 39.3), causing me to seek your face always.[11]

Significant Distinctions: The Word and Words

For Augustine, God's incarnate revelation of himself in time is grounded in the eternal begetting of the divine Word. Augustine therefore seeks to understand the *eternal*—what we would call *immanent*—relationship between the Father and the Son by investigating the production of an *inner* word in the human mind. Marshaling an array of scriptural texts that equate "thinking" and "saying,"[12] he shows the appropriateness of word imagery for human mental processes: "Even if no words are spoken, the man who is thinking is of course uttering in his heart."[13] With regard to internal thought, Johannine linguistic imagery flows together with the otherwise dominant visual metaphor that Augustine derives from his Neoplatonic and Stoic philosophical formation:[14] "When these things happen outwardly through the body, speech is one thing, sight another; but when we think inwardly they are both one and the same."[15] But here we must be clear: Augustine is legitimating word imagery for the mental act of thinking (*cogitare*) and its fruit, a thought (*cogitatio*), and setting this production of an inner word apart from the oral word production one might naturally think of. External communication, Augustine maintains, only constitutes the sign of the thought, or the sign of the word ("*signum . . . verbi*"). The thought itself is more properly referred to as the word.[16]

The distinction between the inner word and external language underscores the former's quality as an image of the divine Word. Augustine elucidates this parallel by way of what Brachtendorf calls the "congruence principle" of truth[17] based on the "Yes, yes; no, no" of Mt 5.37. External language signifies only the knowledge it is intended to convey. But when the inner word is begotten immediately in the mind from the *notitia* of memory, "this knowledge is uttered exactly as it is."[18] Augustine argues that a true word is one that contains what is in memory. Here he finds a similarity between the created image in human beings and God's eternal image in his Son: "In this way this likeness of the made image approaches as far as it can to the likeness of the born image, in which the Son is declared to be substantially like the Father."[19] Just as the Son is consubstantial with the Father, so the inner word is true because it is the knowledge that was contained in memory.[20]

However, the similarity of the image indicates several points of dissimilarity. God's Word is necessarily true,[21] whereas a human being's inner word can be false if the content of memory is deficient. Human beings can acquire knowledge through either empirical or intellectual experience, but they also forget much of what they learn.[22] Moreover, they can think of only one thing at a time. The mind runs back and forth, as it were, from object to object until it strikes upon a true word, yet even that thought lasts only until the mind turns its attention to something else.[23] The human inner word is movable, from one content to another, and mutable, in that the word changes form according to the object toward which it is oriented.[24]

God, however, does not learn through the senses or through himself, let alone forget anything.[25] Moreover, Augustine denies to God any of the discursivity that marks the human mind in this life, since "who could fail to see what a vast dissimilarity there is here to that Word of God which is in the form of God without first being formable and afterward formed, and which could never ever be formless, but is simple form and simply equal to him from whom it is and with whom it is wonderfully co-eternal?"[26] Augustine argues that for this reason the Son is called the Word of God rather than the *cogitatio* or thought of God, inasmuch as the *cogitatio* is characterized by a movement from one object to another.[27] Ultimately, the crux of the distinction between the divine Word and the inner word rests in the simplicity of the eternal Trinity. God does not *have* true knowledge and a true word as a human being does. Rather, God *is* knowledge and truth eternally and unchangingly.

This distinction is crucial for several reasons. Like Hegel, Augustine relates the discursiveness of the human mind to the fall. However, for Augustine, the multiplicity and fragmentation of the mind is understood as an undesirable consequence of sin,[28] because pride disrupts unity with God and others in the fall. Hence Augustine's consideration of the back-and-forth nature of human thought is colored by an eschatological hope to move beyond the fragmentation of the mind, to that heavenly state in which, he speculates, "our word will never be false.... [And p]erhaps too our thoughts will no longer chop and change . . . but we shall see all our knowledge in one simultaneous glance."[29] Nonetheless, Augustine insists that even when the human's likeness to God has been restored, "not even then shall we be equal to him in nature,"[30] since God's Word is eternally form, whereas the human inner word will have been re-formed, such that it shall henceforth persist as true and unchanging.[31]

The upshot of the distinction is that Hegel's spoken linguistic paradigm has no currency, where Augustine is concerned, at the level of the immanent divine. The simultaneity of all things in eternity stands in contrast to the flux and distention of time. There is no eternal divine history and development as in Hegel. Rather, God in eternity serves as the fixed point of orientation for a world struggling through the vicissitudes of change and becoming. Furthermore, at the anthropological level, Augustine suggests an eschatological restoration of the image that extricates it from the back-and-forth motion besetting human thought in this life. Whether in the immanent divine or the human mind in its beatific state, then, the word is not a fleeting moment on the way to truth's pneumatic realization, but rather the everlasting actuality of truth and its re-formed likeness henceforth conformed to it.

Love's (Re)Orientation and the Bridging of the Gap

Hegel's integration of an oral linguistic model into his logic brings thought and language closer together in their self-revelatory, event character and shows their intrinsic connection to reality, insofar as thought, precisely because of its linguistically informed dynamism, actualizes the union of subject and object in the self-conscious totality of absolute knowledge. In its full metaphysical breadth, this linguistic dynamic determines and animates all of reality in a fully knowable and speakable whole, such that Hegel finds an intrinsic connection between the immanent Trinitarian sphere and the finite particular world, mediated through the transitory moment of the incarnate Christ and rendered fully explicit in absolute Spirit. In other words, God and the world are not extrinsic to each other in Hegel's system; his linguistic logic overcomes that divide.

Such a spoken linguistic logic has no place in Augustine's Trinitarian theology at either the level of the immanent divine or the level of its image in the human mind in its restored state. For Augustine, this independence from external language undergirds their likeness. We have seen how the *verbum mentis* is isomorphic to its content in memory, just as the eternal Word is one in nature with the Father. Translation of the inner word into external speech, however, results in a loss of data on account of the mediated and embodied form of transmission. Augustine thus argues that the inner word does not belong to any particular language. Nor does it consist in the thoughts one can have of sounds of a particular spoken language or the visible signs used to write it.[32] This implies for the human being an originary freedom akin to that which God possesses apart from his creative and salutary work. "In other words," John Cavadini observes, "the individual's status as *imago Dei* is not dependent upon what we might think of as a particular cultural identity. It is an eternally valid precultural reality focused on a capacity for self-awareness and self-expression which is productive of culture—of signs and sign systems—but not reducible to any particular cultural expression."[33] This freedom, to the extent that Augustine insists that the mind's finite preoccupations are evaluated in the light of eternity,[34] does not appear to be the brute formal freedom Hegel so disparages.

But does this independence from the structure and limits of external language mean that the inner word is not in some sense expressive? Markus contends that it is expressive in a way that cannot be divided into two distinct processes, first of creation and then translation, but rather as a single expression that informs and determines thought according to an innate metaphorical character of language.[35] Here Markus touches upon a crucial aspect of Augustine's Trinitarian thought: the intentionality of the word, that is, the role of the will and the orientation of one's love. Augustine is clear:

"This [inner] word is conceived in love of either the creature or the creator, that is[,] of changeable nature or unchangeable truth; which means either in covetousness or in charity."[36] Covetousness is a love of the creature for its own sake; charity is love of the creator and of the creature in relation to its creator.

It is this aspect of love that perhaps sets Augustine apart most definitively from Hegel. Whereas Hegel connects what is inside and what is outside through an integration of language into the movement of reason, Augustine can rather be seen to do so through the movement of love. To be sure, this leaves empty handed those who seek a precise description of the mechanism whereby the inner word is translated into external language and actions, but that, as Markus readily concedes, is not Augustine's major concern: "In Augustine's contemplation of [the divine] mystery, words and thoughts were bound to converge in pointing toward the one ineffable source of light: what mattered to him is what they were pointing at, even if they happened to be pointing there from many different places and directions."[37] Vis-à-vis Hegel this remaining gap might in fact be a virtue, when viewed from a theological perspective. That is—to shift to the divine plane—the fact that one cannot offer a necessary rational explanation of creation and salvation is precisely the point: they are free acts of love. Such is at least part of the reasoning behind Augustine's distinction between the inner word and external language. Yet in spite of the nonsemantic character of the inner word, the movement of love still establishes continuity between inner expression and external signification. That continuity enables Augustine to speak legitimately of the rhetoric of God and human beings' task of conforming themselves to God's words and deeds through their own word production. In that regard, Augustine's distinction between God and the world could possibly ensure a more Trinitarian sense of divine rhetoric in the concomitant, persistent, and transformative interaction of God's Word and Spirit, which in turn grounds a more Trinitarian form of Christian life in its power to re-form the individual's and the community's words and spirit.

Indeed, Augustine underscores the creative similarity between the divine Word and its human image. He follows Jn 1.3 in linking the divine Word and the creation of the world: "Just as ... God made all things through his only begotten Word, so too there are no works of man which are not first uttered in the heart."[38] Of note is the trajectory of movement, from the inner person outward, and the begetting of a word in the mind as the inner ground of words and actions in time. In spite of the "data corruption," as it were, between a person's inner and outer word, Augustine extends the congruence principle, as much as is possible, to one's creative work in the world: "Here too, if it is a true word, it is the beginning of a good work. And a word is true when it is begotten of the knowledge of how to work well.... Otherwise such a word will be a lie and not the truth, and from it will come a sin, not a right work."[39] God's act of creation, then, serves as Augustine's first model for a good work, one in which there is a correspondence, though clearly not any identity, between the Word of God and the goodness of creation.

Such a positive correspondence stands in contrast to the connection Hegel draws between the logical utterance of the divine Word and its outward expression in the creation of the world, a kenotic determination marked decisively as a fall into evil. To be sure, Hegel also establishes a "congruity" between the eternal birth of the Word and the creation of the world, but one that operates according to the logic of spoken language, in which the descending trajectory of the Word, the expressive differentiation, finite determination, and definition of the divine, occurs as a necessary moment of self-alienation aimed at the final reconciliation of God to himself through the world. In Hegel's system, the creation of the world, on account of its integration into the outward expression of the divine Word, ultimately reveals *God's* fall into evil. In *De Trinitate*, however, when creation appears as a good work because of its ground in the divine Word, Augustine underscores the lack of necessity in the external expression of both the divine Word and the human inner word:

> There is also this other likeness to the Word of God in this likeness which is our word, that we can have a word which is

not followed by a work, but we cannot have a work which is not preceded by a word, just as the Word of God could be, even without any creation coming into existence, but there could not be any creation except through the Word through which all things were made.[40]

What is clear is that the Word of God is marked by fullness prior to and independent of the creation of the world. By contrast, Hegel's immanent Trinity is characterized by lack, by its abstraction and consequent need to objectify itself in creation as part of the process of self-actualization. But precisely the fullness of the divine Word and its distinction from its work ground the goodness of that which depends on it—the work of creation is good because God's Word *is* truth and goodness.

Hegel's affirmation of the goodness of creation is eschatological, in the pneumatic realization that the finite universe constitutes a moment in the divine. The fall into evil becomes the logical presupposition of redemption and actualization of that goodness, an inherent part of the divine narrative. By expanding the range of the christological moment in his Trinitarian narrative to include both the fall (creation) and redemption (incarnation of the Word), Hegel strives to offer a rational account of the different events in the Christian story, especially of what could seem to be otherwise arbitrary and unconnected divine works *ad extra*.[41] Augustine, contrariwise, shows the goodness of creation to be present at its beginning. This stems from the full and present goodness and love of God its creator and from the fact that, precisely as an act of goodness and love, as an expression of who God is, creation is something God does not have to do.[42] Augustine cannot offer a rational explanation connecting the narrative moments of creation—fall—redemption—glorification according to some form of internal necessity. Evil for him cannot be explained, because it is the fruit of a proud and defiant will, for which no one, Augustine contends in his *City of God*, can find an efficient cause.[43] It has only the deficient cause of disordered self-love. But if, as a result, Augustine is left recounting what God has done rather than why, this does not preclude his giving a reasonable account of God's work according to the more aesthetic, rhetorical categories of harmony and fittingness. It is therefore more illuminating than surprising that in book 15 of *Trin.* Augustine, after describing creation as God's good work through his Word, immediately offers a rationale for the redemptive incarnation of the Son instead of the Father or Holy Spirit:

> And the reason why it was not God the Father, not the Holy Spirit, not the trinity itself, but only the Son who is the Word of God that became flesh (although it was the trinity that accomplished this), is that we might live rightly by our word following and imitating his example; that is, by our having no falsehood either in the contemplation nor in the operation of our word. However, this is a perfection of the image that lies some time in the future. To achieve it we are instructed by the good master in Christian faith and godly doctrine.[44]

As Cavadini points out, by "doctrine" (*doctrina*) Augustine does not so much mean some discrete set of information as, rather, the act of teaching itself.[45] Christ's teaching, in Augustine's view, is instantiated most definitively in the self-emptying movement of love toward humankind in the incarnation. There God speaks to human beings in the world of space and time. Augustine thus maintains that the model of external (oral and written) language has its proper referent in the birth of the divine Word in the flesh, rather than in the Word's eternal generation:

> Thus in a certain fashion our word becomes a bodily sound by assuming that in which it is manifested to the senses of men, just as the Word of God became flesh by assuming that in which it too could be manifested to the senses of men. And just as our word becomes sound without being changed into sound, so the Word of God became flesh, but it is unthinkable that it should have been changed into flesh. It is by assuming it, not by being consumed into it, that both our word becomes sound and that Word became flesh.[46]

The Rhetoric of Christ: Augustine's Christology

The contrast to Hegel is again apparent. God the Father and his eternal Word are not changed by the Son's assumption of human flesh. However, rather than carving an uncrossable gorge between God and his creation, this distinction opens the freedom across which divine love moves and in which it can transform fallen humankind. This transformation is not instantaneous; it is a task. Humans are called to conform their words to God's Word. But if that task entails following God's movement outward, of aligning one's inner word with one's outer word in the right direction, then this can take place only through a reorientation of one's love toward God. For the word conceived inwardly in love of either creature or creator is born outwardly "when on thinking it over we like it either for sinning or for doing good."[47] But if, as Paul says and Augustine so often repeats, "The love of God has been poured out in our hearts through the Holy Spirit which has been given to us" (Rom 5.5),[48] then our investigation will be at once christological and pneumatological. We need, therefore, to explore in greater detail the effect of the fall upon human word production, according to Augustine, and how he thinks God speaks and acts in order to transform those fallen words and the societies they sustain through the incarnation of his Word and the work of the Holy Spirit.

Pride, Language, and the Love of God

In his early *De Genesi adversus Manicheos* (written in 388/89), Augustine explicitly links the fall into sin and the human need for external signs. In Eden, Augustine argues, the soul was itself an oasis: "God watered it by an interior spring, speaking to its intellect, so that it did not receive words from the outside.... Rather, it was satisfied from its own spring, that is, by the truth flowing from its interior."[49] However, by sinning the soul "swelled out into external things through pride [and] ceased to be watered by an inner spring."[50] Here Augustine describes pride as the erroneous desire to find one's identity in external, temporal things. As a consequence, humans must now labor on the earth. Thus, reading Gn 2.5, "For

God had not yet made it rain upon the earth,"[51] Augustine contends that these fallen souls working the earth now need rain from the clouds, that is, instruction through human words. In order to save humankind, "our Lord deigned to assume the cloud of our flesh and poured out most generously the rain of the holy gospel."[52] In the section immediately beforehand, Augustine links the image of clouds with the words of scripture, whose externality is marked—in surprising resonance with Hegel's characterization of the immanent divine Logos—by the fact that "they are words which sound and pass away after they strike the air." Now humans must study scripture diligently to gain spiritual nourishment. Augustine then connects the prelapsarian spring of water in Gn 2.5 with the one Jesus mentions in Jn 4.14 which "will come to be in [the one drinking] a spring of water springing up unto eternal life."[53] If one drinks of the words of scripture, he or she will be led back to the internal spring of truth. Nevertheless, by citing 1 Cor 13.12, Augustine not only shows how he longs for the eschatological state when the regime of signs will pass away, but also suggests that in this life one never attains fully to the internal spring of truth.

Later Augustine will consider the relationship between pride and language primarily in light of the Babel narrative, leading him to discover the consequence of pride in the diversity of human languages rather than in language as such.[54] We will examine Augustine's interpretation of the Babel story in chapter 4. Here we ought to note that this shift in focus shows how attuned Augustine is to language's function in constructing human communities. While the wellspring of truth in the soul, as seen in *Gn. adv. Man.*, recalls the younger Augustine and a theology more closely related to that of Neoplatonic ascent—a theology of God, the soul, and nothing more[55]—the very fact that he sees its loss issuing in the incarnation and the need for scripture anticipates his later emphasis upon the indispensability of teaching[56] and his re-identification of the quest for truth with the investigation and exegesis of scripture within the community of believers.[57]

Language thus occupies a place of ambivalence in Augustine's theology. While the need for signs is humbling and knowledge of them eminently useful, both of these positive effects are jeopardized by the pride which motivates some to master the art of words or is engendered once they taste the glory it affords them.[58] Moreover, a mastery of words can bring with it a mastery of other human beings, who can be exploited toward nefarious ends.[59]

To get at the root of this ambivalence, we need to look closely at the way Augustine conceives of pride and how it can become engrained in the linguistic bonds of a particular community. Recall how Augustine describes pride in *Gn. adv. Man.*: the soul rejects its interior relationship with God and swells outward in an attempt to establish its identity among temporal things—in effect, it tries to replace God with itself. Alienated from its source of being in God,[60] the soul is alienated from itself as well.[61] In this its "double exil [double exile]," as M.-F. Berrouard puts it,[62] the soul dissipates and fades into nothingness, a more radical *Nichts* than Hegel's exilic double negativity that issues in dialectical identity:

> Since the soul on its own account is nothing—for otherwise it would not be mutable and suffer a falling away from its essence—since therefore it is in itself nothing and whatever being it has is from God, it is enlivened by the presence of God himself in the mind and conscience to the extent that it remains in its order. The soul thus has this inmost good. Consequently, to swell up with pride is for the soul to go out to the utmost extreme and, I would say, to become empty, that is, to be less and less. But to go out to the utmost extreme, what is that other than to throw out what is inmost, that is, to thrust God far from the soul, not spatially, but by the affection of the mind [*affectu mentis*]?[63]

By turning its affection, its love, away from eternal truth to the vain things of the world (*amor ... quae avertit a vero*), the soul seeks to imitate God rather than to serve him (*deum imitari, quam deo servire, anima maluit*).[64] It seeks to imitate God's power as creator. As Ps 32(33).9 proclaims and Augustine repeats multiple times, God's Word is effective: "He himself spoke, and they were made."⁶⁵ Yet it is not just God's power that concerns Augustine in this regard. As early as *De vera religione*, Augustine makes clear that the act and goodness of creation are grounded in God's own supreme goodness, which is uniquely Trinitarian: all creation is from the Father, through the Word, and sustained in and led back to the good through the Gift of his kindness and mercy, the Gift of the Holy Spirit.⁶⁶

According to Augustine, it is precisely this gracious and good will that motivates and links God's creative and redemptive movements outward and is glaringly lacking in the human grab for power. A proud human word, even if effective in the world, viciously inverts God's creative act. By failing to recognize his or her subordination to God in the order of being, the human being distances him- or herself from truth. For Augustine, one's word then becomes merely a word among words, floating in the sea of convention without any firm foundation, and the human being, created out of nothing by God, uncreates itself into nothing by loving itself as if it were God.

This proud act of self-destruction is possible for Augustine only because creation is made freely by God out of nothing.⁶⁷ On the one hand, a distinction is thus drawn between God and creation, but on the other, the goodness of creation is affirmed, whereby the gravity of evil can be highlighted in all its inexplicable, negating character. Augustine's, then, is not a negation subsumed into a broader logical narrative. Hegel of course wants to safeguard the infinity of God and underscore how seriously God takes evil. The question, though, is whether Hegel's yoking together of creation and incarnation under the category of the Son, in an attempt to provide a rational narrative of creation, fall, and redemption, does not in fact result in an ambivalent and fleeting divine Word which, when sublated into the eschatological fullness of pneumatic vision, can no longer stand as a critical point of orientation for human society. Hegel's universal narrative of divine self-justification transfigures the evil and suffering of history into good. As a result, it obviates lament and silences the protests of the suffering. In so doing, though, it also mutes God, who no longer can identify with those who suffer. If God's Word is then only a word among other words, a passing moment of the divine in history, is not the fullness of Spirit that supplants it just another of humanity's delusions, one that, in its proud claim to vision, has lost sight of the radicalness of evil and is consequently as alienating as ever?

Whereas Hegel's narrative unification of the eternal Word and its utterance in time justifies God by silencing the particular perspective of suffering, evil, and injustice, Augustine's distinction between the eternal Word and its dispensational utterance, as I will argue in greater detail below, leaves the space for a greater dialogue, for the voices of human misery to be heard and met with the healing message of divine love. Hegel's theodicy, by shifting the lens through which the agon of history is viewed to the all-encompassing narrative of the divine fall and reconciliation with itself, retrospectively conflates what is and what ought to be.[68] On one hand, Hegel acknowledges the misery and destruction of history, but on the other he can, in the eschatological fullness of knowledge, allow no room for the cry for justice or the hope that something can be other than it is.

Augustine, too, sees history in all its brutality, but he responds with faith and hope in divine providence, which has its foundation in Christ's cross and resurrection, where God seeks to persuade suffering humans how much he loves them. Thus, according to Augustine, God offers his incarnate Word as the universal way toward an eternal peace established without coercion. That way, which Christ shows on the cross, is one of humility that seeks justice before power, to love rightly before necessarily having the means to obtain what one desires. In that gap between the ought and the is, a gap which for Augustine characterizes this life, the Holy Spirit gradually transfigures believers through love.

God's love is meant to correct and heal pride, which Augustine describes in *Trin.* 13 as the distorted love of power over justice. The proud human sets him- or herself up as the arbiter of value in opposition to the order of goodness and truth.[69] In humanity's fallen state, this distorted lust for power becomes—Cavadini puts it well—"obsessive." As an unjust distortion of relationships, it affects humans' means of communication as well as the cultures built upon them.[70] Because for Augustine only knowledge that is loved brings forth an inner word that can be represented in an external system of signs,[71] each system humans create will bear the stamp of and perpetuate the love in which it was conceived.[72]

There is thus, according to Augustine, no innocent and neutral expression of knowledge. Superstitious disciplines such as divination and astrology are, on Augustine's account, so thoroughly corrupted because they are aimed at the worship of finite things and rest on distorted value judgments agreed upon in a "common language" with demons.[73] Indeed, even one who has come to immutable truths through the liberal arts, if such knowledge serves only to "puff up" (1 Cor 8.1), to inflate one's pride, if that person is one "who does not turn all this [knowledge] to praise and love of the one God from whom he knows it all proceeds; such a person can seem to be very learned, but in no way can he be wise."[74] The philosopher, whose ascent through the disciplines concerned with temporal things has finally issued in contemplation of spiritual realities, cannot escape his or her condition of being situated in a fallen world; the higher one climbs, according to Augustine, the harder one falls, as pride leaves him or her enamored of the power and glory afforded by intellectual vision.[75]

The proud soul, Augustine argues in *Trin.* 12, grasps after the whole. It seeks to make itself creator and rule by its own laws. Had that soul been satisfied with its creaturely status, it could have shared happily in the whole of creation. By its proud attempt to give itself an independent, total perspective, however, it ends up obsessed only with itself, thinking it is defying the laws of the universe through those things it can know, feel, and do with its body, over which it ironically has only partial control.[76] But when everyone claims mastery over one's own little universe, everyone ends up with the situation Augustine describes at the beginning of his *Confessions*, in which all is nothing more than fragmented words grounded in convention, words with no connection to reality or any real bond with each other. Then everything, even philosophy, devolves into the rhetoric of "smoke and wind,"[77] in which beauty of form trumps truthfulness of content. Socially bound, yet vacuously self-centered humans are swept up into "the flood of human custom,"[78] encouraged to learn "the eloquence essential for persuasion and argument,"[79] where not the beauty of the words, but the "wine of error" that fills them is blameworthy on account of the intoxicating allure of praise and glory.[80]

Into this subtly precarious situation, as Augustine describes it, where even the most collaborative of human cultural endeavors is marked, often unnoticeably and hence even more insidiously, by the promotion of errant self-love and its degrading hierarchy of utility, Augustine believes that God speaks. Uncreative humanity, so obsessed with power and hurtling ever deeper into nothingness, needs to be startled out of its obsession in a creative way. If the first creation was, on Augustine's account, a Trinitarian act of divine goodness, then humanity's reordering of being, inasmuch as it turns away from God's goodness, is also a Trinitarian problem. Thus, for Augustine, God's re-creative solution will be Trinitarian. That solution cannot be simply a matter of knowledge, but must simultaneously entail a reordering of one's loves.

The Birth of the Word

For Augustine, God takes humanity so seriously that he humbles himself in the incarnation. Whereas humans lust after power and, as a consequence, are alienated from themselves and others, the eternal Word of God was spoken in time and became fully human, in order to acquaint humans again with their own humanity through the example of humility: "That God became a man; you, man, know that you are a man. All your humility is this, that you know yourself."[81] But humility is just as much a matter of will, of saying no to oneself and yes to God. "Therefore," Augustine explains, "because God teaches humility, [Christ] said, 'I have come not to do my will, but the will of him who sent me.' For this is a recommendation of humility. Pride, of course, does its own will; humility does the will of God."[82]

Christ, the "master of humility" (*magister humilitatis*), teaches through the entire act of incarnation, from the moment at which the eternal Word of God is first spoken into the world as a human being born of a woman.[83] The original creation was an act of God's goodness, carried out through the Word and sustained in the good by the Gift of God, the Holy Spirit. So too, as Augustine states in *De fide et symbolo*, did the Son of God assume flesh from the Virgin Mary according to the temporal dispensation for human salvation and restoration, a dispensation in which God's goodness (*benignitate*) is at work.[84] The Holy Spirit is also operative in this saving act of humility: "For by the gift of God, that is, by the Holy Spirit, such a great humility of such a great God has been granted to us that he deigned to assume the entire human being in the womb of a virgin."[85]

The later Pelagian disputes help Augustine clarify the significance of the gift of the Holy Spirit in the incarnation of the Word. In his *Enchiridion* Augustine argues that Christ's human nature was not taken up by the eternal Word on account of any good works or intentions, but purely by the gift of grace.[86] According to Augustine, God takes the initiative in resuming the conversation with human beings, in speaking to them in human words. Augustine underscores how the incarnation reveals the triune God, a God already self-conscious, free, loving, and good. In this way God can offer the free gift of grace manifest in the birth of the Word. And in this way humans come to know God as eternally triune. The gift of the Spirit in the incarnation of the Son reveals that it was only the Son, and not the Father or the Holy Spirit, who took on flesh.[87] At the same time, the Holy Spirit is manifest precisely in his role as *gift*. This Trinitarian operation of the incarnation shows that it is God who saves by grace, and that because it is God's grace, it is given in a uniquely Trinitarian way:

> For the same Jesus Christ, God's only-begotten, that is, only Son, our Lord, was born of the Holy Spirit and of the Virgin Mary. We know also that the Holy Spirit is a gift of God, a gift equal to the giver, and so the Holy Spirit is also God, no less

than the Father and the Son. And by the fact that the human birth of Christ is from the Holy Spirit, what else is manifested but grace itself?[88]

For Augustine the Holy Spirit is operative in Christ's incarnation, not potentially but actually. The relationship between word, reality, and Spirit thus takes a different shape in Augustine than it does in Hegel. From the outset, Hegel's Trinity is structurally semantic, though initially only potentially. That is, the seriousness with which God takes the world, the connection between reality and words, is realized only pneumatically and eschatologically, when the word has vanished as a sound but the truth is now known through the word's mediation. The Father and the Son are necessary moments, albeit necessarily passing in their individual instability. Their very structure thereby anticipates their reconciliation in Spirit. Consequently, Spirit, once actualized, is for Hegel the fullness of God where the difference between the abstract Father, the logical underpinning of reality, and the finite world, identified with the Son, has been overcome and these two moments are recalled analeptically in their self-conscious unity.

This difference between Hegel and Augustine is illustrated well by considering the relationship between Christ and the Spirit in light of the savior's personality. For Hegel, to insist upon the existence of a discrete personality of Christ following his death misses the point of the incarnation. Because the very structure of the spoken word, indeed of all finite creation, transcends itself and anticipates its reconciliation with God in Spirit, clinging to a resurrected personality of Christ makes him into a word unable to connect its hearer with the truth. Without the Spirit, only Christ is known to be united with the divine. In other words, if Christ does not withdraw—if people do not permit him to be a finite human being—in order that the Spirit might descend, there is no way for other human beings to know the truth conveyed by Christ, namely, the truth that all human beings are united with God. Human beings in that case have no way to attain real salvation.

For Augustine, on the other hand, the Spirit's grace is essential in forming the one person of the savior Jesus Christ. As he writes in the *Enchiridion*:

> The manner in which Christ was born of the Holy Spirit not as a son and of the Virgin Mary as a son shows us the grace of God by which a man, without any preceding merits, at the very beginning of his natural existence, was joined to the Word of God in so great a personal unity that the Son of God was Son of Man and the Son of Man Son of God and thus in the assumption of human nature grace itself, which cannot allow any sin, became in some way natural to that man. It was right that this grace should be signified by mention of the Holy Spirit because his mode of being God is such that he is . . . called Gift of God.[89]

Here we need to keep in mind Augustine's teaching on original sin. Despite the criticism Augustine's doctrine has garnered, one can see in it how the Holy Spirit plays a role for Augustine in forming the beauty of God's healing plan. Whereas all human beings are now born in fleshly concupiscence because of Adam's sin, God took to himself a truly human being, both soul and body, "one however whose conception from a virgin was inaugurated by the spirit not the flesh, by faith not lust."[90] Here, as Verhees points out, Christ's sinlessness is not merely a consequence of the Spirit's having preserved Mary from lustful urges. One ought to recognize the positive, free operation of the Spirit in uniting the man Jesus to the divine Logos.[91] The grace of the Holy Spirit thus gives to the human nature of Christ the justice of God.[92] Furthermore, the grace of the Holy Spirit preserves Christ from any evil during his earthly life.[93] He did not have to struggle with the urges of the flesh against the spirit as does vitiated humankind. And he did not struggle in his humble obedience to the Father, in the subordination of his own will even unto death on a cross.[94]

A second Adam, Christ remakes and reorders humankind, according to Augustine. By the humility of the incarnation, "which so offends the proud," God creatively affirms the value of humanity:

The Rhetoric of Christ: Augustine's Christology 75

the incarnation "affords man [a view] of the place he should have in God's foundation, seeing that human nature could be so joined to God that one person would be made out of two substances."[95] This "one person ... of two substances" is essential to the Trinitarian affirmation and re-creation of the human being. Augustine's more traditional christological formulation clearly differs from the single nature Hegel posits of Christ.[96]

Augustine maintains a distinction between Christ's two natures and hence between the human and the divine. That distinction, however, opens the space where the Holy Spirit affirms human value by reestablishing the proper order of being. This is evident objectively in the way Augustine talks about Christ's two natures in relation to the Spirit. In *Jo. ev. tr.* 74, for example, he argues that, whereas the eternal Word is equal to the Father and the Holy Spirit by his very nature and has no need of grace, the human being Jesus "was assumed into the unity of the person of the Only Begotten ... by grace, not by nature."[97] Augustine explicitly points to the work of the Holy Spirit in Christ's role as mediator: "For not without the grace of the Holy Spirit is the man Christ Jesus the mediator of God and human beings."[98]

The Holy Spirit, according to Augustine, affirms humanity's value insofar as he freely elevates Jesus' human nature to personal unity with the divine Logos. Augustine underscores the significance of Christ's full humanity: "God could of course have taken a man to himself from somewhere else, to be in him *the mediator of God and men* (1 Tm 2:5), not from the race of that Adam who had implicated the human race in his own sin," but God deemed it fitting, through the grace of the Holy Spirit, to take up into unity with his Son an innocent human being, by whom to conquer Satan.[99] At the same time, the Spirit's affirmation of humankind in the incarnation of the Word is also a way for God to reorder humans according to their proper place in the order of being. For this reason, Augustine stresses that the eternal Word is divine by nature, but the man Jesus united to the person of the Word by the grace of the Holy Spirit. Salvation through Jesus Christ is a gift of God himself, the Holy Spirit.[100]

According to Augustine, the sanctification that Christ the mediator possesses from the moment of his birth in time receives further confirmation at his baptism in the Jordan. That baptism helps confirm for Augustine Christ's two natures, since Christ imparts the Spirit in his divinity but receives the Spirit as a human being.[101] In this latter affirmation of Christ's full humanity, Augustine also underscores Christ's status as the only mediator between God and humans. Only Christ possesses the Spirit in his fullness, and only Christ comes to his baptism already full of grace.[102] In *Jo. ev. tr.* 74.3, Augustine argues that Christ received the grace of the Holy Spirit without measure, whereas human beings receive it according to a discrete measure.[103] The Holy Spirit in this way solidifies Christ's status as permanent mediator upon whom all depend for their salvation. For Augustine, the Holy Spirit builds up Christ's body in love by drawing together a community around, with, and in the Word that God has spoken.

Whereas Verhees suggests that Augustine's discussions of the Spirit at Christ's baptism add little or nothing beyond confirmation of the operation of grace in the incarnation, I think that, when viewed from the perspective of divine speech, Christ's birth and his baptism are inextricably linked for Augustine. Believers, who receive the gift of the Spirit in a limited fashion from Christ, the only one who can give the Spirit, are thereby reborn through baptism into Christ's incarnation, his body understood ecclesially.[104] Augustine connects Christ's birth and that of the church: "'May there be,' [Mary] said, 'one conceived in a virgin without the seed of man; may he be born of the Holy Spirit and a woman untainted, he in whom the Church may be born again untainted of the Holy Spirit.'"[105] Such rebirth takes place through baptism:

> It is written of [Christ] more openly in the Acts of the Apostles, *that God anointed him with the Holy Spirit* (Acts 10:38), not of course with a visible oil but with the gift of grace which is signified by the chrism the Church anoints the baptized with. Nor, to be sure, was Christ only anointed with the Holy Spirit when the dove came down upon him at his baptism [for he

already possessed the fullness of the Spirit at his birth]; what he was doing then [at his baptism] was *graciously* prefiguring his body, that is his Church, in which it is particularly those who have just been baptized that receive the Holy Spirit.[106]

Augustine shows how the internal grace, by which the Word of God took on at his birth a human soul and body, is the same internal grace, albeit in a smaller dosage, by which believers, through the external sign of baptism, are reborn into his ecclesial body, the same body, mystically speaking, that was baptized in the Jordan.

Returning then to the question of language, we can say that, according to Augustine, God speaks in human terms, that his eternal Word becomes semantic through the grace of the Holy Spirit. God's speech in human language is grace, a gift of God himself.[107] The nature of divine speech, for Augustine, is thus Trinitarian in shape, and that shape is intimately related to the two natures in the one person of Christ. In this respect D. W. Johnson sees in Augustine's distinction of language into meaning and sound, and in the corresponding distinction of natures in Christ, lingering Platonic dualism and a denigration of human nature. Johnson detects this most "notorious[ly]" in *doc. Chr.* 1.34.38, where, he thinks, Augustine interprets Christ to be urging humans to go beyond all temporal things, including the incarnation.[108]

The passage, however, deserves a second look. Adducing Jn 14.6, "I am the way, and the truth, and the life,"[109] Augustine paraphrases Christ's words: "It is along me that you come, at me that you arrive, in me that you abide."[110] The dynamism inherent to Augustine's Christology is apparent. The bishop of Hippo then argues that Christ "did not wish us to cling feebly to any temporal things, even those he took to himself and carried for our salvation, but rather to run along and through them, and so deserve to be swiftly and finally conveyed to him himself, where he has deposited our nature, freed from all temporal conditions, at the right hand of the Father."[111] It is best to understand this text as an exhortation to avoid two different mistakes. On the one hand, it is imperative to see how, in Christ, God shows humans that there is something more than just the temporal and material world. Hence, humans ought not to see only the external Christ, ought not to use Christ merely as a word among words, but rather to see how the Holy Spirit has made him a word bearing the truth, to see that the human Christ is also the eternal Word of God. On the other hand, moving along and through the temporal Christ leads one gradually to eternity, "where he has conveyed [human] nature."[112] Augustine does not denigrate human nature and wish to leave it behind, but rather hopes for its re-creation and elevation.

Thus, Augustine argues, "There is one road, and one only, well secured against all possibility of going astray; and this road is provided by one who is himself both God and man. As God, he is the goal; as man, he is the way."[113] The distinction in natures and the unity of person are vital. With the human mind darkened by sin and in need of external guidance, Christ takes on the role of the Good Teacher, and comes to human beings as one of their own, as God's word spoken to them through the very external things they either idolize or disparage as beneath them—for when one scoffs at what is below one, the danger of reducing oneself to that level increases directly with the risk of self-idolatry. To hear God speaking in a human way, according to Augustine, requires that one come to know what a human being is, and that takes humility. It takes a change of heart, wrought by the Holy Spirit, to be able to accept the gift God gives in Christ through that same Spirit.

On Augustine's account, God respects humans even more than they respect themselves, for God forms his word according to humans' social and developmental nature. The distinction between Christ's human and divine natures not only facilitates humanity's self-knowledge, but is also honest enough to show them that they have not yet reached their goal. A single-natured Christ, the integration of an oral linguistic paradigm into the very nature of the divine, which in Hegel's case was meant to show how seriously God takes the finite world, does not avert the aforementioned danger of idolizing either the world or oneself as identical with God. Nor does it open the space in which the Holy Spirit can effect transformation, for in Hegel's paradigm the culmination of Spirit is the attainment of the end. For Augustine, by contrast, Christ's own united personality is that on, in, and toward which the Christian is moving as long as she is in this life. Yet the turn toward the external, Christ as way, and the simultaneous postponement of Christ's divinity as goal, do not for Augustine mean utter alienation from self or from God. Only by gradually conforming one's inner word to Christ in the context of his body, the church, does one come to know oneself as created in the image of the Trinity. At every formative step along the way toward God the Father in Christ the Son, the Holy Spirit guides and reshapes one's heart. It is a complex Trinitarian movement, according to Augustine: the Holy Spirit turns the heart outward to the incarnate Christ in order that one might be transformed inwardly, with the ultimate hope of following the glorified Christ toward full external restoration as well.

Christ's Death and Resurrection: The Persuasion of Love and the Power of Justice

That very hope is at stake when Augustine casts God and the devil as speakers employing competing oratorical strategies to persuade human beings to follow them on either the path of life or death. The devil, according to Augustine, is the master of deceit, promising life but bringing only death. God, by contrast, speaks to human beings in the loving humility of his Son. The curative reformation of humanity through Christ's death and resurrection gives people reason to hope in new life.

Augustine describes humans as a willing audience, eager to listen in their search for the truth. This yearning for life and truth animates the human soul even in its fallen state: "But we were exiled from this unchanging joy, yet not so broken and cut off from it that we stopped seeking eternity, truth, and happiness even in this changeable time-bound situation of ours—for we do not want, after all, to die or to be deceived or to be afflicted."[114] In book 13 of *Trin.*, Augustine is more explicit: all human beings know what the happy life is and desire it. The problem for Augustine lies rather in the fact that people do not know the way toward that end, because their will to happiness is disordered, that is, they love in the wrong way.[115] Since that wrong way amounts to a preference for power over justice, Augustine might say that as listeners humans bring with them a set of presuppositions that affect their ability to understand and interpret the speech they hear. Yet perhaps the term "presupposition" is too tame for Augustine. He insists that since the fall human nature has been vitiated, and humans cannot extricate themselves from their sinful state. They suffer from blindness which clouds the light of God in their rational minds.[116]

On Augustine's account it is only through God's speech that human beings can ever hope, even minutely, to understand that—and how—God speaks to them. Only God can illumine darkened human minds, and such enlightenment results only from "participat[ion] in the Word."[117] Humans, however, are so unclean that this ability to hear God's divine speech lies beyond their grasp. Augustine argues:

> The only thing to cleanse the wicked and the proud is the blood of the just man and the humility of God; to contemplate God, which by nature we are not, we would have to be cleansed by him who became what by nature we are and what by sin we are not. By nature we are not God; by nature we are men; by sin we are not just. So God became a just man to intercede with God for sinful man.[118]

The way Augustine frames it, God is like a great rhetorician vying for human attention, and the incarnation, the Word of God become flesh, constitutes his most essential argument: "First we had to be persuaded how much God loved us, in case out of sheer despair we lacked the courage to reach up to him. Also we had to be shown what sort of people we are that he loves, in case we should take pride in our own worth."[119] To make his point, God underscores, according to Augustine, the stark contrast between human pride and divine humility. On the one hand, humans ought not to be deceived about their own power. However, acknowledgment of sin is not grounds for despair, but rather for courage, because God himself has provided the vehicle of ascent. Augustine writes, "So he dealt with us in such a way that we could progress rather in his strength; he arranged it so that the power of charity would be brought to perfection in the weakness of humility."[120] For Augustine, God's argument is all the more persuasive because it is the free, unmerited gift of God's very self.[121]

Augustine is aware that without that grace the power of charity (*virtus caritatis*) in the weakness of humility is not self-evident. Hence the question arises in *Trin.* 13 as to whether there was any other way God could have set humanity free besides becoming human and suffering death. The task, Augustine claims, is not simply to show that the incarnation is consistent with God's nature and goodness, but that this way, among all those God could have chosen, was the most fitting in order to cure the illness besetting humankind. In other words, Augustine feels compelled to show just how seriously God takes humankind, not simply by saying that God is by nature good, but by saying that God's love can draw greater good out of evil precisely by acknowledging that evil is not how things ought to be and by thus reorienting the human heart toward the pursuit of justice.

This entails for Augustine an emphasis upon how God does not change, how he is eternally loving and just.[122] Accordingly, Augustine argues, when humankind fell into sin, God justly turned it over to the authority of the devil and death. But because the error of the devil and those who followed him was a grab for power without first attending to the rightness of the will behind that acquisitiveness, God's restorative action on behalf of humankind had to reveal the goodness of divine love in accordance with eternal justice. That is, although God could easily have overpowered the devil in winning back humankind, Augustine contends that God shows in Christ's death and resurrection that the right order, that which can really satisfy humanity's desire for truth and happiness, depends first upon establishing a properly oriented love and only then upon the ability to get what one desires. "Justice," Augustine argues, "is a property of good will."[123] Justice ought to precede power, according to Augustine, because "the perversion should be avoided of a man choosing to be able to do what he wants and neglecting to want what he ought."[124] Power ought to be desired for the conquest of vice, not of other human beings. The latter desire, even if realized in the world, is an inversion of reality whereby those wielding temporal power are themselves conquered in accord with the truth of their being.[125]

For this reason, Augustine argues, God uses justice to redeem fallen humanity. The devil could find no fault in Jesus, yet killed him all the same. Christ's innocent blood was shed for human sins, which were deserving of death, and the devil lost his rights over fallen humanity. Justice overpowered the devil. The persuasiveness of God's action, in Augustine's view, relies upon Christ's two natures: "Unless he had been man he could not have been killed; unless he had been God no one would have believed he did not want to do what he could do . . . nor would we have believed that he was preferring justice to power, but simply that he lacked power."[126] The immutable God, in a manner consistent with his own being as love, shows the proper order of love to mutable humanity. Furthermore, Augustine makes clear that divine persuasiveness has need of Christ's objective death and resurrection. By his death Christ manifested divine justice, since he voluntarily suffered an innocent death so that justice might be done on behalf of humankind. By his resurrection he showed God's power over death—hence the priority of justice over power—and the promise of power to those who through faith and love have purified themselves in accord with justice. Augustine concludes:

> In this way the justice of humility was made more acceptable, seeing that the power of divinity could have avoided the humiliation if it had wanted to; and so by the death of one so powerful we powerless mortals have justice set before us and power promised us. He did one of these two things by dying, the other by rising. . . . He overcame the devil with justice first and power second, with justice because *he had no sin* (2 Cor 5:21; 1 Pt 2:22) and was most unjustly killed by him; with power because dead he came back to life never to die thereafter.[127]

The promise of power, of resurrection and the attendant ability to do what one wills, highlights a significant distinction between Augustine and Hegel. Hegel rejects an objective resurrection and ascension of Christ as deleterious to the achievement of self-conscious freedom, and consequently sees those events realized in the pneumatic community. Augustine, by contrast, insists upon Christ's own bodily resurrection and ascension. These are not realities whose objective identification with the person of Christ and subjective character of promise stand in the way of reintegrating the human person and reuniting him or her with God and the broader human community. Rather, they are for Augustine the way in which God's Word is fully human and fully restorative, because God's Word and the Spirit by whom he enters history continue to offer a liberating point of orientation, a way of humility, whereby the myth that the unity of will and power is attainable in this life is debunked. That unity rests, according to Augustine, in the proper ordering of creation under its creator so that, through the Spirit, human beings can truly participate in God's Word, who has raised up the whole of humankind, soul and body.[128]

For Augustine, then, God's eloquence is truly subtle. It operates by drawing contrasts, by juxtaposing unfounded human pride with divine humility, yet in so doing it effects a sublime harmony that only the creator can achieve. In fact, consistent with the divine goodness he sees motivating God's act of creation, Augustine finds the manifestation of and sense for what the Greeks call ἁρμονία built into the human person.[129] Augustine's example of offended sensibilities at the sound of discordant voices demonstrates, moreover, that God's communication with human beings is not simply a matter of knowledge, but involves the affects as well, thereby supporting further a claim of joint, yet personally distinctive, operation of Christ and the Holy Spirit in both the objective and subjective aspects of God's redemptive work. When humans create discord through their sin, says Augustine, God speaks even more beautifully, but no less seriously, in Christ's death and resurrection: "It was surely right that the death of the sinner issuing from the ... necessity of condemnation should be undone by the death of the just man issuing from the voluntary freedom of mercy, his single matching our double."[130]

Humans, according to Augustine, suffer two deaths as a consequence of the fall: one of the soul and one of the body. The death of the soul occurs when it is separated from God by human sin. Death of the body ensues as a punishment for this sin and consists in the sundering of the soul from the body. Without the soul, the body falls victim to corruption; it rots and fades away.[131] Christ, on the other hand, suffered only one death, that of the body. His spirit never died, since he was sinless and never separated from the divine Godhead. Hence he also experienced only one resurrection of the body. Indeed, Augustine elsewhere suggests the Holy Spirit's operation in that one resurrection of Christ. Expositing Ps 108(109).24b as it appears in his Latin text, "And my flesh was changed, because of oil," Augustine suggests the Holy Spirit's role in the glorification of Christ's risen flesh: "That means, because of spiritual grace. Christ's name derives from chrism, and chrism signifies anointing. His flesh was changed because of oil, but for the better, not the worse; it was changed from the ignominy of death into the glory of immortality as it rose. . . . The Spirit may be symbolized by water, which evokes cleansing or irrigation, or by oil, which suggests joy and the fire of charity."[132]

By means of his single death and resurrection, Christ nullified the two deaths humans endure and thereby made possible for them a double resurrection, first of the soul from ungodliness and then, at the eschaton, of the body.[133] Augustine labels Christ's passion and resurrection a *sacramentum*, a sacred sign, which both points to and conveys the mysterious reality of redemption. Christ could not die in his eternal reality, and hence the external, historical event of Christ's Pasch, his movement from death to life in the form of a servant, signifies the internal passage of the soul from death in sin to life in justice. With regard to the soul, death, as Hill has observed, refers in fact to two sides of this transformative process.[134] On the one hand, Augustine refers Jesus' cry of Godforsakenness (Ps 21[22].1; Mk 15.34) to the death of the soul on account of sin. On the other hand, he relates the crucifixion of the old man mentioned in Rom 6.6 to the believer's death to sin through repentance and self-discipline: "a kind of death to erase the death of ungodliness in which God does not leave us."[135] According to Augustine, the death of spirit is thus equivalent to spiritual regeneration, of which Christ's bodily resurrection is also a sacrament. Hence we have an interesting Augustinian parallel here to the doubly negative movement of Hegel's dialectic, but one that can hold together Christ's objective bodily resurrection and its subjective reference to the believer. In that regard, Augustine avails himself of Christ's postresurrection exhortation to Mary Magdalene in Jn 20.17: "Do not touch me, for I have not yet ascended to my Father." Christ's words to Mary Magdalene are intended to turn her attention away from any strictly materialistic conception of Christ and to enjoin her to strive to know him according to his eternal unity with the Father. Christ's bodily resurrection is a sacrament of the inner person when linked with Augustine's citation of Col 3.1, which sets resurrection in Christ in a conditional relation to the quest to know spiritual realities.[136]

This same movement toward spiritual reality animates Augustine's explication of Christ as a model of the outer person. Citing Mt 10.28 and Col 1.24,[137] Augustine enjoins an identification of bodily suffering with Christ's crucifixion in order to train one's focus on the soul, which can be killed only by internal means. However, in contrast to the hortatory exemplarity of Christ's death, Christ's resurrection functions for Augustine as a model of the outer person inasmuch as it confirms the reality of bodily resurrection, seen in Christ's glorified body and awaited by the just at the end of time.[138]

For Augustine, then, God in his eloquence counteracts the discord of the fall by reestablishing concord in Christ's passion and resurrection. As both sacrament and model, Christ's death and resurrection are aimed outward and spoken in love to human beings. Consequently, Augustine argues, the harmony Christ brings about bears not only on the individual, but on the whole body of believers. Here, too, pneumatic implications in Augustine's thought cannot be overlooked. In and through this one savior, humans, previously divided by their passions and desires, are made one in faith and joined together in Christ's spiritual body.[139] Christ in this way brings about harmony and union not only by sharing a common nature with humanity, but also by forging in it a common will, informed by charity and aimed at the true happiness found only in God. Here in the union of nature and will, Augustine maintains, re-formed humanity can begin to reflect and share, as much as is possible for God's rational creation in this life, in the eternal life and love of the Trinity: "Just as Father and Son are one not only by equality of substance but also by identity of will, so these men, for whom the Son is mediator with God, might be one not only by being of the same nature, but also by being bound in the fellowship of the same love."[140]

But such a renewed society, slowly built up in love around God's incarnate Word, must counteract the disordered love that, according to Augustine, has become variously encoded in the communicative bonds of culture ever since humanity established a conventional language, as it were, with the devil. In Augustine's evaluation, that greatest of the fallen angels promised life, but delivered only death. The devil's manner of speaking is deceptively harmonious, Augustine thinks, for in the end it causes greater discord and separation from God and one another. Whereas Christ matches humans' double death with his single life-giving death and resurrection of the body, the devil, who lacks a body and therefore cannot die in the flesh, facilitates humanity's double death with the single death of his spirit. As Augustine puts it: "He too [the devil] brought his own single death to bear in order to operate our double death. By godlessness he died in spirit, though he did not die of course in the flesh; but he both persuaded us to godlessness and insured that because of it we should deserve to come to the death of the flesh."[141] According to Augustine, the devil, lord over his "dominion of deceit," sets many snares for human beings in the form of special rites or sacrifices that promise purification but in fact do nothing but defile the participants, because those rites are not based upon praise and thanksgiving to God, but rather upon the belief that an individual can save him- or herself.[142] In effect, Augustine concludes, the devil erects an entire semantic framework by "which he hoodwinks the proud" into believing the myth of their own autonomy.[143]

The Rhetoric of Christ: Augustine's Christology

Here one ought to observe, moreover, a clear contrast between Augustine and Hegel with regard to the figure of Satan or Lucifer as well as the serpent in Gn 3. In *LPR* 3 Hegel adduces the seventeenth-century mystic Jakob Böhme, who conflates the figure of Lucifer with the Son and integrates the former's fall into an account of the creation of the world qua divine fall.[144] This Luciferian fall thus marks the negative, evil aspect inherent in the moment of the Son. But for Hegel, Satan or Lucifer represents a productive antithesis integral to the self-actualization of the divine. As such, the negative moment of evil or wickedness expressed in the fall is also constitutive of divine reconciliation and truth. Accordingly, Hegel can separate Satan, as a figure of evil, from the serpent of Gn 3; the serpent, on Hegel's reading, speaks truth in his promise to Adam and Eve that they would become like God through the salutary knowledge of good and evil. "So the words of the serpent were no deception,"[145] insofar as the fall was a necessary part of the process whereby humans, and more fundamentally, God, achieve autonomous selfhood and freedom.

By contrast, Augustine is clear that Lucifer and his errant pride stand in unproductive antithesis to God. The goodness of creation precedes his fall and that of humankind.[146] It is not the opposition between Lucifer and God that itself results in reconciliation and love, but simply the love of God that can freely identify with fallen humanity and heal it in spite of the devil and in spite of the reality of sin and death. For Augustine, the serpent is clearly a mouthpiece of Satan,[147] and the serpent's words are through-and-through deceptive.[148] Truth is embodied rather in Christ, the Word of God spoken in the world, to whom human beings are called to listen humbly.

As a nonproductive antithesis to God, the devil's talk proves inefficacious, according to Augustine, because while the devil could "apply his single death to our double one, he certainly could not apply that single resurrection which would provide the sacrament for our renovation and the model for the general awakening."[149] The devil, lacking a body, had no part in human death and resurrection in the same way that Christ did. Augustine argues that only Christ, whose spirit never dies, could raise his dead flesh to life again and thereby promise a wholly reintegrated life to those who believe in him. Many of the proud deny Christ on account of his bodily death and consider the devil stronger because he did not suffer a death of the flesh, but in so doing they are themselves deceived, because it was through Christ's humility and obedience unto death that the devil actually lost his claim on humans and death itself was conquered.[150] The devil, contends Augustine, thought himself greater than humankind, since he could not die a physical death, and consequently he regarded himself as greater than the incarnate Word who also died. But Christ, who was completely innocent, suffered death willingly, and his death thereby became the true and pure sacrifice by which he reclaimed humanity for his own.[151]

In this way Augustine argues that God's one true Word in the world breaks the semantic regime of pride, but not in a way that circumvents or abolishes signs. Demons promise such circumvention in touting the alleged strength of their incorporeality.[152] But on Augustine's analysis, the reverse becomes the case: the devil could not corrupt Christ's spirit, Christ's love of the Father, and thus he, the devil, could silence only the external human being in death. Moreover, because the devil did not attend to the pride manifest in his premature claim to victory, what authority he may have had over human beings dissipates permanently into the flux of external sign, as he is, according to Augustine, henceforth banished from the human heart and relegated to control over the exterior.[153] The love of God, on the other hand, makes it possible, Augustine maintains, to begin to speak words of substance, really to struggle and take seriously this fluctuating and unhappy life, in the hope that those words will be transfigured one day, completely oriented toward God and hence completely meaningful.

If pride, then, which enables people to accept the devil's dissembling rhetoric so readily, is in Augustine's view the common condition of fallen humanity, faith—an act of humility in response to God's own humbleness, love, and mercy in the incarnation—is that which purifies the proud sinner. There are some philosophers, Augustine observes, who laud their ability to ascend intellectually beyond created realities. Such thinkers look condescendingly upon those who live by faith, especially faith in a man who died on a cross and in the resurrection of the body. In response Augustine argues that faith is the only way to arrive at understanding and truth: "What good does it do a man who is so proud that he is ashamed to climb aboard the wood, what good does it do him to gaze from afar on the home country across the sea? And what harm does it do a humble man if he cannot see it from such a distance, but is coming to it nonetheless on the wood the other disdains to be carried by?"[154] In focusing so intently on attaining a vision of the eternal realm, the philosophers overlook the fact that God has spoken in history through his creation, a process culminating in the incarnation. Their vision of the eternal in no way enables them to speak about the course of history, about what is to come. Augustine contends that only the prophets, whom God had chosen and to whom he revealed part of his eternal plan, were able to announce Christ's coming.[155]

Faith for Augustine is primarily faith in this economy of salvation. Nevertheless, Augustine distinguishes between those things that are believed and the faith by which they are believed. The latter is not externally sensible, but is known internally and certainly to each person. Such internal knowledge is inevitably vulnerable to the pitfalls of communication. One cannot know the faith of another with the certainty one has of one's own faith: "So everyone sees his own faith in himself; he only believes and does not see it to be in someone else, and he believes all the more firmly, the more he is aware of its fruits, which it is of the nature of faith to produce by *working through love* (Gal 5.6)."[156] This passage brings to light two vital points. In the formation of community, faith is essential. Direct sight of another's knowledge is an eschatological good; hence, in building up the body of believers, one is constantly humbled by the need to listen to the other and believe him or her. However, that faith is awakened and strengthened by its working in love. Knowledge alone cannot overcome the gap between inside and out; it cannot explain the incarnation of God's eternal Word. Consequently, rational dialectic cannot on its own nourish genuine relationships between different individuals or between those individuals and God. On Augustine's analysis, a more fully Trinitarian reformation is needed.

The economy of salvation, climaxing in God's incarnate Word, demands for Augustine a humble faith, a belief in God's external word now in the hopes of seeing his eternal Word at the end of time. Yet that economy, especially the death and resurrection of Christ, initiates and sustains faith because it is a persuasive manifestation of love. Furthermore, it is love, the gift of the Holy Spirit, that propels one toward a deeper understanding of the unchanging truth—in Augustinian terms, from knowledge (*scientia*) toward wisdom (*sapientia*). For this reason, *Trin.* 13, a book devoted to an exploration of temporally oriented faith (in the mode of *scientia*), discusses at great length the need for a good will. Indeed, the love of justice thus draws believers together ever deeper into the body of Christ. According to Augustine, it is God's Word, spoken in the world through the love of the Holy Spirit, that continues sacramentally to break open every cultural system, every concrete body of knowledge, to reorient and enflame one's love in the hope that justice will reign in accord with Christ's example.

IN PART I, we have started to explore how Hegel and Augustine each talk about God—specifically, how each speaks about God speaking and acting in the world through Christ. We saw how both Hegel and Augustine adopt Johannine Logos imagery. Both, moreover, utilize the concept of Logos in its dual meaning as an element of thought and a word in speech. Yet, whereas Hegel consciously integrates these two elements across the breadth of his Trinitarian theology, Augustine maintains a distinction in the scope and locus of their applicability. The result is two very different Trinitarian and christological grammars, or sets of rules concerning how to speak adequately and responsibly about God in human language, rules that fundamentally affect the way in which those who speak according to them relate to God and to each other.

By integrating the movement of the spoken word—a dynamic of self-distinction and self-transcending reunification considered by Hegel to be the motor of historical development—into the logical structure of reason itself, Hegel deems it possible to discover meaning in all of history, including even the most apparently senseless evil and death. Theologically, that move entails an identification of the world and its history with the Son of God, the second, necessarily fleeting moment of Hegel's philosophically reconfigured Trinity. It means that that part of creation conscious of itself, humankind, comes to know itself too as a *fleeting word*—fleeting, that is, in its finitude—indeed as *the* Word that, in passing away, has its truth and freedom in the knowledge of itself as one with God, as absolute *Spirit*.

Because the strife of history itself issues in the eschatological fullness of knowledge, and because that strife comes to make sense through what we have called Hegel's logic of Christ, or better, his logic of Spirit, that logic is appropriately characterized as a theodicy. However, we also observed that Hegel's integration of evil and its reconciliation into the all-encompassing narrative of divine self-actualization risks vitiating his account of evil, insofar as he disallows the application of moral or ethical criteria to the interpretation of God's action in history and thereby suppresses the voices of those who lament and cry out for justice.

Contrariwise, I have tried to show in chapter 2 of Part I how Augustine's traditional christological narrative, in its very representational and Trinitarian form, offers a broader, more transformative theological foundation for individual and communal Christian life in the world. Augustine, like Hegel, employs the image of the spoken word, but unlike Hegel, he restricts its application to the incarnation of the eternal Logos in the historical Jesus. Augustine thereby relinquishes the possibility of any necessary rational account of the eternal triune God and his action outward in history. Nevertheless, the consequent difference between God and the world issues not in epistemological or ethical paralysis before a fathomless abyss, but rather forms the opening in and across which real relationships can be built up in the freedom of love, a love that is, moreover, consistent with the truth of God's triune being as Father and Son united in the bond of the Holy Spirit.

Augustine's use of oral linguistic imagery in his Christology thus provides an account of Christian life in which dialectical tension is not resolved, but rather persists as long as one is in this world. This tension between God and the world, the now and the not yet, always maintained and yet mysteriously bridged in the incarnate Word of God through the love of the Holy Spirit, gives Christian life its dynamism. Perhaps, too, it gives Christian life greater freedom than Hegel's Trinitarian theology, precisely because Augustine's critical assessment of human sinfulness does not allow for any temporal resolution to the drama of history. That is to say, Augustine takes seriously the inexplicability of evil and suffering that is rooted in unjust love of self. He does not strive to make sense of that evil by incorporating it into a grand narrative of divine self-development. Even though Augustine speaks at points of how God can render human history "beautiful" through an aesthetic of fittingness, the overall thrust of his thought remains resistant to any type of theodicy.[157] Rather, Augustine insists, God's response of love in the incarnation brings good out of death, which nonetheless remains inscrutably evil. That re-creative act is something only God can do. Only God's Word spoken humbly in the world through the love of the Holy Spirit can remake humankind by constantly liberating it from its fatally erroneous claims of absolute authority.

Yet Augustine's insistence that no person, state, or culture can claim the fullness of vision is not, as Hegel would argue, pie-in-the-sky escapism. To the contrary, the exhortation to humility and love that Augustine sees manifest in Christ's incarnation and death—a death, indeed, intended to persuade us to love justice before power—is none other than instruction on how to live rightly in the world. To live rightly in the world means that one does not absolutize the world. It means that one lives with an openness to the transformative love of the Spirit that turns one's heart toward Christ, that slowly conforms one's words and actions to God's Word, in the hope that God will re-create the world in accord with the justice that he is.

PART II

PENTECOST

Part II explores how Augustine and Hegel each approach the Holy Spirit's Pentecostal witness to Christ as the theological and historical foundation of the Christian community of faith. Pentecost in this context will mean not only the particular event recorded in Acts 2, but also pneumatology more broadly conceived. In Part I we saw how Hegel's and Augustine's respective ways of speaking about Christ were situated within different Trinitarian and soteriological contexts. The divergence between the two thinkers when it comes to what God has said and done in Christ consequently affects what they say about the Holy Spirit too. Because both of their distinct Trinitarian paradigms set about to describe a God who is in free and conscious relationship with his human creation, their theological content is inextricably intertwined with the way human beings come to know and love their creator and the way that knowledge and love are communicated. Indeed, we remain concerned here with the relationship between the Word and words. In that regard, the issue of pneumatic witness that we seek to explore in the next two chapters under the general heading of Pentecost is one in which both the content and form of witnessing are at stake.

As with his Christology, Augustine's pneumatology is, on the whole, much more biblically based, comprehensive, and complex than Hegel's. It contains material elements that Hegel does not address. Nevertheless, because the resultant disparity bears upon the kind of Christian witness that is possible according to their respective Trinitarian paradigms, it gives impetus to our comparison. That is, Hegel's very critique of the type of representational theology exemplified by Augustine is itself pneumatological in character and must therefore be taken into account.

Hegel's critical standpoint is, to be sure, afforded and sustained by his different historical context. In the wake of the disruptive political and social changes of the modern period, including the French Revolution and political unrest in the German states, as well as the Enlightenment and especially the Kantian philosophical critique, the young Hegel sought to mine his culture's Judaeo-Christian heritage for resources with which to effect a reunification of the subject with God and the surrounding world. In his early text *The Spirit of Christianity*, however, he reaches an impasse. There Christ is a tragic figure who cannot reconcile himself to the unspiritual positivity of his Jewish culture and, by withdrawing, must submit to the fate of an unfulfilled life and ultimately his own destruction. Christ's followers try, similarly, to preserve their purity from the world around them, but in establishing the historical figure of Christ as the locus of their unity, they end up perpetuating the same Jewish positivity they had sought to avoid.[1] The concepts of love and life that Hegel proposes in that text to bridge the gap between the divine and the human and the church and the world falter. Hegel cannot yet reconcile the transformative, unifying aspects he finds in Christianity with the multidimensional political and social realities he encounters in the world.

In his mature system he ultimately shifts the locus of unity from love to reason. There he can retain the autonomy for which Kant had argued and bring about a union between the subject and the world. Toward that end, Hegel devises his own logic in which Christ comes to function as the fleeting middle term, the transient Word, in a dialectical process of divine becoming. Hegel's reassessment of Christianity and its role in the actualization of Spirit, however, does not affect his general critique of the early church's Trinitarian theology and its social implications. One of the primary features Hegel consistently discerns in early Christianity is recourse to sensual immediacy, which issues in an alternating struggle between the empty bond of love that unites the group over against the world and, as interaction with the world becomes inevitable, the increasing externalization and sensual objectification of that communal bond, especially in the individual figure of Christ and his figural-historical extension in the institutional church. Put in terms of Hegel's Logos theology, the early church mistakes the man Jesus for the divine Word, and in so doing they evacuate the Word of any real meaning. The language around and through which they build up the church is fundamentally flawed. Traditional Trinitarian theology has social consequences that, to Hegel's mind, stand in the way of freedom. By contrast, Hegel thinks that the language of Spirit, articulated in terms of his mature system, positively shapes the formation of community, a community based on the act of mutual recognition and engagement in the world. Indeed, ultimately, the only perspective that matters according to Hegel is the universal rational vision ultimately achieved by the divine in the modern state.

Yet when we turn our attention to Augustine in chapter 4, we begin to see how he—as an exponent of the Trinitarian tradition Hegel deems in need of philosophical reconstruction—in fact offers a dynamic and liberating view of the Holy Spirit's operation in the world. Given Augustine's emphasis upon the social force of language, which we explored in chapter 2 with regard to the divine rhetoric of the incarnation, our investigation again orients itself around human communication, but this time in its relation to the work of the Holy Spirit, particularly with regard to how the Spirit empowers human beings to participate in God's rhetoric of love.

Several differences between Hegel and Augustine emerge in Part II. In the latter's pneumatology, a different relation between Christ and the Spirit maintains at the same time an ontological distance between Christ and his followers. Conditioning that distance for Augustine is a broader christological narrative that includes the resurrection and ascension in contrast to their attenuation and conflation with Pentecost in Hegel's account. In Augustine the Holy Spirit bestows freedom, but a freedom founded upon the distance between the divine and the human rather than upon their dialectical identity. Whereas that dialectical identity underscores the fundamental relationship between Spirit and knowledge in Hegel's pneumatology, Augustine, although not denying the role of the Holy Spirit in enabling knowledge, places the emphasis upon the Spirit's gift of love. That love entails, moreover, an understanding of forgiveness and reconciliation—marked as they are by their character as gift—that is different from that of Hegel, where evil and its forgiveness are both moments in one single ontotheologic of divine becoming.

For both Augustine and Hegel the Spirit works to build unity between human beings beyond the bounds of the institutional church. But for Augustine the unity that the church strives to achieve is a reflection of the divine unity rather than God's actual concretion in the world. What is more, while in Hegel that concretion of the divine in the world ultimately leads to an identification of church and state, such an identification is not possible for Augustine. Indeed, Augustine's pneumatology makes possible the ultimate sacrifice of martyrdom as a relativization of worldly claims to absolute authority. Precisely therein, Augustine shows how, in the pneumatically empowered act of witness to Christ, a witness animated by a love which sometimes must contradict the world even unto death, the Holy Spirit acts freely and liberates the faithful to build up the body of Christ.

Chapter 3

HEGEL'S LANGUAGE OF SPIRIT AND ITS SOCIAL REALIZATION

For Hegel, the true, speculative understanding of Christ comes only through the witness of Spirit to Spirit.[1] This witness, which begins to enable the proper means of speaking about Christ, unites individual subjects in the one universal truth. It thus establishes the spiritual community. But what, for Hegel, constitutes true pneumatic witnessing, and what kind of community does he aim to achieve? How, moreover, does this differ from what Augustine considers appropriate pneumatic speech, the kind that he thinks gives shape to a community of love for God and neighbor?

We can better position ourselves to answer these questions if we start our analysis with one of Hegel's Catholic contemporaries, Franz Anton Staudenmaier, who ultimately concludes that Hegel's mode of speaking about the Spirit jeopardizes its very character as a critical witness to God's Word in the world. With this critique in mind, we can then try to understand why Hegel formulates his logic of Spirit the way he does by investigating his Protestant, specifically Pietist, religious and social background. This historical religious context, with its emphasis on social reform and anti-Augustinian, Pelagian bent, will help us to explain why Hegel readily links social malaise with a traditional, here Catholic, way of talking about the triune God.

By contrast, Hegel seeks a means of pneumatic speech commensurate to the self-conscious freedom he sees realized in the modern world. It is here that we adduce Hegel's discussion of evil and forgiveness in the *Phenomenology of Spirit* as a prime text for discerning how, for Hegel, language itself can serve as a theophany of Spirit. However, it is here also that Staudenmaier's critique will be especially pertinent. Must we not situate Hegelian community, formed through the mutual recognition of autonomous rational subjects, into a broader narrative theodicy that in fact cannot or will not recognize the voices of those who cry out for justice? This question seems apt when we lastly observe how Hegel rejects the witness of the early Christian martyrs as fanatical and effectively replaces them with the figure of the hero, who is for Hegel a witness to reason or Spirit by sacrificing his or her particular human perspective in order to achieve the universal, divine end, an end, we have seen, that legitimates itself apart from any particular appeals for justice.

Franz Anton Staudenmaier: Hegel and a Pneumatic Catholicism?

As Hünermann, Franz, and O'Regan have shown, the young Staudenmaier (1830s) was receptive to Hegelian thought as a resource for Catholic theology, but not unqualifiedly so.[2] Staudenmaier understood Hegel to be the philosophical force of the day with whom an intellectually serious Catholicism would have to come to terms. Hegel's systematic understanding of *Wissenschaft*, with its unity of form and content elucidated by way of developmental categories, appealed to him as a way to render due justice to the positive historical content of Christianity and to the living God who reveals himself through it.[3] He lauded Hegel for having transcended Protestant subjectivism and Enlightenment rationalism, which in their pure arbitrariness or static formalism were lacking in objective content. Finally, Hegel articulated for Staudenmaier a pneumatic vitality capable of enriching the Catholic understanding of tradition. Such Spirit, Staudenmaier thought, could deflate pride and revitalize the ossified institution of the church. For both thinkers, the activity of the Spirit, as the agent of transformation, vitality, and revelation, could not be foreclosed in modernity.[4]

All the same, Staudenmaier's enthusiasm for Hegel was tempered by theological reservation. When Staudenmaier takes up Hegelian language or concepts, he often modifies them according to Christian theological principles. Hence *Geist* for Staudenmaier is one of life and love more than of reason, and when he describes the Spirit's operation in the world, he avoids a dynamism motored by logical necessity.[5] In this way he hopes to avert Hegel's tendency to identify the content of theology and philosophy so much that the former becomes expendable. Staudenmaier likewise strives to avoid Hegel's determination of the divine according to a dynamic logic that renders the act of creation necessary and thereby jeopardizes divine and human freedom. This desire to preserve the integrity of freedom prevents Staudenmaier from going as far as Hegel's pneumatic ecclesiology in erasing the line between the divine Spirit and the *Gemeinde*, or spiritual community.[6]

This moderated approach to Hegel is on display in Staudenmaier's earliest work, *Der Pragmatismus der Geistesgaben; oder, Das Wirken des göttlichen Geistes im Menschen und in der Menschheit*, written in 1827 but first published as a book in 1835.[7] Language of Hegelian provenance is there employed within the context of a Pauline theology of spiritual gifts drawn from 1 Cor 12–14. At the outset, Staudenmaier sets forth a fourfold pneumatological program: (1) to help each human being grasp him- or herself as a free, conscious, individual personality, that is, as (2) a particular divine revelation and as (3) a living member of an actual kingdom of God, and thereby (4) to present a truly Christian view of the world, with regard both to its current relations and to their pneumatic transfiguration.[8] Adducing 1 Cor 12.4–6 as his programmatic guide, Staudenmaier argues in that work that the Holy Spirit helps realize the unique idea of the individual human being through the tripartite operation of gift (*Gabe*), vocation (*Beruf*), and strength (*Kraft*).[9] Particular internal elements of the individual's inborn living Word, his or her concept, are transfigured, animated, and expressed outwardly in act (*That*), whereby the individual is brought back into harmony with him- or herself and with God and becomes a free, self-conscious personality in accord with his or her God-given idea.[10]

This attainment of freedom is a task, the development of character, which Staudenmaier calls holiness.[11] Through the sanctifying action of the Holy Spirit, each person becomes a particular revelation, a freshly spoken word of God.[12] In this respect Staudenmaier shares with Hegel an agonic, developmental understanding of personality, but his Christian commitments prevent him from following Hegel all the way. Without mentioning Hegel explicitly, Staudenmaier is clear that the revelation of God in finite spirits is not to be understood as though God's full essence existed in that revelation. The human mind, Staudenmaier insists, cannot plumb the depths of God.[13] Indeed, in a telling Augustinian turn, Staudenmaier contends that, given the incomprehensible profundity of one's own personality, it is laughable to attempt to measure the divine personality by its anthropological analogate.[14] In other words, he (1) resists Hegel's eschatological identification of infinite and finite *Geist* and (2) underscores instead the limited representational character of the human being as *imago Dei* so as to preclude claims to any definitive knowledge of the divine based on merely anthropological inquiry.

For Staudenmaier, individual sanctification develops in tandem with the formation of the kingdom of God, inasmuch as each individual complements and completes the other in the whole, and through the whole each comes to a deeper knowledge of one's own individuality. Like Hegel, Staudenmaier argues that the Spirit actualizes the ideal in the world. Hence Staudenmaier takes seriously the familial and various national spirits in addition to individual vocations. Moreover, the harmony of ideal and real obtains in society and among nations according to the one idea of humanity. Again, however, Staudenmaier's theological commitments delimit his overlap with Hegel. While Staudenmaier's language is reminiscent of Hegel when he claims that in Christianity differences among individuals, groups, and nations "appear as immanent determinations, as moments of the idea, and together they constitute the one, systematic totality of the spirit of humanity,"[15] he also distances himself from what he views to be the deleterious consequences of Hegelian philosophy: God is not to be understood as coming to consciousness of himself through his creation. Staudenmaier consistently underscores the distinction between God and his creation and God's specific personal relationship to each created thing.[16]

In Staudenmaier's view, the ideal unity that realizes itself in history does not, as in Hegel, require the sublation of Christianity into philosophy or into the ethical world (*Sittlichkeit*) of a modern German Protestant social milieu. Rather, unity obtains only in Christianity, through the love given by the Holy Spirit.[17] However, the historical realization of the kingdom of God is not yet complete; Staudenmaier's affirmation of Christianity's continued eschatological distention assigns to *hope* a catalytic function in history and the development of human character.[18] It also reserves for the church a preeminent transformative, or *transfigurative*, role to play in society and history. Whereas in Hegel the Spirit exerts a critical force upon a church standing in the way of its realization, for Staudenmaier the church retains the ability to raise a critical voice toward secular power. For this reason, Staudenmaier enjoins Christians to speak the truth with courageousness (*Tapferkeit*)[19] and emphasizes that the historical formation of character requires a bold (*muthig*) struggle with the world.[20] The Holy Spirit thus transforms people into living words of God.

If in *Pragmatismus* there is clear, if not vociferous, theological modification of Hegel's thought, the tone of denunciation becomes much more pronounced later in Staudenmaier's career. It occurs in the context of tumultuous developments among Hegel's followers. Staudenmaier witnessed the emergence of such Young-Hegelian thinkers as Feuerbach, Strauss, Bruno Bauer, and Heine, and he came to the conclusion that their atheistic and materialistic worldviews could be traced back to Hegel.[21] The understanding of *Wissenschaftlichkeit*—marked by a systematic character, truth as totality, and the identity of method and object—that had attracted the young Staudenmaier gradually drives him in his mature years to reject Hegel's thought as logical pantheism.[22] By "logical" Staudenmaier has in view Hegel's narrative rendering of the divine in which a necessary organic process of development has become axiomatic. The accusation of pantheism refers in a narrow sense to the reduction of creation to a necessary moment in the process of divine becoming. But in a broader sense, Staudenmaier also uses the term "pantheism" to designate what he deems to be Hegel's thoroughgoing systematic distortion of Christian faith.[23]

Staudenmaier gives his most sustained treatment of Hegel's alleged pantheism in his *Darstellung und Kritik des Hegelschen Systems* (1844). There he concludes that Hegel's radical identification of God and the world through a movement of logical dialectic precludes the true personality of God and individual humans as well as any genuine and free relationship of God to human beings and humans with each other.[24] When the creation and salvation of the world become necessary components in the movement of divine self-actualization, God loses his sovereignty and freedom.[25] Conversely, the world is unduly raised up beyond its creaturely status.[26] In that way it is in fact devalued, as it becomes simply a means to a divine end.[27]

According to Staudenmaier, Hegel's logical transfiguration of the positive content of Christian faith not only undermines his insistence on the identity of content between Christianity and his Idealist philosophy. More fundamentally, it is in Staudenmaier's view completely incompatible with Christian belief, a belief indispensably linked to the self-revelation of the personal God of the Bible, who freely creates and saves the world out of love.[28] Without this personal spiritual ground, Staudenmaier thinks there is really no use speaking of a church, or for that matter any distinctive spiritual community.[29] The identification of Spirit with the pneumatic community overimmanentizes the divine and erases the distinction between infinite and finite spirit necessary for true communal relationships. The teleological-historical actualization of Hegel's dialectic, moreover, separates the spiritual community from its historical roots, its scriptural and creedal foundation, and in the modern period risks associating that community too closely with the state. Hegel ultimately reduces the Spirit, Staudenmaier worries, to the impersonal bond of a group of people. The church's critical voice is thereby lost in the cacophony of the day.

By 1848 in Germany this cacophony was very real to Staudenmaier and threatened to issue in complete social breakdown. Like Hegel, but in a different way, Staudenmaier was convinced that that fragmentation had theological roots. Hegel's depersonalization and making immanent of Spirit, which Staudenmaier thought went hand in hand with modernity's focus on unfettered intellectual inquiry and autonomous self-determination, risked unleashing anarchy in society. Against this background, the church could stand as a critical bulwark, Staudenmaier claimed, only to the extent that it recognized Christ as its foundation and held him to be both the epitome of personhood and its source of unity. Only in that church, where each individual is affirmed in the freedom of a personal relationship to God and other human beings through the love of the Holy Spirit, did Staudenmaier think one could avert the "Babylonian confusion of concepts and life."[30]

The integrity and critical voice of the church amid the bedlam of Babel is thus maintained for Staudenmaier when it rests upon an authentically Trinitarian foundation—one he thinks is glaringly lacking in Hegel's philosophy, with its pneumatological bias. When he analyzes Hegel's *Lectures on the Philosophy of Religion* in his 1840 text *Philosophy of Christianity*, Staudenmaier therefore underscores Hegel's transposition of the three Trinitarian persons into moments in a process of divine becoming, which, in its inclusive breadth, erases the boundary between the immanent Trinity and its operations in time.[31] Staudenmaier concludes that the best way of describing Hegel's articulation of the Trinity is as a logical form of Sabellianism, characterized as it was historically by the emphasis upon the single personality of the divine expressed merely in different modes across salvation history. Whereas Hegel endorses only a developmental divine monologue issuing in the predominance and immanence of Spirit at the expense of the Father and Son, Staudenmaier stresses the mystery of the divine life as a perichoretic fullness of divine love between the three divine persons. It is this fullness of divine life and love, apart from its expression in history, that, in Staudenmaier's view, makes possible the life of the church and empowers each individual therein to develop into the fullness of personhood through a life of love.

But we ought then to ask of Hegel: what forms of life emerge from his concepts? On Staudenmaier's reading, there can be no sanctifying Spirit in Hegelianism. Staudenmaier's judgment compels us to look at Hegel's narrative and its implications. In order to do so adequately we first need to consider the religious context in which Hegel's philosophy developed.

Württemberg Pietism, Sanctification, and Political Recollectivization

Early Pietism arose in the latter half of the seventeenth century as a critique of the official Lutheran church, its preaching, allegedly dry doctrinal and polemical theology, and the routinized religious practice of its members, in which not the Word but the enlivening Spirit was perceived to be lacking.[32] Philipp Jakob Spener, author of the *Pia Desideria*, a 1675 text which was to become programmatic for Pietism, identified the problem as the barriers humans put in the way of God's continuous bestowal of spiritual gifts. At the heart of all his reforms stood the effort to eliminate the obstacles blocking the Holy Spirit, as is evidenced especially in his attempt to recognize a wider range of pneumatic operation beyond the ministerial office of the church. However, as Wallmann observes, "it is no contradiction when, from the expansion of the Holy Spirit's potential range of activity beyond the confines of the ecclesial office, there results a narrowing of the Holy Spirit's actual field of operation."[33] Unlike Luther, for whom all baptized Christians were members of the spiritual priesthood, Spener considered only those who have experienced the anointing of the Holy Spirit to be spiritual priests. Consequently, he spoke of the "ecclesiola in ecclesia," a specially sanctified group within the larger church community.[34]

Following Albrecht Ritschl, Alan Olson wonders whether Pietism's tendency toward spiritual elitism harbors a potentially divisive social effect that undermines Luther's emphasis upon the sanctity of all vocations, religious and secular, and his doctrine of freedom that so informed the Reformation spirit. The debate between Lutheran Orthodoxy and Pietism revolved around the role of the Holy Spirit in sanctification. Pietism's predominating pneumatic focus, the Orthodox worried, might distract from the centrality of Christ and result in an overly subjective concern with attaining immediate confirmation of one's salvation and the pursuit of holiness. But for Ritschl the conflict posed broader social consequences than the theological frame of the dispute might initially suggest: the subjective emphasis of Pietism put in jeopardy the very German Protestant social order founded on the Lutheran affirmation of freedom and vocation by reintroducing in effect a quasi-monastic quest for personal holiness. Such subjectivism threatened to sunder the unity of the religious and secular realms achieved in the Reformation.[35]

However, as Laurence Dickey has shown, Württemberg Pietists of the late eighteenth century were not only concerned with personal sanctification, but in fact saw themselves engaged in the communal and political task of reform, indeed of completing a second Reformation.[36] Dickey argues that it was this active socio-political orientation of Württemberg Pietism that shaped the development of the young Hegel's religious and political views and his concept of *Sittlichkeit*, or ethics. For his project, Dickey retrieves categories from the Pelagian controversy that shaped much of Augustine's later thought. He thereby shows how the dispute between Pietists and Lutheran Orthodoxy stands as one significant historical link between the post-Reformation, post-Enlightenment Hegel and the North African bishop Augustine writing at the end of the Roman Empire:

> The idea of Christian reform [exemplified by the Alexandrian tradition of Clement and Origen] presupposes three things about *homo religiosus*: (1) he must possess a capacity

for *homoiosis* after the Fall; (2) he must be actively committed to the pursuit of "relative perfection" in time; and (3) he must conceive of the *end* of that perfection in terms of eschatological fulfillment in the Kingdom of God on earth. . . . These three conceptions figured prominently in the thought of Lessing, Kant, Schiller, and Hegel. Yet, even before them, among the early Württemberg pietists, these conceptions had been used to challenge the theological anthropology of orthodox Lutheranism. That anthropology . . . had been heavily influenced by Augustine's ethical and eschatological teachings. It cannot be surprising to learn, therefore, that when the *Aufklärer* began to contest orthodox anthropology they drew on anti-Augustinian ethical and eschatological sources.[37]

Dickey concedes that, while the terms "Pelagianism" and "Augustinianism" are helpful in explaining types of Christian thought, they are not immediately identifiable with the thought of the historical Pelagius, Julian of Eclanum, or Augustine. Even so, the distinction he demarcates between "theocentric" Augustinianism and more "anthropologically oriented" Pelagianism appears generally valid. Augustine, after brief flirtation with Eusebian-esque imperial theology, evidences in his later thought a more acute sense of the ambiguity of historical and political flux with regard to its soteriological value.[38] This view is informed by an anthropology increasingly sensitive to human weakness, to the inability of fallen humanity to believe and love apart from God's help. Pelagianism, on the other hand, viewed such anthropology as conducive to ethical lethargy.

The Pelagian anthropology characterizing the thought of German Enlightenment figures receptive to Christianity eschews an Augustinian understanding of grace. Kant's *Religion innerhalb der Grenzen der blossen Vernunft*—a book we know the young Hegel thought about a great deal—offers a good example. There Kant explicitly restricts the works and means of "grace" to *parerga*, which are inessential to *Vernunftreligion* and merely "border on it."[39] Kant distinguishes between two types of religion: (1) those consisting of obedience to divine commands simply with a view toward currying divine favor and gaining a reward of happiness ("mere worship") and (2) those he calls *"moral religion, that is, the religion of good life-conduct."*[40] The former is an ignoble form of piety that devalues the human potential for good and instead pins its hopes upon God for forgiveness of sins, moral transformation, and the reward of happiness. By contrast, moral religion (and Kant thinks Christianity is the only historical religion one can label moral) has as "a fundamental principle that, to become a better human being, everyone must do as much as it is in his powers to do; and only then ... if he has made use of the original predisposition to the good ... can he hope that what does not lie in his power will be made good by cooperation from above."[41] Kant therefore does not explicitly reject "grace" altogether. But he argues that the only way hope in divine assistance can be rendered compatible with religion based on the universal law of reason is if that hope rests upon one's own efforts to become worthy of God's grace. Grace cannot be the starting point of ethical action.[42] With Kant's universally valid and rationally discernable ethical religion, then, we are a far cry from Augustine's claim that God first had to persuade us of how much he loved us by dying on the cross: "'It is not essential, and hence not necessary, that every human being know what God does, or has done, for his salvation'; but it is essential to know *what a human being has to do himself* in order to become worthy of this assistance."[43]

But Kant's concern here extends beyond individual morality. The two forms of virtue—one in which obedience to the letter of the law is motivated by happiness and one in which the law has been internalized and is followed according to its spirit for the sake of holiness or virtue itself—are situated onto an ethico-historical trajectory in which the right formation of a people by means of a reformed Christianity is at stake.[44] As Dickey argues, Kant is setting before his readers a decision of momentous social, historical, even eschatological import, arguing as he does in books 2–4 of *Religion* for the choice of virtue and holiness over legalism and self-interested happiness.[45] The idea of the kingdom of God inspires ethical action here and now because it is grounded upon the hope that it can be realized through human effort, that its realization is possible because it rests upon the ought dictated by the universal law. This eschatological hope rests, then, on the perfectibility of humankind and human society in history, on the possibility of *homoiosis* or "assimilation to God."[46]

In this evolutionary eschatology and assimilationism as part of a program of religio-political reform, Dickey sees Kant's interests converging with, if not directly influencing, those of Hegel in the early 1790s. But the point of his broader argument is to show that these interests were not entirely unique to Kant or Hegel, but rather need to be situated against the backdrop of a this-worldly, socially oriented Pietism.[47] Originating from amid the rubble of the Thirty Years' War, Pietism shared with other Lutheran reform movements, such as that of Johann Arndt, an impulse toward social activism.[48] Following Spener's visit to Tübingen in 1662, Pietism gradually established itself in Württemberg, becoming an intellectual and cultural force through such Tübingen Pietist theologians as Christoph Reuchlin and Johann Albrecht Bengel.[49] The form of Pietism espoused by Bengel and in line with Spener's theology, a form which Olson labels devotional Pietism, was characterized by its down-to-earth, practical orientation, what Dickey terms a *praxis pietatis*. Questions of applying the moral law in this tradition were determined by the *sensus communis*, a shared understanding of value and right action within the community.[50] Württemberg Pietists conceived of themselves as a holy people in covenant with God, and this self-understanding was situated within an evolutionary, this-worldly eschatological outlook in the Joachimite tradition, an outlook that had continuous reformation in the process of assimilation to the divine as its telos.

In contrast to Ritschl's negative assessment, then, Dickey argues that Pietism's collective outlook is anything but subjective, as it entails the giving of oneself to the work of achieving the common good and the gaining in turn of an elevated collective consciousness. The Pietist reformers, according to Dickey, understood the limits of historical progress, but still had faith that certain individuals could educate the people and persuade them to take up, voluntarily, the task of realizing their religious telos as a people in covenant with God. These views influenced the young Hegel in the 1790s and beyond as he strove to combine a Protestant program of active reform with an increasing awareness of the inadequacy of the existing political institutions to support real change.⁵¹

Our brief consideration of the Pietist theology of sanctification has, however, indicated several possible points of internal tension. As an effort to expand what was understood to be the Holy Spirit's sphere of operation, Pietism strove to remove obstacles restricting the Spirit's range of movement. But the extension of that range beyond the bounds of the institutional church and its liturgical worship threatened at the same time to result practically in a contraction of its perimeters to those who had verifiable experience of spiritual regeneration. On the other hand, the practical, even Pelagian, orientation of Pietism's affirmation of the Spirit was linked in Württemberg to a covenantal collective self-understanding informed by the evolutionary-Joachimite eschatological tradition. This alignment, however, raises the question of whether the expanded operation of the Spirit in Württemberg Pietism did not risk becoming confused or even conflated with Protestant social culture and politics. In Trinitarian terms, we might ask whether here, too, the Word exhibits an ephemerality, akin to that in Hegel's oral linguistic model of the immanent Logos, which results in an exaggerated immanence of Spirit, an immanence which bars human language from any critical transcendent referent. We close this section with a telling example: Dickey adduces studies showing the common connection in the thought of early modern Europe of the Christian notions of μάρτυς and *caritas* with the classical notions of ἥρως and *amor* (*patriae*). "And so," Dickey observes, "they were [linked] in Hegel."⁵²

CATHOLICISM AND CHRISTOLOGICAL STAGNATION

It is not surprising, then, that in Hegel's early works we find him struggling to find a way to reconcile "church and state, worship and life, piety and virtue, spiritual and worldly action."⁵³ In *The Spirit of Christianity*, from which the previous quotation is taken,

Hegel's critique of Kantian ethics—namely, that a purely formal categorical imperative lacks any mechanism whereby to realize itself in the world because it subjugates the moment of particular inclination—is motivated by a communally inflected concept of freedom sustained and actualized by love. A purely formal imperative cements heteronomy within the individual and thereby prevents free reconciliation with others. No one can love a universal idea. In contrast, Hegel appeals to Jesus' teaching of brotherly love (Jn 13.34–35).[54] This concept of love is pneumatological and bears the marks of Pietism.[55] Hegel identifies this community of love with the kingdom of God and attributes its formation and growth to the outpouring of the Holy Spirit:

> What Jesus calls the "Kingdom of God" is the living harmony of men . . . the development of the divine among men, the relationship with God which they enter through being filled with the Holy Spirit, that is, that of becoming his sons and living in the harmony of the developed many-sidedness and their entire being and character. In this harmony their many-sided consciousness chimes in with one spirit and their many different lives with one life, but, more than this . . . the same living spirit animates the different beings, who therefore are no longer merely similar but one; they make up not a collection but a communion, since they are unified not in a universal . . . but through life and through love.[56]

However, throughout his writings Hegel thinks that the kingdom of God and the bestowal of divine sonship have not yet been realized in the early Christian community. The central problem that restricts the formation of truly spiritual community after Pentecost lies in the inability of Jesus' disciples to understand the need for his departure as a condition for the advent of the Spirit. In *The Spirit of Christianity*, Hegel observes that the love binding the early Christians was a restricted love aimed at maintaining their purity from the surrounding Jewish milieu. Yet as the group began to grow, the bounds of the community increasingly overlapped with the secular world. The early church therefore sought to objectify its unity in the historical man of Jesus and his empirical bodily resurrection. However, by exalting the historical, exclusive particularity of Christ, by elevating the *forma servi* into heaven rather than seeing it as the passing veil of the divine nature, the early Christians prevented the genuine reconciliation of subject and object and of different individuals in collective spiritual self-consciousness.[57] Hegel concludes *The Spirit of Christianity* with the observation that, throughout the history of the church, Christians have been unable to bridge the gap between themselves and the world.[58]

Hegel's criticism of Catholicism is especially pertinent to the theme of Pentecost. At issue is the externality that pervades Catholic theology and sacramental worship. Hegel thinks that the basic outlook of Judaism, which seeks its unity and independence in a transcendent God over against whom all finite relations are annulled and subjected to a strict legalism, persists in Catholicism. Catholicism "enjoys the actuality of the most multiplex consciousness and unites itself with the fate of the world," to which God stands in contradiction, such that there is "felt opposition in all actions and expressions of life which purchase their righteousness with the sense of the servitude and the nullity of their opposition."[59] In the *Phenomenology of Spirit*, Hegel describes medieval Catholicism as the "unhappy consciousness" still unable to unite its finite consciousness with the infinite divine. To be sure, Christianity distinguishes itself from Judaism insofar as God has taken empirical shape in Christ. But inasmuch as the incarnation is seen to happen only in Christ, all other human beings remain separated from God. For the unhappy consciousness, God is conceived as an immutable infinite and hence as completely distinct from the world. Conversely, both the incarnation of Christ and the outpouring of the Spirit among the members of the Christian community are understood as merely historical events, rather than as moments of the Trinitarian divine.[60] As Hegel makes clear in *PS* VII and *LPR* 3, the root of the problem lies historically in the early church's attachment to the historical person of Christ, the result of which is "spiritual opacity" and heteronomy.[61]

The withdrawal of Christ in sensible form is a necessary step toward the realization of God's kingdom and the attainment of freedom as God's children, in that the subject, the spiritual community, is thereby able to know itself in this truth content. If Christ remains, then the truth maintains an external relationship to the subject. The Christian community, however, proves as yet unable to escape its need for sensible immediacy, the now of presence. Its representational thought knows reconciliation only as an extrinsic act performed by Christ in the past.[62] Because Christians cling to Christ's sensible particularity, they represent him as bodily resurrected, ascended, and dwelling in heaven, whence he will one day return.[63] In the meantime, they attempt to effect a sensible presence by such media as relics or pilgrimages to sites associated with Christ's historical existence.[64] The search for Christ's body during the Crusades, which finds only the empty tomb, indicates well the inadequacy of such representational thinking.[65] In effect, the Christian subject knows him- or herself to be reconciled only implicitly now by an external sacrifice carried out by a distinct subject. This reconciliation remains confined to the heart and awaits its realization in an eschatological future. A disconnect thus persists in the community between religious consciousness and immediate consciousness. The former knows its implicit unity with the divine, while the latter is conscious of a world still groaning for transformation.[66] The early Christian community remains separated from both God and the world.

Hegel thinks that this divide poses dire consequences for ethical action and the formation of civil society. Within Catholicism the result of institutionalized objectivity is a systematic passivity in worship and doctrinal and social formation that denies subjectivity and freedom:

> The *Catholics* venerate the host as such, even when [it is] not [being] partaken of. The same [is] true of doctrine, [where they demand] not insight but obedience, stern objectivity, subjection, and the doing of works. This form of external objectivity with respect to what subsists in and for itself is not limited to

this sacrament but occurs elsewhere in accord with the same principle. Thus, the doctrine of the church stands there rigidly on its own, to be taken into the possession of the church by its members in a purely receptive fashion, as the ongoing development and tradition of the church itself. Equally [if not] more unconditional is the demand for action, for works. The laity are excluded from having any say in the development and self-understanding of doctrine. Thus [it functions as] law for the faithful, [who are expected] to conduct themselves in a receptive fashion. Grace, the dispensation of grace and of the sacraments, [falls to] a particular office. The church [is] the external proprietor and dispenser of the means of grace. Hence this grace [is] a "mass."[67]

The general passivity of the Catholic laity leads to opposition between the religious and the secular spheres, with a twofold result: (1) the church strives to dominate secular and political affairs and is thus itself sometimes suppressed; (2) political power over passive Catholic populations, as in South America, is gained through violent revolts and retained by means of force and oppression. Contrariwise, Protestantism, by sanctifying all religious and secular relations and works, gives rise to a general trust between individuals, civil stability, and a government emerging organically from the people's sense of its free self-consciousness.[68]

Christianity as a religion possesses the truth, in Hegel's view, but historically it remains nascent and undeveloped until well into the Reformation period. In this way Hegel can underscore the genuinely spiritual element of the historical Pentecost. This is evidenced by his rejection of miracles as a means of verifying Christ's divinity and unity with the Father. Following Reimarus and Lessing, Hegel thinks the appeal to historically contingent miracles cannot be used to establish eternal rational truths. Rather, Spirit gives witness to Spirit for spirit. That is, at Pentecost only Spirit can testify to the unity of the finite moment of the Son with the eternal moment of the Father as absolute Spirit. The early Christians, however, do not yet grasp the full universal implications of the unity between the divine and the human. They restrict this union to the incarnate Christ and thereby leave no route for all humans to achieve sonship in the kingdom of God. Humanity is not yet understood as a moment in the broader Trinitarian narrative of divine becoming.

Standstill at the moment of finitude, Christ in *forma servi*, distorts for Hegel the dynamic grammar of divine self-realization. The damage that results is found not only in the extrinsic relation of subject and object, but also in the divisions that persist between individuals and groups. Such division, Hegel thinks, does violence to love and reason, violence that can even rear its ugly head in the physical aggression of one group against another. In *The Spirit of Christianity*, Hegel faults the first followers of Christ for fostering an exclusive love that separates them from the broader society. With jealousy they protect the *Holy* Spirit—God in them as a distinct and pure community. Thus they are unable to recognize themselves in the spirit of the culture, in the diverse vocations and circumstances that constitute the world around them. In order to avert the possibility that their love, their Holy Spirit, might dissolve into the differences and petty bickering of mundane existence, they withdraw from society.[69] They cannot reconcile their abstract unifying love with the multifarious roles and relations of the world. Hence when their growth pushes them into contact with the world, there remains a relationship of contradiction, dominance or subservience, and ultimately violence and aggression.[70] This critique of religious "love" as overly emotive and sectarian, here attested explicitly in Hegel's early *Spirit* essay, remains in his mature thought. Its persistence is especially on display in explicit comments regarding the early Christian martyrs from the *Aesthetics* and *Lectures on the Philosophy of History*, to which we now turn.

Grace and Forgiveness: The Hero as Hegelian Martyr

In light of his critique of the early church, it appears that Hegel would draw a line from early Christian martyrdom to the grave consequences that ensue when Christianity (in particular, Catholicism) gains political power and the means of repression. These are forms of religious social life born out of a Christianity not yet *free*. For Hegel such social malaise stems from the way Christians talk about God. That is, Hegel thinks that theology, in this case Trinitarian theology, can have dire consequences. In the foregoing section we saw that this social division and heteronomy were rooted, in Hegel's view, in an underdeveloped historical representation of the Trinity, in which the person of Christ assumes a position of primacy and, as a consequence, the Holy Spirit is identified increasingly with a church hierarchy seeking to maintain control over its congregants through its function as the sole mediator of grace and forgiveness.

We could also put this in terms we explored in chapter 1. Hegel employs oral linguistic imagery, wherein the second Trinitarian moment of the Son necessarily gives way to the Spirit, to show that, for truth to be universal, it must encompass the whole finite world but not be identified exclusively or permanently with any single part of it. There is another reason why he uses such imagery as well: one must be able to speak about the truth in a way that is universally accessible and comprehensible, and the only means of doing so for Hegel is the universal language of reason. That, in fact, is a major problem with the martyrs, on Hegel's analysis. Hegel is, to be sure, willing to acknowledge that the early Christian martyrs served a historical purpose in advancing the spread of Christianity, but to his mind such a form of religious witness has no place anymore in the modern liberal democratic state, where Spirit, reason, is present and real universally. Such religious action, whether motivated by love or not, cannot be rationally justified to others in the socio-political condition of modernity. Love cannot explain itself.

Hegel detects a connection between Trinitarian theology, martyrdom, and religio-political oppression; as a theoretical counterproposal, he introduces the world historical individual, who becomes the true martyr of Spirit on its way to free self-conscious realization in the modern state. We will first examine the way in which Hegel, following Kant, reconstructs the traditionally pneumatological themes of grace and forgiveness before next contrasting the role of the Spirit in the lives of the ancient Christian martyrs and the heroes of history.

The dialectic of forgiveness and reconciliation is for Hegel realized socially and in the world, a world that is not perfectly beautiful or morally pure. Consequently, when Hegel comes to speak of evil and its forgiveness in the *Phenomenology of Spirit*, his depiction involves the figure of the "beautiful soul," who withdraws from the world in order to maintain his or her purity.[71] This figure thus parallels what Hegel deems to be the lack of engagement with the world, with the ethical (*sittlich*) and political realms of the state, that characterized the early Christian church and negatively affected its relation to the state throughout the medieval period. Hegel argues that the beautiful soul's effort to preserve itself apart from the world ironically results in its destruction, because there can be no actual (*wirklich*) existence apart from the world: "It lives in dread of besmirching the splendour of its inner being by action and an existence; and, in order to preserve the purity of its heart, it flees from contact with the actual world.... In this transparent purity of its moments, an unhappy, so-called 'beautiful soul,' its light dies away within it, and it vanishes like a shapeless vapour that dissolves into thin air."[72] Nevertheless, the self-destruction of the beautiful soul marks the necessary sublation of a moment in the narrative of Spirit's self-actualization. The vivid and dense account of forgiveness contained in *PS* §§666–71 must thus be read on multiple levels at once: (1) that of the dynamism of individual self-consciousness, (2) that of human intersubjectivity, of the community of individual self-consciousnesses, and finally (3) that of the divine—in whose narrative the first two anthropological levels are but moments—on its way to freedom and truth in self-conscious existence.[73]

In the *Phenomenology* Hegel is in dialogue with Enlightenment moral thought. A contradiction within the moral consciousness and between moral consciousnesses has arisen and must be overcome. As one thinks about one's action, one judges (*urteilen*)[74] it, breaking it up into its universal and particular components. On the one hand, it is judged according to universal duty; on the other, it is through this particular act of this individual that the universal law is always realized in the world. Hegel thus sets up the account of evil and its forgiveness. Judgment according to a universal standard, qua universal, entails abstraction from every determinate content. Here the figure of the beautiful soul who has fled from the world in order to preserve his or her unity with the universal has its place. This universal consciousness looks *judgmentally* upon each particular act claimed to be performed in accord with duty.

To Hegel's mind, the one judged, the acting agent, is in one sense rightly judged. The abstract universal, because it lacks determinate content, is open to any content. In the absence of an objective standard, then, actions performed in the name of duty to conscience become arbitrary and subjective. They are thus dishonest and hypocritical, insofar as it is claimed that the action expresses universal duty, when it is in fact the externalization of an individual's inner feeling of self-certainty. Yet by judging such evil, the so-called beautiful soul ends up lowering itself to the same level. The standard, by which it judges the selfish intentions of the evil consciousness, is its own law, not a universal. And its judgment is passed solely in an intellectual milieu. Hence here, too, words and actions do not correspond; the judging consciousness gives voice to empty words that are not backed up by any action. The judging consciousness sunders the unity of the action, the universal from the particular, and hypocritically deems the unreality of its judgmental nonaction a greater form of reality than that of action in the world.[75]

Yet because judgment is passed in the universal medium of thought, Hegel thinks the contradiction it brings forth can be surmounted. The juxtaposition of the two consciousnesses in abstract thought alone enables the acting consciousness to recognize its own baseness and hypocrisy in the judging consciousness. Aware of its evil and selfishness and, thus, its identity with the one judging, the acting consciousness confesses their identity. Confession is not utter annihilation of self, but rather its affirmation and elevation in the universal existence of Spirit:

> His confession is not an abasement, a humiliation ... of himself in relation to the other ... this utterance is not a one-sided

affair, which would establish his disparity with the other: on the contrary, he gives himself utterance solely on account of his having seen his identity with the other; he, on his side, gives expression to their common identity in his confession, and gives utterance to it for the reason that language is the *existence* of Spirit as an immediate self.[76]

In confessing, the acting consciousness gives expression to who he or she is, not something alien, since language expresses the immediate self. Yet, in uttering this confession, one simultaneously gives up mere particularity and manifests his or her universality. The confession, "I am thus," made in the universal medium of language, invites the other to recognize him- or herself therein, so that the "I" might become a "we," a dialogue, and the universality of Spirit might be real.[77] There is, we might say, a demand for the individual to identify with the fleeting moment of the spoken Word, whereby individuality passes over into the universality of Spirit.

But the judging consciousness refuses to recognize this unity of nature. With a hard heart, the confession is rejected and the situation reversed, as the unrepentant judge is now known to be evil him- or herself. This judging consciousness falls into contradiction with itself, declaring pompously the beauty and superiority of its inner being, giving voice to its judgments while refusing to speak what is in fact true, that it shares a common evil nature with the other inasmuch as they both are caught in the particularity of their respective deeds or nondeeds. In this way, the judge him- or herself prevents the confessor from attaining to the universality of Spirit manifest in language, for the judge does wrong in continuing to reduce the sinner to the particularity of his or her action. The judge "denies Spirit; for it does not know that Spirit . . . is lord and master over every deed and actuality, and can cast them off, and make them as if they had never happened."[78] In contrast, what words the beautiful soul does pronounce, words merely of judgment, remain uncreative. Their utterance, like the eternal generation of the Word in the abstract, unliving moment of the Father, is simply an ephemeral "sound that dies away."[79] Ultimately, the contradiction within the beautiful soul, its desire for actual existence and inability to achieve it, leads to "madness," the dissipation of self into mere, indiscriminate being.[80]

Nonetheless, this involuntary dissipation of the abstract judging self, of its selfish, subjective judgment, paves the way for genuine reconciliation, because the hard heart that had clung to its superiority now softens, thereby elevating itself to the universality it shares with the confessor. The latter gives up the particularity of its action through its confession, while the former gives up the particularity of its self-conception in the words of forgiveness.[81] Spirit then exists actually, in the concrete community of reconciliation formed by language, in a way that sublates and unites the one-sided particularity of both thought and action motivated by subjective intention: "The word of reconciliation is the *objectively existent* Spirit, which beholds the pure knowledge of itself *qua universal* essence, in its opposite, in the pure knowledge of itself *qua* absolutely self-contained and exclusive *individuality*—a reciprocal recognition which is *absolute* Spirit."[82] Hegel thus makes clear how his account of evil and its forgiveness must be understood at the level of individual consciousness, in the human community, and ultimately at the level of inclusive divine, of God who now begins to take shape, to know himself, in the community of finite consciousness. Spirit knows itself as one, as individual, but as the one absolute Spirit that concretely includes all reality.

Consistent with the linguistic character of Hegel's Christology, the language of forgiveness as the ground of self-conscious community is pneumatologically theophanic: "The reconciling *Yea*, in which the two 'I's let go their antithetical *existence*, is the existence of the 'I' which has expanded into a duality, and therein remains identical with itself, and, in its complete externalization and opposite, possesses the certainty of itself: it is God manifested in the midst of those who know themselves in the form of pure knowledge."[83] Noteworthy in comparison to Augustine is not as much the concrete social character of forgiveness in Hegel's account as certain characteristics of its strong pneumaticism. The term "in the midst of" in the quotation above does not refer to a dialectic of transcendence and immanence in which the dialectical tension must be maintained, but one in which the tension is overcome in the fullness of the Spirit's presence and immanence in the pneumatic community. The community itself is the concrete form of Spirit's universality. That community, if it is truly spiritual, takes the form of a democracy of Spirit, in which reconciliation effects the knowledge of the equality of all individuals. Finally, the governing operation of Spirit is knowledge rather than love. According to Hegel's logical construal of Spirit, God's reconciliation with himself takes the character of theodicy. The contradiction of evil becomes necessary for understanding good, for divine reconciliation, peace, and freedom. Because for Hegel rational autonomy is the goal, there is no sense of forgiveness as gift.

From Augustine's perspective, though, we might ask whether the rationalization of divine grace results in the loss of critical dialogue with God's Word. Such dialogue requires distance between the Holy and human spirits, and is put in evidence more by the language of thanksgiving and praise than of mutual recognition, more by an anthropology of listening than recognizing. Might not this distance between God and humanity reduce the chances that humans whitewash past and present injustice in the name of some "greater" end that they themselves can achieve through their own rational efforts? Is not such absolute knowledge then just a recipe for forgetting? These are questions we ought to keep in mind as we now look at Hegel's devaluation of the early Christian martyrs as ethical role models and his elevation of the heroes, or world historical individuals, as truer witnesses to reason or absolute Spirit.

The reconciliation Hegel describes does not, in his view, obtain fully and explicitly at the time of Christ or the early church. In his mature system, it is realized objectively in Christ, but not actually in the world. That realization is the proprium of Spirit, one that must develop through history until the advent of the modern European (German Protestant) state. Prior to that, the Christian community remains in a state of unreconciled difference, the results of which we have traced out in Hegel's critique of Catholicism. It is in this respect that one can see at least part of the reason Hegel comes to show a preference for knowledge over love in his pneumatology. The early Christian community, according to his diagnosis in the *Spirit of Christianity*, remains sundered and exclusive. In an effort to preserve the purity of its love, the community defines itself over against society and the state. Herein Hegel discovers a major weakness in the concept of love—its proximity to the immediacy of sense, which leads to passivity and a hierarchical, heteronomous social structure.

In his *Philosophy of History* and *Aesthetics*, Hegel reflects further on the early Christian church. Jesus had, as we have seen, proclaimed the kingdom of God and forgiveness of sins with "transcendent boldness" to a largely unreceptive Jewish audience.[84] In this first phase of the founding of the Christian community—reported in the Gospels—the message preached is that of the infinity of the divine Spirit and the nullity of all that is merely finite. The radicalness of the message, of the need to turn away from all that is of this world, was necessary if people were first to be broken of their sensible attachments.[85]

After Jesus' death, it was the fate of the Christian community that it first emerged and grew in the Roman world. The same radicalness with which Jesus preached the infinity of Spirit and the nullity of the finite governs the community's relation to the Roman state, too. The first Christians separated themselves from it and abstained from commenting upon its affairs. Their rejection of the absolute dominion of the emperor, especially over spiritual matters, aroused suspicion and persecution from their non-Christian compatriots. In spite of the persecution and death they endured at the hands of the Roman state, Hegel thinks that the early Christians experienced an "infinite inward liberty" in their detachment from the affairs of the secular world.[86]

Yet this freedom he ascribes especially to the early Christian martyrs is the deficient freedom of the beautiful soul who withdraws from the world, as evidenced by Hegel's discussion of Christian martyrdom in his *Aesthetics*. Martyrdom marks for Hegel the first phenomenon in which finitude is transcended in the "spirit of the community."[87] And yet Hegel finds this appearance of the communal spirit to be a selfish phenomenon, a merely "*external repetition of the Passion story*" aimed at attaining salvation for the individual alone.[88] For the martyr, the negative aspect of Christ's history—the negation of human finitude as evil and unworthy of the divine—predominates: "In martyrdom this negative—grief—is an end in itself, and the magnitude of the transfiguration is measured by what the man has suffered and the frightfulness to which he has submitted."[89] Because the inner life of the martyr remains undeveloped, the meaning of Christ's death is taken literally. What is annulled is the martyr's natural existence, not his or her inner particularity of spirit.[90]

In light of Hegel's oral linguistic Trinitarian paradigm, we can perhaps understand why he thinks that the words spoken by the martyrs through their mouths and their bodies are inefficacious. Recall that it is at the level of Trinitarian depth grammar that Hegel begins to utilize the image of the spoken word. In other words, the fleetingness of the Logos is grounded in Hegel's Trinitarian logic, which undergirds his analysis of all reality. Hence it is not just extrinsic material reality that must pass away, must die, but also Spirit: on the one hand, the logic of the Father and, on the other, the particular Spirit—here of the martyr of one nature with Christ—in their mutual abstraction from each other. The martyr, in Hegel's view, misses the fact that the universality and truth of the divine Logos is secured by its necessary fleetingness as a "finite Word" and subsequent resurrection in Spirit. Only when Hegel's Trinitarian logic is known as the truth of the world, only when it is known that his logic is what explains all of reality, including nature and human society, does one really speak words in and through the Spirit. Only then does one speak truly in a manner comprehensible to all rational human beings. Otherwise, the witness of the martyrs is inevitably misunderstood. In their insistence on the static presence of Christ, on the permanence of the Word, they, in Hegel's view, lose the ability to speak almost any words at all.

In contrast to Hegel's socially, worldly oriented understanding of sanctification, the sanctification and transfiguration the martyr seeks consists, Hegel thinks, in an escape from the world.[91] The love, the feeling of unity the martyr feels with the divine, is abstract and unhealthy: "This deep feeling of faith and love in [the martyr's] spiritual beauty is not the spiritual health which permeates the body healthily."[92] Moreover, whatever genuinely spiritual element is contained in the martyr's self-negation becomes not just a desire for the death of the body, but a devaluation of the finite world as a whole. The martyr views "ethical life in the family, the bonds of friendship, blood, love, the state, [and one's] calling" as incompatible with and even damaging to piety.[93] In this disdain for the ethical world, Hegel thinks, the martyr is not actually reconciled with God, because he or she has given up real relationships with other people:

> The ethical organization of the human world is ... not yet respected, because its parts and duties are not yet recognized as necessary and justified links in the chain of an inherently rational actuality. . . . In this respect the religious reconciliation itself remains here in an *abstract* form, and it is displayed in the inherently simple heart as an intensity of faith without extension, as the piety of a heart lonely with itself which has not yet framed itself into a universal and developed confidence and into a discerning comprehensive certainty of itself.[94]

An individual truly confident in faith recognizes the rationality and holiness of the ethical world and its attendant responsibilities as giving actual shape to love.[95]

The martyr, however, considers grief to be an end in itself—grief all the more intense and salutary the more relationships one has had to renounce. This pious compulsion to deny the world is for Hegel the link between martyrdom and the potential for violence: "The richer the heart that loads itself with such trials, the more it possesses a noble treasure [of diverse social relationships] while yet believing itself forced to condemn this possession as null and to stamp it as sin, all the harsher is the lack of reconciliation, a lack that can generate the most frightful hysteria and most raving disunion."[96] To Hegel's mind, the renunciation of relations in the world for the sake of holiness and morality is in fact immoral and selfish because one ends up alone and divisions among people persist.[97] The fact that such world-renunciation cannot be the path to actual reconciliation is egregiously evidenced in the ways it opens the door to actual violence. In *LPR* 3 Hegel finds repression at work: "Social groups and bodies will always arise among a people—among a people, a community, that [shuts] itself off, in the world too, in opposition to rational cohesion and existence—[sects that] take this distillation of the entire established order back into the simple heart, into simple love, and behave outwardly in merely a forbearing, submissive manner, offering their necks [to the executioner]."[98] Hegel views this type of sectarian withdrawal as inherently unstable and dangerous. The internal energy built up during persecution eventually expresses itself in a commensurate outward act of violence toward others, one that is realized on a social scale when Christianity gains political power and the means of force.[99] Thus, Hegel concludes that even though the church made explicit in the Roman world the truth of divine-human reconciliation—and its implications concerning the equality and freedom of all human beings—in theoretical form, in its teaching, it was the vocation of another Christian people, the Germanic, to create a state founded upon that Christian principle, whereby actual reconciliation between religion and the world comes about.[100]

In summary, on Hegel's reading, early Christian martyrdom is marked by its negative character: (1) the martyr seeks to imitate the negative aspect of the passion narrative, Christ's death, through his or her own external death; (2) in so doing, the martyr seeks freedom from the world; (3) the result is a purely subjective, and hence selfish, freedom that is in Hegel's view not a real freedom in accord with reason. Hence the martyr has only minimal to no connection with divine reconciliation, with Spirit. Hegel's systematic "counterproposal" to the early Christian martyrs—the heroes or world historical individuals, such as Alexander, Caesar, or Napoleon—could, by contrast, be understood in a legitimate sense as figures who have sublated the negative and reached the side of the resurrection, the positive pneumatic upshot of Hegel's historical dialectic.[101] Their purpose is to give reality to the world. They perceive the dissatisfaction of spirit in its present conditions and are the first to make explicit the desires of their compatriots. The latter do not yet know what they want. In their dissatisfaction, they persist in an unreconciled negative state, whereas world historical individuals "knew what they wanted, and what they wanted was of a positive nature."[102]

Heroes are individuals of practice who pursue their goals passionately.[103] However, from the perspective of the "moral valet," as Hegel puts it, the hero is ambitiously self-interested. Apparently, this is the category into which Hegel would put Augustine, thereby evacuating the latter's analysis of the role pride plays in history of any rational force.[104] The moral valet, like the one mentioned by Hegel in the introduction to *LPH*, acts like the judgmental individual from *PS* who effectively reduces the person acting in the world to the particularity of his or her sins.[105] In *LPH*, Hegel argues that the judgmental valet equates the consequences of the hero's action with his or her personal goals—the acquisition of power or renown with the desire for it, and so on. Yet in striving to call into question the moral rectitude of historical individuals, Hegel thinks, the one casting judgment inhibits his or her ability to see the unity of personal ends with those of universal reason. Spirit, the universal, can realize its ends only by means of the particular, and passion is what drives the world historical individual to strive wholeheartedly to actualize the universal in the world. Thus, from Hegel's point of view, the hero does pursue personal ends, but they are the same as that of Spirit.[106]

Here, then, various themes we have followed in this chapter with regard to Hegel—practical social reform, Christ's sacrifice of individual personality, confession and pneumatic reconciliation—come together to form Hegel's understanding of pneumatically inspired witnessing or martyrdom and its significance in the history of Spirit. The hero knows the spirit of his or her nation, its dissatisfaction in its present circumstances, and he or she strives passionately to render explicit and actualize the implicit desire of the people for change. Like the historical person of Christ, though, the world historical individual qua individual must sacrifice him- or herself: "It is what we may call the **cunning of reason** that it sets the passions to work in its service, so that the agents by which it gives itself existence must pay the penalty and suffer the loss.... The particular is as a rule inadequate in relation to the universal, and individuals are sacrificed and abandoned as a result."[107] Reason exacts a high toll: throughout history individuals are used and then cast aside, in order that the universal may show itself as universal Spirit, Spirit inclusively concrete and real. In this way, moreover, the hero averts the selfish deficiency of the beautiful soul and the martyr—empty subjectivity—because through the hero's actions the interest of the spirit of the nation becomes objective and knowable in its universal necessity.[108] This necessity is compatible, Hegel thinks, with the positive freedom that historically attains reality only in the context of the modern state, a reality in which truth—the rational unity of the universal and the particular—finally prevails:

> Justice, ethical life, and the state, and these alone, are the positive realisation and satisfaction of freedom. The random inclinations of individuals ... on which restrictions are imposed [are] mere arbitrariness [and hence not freedom].... Whatever worth and spiritual reality [the human being] possesses are his solely by virtue of the state. For as a knowing being, he has spiritual reality only in so far as his being, that is, the rational itself, is his object and possesses objective and immediate existence for him.... For the truth is the unity of the universal and the subjective will, and the universal is present within the state, in its laws and in its universal and rational properties.[109]

But, Augustine might ask of Hegel—as he does when deconstructing Rome's myth of origins—how many have to die to achieve your universal divine end? And is it desirable, let alone Christian, to attribute the bestowal and reality of humanity's spiritual worth to the composition and execution of rational human laws?

Hegel's Language of Spirit and Its Social Realization

THE LANGUAGE OF SPIRIT in Hegel's philosophy aims at social and political transformation through its function of *witnessing* to the movement of reason. Hegel's early thought emerged in the context of Pelagian pneumaticism and religio-political activism. Against that backdrop Hegel's critique of Catholicism shows how the social orientation of his thought rests on the basis of a philosophically reconfigured Trinitarianism. In particular, Hegel thinks a damaging lack of freedom and social instability result from traditional Trinitarian theology with its overemphasis on the person of Christ and consequent attenuation of Spirit. When this critique of Catholicism is considered in tandem with the conclusions of chapter 1, Hegel's practical motivation for reformulating his Christology and pneumatology according to a logic of the spoken word becomes clearer. Indeed, that Trinitarian "logic," as a means of speaking about Spirit, plays out in Hegel's understanding of Spirit as fully immanent in the community—community, moreover, whose universalizing spirit drives toward the formation of a concrete state. Yet Hegel's fleeting Word empowers certain types of language and forecloses others. Hegel's judgment results effectively in the loss of martyrdom as a legitimate option for Christian life—in other words, as a spiritually motivated expression of love—because he sees martyrdom as escapist, as a denial of the rational Spirit in the community. For Hegel, the heroes are the vital agents of change, because through their singularly passionate drive, they give concrete universal reality to the rational ideal, in whose light their otherwise vastly destructive actions come to make sense.

As we turn now to Augustine, however, we need to think critically about Hegel's conclusions. Should martyrdom, if interpreted less in the light of knowledge and more in the light of love, be characterized as negative and world denying, or does it serve instead a vital critical function, a function grounded in a theology of the cross shaping a fundamentally positive, Christoformic way Christians are to speak and act in the world? This question leads to a second: whether the positive intention motivating Hegel's world historical individuals does not identify them too closely with a particular culture or state, even in incipient form, to be open to the transformative movement of the Holy Spirit. For it is the Holy Spirit who, according to Augustine's theology of martyrdom, empowers the early Christians in their witness to Christ even unto death, that is, the witness to the cross's critique of all human claims to absolute autonomy, but also to Christ's free re-creation of humankind out of love.

Chapter 4

AUGUSTINE

The Holy Spirit and the Transformation of Language

Hegel's intrahistorical eschaton in the post-Reformation, post-Enlightenment period—that is, the social realization of the presence of God, the fullness of knowledge and freedom in the world—was grounded in his philosophically reconstructed Trinitarian paradigm, in which the christological moment is surpassed and sublated in Spirit—God fully actualized in the community. Augustine, in contrast, characterizes Pentecostal, pneumatic witness in terms of how pride disrupts human communication and social relations. First, we will focus on his interpretation of the biblical account of the Tower of Babel in *civ. Dei* as well as in certain passages on language from *Trin*. Thus our exploration of this theme corresponds primarily to the previous chapter's analysis of Hegel's theological critique of Catholicism. Augustine traces the violent breakdown of human society to an inexplicable, disordered self-love rather than to one-sided knowledge.

This results in different understandings of Pentecostal appropriation and witness. In certain passages in *Trin., en. Ps., Jo. ev. tr.*, and *ep. Jo.*, Augustine not only recounts the historical event of Pentecost, but also points out specific features of pneumatically inspired speech. Augustine sees at Pentecost the Holy Spirit's work in reestablishing the linguistic and social unity lost at Babel. However, the Spirit's primary unifying work is achieved less through knowledge and more through the reorientation of one's love toward the person of Christ.

This reorientation of love is integral to Augustine's theology of martyrdom, understood as the paradigmatic witness to Christ. Augustine develops this theme in several sermons he preached on the feast of Saint Stephen as well as in passages from *Jo. ev. tr.*, where he explores the apostle Peter's transformation from one who denies Christ to one who courageously witnesses to his Lord even with his life. In contrast to Hegel's devaluation of the martyrs as selfish fanatics who seek their salvation in a freedom *from* the world, Augustine's interpretation of martyrdom shows how true martyrs seek not their own glory but Christ's. The witness of martyrdom is possible, for Augustine, only through the grace of the Holy Spirit. And because the *bodily* death of the martyr is an expression of love, it is at once an affirmation of the goodness of God's creation and a critique of human societies marked by sin.

Pride and the Fragmentation of Language and Society

In his massive work of history and cultural critique, *City of God*, Augustine indicates his sense of humanity's inherently social nature. Yet he also insists that human beings were created with the freedom to obey God and become immortal like the angels or to disobey their creator and succumb to death like the animals. Humans chose the latter, and the innate kinship they possess meant that the fall had grave social ramifications. Indeed, Augustine laments the subsequent dissipation of human society to a level below even that of the wildest beasts. In his eternal gaze, however, God foresaw also the formation of a new society through his grace, one which would embody the unity and peace among its many members that God had first manifested in the creation of humanity from one individual.[1] Augustine distinguishes between these two societies by the orientation of their love or will.[2] One city, as he calls it, promotes love of self, while the other submits its will to God.

The disintegration of fallen human society manifests and perpetuates itself in and through the parallel fragmentation of language.³ Interpreting the story of the tower of Babel (Gn 11.1–9), Augustine highlights pride as the source of linguistic diversity. The tower which Nimrod—whom Augustine holds to be the leader of the people building the structure—sought to erect against God is a sign of "impious pride."⁴ Nimrod does not want (*noluit*) to understand God's commands, so God accordingly frustrates the means—namely, his *lingua*—whereby he, Nimrod, gives commands and seeks to exalt himself. Augustine thus emphasizes that the way of ascent—a pattern established preeminently in Christ—is humility which elevates the heart to God: "What harm could be done to God by any spiritual self-exaltation or material elevation however high it soared? The ... genuine highway to heaven is constructed by humility, which lifts up its heart to the Lord."⁵

To orient the heart toward heaven, Augustine deconstructs the goods of this world in *civ. Dei* 19. His litany of woes is a grand story of disintegration, the loss of harmony and peace at all levels of created reality. At the level of human society, following the household and city, Augustine observes that the barrier to communication posed by linguistic difference is so great that it trumps any feeling of human kinship. Human efforts at restoring peace through the bond of common language—Augustine has the expansion of the Roman Empire in view—are fraught with disastrous consequences. He points to the bloody wars aimed at conquering foreign peoples. Even worse, long after those initial wars of conquest, internecine conflicts still rage within the borders of the so-called unified realm. Finally, the unavoidable necessity of waging even just wars reveals the extent to which the sense of common human nature has been downtrodden under the weight of injustice.⁶ It is telling that, within one brief section of the book, Augustine can move so quickly from linguistic diversity to the bloodshed of war. It is equally telling that he thinks that human efforts to remedy the situation are of limited use at best and utterly disastrous at worst. Set against the backdrop of his exegesis of Babel, moreover, the line between a proud will on the one side and inhumanity and injustice on the other is clearly drawn.

One must avoid the misunderstanding, however, that Augustine attributes human injustice to language itself. Indeed, when exploring the relationship between love and knowledge in book 10 of *Trin.*, he gives the example of someone striving to learn the meaning of a word he or she does not yet know. Of interest here is what Augustine thinks a person can know by the light of truth in his or her own mind: "It must be that he knows and sees by insight in the very sense of things how beautiful the discipline is that contains knowledge of all signs; and how useful is the skill by which a human society communicates perceptions between its members, since otherwise an assembly of human beings would be worse for its members than any kind of solitude, if they could not exchange their thoughts by speaking to each other."[7] Naturally, Augustine links this ideal discipline that knows the meaning of all signs to the advantage ensuing from the knowledge of all human languages, whereby linguistic difference would no longer stand in the way of communication.[8]

Language is thus viewed by Augustine as a great good, especially as a component in the building up of human society. It is a tool necessitated, however, by the human inability to communicate directly from mind to mind. In this way there is a link between human language and human corporeality. Pertinent in this respect are the Augustinian images we have discussed in chapter 2: the incarnation as divine rhetoric and Christ as *sacramentum* and *exemplum*. Indeed, in *Jo. ev. tr.* 27.5 Augustine suggests this connection. He is addressing Jn 6.63, "It is the spirit that gives life; the flesh profits nothing."[9] Augustine inquires:

> If Christ profited us much through his flesh, how does flesh profit nothing? But through the flesh the Spirit has accomplished something for our salvation. The flesh was a vessel; observe what it had, not what it was. The apostles were sent; did their flesh profit us nothing? If the flesh of the apostles profited us, could the flesh of the Lord have profited nothing? For from where does the sound of a word [come] to us except through the voice of the flesh? From where [comes] the pen,

from where the writing? All these things are works of the flesh, but with the spirit playing it, its musical instrument, as it were.[10]

Immediately before this excerpt, moreover, Augustine likens the verse from John to the Pauline injunction that knowledge (*scientia*) puffs up, but love (*caritas*) builds up, such that knowledge benefits through love. Human words, audible and written, then, are works of the flesh. As such they are vessels like the flesh. What matters is the orientation of the will or love, that is, the spirit that animates their utterance. Indeed, references to pneumatic operation in the incarnation and in the apostles and their preaching and writing after Pentecost are obvious in the passage above. The Spirit's love in Christ's incarnation and at Pentecost makes the apostles' linguistic production—a production that extends beyond mere words—beneficial.

By contrast, pride and self-glorification oppose the Spirit and render language useless, even gravely injurious. In an early exposition of Ps 8, Augustine characterizes scripture as divine condescension, God's speaking to humans in human language. It is interesting to observe how he sets divinely inspired speech apart: "Those books ... are indeed the works of God's fingers, for it was by the operation of the Holy Spirit in the saints that they were written. Those who sought their own glory rather than the salvation of humankind spoke without the Holy Spirit, in whom are depths of the mercy of God."[11] Here we ought to note at least two negative characteristics of the language of pride: it is spoken *sine spiritu sancto* and not for the benefit and salvation of others. In fact, when proud speech is used to undermine or even destroy the Christian community, it can be fatal. In such a case Augustine means spiritually fatal, the worst kind of death for a human being.[12]

Pentecost and the Conversion of Language

The fragmentation of Babel is inverted at Pentecost. Investigating Ps 54.10 (55.9),[13] "Engulf them, Lord, and confuse their languages," Augustine contends that it is good that those whose unity is predicated upon an evil will have their plans frustrated by barriers to their communication. He recalls the tower of Babel, a proud plan issuing in the diversity of languages as its punishment. Earlier "there had been only one tongue; and one tongue was expedient for people who were of one mind, one single language was right for humble people."[14] Once they set their hearts on a wicked plan, however, God divided their languages in order to prevent its realization. Augustine is fully aware of the way in which society can amplify human evil. The diversification of language is, accordingly, in its prophylactic purpose, an act of mercy on God's part.[15] But God's Holy Spirit works to restore humility of heart and to build up around it a new society:

> Through proud persons human languages were diversified, and through the humble apostles languages were harmonized; the spirit of pride fragmented language, and the Holy Spirit gathered dispersed languages into one. When the Holy Spirit came upon the disciples they spoke in the tongues of all who heard, and were understood by all. The fragmented languages were reunited. If there are still pagans on the rampage today, it is just as well that they speak different languages. If they aspire to one common language, let them come to the Church, for here though we differ in our natural tongues [*in diversitate linguarum carnis*], there is but one language spoken by the faith of our hearts.[16]

The value of language hinges upon the spirit that animates it. Pride sundered the unity of the languages of the flesh. The Holy Spirit unifies language again at Pentecost by spiritualizing it. Yet, as in the case of the human body, Augustine does not devalue the languages of the flesh (*linguae carnis*), but rather orients them through the faith of the heart. Implicit therein is the same eschatological tension we have seen elsewhere between the interior and the exterior person. Furthermore, given the ecclesial sense of the resurrection and ascension we have already seen and the linguistic function of bonding people together, this eschatological tension between interior and exterior across which the restoration of unanimity operates must be interpreted in both an individual and communal register.

The spiritualization of language, the one language of the heart, has as its content the spiritual vision of Christ afforded by faith and given by the Holy Spirit at Pentecost. At this juncture the thought of Hegel and Augustine might appear to intersect. With his eschewal of external, sensual evidence as verification of the truth of faith, Hegel gestures toward a second form of kenosis—in addition to the finite determination of the abstract concept of God—manifested in Christ's death: the Son's divestment of finite particularity, or his withdrawal from sensible presence. Here Hegel—building, it seems, upon Christ's words in Jn 16.7—establishes a conceptual link between Calvary and Pentecost: "This transition [from the sensible particular to the spiritual] is what is termed the *outpouring of the Spirit*. It could occur only after the Christ who had become flesh had withdrawn, after his sensible, immediate presence had ceased; then for the first time the Spirit issued forth."[17]

In Hegel's view, this is the challenge facing the early church: coming to terms with Christ's departure in a bodily sense and the transition to spiritual presence. The problem is that they retain faith in the historical individual Jesus and his elevation into heaven, rather than understanding the transferred locus of the resurrection and ascension to be the spiritual community itself. Augustine, with his distinction between Christ in *forma servi* and *forma Dei*, and with his strong insistence upon faith in the bodily resurrection, both of Christ and of Christian believers in the future, would seem to be an egregious example of such detrimental externalization. But in fact, Augustine's reading of Jn 7.39 and 16.7 points toward a wide arena of pneumatic operation that, precisely because it is linked with Christ as a *sacramentum* and *exemplum* of the believer's resurrection, comes to encompass both internal faith and external transformation of the body, both individually and communally in the body of Christ, the church. In this way, too, external language, as the means whereby the communal body is built up, can become, on Augustine's account, the occasion and locus of inward spiritual transformation.

Christ's glorification, in Augustine's theology, entails a continuity between the resurrection and ascension in the upward-oriented trajectory of the incarnate Word (in contrast to the descent in humility).[18] This continuity is especially evident if we extend the Augustinian concepts of *sacramentum* and *exemplum* to his interpretation of the ascension. Then it becomes clear how for Augustine the turn toward the spiritual reality behind the bodily and material which is adumbrated by the ascension is not a rejection of the created world as evil, but rather a right ordering of created goods in the heart—that is, a right ordering of one's love. Such an ordering emerges in *Trin.* 4.6, where Augustine distinguishes between the resurrection as *sacramentum* and as *exemplum* to make sense of a scriptural conundrum. On the one hand, Jesus instructs Mary Magdalene in Jn 20.17 not to touch him, since he has not yet ascended to the Father, whereas in Lk 24.39 he encourages his disciples to touch his resurrected body. In Augustine's interpretation, Christ's resurrection body functions sacramentally for the interior person when interpreted jointly with the ascension, but in an exemplary way when associated with his tangible bodily presence in the world.[19]

On the other hand, Christ's glorified bodily presence points already to its absence as a way of showing the order of spirit over flesh and God over all. Christ, as the eternal Word, is always with his Father in heaven. Thus, just as Christ's resurrection body is a sacrament of the inner person's spiritual regeneration, so Christ's bodily ascension into heaven functions as a sacrament of the Christian's ascent to heaven in the heart. The exemplarity of Christ's death and resurrection, on the other hand, shows how the bodily enactment of this right ordering, in the disciplining of temporal, corruptible flesh, is a means toward the glorification of the body in eternal life. Thus, the exemplarity of Christ's resurrection body includes the ascension when it orients the faith, hope, and love of the Christian toward his or her ultimate end. Indeed, this sacramental and exemplary operation of Christ's resurrection and ascension are further apparent, even if not explicitly labeled as such, in *Trin.* 4.24, when Augustine argues:

> Our faith has now in some sense followed him in whom we have believed to where he has ascended, after having "originated," died, been raised to life, and taken up. Of these four stages we already knew the first two in ourselves; we know that men originate and die. As for the second two, being raised to life and taken up, we can justly hope that they are going to happen to us because we have believed that they happened to him. So because what has originated in him has passed over into eternity, so too will what has originated in us pass over when faith arrives at truth.[20]

In the Christian life now, the internal transformation that reorients itself toward God is worked out further in the struggle to conform the exterior person to the right order manifested in Christ, such that in the end the Christian will live with him eternally as a spiritual whole, soul and body together.

The dynamism with which Hegel and Augustine interpret the ascension therefore issues in very different pneumatic inflections. For Hegel the resurrection and ascension entail the negation of Christ's individual personality in such a way that their locus is transferred to the actualization of Spirit in the community. By contrast, the dynamism is for Augustine more extensively christologically conditioned, in that Christ is himself the way toward and in which the Spirit leads, insofar as faith orients itself toward the *forma servi* in the hopes of attaining to final vision of Christ in *forma Dei*. Two important consequences emerge: (1) far from resulting in pneumatic truncation, the elevation of Christ in *forma servi* to heaven, along with the attendant eschatological tension, in fact opens the personal and ecclesial space in which the Spirit can sanctify within but at the same time independent of any particular cultural parameters; (2) the relationship of Christ and the Spirit results in a more genuinely Trinitarian understanding of God and his relationship with human beings.

This is evident in *Trin.* 1.18, where Augustine grounds the ascension in the ontological unity and equality of Father, Son, and Holy Spirit. At the same time, the affirmation of equality of persons in the Trinity underscores their differentiation as well. With regard to Jn 16.6–7,[21] Augustine contends, "But the point is, he did not say this because of any inequality between the Word of God and the Holy Spirit; it was as though he was telling them that the presence of the son of man among them would be a hindrance to the coming of the one who was never an inferior, because he never *emptied himself, taking the form of a servant* (Phil 2:7), like the Son."[22] The equality of Son and Holy Spirit undergirds the distinctiveness of their missions and hence also knowledge of the one God as triune.

Augustine's purpose here is not merely ontological or christological, if those categories are interpreted in a static sort of way. It is much more dynamic. Just as Augustine endeavors to show that the incarnation does not denote the inferiority of the Son to the Spirit, who has not become human, so Augustine's predilection elsewhere to attribute to Christ the sending of the Spirit at Pentecost[23] does not, in light of this text, show any dependence or inferiority of the Spirit to the Son, but rather affirms the Spirit's equality. *Trin.* 1.18 reveals that it is the Holy Spirit who teaches Christ's equality with the Father. This is a dynamic process of coming to know. The link between the ascension and Pentecost in pointing toward Christ's equality with the Father blazes the trail of the Christian life. As in *Trin.* 4.6, Augustine here adduces Jn 20.17,[24] but with a fuller explanation: "Touching concludes as it were the process of getting acquainted. [Christ] did not want this heart, so eagerly reaching out to him, to stop at thinking that he was only what could be seen and touched. His ascension to the Father signified his being seen in his equality with the Father, that being the ultimate vision which suffices us."[25] Christ ascended so that the human heart would not only be satisfied with him in *forma servi*, so that the heart's striving would not stop, but rather so that it would journey deeper into the mystery of Christ. In his very assumption into heaven, Christ's *forma servi* is shown as the way toward the goal of vision: Christ in *forma Dei*.

In terms of the oral linguistic imagery explored in Part I, Augustine restricts the use of such imagery to discussion of the incarnation of the Word, while he disallows its application to the Word's eternal generation from the Father in the immanent Trinity.

This is important because just as Augustine argues that the equality of the divine three undergirds the distinction and exposition of the divine missions, so too does that equality mark out a strong distinction between the human and the divine. And it is that distinction, coupled with the equality of the Son and the Spirit with the Father, which imbues Augustine's Trinitarian and ecclesiological thought with its dynamism. Augustine's use of oral linguistic imagery for the incarnation and his description of the Holy Spirit's work in making incarnational language possible qua an expression of grace and love both affirm the broad scope of human language and culture as potential salutary loci of divine grace. Yet the clear prohibition against the transfer of such linguistic imagery into a more fundamental discussion of the divine life apart from the world is intended by Augustine to ensure that no particular instantiation of human language is ever regarded as fully expressive of and adequate to the mystery of the Trinity *in se*. What is more, that prohibition is meant to prevent the identification of any particular human linguistic or cultural production with the divine itself.

Augustine sets up, rather, a relationship of similarity-in-difference between human language and the eternal generation of the Word. That relationship is given shape and animated by Augustine's pro-Nicene Trinitarian theology: it takes place within the two-natured person of the Word and is held together by the Spirit, who is equal to the Father and the Son. Through the inspiration of the Spirit, human language spoken within and constructive of the communal body of Christ is conformed to the incarnational (oral linguistic) language of God, language that is sacramental and exemplary in its inculcation of humility and love. Yet the goal is that, by speaking audible human words consistent with God's humble language of the incarnation, humans might one day be prepared to grasp more fully the mystery of the eternal Trinity, what it means for the Son to be generated from the Father in unity of the Spirit without ever passing away like a word spoken in time. That goal, toward which the Holy Spirit drives believers through the gradual transformation of their external, spoken words, is what invests the Christian life with its forward motion. Thus, the mature

Augustine's insistence that in this life humans can only strive to speak language in conformity with God's incarnational language, without ever speaking knowingly, only believingly, of the eternal Trinity, is not characterized by stasis or hierarchical institutional ossification—precisely because Augustine does not allow the incarnate Word to pass over into Spirit, but rather holds them in fruitful dialectical relationship, inasmuch as the Spirit continuously builds up the body of Christ while always exceeding its bounds, inasmuch as the Spirit inspires faithful human words while always resisting exhaustive exposition through those words. In other words, the Holy Spirit enables Christians to come to know the Trinitarian God through faith in the incarnate Word; the Spirit does not yet provide full intellectual vision.

This dynamic coming to know in faith is transformative and fruitful. Augustine believed that the man Jesus had received the Spirit from the moment he was born in the flesh.[26] Thus the reason, for Augustine, that Pentecost is postponed until after Christ's glorification rests not in something lacking in the man Jesus, but in the disciples, who by Christ's resurrection and ascension gain the capacity to receive the Spirit. In *Jo. ev. tr.* 94.4 the word Augustine uses for capacity is *capax*, which, from an epistemological perspective, points to the mind's ability to grasp something, in this case, to grasp the reality of Christ beyond spatio-temporal limits.[27]

This spiritual vision, in the present mode of faith, bears upon the nature of language and its reorientation at Pentecost. We can see this connection in relation to Augustine's discussion of glorification in *Jo. ev. tr.* 100. Augustine there explains Christ's words in Jn 16.14, "He [the Holy Spirit] will glorify me because he will receive of mine and announce it to you."[28] Augustine writes: "'He will glorify me,' can be understood in this way: by pouring out love in the hearts of believers and by making them spiritual, he revealed to them how the Son, whom they only knew before according to the flesh and, as men, thought him a man, was equal to the Father."[29] Later in this same tractate, Augustine equates *claritas* and *gloria*. The equation is possible because in Latin *claritas* means both visual brightness and renown. The first reading of Jn 16.14 that Augustine provides corresponds perhaps to the visual or epistemic sense of *claritas*, a brightness through which the transfigured *forma servi* of Christ points toward his unity with the Father. In other words, at Pentecost the Holy Spirit spiritualizes the apostles and opens their eyes to that which they could not see when Christ was present with them in the flesh.[30]

But the other meaning of *claritas* suggests an oral, mediated component as well, whereby the content of the first is conveyed to others. In this regard Augustine offers a second reading of Jn 16.14: "So then he said, 'He will glorify me,' in such a way as though he were to say, 'He will take fear away from you and will give love, with which, proclaiming me more passionately . . . you will commend the honor of my glory through the whole world.'"[31] The gift of the Spirit at Pentecost is thus not only that of spiritual vision, the grasp, however limited now, of Christ's eternal reality, but also the gift of courage that comes with the love of God and is bestowed upon the apostles to speak of Christ with praise, to glorify him throughout the world.

In the language of praise motivated by the love of the Holy Spirit, we gain insight into how Augustine thinks that same Spirit transforms human beings and conforms their words to the Word of God, that is, how love draws temporal human beings to the eternal truth and at the same time motivates them to strive for justice in the world. For both Hegel and Augustine, language of Spirit is language in accord with the truth. Both fear dishonesty and especially self-deception. We saw how Hegel diagnoses such dishonesty in the purely subjective judgments of conscience, on the one hand, and in the pious yearning for the grace won objectively by Christ, on the other. Hegel thinks he attains to the truth in the dialectical unity of these two sides, through the language of forgiveness and reconciliation, whereby the subject knows him- or herself as the objective truth of Spirit in the world. Such an understanding of pneumatically achieved reconciliation, however, differs from what we will see in Augustine in several respects: (1) the forgiveness communicated in Hegel does not possess the character of gift, (2) because reconciliation results in self-recognition and the realization of a radical human identity with the divine, (3) thereby obviating any pneumatic language of praise, conceived as the free expression of gratitude and love to God for the gift of salvation.

Augustine, too, insists that the language of Spirit is effective in reconciliation only when grounded in truth. He is acutely aware of the danger of deception that any humanly spoken language of praise and glory brings with it.[32] Especially egregious in its potential for the deception of both the one praising and even the ethical agent—and in that sense parallel to Hegel's analysis of the purely subjective conscience—is the case in which someone acts justly not for the sake of justice itself, that is, for God, but for one's own advancement. There justice is being exploited—and not always consciously—for self-promotion. It is that very potential for the abuse of virtue that requires a critical distinction between God and human beings.

That distinction, we recall, undergirds Augustine's incarnational rhetoric. We saw in the first chapter how, according to Augustine, Christ, the Word of God spoken in the world through the Holy Spirit, counteracts pride with humble love, how he overturns the human lust for power by saving humankind through humility in accord with justice. The incarnate Word of God is at once instructive and persuasive. God teaches the truth, the priority of divine justice, and persuades humans to love that truth and hence to seek after his justice. This instruction and persuasiveness are possible because God is distinct from human beings, because only as God can Christ humble himself to conquer sin not through the power he has but through the justice that he is as God. At the same time, God's Word is effective, is transformative of human words and culture, because it is spoken through the same love, the same gift of the Holy Spirit that is poured into the hearts of the faithful.

The human response to God's Word is shaped by the Holy Spirit's character as gift. The Spirit gives the believer the courage to humble him- or herself in grateful witness to truth and justice. That witness, as praise, is animated by a love that moves outward, but that, in that very movement, transforms the one speaking and acting in love by conforming him or her ever more to God's just Word in Christ. In this way, we can interpret what Augustine means by the benefit of praise. When glory is given to someone who is just through God and for God's sake, that attribution of glory is true, Augustine says, because true justice is found only in God. The benefit of praising a just individual, however, accrues not to the one praised, but rather to those offering the praise, "because they judge rightly and love a just man."[33] A fortiori the just death of Christ benefits not him, but those who now praise him for winning their salvation.[34] What for Hegel is another source of dishonesty—the praise of an objective Christ through whose action one hopes to receive forgiveness—becomes through the love of the Holy Spirit the standard, goal, and context of subjective transformation, of growth in the love of and seeking after justice. What, to Hegel's mind, is the hypocritical language of a passive faith, language of praise and thanksgiving at the gift of God's grace,[35] is in fact the means of transformation that in fact preserves the independence and freedom of God and the believer. For it is God's gift of himself in the love of the Holy Spirit that transforms but does not absorb the believer. And this praise, as a linguistic function of grace, is, as we shall see in what follows, not a hindrance to ethical action in the world, but—because it is a courageous expression of honest and free love of justice maintained by the critical yet paradigmatic distance of the just Word of God—precisely what impels the believer to action.

By means of a pneumatic lens, then, Augustine illumines the christologically conditioned dynamic of ascent through humility. The consequences of this pneumatic elucidation affect human language and the community it sustains. In *Jo. ev. tr.* 6.1–3, a homily aimed at the Donatists in the dispute over baptism, Augustine comments on the relationship between the two visible manifestations of the Holy Spirit in the New Testament, his appearance in the form of a dove at Jesus' baptism (Jn 1.32–33)[36] and as tongues of fire at Pentecost (Acts 2.1–4). The unifying love of the faithful *in* Christ gains expression, Augustine says, through the moaning of the dove.[37] In addition to his zoological reasoning, Augustine finds scriptural confirmation for the moaning of the Spirit in Rom 8.26:

"For we know not what we should pray for as we ought, but the Spirit himself intercedes for us with unspeakable moanings."[38] He argues that the Holy Spirit does not moan in his eternal unity with the Father and Son, but rather "he moans in us because he makes us moan."[39] In so doing the Holy Spirit teaches the Christian to place his or her hope in God and the salvation—not yet fully attained—that only he can offer. Those, by contrast, whose hearts are turned toward the here and now Augustine describes as ravens, since their voices are full of shrieking at temporal delights. Yet the one who moans "knows that he lives in the midst of the affliction of this mortal life, and that he is exiled from the Lord, that he does not yet possess that unending beatitude which has been promised to us, but that he has it in hope, and will have it in fact, when the Lord comes with shining brightness [*praeclarus*] in his manifestation, who before came hidden in his lowliness [*humilitate*]—he who knows this is the one who moans."[40] The moaning that the Spirit teaches is oriented along the trajectory of humility set by Christ and is characterized by its longing for eternity. It is not the moaning of the person who suffers temporal woes and, once they are past, becomes happy again. Such fickle people put their own desires first. The dove, however, seeks what belongs to Christ.[41]

The contrast Augustine then draws between the Holy Spirit's appearance as a dove and as tongues of flame at Pentecost indicates several facets of pneumatic indwelling and spiritual utterance: "Here we saw a dove upon the Lord; there parted tongues upon the assembled disciples; in the one, simplicity is shown, in the other, fervor."[42] Both aspects are necessary. Indeed, Augustine points out, some simple people are also lazy.[43] He therefore adduces the martyr Stephen as an example of both characteristics: "Not such a [simple, but lazy] one was Stephen, full of the Holy Spirit. He was simple, because he harmed no one; he was fervent, because he reproached the impious."[44] Augustine finds Stephen's simplicity evidenced in the latter's prayer for God to forgive his assailants, and he finds Stephen's fervor in the very vehemence with which he, Stephen, admonished them for resisting the Holy Spirit. The Holy Spirit leads Stephen to follow Christ's example of humble forgiveness: "For earlier his master, upon whom the dove descended, had done that [i.e., forgiven his killers]; hanging on the cross, he said, 'Father, forgive them, for they know not what they do' [Lk 23.34]. Therefore in the dove it has been shown that those sanctified by the Spirit should have no deceit; in the fire it has been shown that their simplicity should not remain frigid."[45] Negatively, the simplicity of the Holy Spirit entails the desire not to harm anyone—and by harm Augustine means the really grievous deceit whereby people are drawn away from the universal church and lose connection to the presence of Christ and the gift of the Holy Spirit. Positively, this simplicity is manifest in the Spirit's gift of love that binds believers together in unity. This love, this orientation away from self toward others, is expressed in words of admonishment aimed at the impious in need of salvation and in words of invigoration directed at those already united in the simplicity of the dove but who themselves have gone cold.

The transformation grounded in the gift of love at Pentecost thus moves in two directions, according to Augustine. On the one hand, Pentecost and especially the miracle of speaking in tongues ground the expansion of the church, its universalization as it spreads throughout the world. In this sense the Holy Spirit comes to encompass every language spoken by human beings through the preaching of the apostles. At the same time, though, the Spirit is also the love that unites the individual members of the community. We can see both these aspects of the Pentecostal mystery come particularly to the fore in Augustine's disputes with the Donatists, who in his view deny the universality of the church by restricting its geographic extent to North Africa and reject its unity by separating themselves from that universal church.

To undermine their geographic exclusivity, Augustine turns in *ep. Jo.* 2 to Lk 24.47, noting that Christ suffered, died, and rose again "for penance and remission of sins to be preached in his name through all the nations, beginning at Jerusalem."[46] He enjoins his congregation: "Let no one doubt about the Church, that it extends through all nations. Let no one doubt that it began at Jerusalem and has filled all the nations."[47] In the aforementioned text this emphasis on the church's universality forms the second part of a double affirmation concerning Christ's resurrection as the beginning of the church as the bride and body of Christ.[48] Christ not only gave to the doubting disciples his risen flesh to touch, but also explained how the scriptures predicted his death and resurrection and were now fulfilled. He did this with a view toward later believers whose faith, long after his ascension in the flesh, would be confirmed by the text of scripture itself.[49] Just as the prophecies of scripture are shown to be fulfilled in the resurrected body of Christ, so they are further fulfilled in the universality of his body, the church.[50]

Augustine accordingly chastises the Donatists for their blindness, a blindness that betrays a dearth of paschal and Pentecostal understanding.[51] They mourn Christ's death. Rejecting a literal interpretation of the city of Jerusalem,[52] they deny any communion with the place where Christ was killed.[53] By means of his concept of the church as Christ's body and his rhetorical interpretation of Pentecost, however, Augustine is able to confound Donatist claims upon Christ and his gift of the Holy Spirit. Relative to those who put Christ to death, a Christ they knew only as a man, the Donatists commit much graver evil by injuring Christ in heaven, the same Christ present in the hearts of his faithful: "Godly and merciful men, they grieve much that Christ was slain, and yet they slay Christ in men!"[54] Their insistence upon a figurative reading of the external, earthly Jerusalem issues, surprisingly, in the spiritual, inner death of Christ in the believer. Augustine's understanding of the church as the body of Christ undermines the Donatist claim to honor him.

Moreover, while Augustine might concede that the Donatists recognize scriptural testimony regarding Christ's death and resurrection, he would also emphasize how they miss the same testimony in respect to the universal expansion of the church following Pentecost. In surprising resonance with Staudenmaier's critique of Hegel, who, for all his attentiveness to history, disconnects the spiritual community from its historical roots, Augustine argues that the Donatists, in their schismatic fury, reject the root, that is, Jerusalem, from which they had been cut off. But in contrast to the "godly and merciful" Donatists, Christ had mercy upon Jerusalem and established it as the origin of the church in its universality.

In that regard the Donatists fail to recognize how the miracle of speaking in tongues, which took place in Jerusalem at Pentecost, serves as a sign of the future universality of the church.[55]

Neither the unifying nor the universalizing force of Pentecost, however, negates difference within the body of Christ. Indeed, Augustine's analysis of signifying pneumatic manifestation reveals how, precisely within this dialectic of diastolic and systolic movement, the Holy Spirit bonds believers together while concomitantly affirming difference within the body. At the broader social level, this unity in multiplicity is evident to Augustine in the distinct manifestations of the Spirit. In *Jo. ev. tr.* 6.10, he emphasizes that Christ sends his apostles to all nations to preach and baptize in the name of the Trinity: "The apostles were sent to the nations; if to the nations, to all tongues. The Holy Spirit, parted in tongues, united in the dove, signified this. On this side tongues are parted; on that the dove joins them together. Have the tongues of the nations achieved harmony and only the tongue of Africa become disharmonious? What is clearer, my brothers? In the dove is unity; in the tongues of the nations is community."[56] Playing on the dual meaning of *lingua* both as the organ with which one speaks and as a language,[57] Augustine draws together the distinct tongues of fire and the miracle of speaking in tongues at Pentecost and compares them to the Holy Spirit's appearance as a dove at Christ's baptism. In the church, the Holy Spirit is in the process of drawing all people to Christ, of conforming all languages to the unity of love without negating the differences between them.

This for Augustine involves an explicit re-collection of Babel's fragmentation. In *Jo. ev. tr.* 6.10, he argues that those constructing the tower sought to avoid perishing in another flood. But they knew that by the flood God intended to wipe out all wickedness from the earth; hence their construction project really constituted an attempt to avoid conversion of heart. But self-exaltation cannot lead to genuine community, peace, and mutual understanding. The only way, then, for genuine unity to arise is through humility, through the movement away from self taught to and made possible for humankind by Christ's own self-abnegation:

If pride created differences of tongues, Christ's humility has joined the differences of tongues together. Now what that tower had dispersed, the Church binds together. From one tongue came many; do not be amazed, pride did this. From many tongues comes one; do not be amazed, love did this. For, although there are different sounds of tongues, in the heart one God is invoked, one peace is kept intact.

How then ... ought the Holy Spirit, as representing a unity, have been shown except through the dove ... ? How ought humility [have been shown] except through a simple and moaning bird, not through a proud bird, exalting itself like a raven?[58]

Pride issues in disintegration: of the individual, of relationships, of community. The diversity of language encapsulates this disharmony. But precisely this multiplicity is taken up by the Holy Spirit at Pentecost in the divided tongues of fire and converted. The humility of Christ and the love of the Holy Spirit put diverse languages back into proper relation—oriented toward God—and thereby make possible the formation of genuine community in which mutual understanding and thus unity in difference can emerge.

In *Jo. ev. tr.* 32 Augustine offers a further interpretation of the miracle of speaking in tongues that, by means of a connection with Paul's discussion of the distinct gifts of the Spirit in 1 Corinthians and the love poured into the hearts of believers by the Holy Spirit in Rom 5.5, affirms simultaneously the unity of the body of Christ and the particularity of its members. Augustine recounts the double sending of the Holy Spirit by Christ after his resurrection and ascension, respectively, and notes the historical novelty of the Spirit's appearance at Pentecost on account of the miracle of speaking in tongues, a feat never witnessed before. But this raises a question for him with regard to later generations of believers: "Well now, brothers, because he who is baptized in Christ and believes in Christ does not now speak in the languages of all nations, must it be believed that he has not received the Holy Spirit?"[59] By no means, Augustine answers. Yet the question could be put another way: if it is the case that the Holy Spirit is also received by later generations of believers, why then do they not speak in the tongues of all peoples? Augustine responds: "Because now the Church herself speaks in the languages of all nations. Before the Church was in one nation, when it was speaking in the languages of all. By speaking in the languages of all it signified the future, that, by growing through the nations, it might speak in the languages of all."[60] The historical event of Pentecost and its effects are now carried forward and fulfilled through the personalization of the church—formed into the one person of Christ—in his unity and universality.

This has a number of consequences. First, it means for Augustine that the Holy Spirit is not received outside the church, since only within the church does one speak in all tongues. Such a claim, however, suggests that the unity and universality of the church is different from that of an international organization spread throughout many nations and encompassing multiple human languages. This is a vital point in our comparison with Hegel, for whom the unity of Spirit is realized concretely in the state. For Augustine, that unity is rather a function of the love that unites and universalizes, and that links and reorders both the interior, the heart, which speaks spiritual language, and the exterior, the corporate body held together by spoken human language. This love mediates between the individual and the whole, granting each member a claim upon what the whole church has been given, such that, in the church, each member speaks all the languages spoken by the whole body: "The Church, spread through the nations, speaks in all languages; the Church is the body of Christ, in this body you are a member. Therefore, since you are a member of this body, which speaks in all languages, believe that you speak in all languages. For the unity of the members is made into its oneness of heart by love; and this unity speaks as then one man spoke."[61] If speaking all languages is the sign of having received the Spirit, and one speaks all languages by being united in the church through love, then, Augustine argues, we can believe that the degree to which one loves the church of Christ is also the degree to which one has received the Holy Spirit.

Precisely the unifying function of the love of the Holy Spirit, moreover, affirms at the same time the individual value of each member of Christ's body. In appealing to 1 Cor 12–13 and Rom 5.5, Augustine indeed suggests that only within a community united by the Holy Spirit in the love of God can one know and appreciate the true value of each individual. Yet in contrast to Hegel, Augustine's eschatological orientation, the not yet, and the clear distinction between the divine and the world as well as between the individuals within the world itself, give impetus to the faithful in their striving for God. At the same time, this orientation necessitates the actualization of love in the world. As Augustine notes in *Jo. ev. tr.* 32, Paul teaches in Rom 5.5 that the love of God has been poured into the hearts of the faithful through the Holy Spirit. In discussing 1 Cor 12–13 immediately beforehand, though, Augustine shows that this love mediated by the Spirit is known only by the horizontal trajectory in which its vertical trajectory is found. This love orients itself outward, in service of others. In building up the body of Christ through love, the distinct gifts of the Spirit given to each individual are of benefit; otherwise, they are for naught. Conversely, through this love one benefits from all the unique gifts of the other members of the body, just as one speaks all languages.[62] Contrary to Hegel's claim, the benefit of love that witnesses to divine truth and justice is, according to Augustine, precisely not individualistic in its desire for personal salvation alone. Rather, that benefit emerges only in the building up of the communal body of Christ, where the dissipating "self" held together by pride is gradually reintegrated through its Trinitarianly grounded relationships to others.

Persuasive Testimony: Freedom, Confidence, Action

This body of Christ is reintegrated not by mutual recognition of rational autonomous selves, but by humbly listening to God's Word and responding with love. And contrary to Hegel's fears, such humility does not, in Augustine's view, result in dependence and heteronomy, but rather in true freedom and confidence to witness to the truth in love. We can begin to see this in tractate 6 on the First Epistle of John, where Augustine also takes up the question as to why Christians who had received the Holy Spirit at baptism no longer speak in tongues as the apostles did at Pentecost. If receipt of the Holy Spirit is no longer confirmed by such miracles, Augustine asks—and here we might discover the seeds of a rather pastorally oriented response to Hegel's post-Enlightenment critique of miracles—then how does anyone know the Holy Spirit dwells within him or her? Augustine's answer again points toward the universalizing and unifying love of the church, though here without explicit reference to its mediation of language. He exhorts his congregation to examine their hearts. If they find love of their brothers and sisters there, then they can know that the Holy Spirit abides in them. In this way they adhere to the community of those who, though separated by physical space, are united in orientation of heart, in the love of God, which, adducing Rom 5.5, Augustine emphasizes is given by the Holy Spirit.[63]

The question thus arises concerning how to test the spirit of the community to which one belongs. Augustine appeals to 1 Jn 4.2: "In this the Spirit of God is known. Every spirit that confesses that Jesus Christ has come in the flesh is of God."[64] He observes, however, that any number of schismatic or heretical groups confess that Christ has come in the flesh, but that this conformity cannot mean that they possess the Spirit of God.[65] Consequently, Augustine seeks a further criterion and discovers it in Ti 1.16: "For they confess that they know God, but in their works they deny."[66] Here Augustine establishes a further pneumatological link between what he deems a correct Christology and the realization of love in the world. The Spirit of God, we have seen, gives true knowledge and love of Christ. A genuine understanding of Christ's incarnation, passion, and resurrection presupposes belief in his equality with the Father. In this way Augustine makes clear how the confession that Christ has come in the flesh must issue in actions, that is, in love. The Son, as God, could not die and thus took on flesh in order that he might die and give human beings hope in the resurrection. Death in the flesh is thus God's movement toward humankind. Confession of this movement without love is tantamount to denial because this movement is itself one of love: "'How,' you say, 'do I deny it in acts?' Because Christ came in the flesh precisely that he might die for us. He died for us precisely because he taught much love. 'Greater love than this no one has than that he lay down his life for his friends' [Jn 15.13]."[67] Christ came in love in order to draw humans together. Heretics, in Augustine's view, sunder Christ's body for their own honor rather than for love. They deny Christ and do not have the Spirit of God.[68]

The love that the Spirit pours into the hearts of believers is here not, as Hegel might fear, purely subjective. It has objective content in Christ and the right teaching about him. But that very objective content, as God's persuasive Word of love in the world, does not alienate believers in either an external Christocentrism or a compulsion toward subjective retreat from the world. This is seen when Augustine exhorts his readers to search for the Spirit in actions rather than merely in the sounds of words.[69] Keeping in mind Augustine's description of the transience of the external, historical miracle of glossolalia, we can see how, according to Augustine, one must look deeper than the external sign to the will behind it, to the love of God and neighbor given by the Holy Spirit. Thus while, in one sense, Augustine moves beyond language to a deeper spiritual level, in another he broadens the semantic and social range of Pentecostal pneumatic operation. The unifying and universalizing nature of love given by the Holy Spirit ensures correct speech about Christ, but it is speech that encompasses the entire person. Consistent, moreover, with what we have seen in this chapter, the Spirit's action at Pentecost functions unifyingly across two oft-overlapping dialectical trajectories: the internal and the external, and the individual and the ecclesial body. Augustine's adduction of Rom 5.5 reveals, on the one hand, an internalizing tendency in his interpretation of Pentecost. But this inward movement of love, while perhaps taking priority, is concomitantly externalized as well, inasmuch as the love poured into the heart by the Holy Spirit must be made manifest in words and deeds, both of which come to constitute spiritually guided linguistic and cultural production binding individual believers together in the body of Christ. Finally, as this passage evidences, this Pentecostal semantic of love is consistent with the divine rhetoric of the incarnation, passion, and resurrection, rhetoric that aims to instill a love of justice over power.

In *Trin*. 15.46 Augustine makes the nature of Pentecostal love even more concrete through an interpretation of the double sending of the Holy Spirit, once after Jesus' resurrection when he breathed the Spirit upon his apostles (Jn 20.22), and again after his ascension at Pentecost (Acts 2). This double sending, according to Augustine, "is because charity is poured out in our hearts through this gift, charity by which we are to love God and neighbor according to those two commandments on which the whole law depends and the prophets. It was to signify this[:] that the Lord Jesus gave the Holy Spirit twice, once on earth for love of neighbor, and again from heaven for love of God."[70] Augustine does not view this interpretation of the double sending to be binding, as long as one affirms the unity of the Spirit sent in both instances.[71] In this way he underscores not only the Trinitarian nature of the God toward whom Pentecostal love orients the heart, in confirming the relationship of the Holy Spirit to the Father and the Son—both in the sense of their equality of nature and the unifying function of the Spirit as the Spirit of the Father and of the Son—but also the way in which the same Spirit builds up the community oriented around the love of God.[72]

Tractate 74 on John offers a similar interpretation. The twofold sending manifests the double command of love, that is, of God and neighbor, but in a circular fashion also thereby confirms that love belongs properly to the Holy Spirit. These considerations are steps in Augustine's effort to clarify Christ's words in Jn 14.15–17, namely, that if the disciples love Christ, they will obey his commandments, and then the Father will send the Holy Spirit as an advocate to them. When considered together with Rom 5.5, Christ's words raise the question: "How is it that we love in order to receive [the Holy Spirit], and yet unless we should have him, we cannot love? Or how is it that we shall keep the commandments in order to receive him, and yet unless we should have him, we cannot keep the commandments?"[73] It is not as if one first receives the love of Christ and follows his commands in order to receive afterwards the love of God the Father, for otherwise the Spirit would be sundering the Son from the Father, and one would in fact not be loving Christ, but rather some idol.

The only conclusion, as evidenced by the apostles who loved Christ but had not yet received the Spirit fully, and as confirmed by the appropriation of love in its twofold commanded form to the Spirit, is "that without the Holy Spirit we cannot love Christ and keep his commandments, and that we can and do do that so much the less as we receive him less, and so much the more as we receive him more."[74] Noteworthy, first, is how dynamic Augustine's understanding of Pentecost is. It is not simply a one-time event, either historically speaking or from a subjective, anthropological point of view. Only Christ the mediator has received the fullness of grace from the moment of his birth by the Holy Spirit.[75] But humans receive the Holy Spirit in measure, receiving more until they attain their proper extent of perfection.[76] This entails a growth of love: "He who loves has the Holy Spirit, and by having deserves to have more, and by having more to love more."[77] In sermon 378 on the Feast of Pentecost, Augustine renders this Pentecostal dynamism explicitly eschatological by specifying the nature of Christ's promise of the Holy Spirit.[78] In that sermon Augustine argues that at Pentecost Christ sent the Holy Spirit, whom he had promised to his disciples as a guarantee of eternal life: "What has he promised us? Eternal life, as the earnest of which he has given us the Holy Spirit. Eternal life is the possession of those who have reached home; the earnest is the reassurance of those who are still on the way there."[79] Those who receive the Holy Spirit, then, are on the way. They have not, as have the recipients of *Geist* in Hegel, reached the eschatological pleroma of vision. Augustine's further distinction between an earnest and a pledge nevertheless underscores the pneumatic continuity of love between those on the way and their end goal. Although both a pledge and an earnest are presented as a guarantee that a promise will be met, the pledge is returned once the promise is fulfilled, whereas an earnest is retained and included in what has been promised. For this reason, Augustine calls the Holy Spirit an earnest, which nourishes the hearts of believers as they make their way toward its source.[80] Yet upon arrival they will not relinquish the love they have received; the love of God remains.

By his insistence on the need for the Holy Spirit in order to love God and obey his commandments, the later Augustine indicates his growing sense of the human being's inability to attain faith or love without the assistance of grace. This sensitivity to human weakness comes to the fore especially during the Pelagian controversy and often manifests itself with regard to Pentecost by explicit contrasts between the law of fear given on Sinai and the love of Pentecost that fulfills the law in freedom. With regard to the Spirit's work in both the Hebrew Bible and the New Testament, Verhees has observed that, on the one hand, Augustine explains the newness of Pentecost, when compared to previous theophanies or donations of the Holy Spirit, as consisting in greater universality and openness.[81] The gift of the Holy Spirit is rendered visible in the proclamation of a universal church. After Jesus' glorification there is a wider dissemination of the Spirit in love and spiritual grace.[82]

This universal, revelatory thrust in the consideration of Pentecost's historical novelty, then, is complemented by the spiritual gift of love, which Augustine sets in contrast to the law of Sinai.[83] Augustine makes clear the ecclesial context of this love. He shows that love makes the community possible through freedom, freedom which enables the speech, the preaching inspired by the Holy Spirit, that initiates and sustains the church. Christ has risen and ascended; the head is in heaven. But, Augustine maintains, Christ's feet are still on earth working hard to bring him to all nations. Christ's feet are his apostles and all who proclaim the gospel.[84] But in order that they might preach, that through them the church might become universal, they had to be set free, free from the fear that they were still guilty under the law. Christ, by sending the Holy Spirit, removed legal guilt and bestowed upon them the grace and love through which the law is fulfilled. This love of the Holy Spirit, a gift from God, enables Christians to build a community around justice and giving.[85]

The contrast between Sinai and Pentecost emerges also in an anti-Pelagian context in *s.* 156.14. There Augustine argues against the notion that Christ's grace simply makes it easier to do good. The law, Augustine says, is the nagging pedagogue who has brought believers to Christ, the teacher who does not deceive when he says, "Without me you can do nothing" (Jn 15.5).[86] Linking Rom 8.14[87] and 1 Pt 2.5,[88] Augustine shows that the Spirit is leading believers and thereby building up a living community, his temple. Toward that end the law is insufficient, as it produces only enslaving fear. Adducing Rom 5.5, Augustine indicates that when led by the Spirit, one is led to liberating charity. There are, however, not two spirits, one of slavery and another of freedom. To the contrary, Augustine affirms the unity of Spirit and makes clear that the difference between Sinai and Pentecost consists rather in the way in which the one Spirit relates to human beings: "So it's the same Spirit, but in fear on the tablets of stone, in love on the tablets of the heart."[89] In the former instance, the Spirit imposes an external law, whereas at Pentecost the law is written in one's heart and is thus fulfilled in the freedom of love from the inside out. Here there is none of the detrimental passivity and heteronomy that Hegel diagnoses in the early church.

The language of the heart, then, which we have seen Augustine elsewhere describe as the unifying gift of Pentecost, operates in accord with the law written in the heart. By receiving the Holy Spirit, Christians are adopted as God's sons and daughters. They no longer fear him as a harsh taskmaster, but rather love him as a Father. Consequently, they now call to him, "Abba, Father!" (Rom 8.15). The heart speaks in freedom to God.[90] Its thrust, nonetheless, is universal. Why, Augustine asks, does Paul not merely say "Father," but rather the combined form of Hebrew and Greek? It is because Christ is the cornerstone that the builders had rejected, a cornerstone that through the Holy Spirit now joins two walls, the Jews and the Gentiles, in the peace of love whereby true glory is given to Christ in the witness of praise: "the walls harmonized, the corner glorified."[91]

Through the gift of the Holy Spirit at Pentecost, the apostles are set free from fear. They are given the freedom of love. With this love the disciples receive confidence (*fiducia*) to manifest that love both in word and deed. In *ep. Jo.* 8.10, Augustine seeks to show the unity of the Johannine exhortation to brotherly love and Christ's command to love one's enemies. Their unity rests upon a dynamic understanding of the human person. In contrast to Hegel, Augustine draws a distinction between one's humanity, which was created by God, and one's evil, which one creates for oneself. Love of an enemy is brotherly love because it is oriented toward what the enemy ought to become, the true humanity he has been made by God. One loves an enemy by wishing that he or she not remain an enemy. This means, ultimately, turning one's love away from this world toward eternal life with God. Thus, one ought to desire that one's enemy be with him or her in eternal life. With regard to human beings, God has already done this paradigmatically in Christ, who did not wish that human beings remain forever sinners. Augustine finds God's love of enemy dramatically encapsulated in the transformation of some of Christ's persecutors into believers between the crucifixion and Pentecost:

> Observe how [Christ] himself loved, that is, that he was unwilling that they should so remain persecutors. He said, "Father, forgive them, for they know not what they do." Those whom he wished to be forgiven he wished to be changed; those whom he wished to be changed he deigned to make brothers from enemies, and he truly made them so. He was slain, he was buried, he arose, he ascended into heaven, he sent the Holy Spirit to the disciples. They began with confidence to preach his name; they worked miracles in the name of him crucified and slain.[92]

In a move important to our comparison with Hegel, love of enemies is here explicitly linked with forgiveness of sins, specifically, Christ's forgiveness. It is through that forgiveness that Augustine establishes the unity of love of enemy and brotherly love. That forgiveness is sacramentally transformative. Christ's words of forgiveness are grounded in the act of his passion, death, and resurrection, where the Word of God spoken in the world becomes a sacrament and model for the transformation of all believers. But note that the transformation, the conversion, of Christ's persecutors is occasioned by the confident preaching of the apostles in the Holy Spirit after Pentecost. Miraculous Pentecostal preaching is not merely an external sign meant to incite faith in Christ mechanically.[93] Rather, it is itself sacramentally transformative insofar as it enables participation in Christ's sacramental death and resurrection. Contrary to Hegel, Christ, for Augustine, remains constitutive of Christian faith given by the Holy Spirit. In this way, the Spirit aids human words and actions in conforming themselves to God's incarnate Word. In Augustine's view, were Christ as the incarnate Word to pass away into the kingdom of Spirit, the apostles' words would lose all semantic and especially prophetic value, because the apostles would be making claims about their own abilities beyond what is warranted. They would lose the value of their witness as one of love.

The transformative effect that the apostles' words in the Spirit have rests, therefore, upon the difference between God and humankind, a difference that we have seen is maintained and yet transfiguratively bridged by the Holy Spirit in the two natures in one person of Christ. Put in terms of the imagery used in Part I, moreover, the Holy Spirit bridges the humanly insurmountable gap between the eternal generation of the divine Word and the divine rhetoric of the incarnation, which believers can learn to speak through grace. For Augustine, then, human words and deeds can be the occasion for reconciliation with God in that they point always to the gift of forgiveness in Christ, a gift that was possible only because Christ was not merely human, because through the grace of the Holy Spirit the divine Logos was united personally with the human being Jesus.

Furthermore, the conversion of Jesus' persecutors upon hearing the post-Pentecostal witness of the apostles is possible only because of the disciples' transformation from fear to love and confidence. Only then do the disciples' words and deeds become the vessel of the Holy Spirit, by which the Spirit convicts (*arguere*) the world of unbelief[94] and re-creates human beings in God's image. The disciples' external words of love at Pentecost thus become the occasion for faith in God's healing of humankind in Christ on the cross,⁹⁵ the subject of the disciples' preaching and actions which is so persuasive that it moves even those who had really shed Christ's blood now to draw spiritual nourishment from it sacramentally.⁹⁶ Indeed, Augustine's eucharistic allusion with regard to God's transformative gift of forgiveness is telling and highlights a stark difference from Hegel's understanding of divine forgiveness. The word "Eucharist" means thanksgiving, and Augustine's allusion to it here underscores (1) the gracious character of divine forgiveness and (2) that for Augustine the appropriate human response to God, the human's vocation qua human, as a creature who owes everything to and hence cannot give anything to its creator, is one of confession, witness, praise, and gratitude. Such is a response of humility, a humility that demands courage while one still lives in a fallen world. It is a response, moreover, whereby a human becomes—if we can use a concept from Staudenmaier—a living word of God, one who is transformed by and imitates Christ, the Word who gives life.

The courage given by the Spirit aids in a conversion of heart which is ongoing and as yet incomplete, for Christians begin to be healed now in faith, but hope that their healing will one day be fully perfected in reality.⁹⁷ Consistent with his Christology, in which the one person of Christ is both way and goal, Augustine claims on the evidence of Rom 5.5 that the God in whom Christians believe and hope already dwells in them through the love of the Holy Spirit.⁹⁸ In this way, the transformation mediated by the Pentecostal witness to Christ brings with it a measure of spiritual presence, a foretaste of eschatological vision, while yet making clear that the perfection of love in the fullness of vision remains an unattained goal.⁹⁹

Where Hegel sees alienation, a sundering of the believer's heart from reality, Augustine shows that the gift of love at Pentecost is all-encompassing: the Holy Spirit takes hold of the entire person. The Spirit transforms the disciples. Confidence (*fiducia*) supplants fear (*timor*), and tongues of flame bring fire to the disciples, who now preach in many tongues. Through their confident preaching the Holy Spirit orients others toward the salvation effected by Christ on the cross and, in so doing, convicts the world of unbelief. The Spirit thus uses the words of the transformed disciples to transform other sinners, even the very ones who had put Christ to death. In this Pentecostal orientation toward Christ as foundation, way, and destination, moreover, we have seen how, according to Augustine, the Spirit inspires words not only about Christ, but that point to Christ in both content and form, that is, in their humility and peacefulness, but also in the fervor of love toward an enemy, in the desire that he or she be won over for eternal life. At the same time, though, we have seen the way in which Augustine follows the effects of Pentecostal love beyond words.

Both words and deeds can be understood as a semantic unity issuing from a converted heart. Just as we have seen Augustine speak of Christ's passion and resurrection as God's effort at persuading human beings of how much he loves them, that is, as a divine rhetoric of love, so too does the Holy Spirit at Pentecost empower humans to respond in love to God's incarnational speech, to express themselves genuinely in humble self-giving to others, that is, to embody God's word of love by sharing its persuasiveness with others in their words and in their actions and, in so doing, to build up Christ's body the church. But if human beings are to follow Christ, if not only their words but also their deeds are to proclaim him and imitate him, then first the conversion of the heart by the Holy Spirit, along with its attendant freedom and confidence, is necessary. Indeed, Augustine makes clear in *Jo. ev. tr.* 93.1 that, although Christ strengthened his disciples through his words and his example, they needed to be filled with the Spirit if they were to follow it.[100] The example of Christ is followed most dramatically by those who give their lives for him, the martyrs.

Augustine's understanding of martyrdom, however, differs from that of Hegel. Recall that Hegel views the martyrs as selfish escapists who, in trying to ensure their own salvation, end up dissipating in a subjective void, because they cannot sense the Spirit's presence in the real world. In working out an Augustinian response to Hegel's critique, a good place to start is with the Donatist controversy, which gave impetus to Augustine's mature views on martyrdom. The challenge the schism posed to church unity, the strict moral rigorism of the Donatists, and their appeal to specifically Donatist martyrs in the legitimation of their views forced Augustine to search for a precise definition of the true martyr.[101] The definition he advances is consistent with the nature of Pentecostal language and action we have seen in this chapter: the evaluative criterion rests in the cause for which one dies, in the intention or will, rather than in the external punishment or death. Thus, not every imposed death makes a martyr.[102] The only truly good cause is charity: "Those martyrs who suffered in the time of persecution acted out of love."[103] For support Augustine adduces 1 Cor 13.3: "If I deliver my body that I may be burnt, yet do not have love, it profits me nothing."[104] The immediate connection between 1 Cor 13.3 and Rom 5.5 in *en. Ps.* 118(21).8 confirms the Holy Spirit's role in Augustine's definition of genuine martyrdom. Martyrs have been given the love of the Holy Spirit, which affords them freedom to fulfill the law, the bipartite commandment to love God and neighbor.[105]

In accord with the double command of love, moreover, Augustine stresses against the Donatists that genuine martyrdom is communally situated. Recall how in *Jo. ev. tr.* 6.3 he links the pneumatic images of the dove and tongues of flame with the character of Stephen's preaching during his stoning. As a dove Stephen sought to maintain the unity of the church, manifest in the one language of the heart that transcends and repairs the disintegration of Babel,[106] a disintegration brought about by the pride likewise manifest in the divisive actions of the Donatist martyrs, who suffer and die in the name of Donatus, hence, to Augustine's mind, for human glory rather than out of love for the sake of Christ and the unity of his church.[107] True martyrs, Augustine shows, are not self-seeking or fanatical, because their sacrifice is one of love grounded in the truth of Christ and aimed at benefiting the community of believers.

The link for Augustine between the historical event of Pentecost and martyrdom is perhaps clearest and most dramatic in the figure of Peter. We have already seen examples of how the disciples receive from the Holy Spirit the freedom and confidence to preach and act in love. Augustine highlights this transformative effect on Peter by juxtaposing it with the latter's earlier denial of Christ.

Augustine seems to suggest two not unrelated causes of Peter's denial. Looking first to Jn 13.38, where Christ responds to Peter's promise to sacrifice his life for him with a prediction of Peter's denial, Augustine argues that Peter was not yet able to recognize his sinfulness and need for healing. With a brazen confidence (*temeraria quadam fiducia*), Augustine says, Peter promises to die for Christ, when in fact Christ had come to die for him. Thus Christ predicts Peter's denial in order to show him his need for salvation, to break down his disordered confidence.[108] Augustine contrasts Peter's threefold denial with the risen Christ's thrice-repeated question to Peter in Jn 21.15–19, "Do you love me?" Upon hearing this question from Jesus the third time, Peter is reminded of his denial. That, Augustine claims, is why Peter feels hurt (Jn 21.17): "You are aware, blessed Peter, you are aware of your desertion, in recalling it you are hurt; but after being hurt, rejoice. Let love confess the one whom fear had denied."[109]

We have observed the Augustinian contrast between Sinai and Pentecost, between the fear of punishment under the law and the charity which fulfills the law. Here *timor* focuses explicitly upon the consequence of sin; it is fear of death. This fear is evident when Peter denies his Lord. In fact, *timor mortis* becomes a prominent theme in Augustine's debates with the Pelagians concerning the martyrs' human frailty, specifically, and the limits to human justice and perfection more generally.[110] Augustine argues that the fear of death, rather than death itself, is natural, because death is punishment for the sin that impedes human perfection. This means that not only in his denial of Christ, but also in his martyrdom, Peter still feared death.[111] This unwillingness to die affects all the martyrs, even Paul.[112]

Only Christ, who was without sin, went willingly to death.[113] Consistent with his sense of Christ's death as *sacramentum* and *exemplum* for his followers, that is, of internal transformation augmented by eschatological hope in the transfiguration of the flesh, Augustine maintains that the struggles of the flesh remain for believers, but that now, following Christ's death and resurrection, suffering and death can be turned toward the cause of justice, as the way to eternal life.¹¹⁴ Death, in Augustine's view, cannot be loved, only borne, and it is precisely this patient endurance that constitutes the merit of the martyr. The love of the martyr defeats the fear of death because he or she hopes in the eternal life guaranteed by *Christ's* resurrection.¹¹⁵ This helps further illuminate the link between Christ's death, resurrection, and ascension on the one hand and the gift of the Holy Spirit at Pentecost on the other, in that faith in Christ's resurrection guarantees the hope in one's own resurrection, but is meritorious only if Christ goes away in the ascension and if the believer's own resurrection is delayed, such that faith becomes a struggle, a faith in things unseen.¹¹⁶ The Holy Spirit gives both this vision of faith at Pentecost and the love and hope whereby the martyr is able to imitate Christ despite the fear of death.¹¹⁷

Here, too, appears the contrast between Augustine and the more "active" classical heroic and Pelagian traditions of Württemberg Pietism and the Enlightenment so influential on Hegel's views of religious and political reform. Both the Donatist controversy and disputes with pagans in *civ. Dei* shape a notion of altruistic death that deviates from what had been passed down to Augustine through his culture. As Straw notes, "Ultimately this line of thought would separate him from earlier Christian writers such as Origen, Eusebius, Jerome, and Ambrose who embraced much of the classical tradition on the noble death and simply translated it to martyrology."¹¹⁸ Contrary to the accusations of heteronomy and passivity, though, Augustine's criteriological emphasis upon the love motivating the martyr and its source in the gift of the Holy Spirit, as well as his departure from the classical model of the hero who goes to death willingly and without fear, appears at once to open a greater pneumatic freedom—a freedom to stand over against even prevailing norms of altruistic death—and to mitigate, in the pedagogically humbling stance of constant struggle even with oneself, the chances for the violent and proud vacillations that Hegel so decries.

Augustine's theme of *timor mortis* in the martyrs leads Straw to describe the "ontological distance between Christ and the martyrs."[119] She notes that, in this regard, he differs from the Eastern tradition of Eusebius and Origen, for whom "the martyrs' sanctification is akin to deification."[120] This is significant because Dickey has gone to such lengths to show the parallels between the Eastern (Clementine and Origenistic) traditions of divinization and post-Reformation and Enlightenment ideas of reform. According to Augustine, however, only Christ dies voluntarily, and only his death is redemptive. While shed on behalf of others, the blood of martyrs does not remove sins. Indeed, "the martyr of Christ is far inferior to Christ."[121]

In Peter's martyrdom, Christ's mediation points to profound transformation which enables the dialectic of similarity and difference whereby one can speak at all of God's salvation in Christ and follow him in self-giving love. Linking Rom 5.5 with Jn 15.26–27 and Pentecost, Augustine claims that the love of God poured forth into their hearts will give the apostles "confidence for giving testimony."[122] Peter lacked this confidence when he fearfully denied Christ before the woman. When, by contrast, he confesses his love in freedom to the risen Christ three times in Jn 21, he is beginning to love, Augustine argues, but that love is feeble and limited and needs the Holy Spirit to "strengthen and enlarge it."[123] Thus, at Pentecost Peter received an overwhelming amount of grace that emboldened him and rendered him able to speak of Christ's resurrection. The Holy Spirit, who came in the tongues of all nations, transformed Peter's tongue, and through it, the tongues of those who once killed Christ. And not just in words: Peter had the confidence to preach Christ unto death.[124] What is more, with the fervor of the Holy Spirit, Peter was so persuasive that "of the immense crowd he made Christ's adversaries, his killers ... ready to die for him, those at whose hands he had feared to be slain with him. The Holy Spirit ... did this."[125] Here we see why it is important, for Augustine, that Christ not pass away into Spirit like a spoken word, for it is precisely the dialectical relationship between Christ and the Spirit that enables transformation in Peter and enables him to speak words in conformity to the divine Word. Christ must remain distinct from Peter so that real transformation is possible, so that humans do not misidentify the source of their salvation or prematurely claim that salvation as fully within their grasp. At the same time, the Spirit must bridge that distance between the glorified Christ and the believer with a love that transcends any normal human love, so that in the face of a still fallen world and their own persistence in sin, believers can speak and act in imitation of Christ.

Far from imposing heteronomy, the ontological distance between Peter and Christ is at the same time, for Augustine, the means whereby Peter is bound to Christ and whereby his martyrdom bears any semantic value. Augustine observes that Christ predicts to Peter the apostle's denial and martyrdom: "In foretelling that denial the Lord showed up Peter to Peter; while in that question about love, the Lord showed Christ to Peter."[126] The grace needed to make Peter a martyr is also what binds him to Christ and gives his testimony orientation and meaning. In that way, Christ is seen in Peter the martyr. Augustine's understanding of the church as Christ's body following its head enables him, in an earlier homily, to underscore this spiritual unity even further, albeit now with all its communal import: "The martyrs were killed so that Christ might suffer anew, not in himself [*non in capite*], but in his body."[127] Peter and other martyrs after Pentecost, through their testimony, contribute to the growth of this body by their orientation away from themselves toward Christ, their head.

Following upon the uniquely salvific death of Christ, the words and deaths of the martyrs are, according to Augustine, the means whereby the Spirit spreads the gospel universally. Thus, the martyrs are vessels of the Spirit and the gospel. Before the gospel was recorded in writing, the disciples in a very real way embodied the word given to them by the Spirit. Yet the word of God also transcends and encompasses them. Indeed, for Augustine, a unique facet of the post-Pentecostal martyrs Peter, Stephen, and Paul is that their words and deeds are included in the Christian scriptures. The Holy Spirit has preserved them for the persuasion of future generations; the inspired account of the Spirit's action in Peter's life is, accordingly, delightful and sweet: "If it delights anyone to view a spectacle like this, so sweetly hallowed, let him read the Acts of the

Apostles. There let him be amazed at the blessed Peter preaching for whom he had grieved when he was denying."[128]

Likewise, Augustine considers it a blessing that the martyrdom account of Stephen is preserved in the canonical scriptures and hence more readily accessible to the faithful than the stories of later martyrs.[129] The transformative power of the Holy Spirit is more concretely present to them through the reading of scripture. "You heard the story and saw the spectacle with your hearts," Augustine tells his congregation. "You were spectators of St. Stephen's great contest, in which he was being stoned."[130] They experience the Holy Spirit's persuasive power of love, specifically, a love of enemy through which Stephen and, by extension, Augustine's congregation are linked to the event of Pentecost and to Christ's death and resurrection. Augustine wonders whether Stephen was among those who, after participating in Christ's crucifixion and hearing him pray for those who knew not what they were doing, had their eyes opened and hearts converted by Peter's preaching.[131] Moreover, Augustine finds the love of one's enemy—evidenced by Christ's prayer and possibly heard by Stephen—further replicated in Stephen's prayer for the forgiveness of his killers. Paul, in turn, was present at Stephen's martyrdom and, according to Augustine, must have heard Stephen's prayer, though at the time he was still a persecutor of the church. Nonetheless, he too was included in Stephen's prayer and eventually won over to Christ.[132] In this way, through love of one's enemy articulated in the prayers for forgiveness, Augustine illustrates the link between Christ's passion and Pentecost as well as the means by which the Spirit causes the church to grow through the spoken and bodily witness of the martyrs.

Here again the contrast with Hegel's interpretation of early Christian martyrdom emerges. Hegel views the martyrs' passivity over against the state as a symptom of a deeper-seated wish to escape from the world. This thoroughly negative posture, as a devaluation of one's natural existence and the external affairs of society, eliminates any last rational impediments to the violent outbursts of repressed zeal against the world seen in later Catholic societies. In response to this view, however, Augustine's theology of the Holy Spirit offers us another way of understanding martyrdom: as an interpretation of death that actually ensures a greater spiritual richness and breadth of Christian life. Faith in the person of Christ and hope in the resurrection he has made possible do not devalue the world, but rather affirm its value. Through Christ's death and resurrection and the grace of the Holy Spirit, God brings good out of bodily death. Indeed, by prohibiting the application of oral linguistic imagery to the immanent Trinity Augustine gains a broader semantic range for Christians and the church. While Hegel maintains that without the passing over of the spoken divine Word into the presence of Spirit nothing in the material world holds any value, and hence nothing can be used as a means of expressing the truth, Augustine shows how martyrdom, far from being an escapist death cult, confirms the goodness and signifying character of the broad scope of creation. The transience of Christ's death in Hegel's system, the fading of the Word into Spirit, in fact evacuates other human deaths of their semantic value, for what one is to learn, according to Hegel, is that death is overcome in the fully realized kingdom of reason. For all that Hegel tries to explain them, suffering and death lose meaning in the modern world. Augustine, by contrast, declares in no uncertain terms that human suffering and death are evil, that in themselves they possess no meaning, but that through the sacrament and example of Christ's death they can speak about God. They become the means of both transformation and witness to divine love.

In Augustine's view, the voluntary death of the martyr gains meaning, in spite of death's primal obscurity, when guided by the love of the Holy Spirit. In the witness of the martyr, the Spirit's love speaks boldly, rebuking if necessary, when witnessing to the truth of divine justice. At the same time, it expresses love for one's enemies, including the very people putting one to death, a love articulated in the prayer for their forgiveness and hence grounded in God's love for his enemies, that is, in the forgiveness God freely offers in Christ through the Holy Spirit. In this way, the critical witness of the martyr is in fact a positive expression of the gift of the Holy Spirit, a free fulfillment of the law as the double command to love God and neighbor. For when one loves one's enemies in God, one seeks a reconciliation that transcends the resolution of personal, purely subjective disputes or even the breach of particular societal norms and laws. As an expression of true love of one's enemies, grounded in the forgiveness that God offers to all human beings, martyrdom can overcome the repressed feelings of resentment that Hegel fears. Only martyrdom wrongly understood—motivated, according to Augustine, by love of self rather than love of God and neighbor—could be corrupted into hatred and violence toward other human beings. Genuine love of neighbor, which has its ground in divine forgiveness, in turn realizes itself concretely in the world through the building up of Christ's body, the church, albeit a church body that, through its unity in the person of the Holy Spirit and its goal in the as yet unattained vision of Christ in *forma Dei*, is not identifiable with any particular human state or society. It is thus a church able to be a witness to God's love, justice, and mercy.

According to Augustine, the Holy Spirit transforms Peter's and Stephen's lives after Pentecost. In so doing, the Spirit works to communicate himself also to later generations of Christians, to transform their lives through scripture and the church's preaching of it. Cornelius Mayer, in analyzing Augustine's sermons on the martyr Stephen, situates them in Augustine's theory of signs. This theory, Mayer argues, with its distinction between *signa* and *res*, enabled Augustine to affirm these martyrs and their lives as *signa* while distinguishing them clearly from the *res* toward which they point. Thus Augustine, as a pastor, was able to allow the cult of the martyrs while at the same time reining in its worst abuses. The martyrs and the stories about them are for Augustine signs pointing toward God's saving work in Christ, whose incarnation, death, and resurrection in turn mediate and signify the eternal God outside time and space.[133] The sacramentality and exemplarity of Christ's death and resurrection are what enable the martyr to speak about God in his or her words and actions.

Yet, as we saw in Part I, just as the Holy Spirit, for Augustine, guarantees that the incarnate Word mediates and signifies the eternal triune God and not a false idol, so we ought not to stress

Augustine's distinction between the *signum* and the *res* at the expense of the movement of love, which, when rightly ordered toward God, at once sustains that distinction and can nonetheless thereby build a real relation between sign and thing, between outside and in-, albeit a relation that eludes full rational elucidation. Otherwise there is no possibility that the words and actions of the apostles, martyrs, or any other witnesses to God's love in Christ can be vessels of God's Word, can build up the church as the real body of Christ, or even, most fundamentally, that the historical person of Christ truly reveals the life of the eternal triune God. Hence, without the gift of the Holy Spirit, God does not speak in the world, and the foundation of the church's witness to justice crumbles. The ground of hope in God's renewal of the world is then lost, the ground of hope that makes the spoken and bodily witness of the martyrs—and indeed all genuine love of neighbor—a true expression of God's love and an affirmation of the goodness of life in this world.

HEGEL AND AUGUSTINE develop different conceptions of the Spirit's witness to Christ as the ground of Christian community. For Hegel, the spiritual meaning of Christ's death has to do not merely with external negation, but with the negation of negation, the in-finitization of the finite, in the positive resurrection in the universal Spirit not sundered from the world but inclusive of it. Hegel's goal of real social re-collectivization thus engenders a new form of language aimed at building a community of Spirit, a language of forgiveness and reconciliation that enables the recognition of oneself, of the selfsame universal Spirit, in the other. This language that seeks and offers forgiveness is directed toward the positive reconciliation of Spirit in a community of the resurrection, a community of human beings who recognize the Spirit in themselves, who know themselves as forgivable and indeed forgiven, and who are therefore free and unafraid to build a better society in the world. As a consequence, the true witnesses to Spirit are for Hegel the heroes, the world historical individuals, who sacrifice themselves in order to build something real, to bring about the modern liberal state, toward which, Hegel thinks is now clear, reason has been driving throughout history.

For both Hegel and Augustine, the new community of Spirit is formed around divine forgiveness of humankind. By rendering the Spirit radically immanent in the world, Hegel is able to trace its movements through the vicissitudes of history and to see reconciliation fully obtain when humanity comes to know itself as working out the realization of reason in history. However, we might ask, in the face of the radical evil human societies have perpetrated throughout history, does a tragi-comic narrative of divine fall and reconciliation suffice? From that evil can some meaning emerge in history? Can humans explain evil, or is that tantamount to explaining it away? If absolute Spirit has been made immanent in the community so thoroughly, if the objective criterion of truth necessarily passes into that immanence, if the prophetic voice of scripture and the church pass over into the conceptual language of philosophy and the structures of the state, is not then that evil, the evil integrated into the divine, thus irremediable and unforgivable?

Augustine insists that forgiveness is an unexpected, humbling gift to a humanity inexplicably obsessed with injustice. In that gift, God's transcendence over against the world is preserved, yet because that gift is the love of God through his Holy Spirit, God remains the transformative, personal presence within a human community ever being re-formed. As transcendent and critical, the Word of God spoken through the Holy Spirit continues to awaken the world from its proud blindness. The witness of the martyrs is critical in convicting the world of injustice, but that critique is not as thoroughly negative as Hegel claims. Augustine's more nuanced theology of martyrdom, one whose criterion is love, a love of neighbor grounded in the love of God, shows how the Holy Spirit at once critiques the world through the courageous death of the martyr and precisely thereby builds up a real community in the world. Through the witness of the martyr inspired by the Holy Spirit, a community is built up around the love and pursuit of God's justice manifest by Christ on the cross. It is a community that remains open to God's Word, that knows it can do nothing without God,

Augustine: The Holy Spirit and the Transformation of Language 171

but also knows that now it can and must speak and act on behalf of justice because it has hope.

Parts I and II have traced differences between Hegel's and Augustine's Trinitarian grammars—specifically, how each thinker speaks about Christ and the Holy Spirit—with a view toward the practical ramifications for Christian life and community. Part III will work out in greater detail the different shapes that the Christian community takes in their thought. The paradigmatic case of the martyr has already begun to show their different understandings of pneumatically inspired witness and its role in the community. Part III will continue this line of inquiry by asking how, for each thinker, the Spirit empowers the church community to witness to God's presence in the world.

PART III

CHURCH

Both Hegel and Augustine situate the doctrine of the Trinity at the intellectual and practical heart of Christianity, and both strive to formulate that doctrine in a way that they think most effectively enables and sustains the flourishing of the community formed around it. In Part III our analysis of Hegel and Augustine orients itself around more "traditional" aspects of Christian ecclesiology: the church as the body of Christ and the sacrament or mystery of divine love in the world. In response, once again, to the potential objection that such a method constitutes a gross imposition of non-Hegelian categories upon Hegel's philosophy and thereby obscures his intentions, we reiterate a few points: (1) Insofar as Hegel attempts in his philosophy to remedy alleged problems with the representational Christian theological tradition, it is helpful to investigate how he philosophically reconstructs certain traditional theologoumena, in order to assess (1a) whether his reconstruction deviates from them formally and materially, and if so, to what degree, and (1b) what is lost as a result when Hegel's normative prescriptions are considered from a theological perspective. Toward that end, (2) such an interpretive structure facilitates comparison with Augustine's "representational" ecclesiology and enables us to highlight its theological strengths over against the deficits we identify in Hegel.

Two modes of biblical discourse, lament and praise, will serve as our test case for the theological adequacy of Hegel's pneumatological reconfiguration of traditional ecclesiological imagery and the church practices of biblical exegesis, teaching, and the Eucharist. The purpose in choosing these forms of linguistic praxis is twofold: (1) they exemplify human experiences, such as tragedy, love, or grace, that exceed any exhaustive rational explanation, and (2) they have revelatory and traditional warrant, the continued value of which, in Augustine's view, derives from faith in the incarnation as the expression of God's love for the world. Hegel, in his understanding of spiritual community, obviates these forms of Christian language and practice and thus, through a pneumatological overemphasis on the resurrection, paradoxically undermines his effort to affirm the value of reality. He thereby vitiates the overall value of his concept of community as a resource for the Christian community striving to understand itself in its relationship to God amid a world still marked by evil and suffering.

Over against Hegel's concept of spiritual community, chapter 6 will highlight the strengths of Augustine's "representational" theology of the church, by drawing out the pneumatological implications of a central and strongly christological concept Augustine uses to think about the church: the *totus Christus*. We will consider Augustine's concept of the *totus Christus*, or the whole Christ, especially as it takes shape, he thinks, in the recitation and exposition of the psalms and is sacramentally realized in the Eucharist. Just as God's Word became fully human through the grace of the Holy Spirit, so that same Spirit, Augustine argues, calls believers and unites them in Christ's body, the church, through the words of scripture and the Eucharist. In the community whose life is shaped by those words and that sacrament—signs which, on the evidence of the psalmic language of lament and praise, Augustine sees touching all aspects of human existence—the Holy Spirit draws believers into communion with God's Word and thereby gives them a truly authentic voice.

Chapter 5

HEGEL'S SPIRITUAL COMMUNITY

As in the case of F. C. Baur, it is those who come after Hegel, rather than the man himself, who notice his apparent similarities with Augustine. With regard to the church, Peter Hodgson observes that Hegel, by criticizing a so-called Catholic principle of externality,

> takes a juridical version of Catholicism as normative and overlooks a strong emphasis stemming from Augustine on the Spirit as the "soul" of the church. Hegel basically is not familiar with the Augustinian strand of Catholicism. He himself insists on the necessity of the second moment, that of objectivity and otherness, but adds that it must be "sublated in love." The third moment unifies the abstractness of the Father and the objectivity of the Son in the community of the Spirit ([*LPR*] 2:230–1). *In this Hegel thinks very much like Augustine.*[1]

The previous four chapters ought to render us suspicious enough of the parallels Hodgson detects between Hegel's and Augustine's Trinitarian theologies. By extension, any deeper similarities he might find in their conceptions of the church should also strike us as suspect. This, to be sure, must be argued; Hodgson provides us, fortuitously, with a ready point of access to such an endeavor. If Hegel's critique of Catholicism overlooks important theological sources—namely, those of an Augustinian tradition—that paint a much more vibrant picture of the Spirit's activity in the church, we need not, as Hodgson does implicitly, assume an Augustinian legitimation of Hegel's Trinitarian credentials. Rather, if we attend to the teleological interpretation of history that forms the context of Hegel's opposition to Catholicism, then Hodgson's acknowledgment of the merits of Augustinian pneumatology, especially with respect to Catholic ecclesiology, not only problematizes Hegel's normative Trinitarian reading of history, but thereby recommends Augustine's Trinitarian theology as a worthy response to Hegel's critique of the longer theological tradition.

Yet Hegel's narrative of the history of Trinitarian doctrine, which has his philosophy of Spirit as its telos, has not lost its allure. Indeed, we find such an account concerning the Holy Spirit and the church in Alan Olson's 1992 book *Hegel and the Spirit: Philosophy as Pneumatology*. There Olson argues that "theologians after the fourth century paid little attention to the phenomenology of *pneuma*, focusing rather on the institutional-sacramental mediation of Spirit's authority. This neglect led to the replacement or, more accurately, the displacement of pneumatology by ecclesiology."[2] Instead, Olson claims, Hegel separates these two elements in his philosophy, in order that his pneumatology may not be obfuscated "by wedding it to an outmoded doctrine of the Church."[3] Tellingly, this allegedly obsolete ecclesiology "is replaced, in the *Rechtsphilosophie*, by a far more encompassing post-Enlightenment conception of society and the state—a conception within which art, religion, and philosophy each play integral but not exclusive roles."[4] Olson's reading not only describes, but also positively evaluates Hegel vis-à-vis the longer Trinitarian and ecclesial tradition. We can use this reading, along with that of Hodgson, to lay the structural groundwork for the current chapter.

First, we investigate the theological pedigree of Hegel's conception of spiritual community. Against Olson's very Hegelian claims that (1) Hegel is more Lutheran than the Lutherans themselves and that (2) his philosophy offers the speculative exposition of Spirit that had been egregiously lacking in Christian theology, we will see that Hegel's brand of Lutheranism derives less from Luther and more from very different mystical, apocalyptic, and socially oriented strands of Reformation thought. By driving a wedge between Hegel and Luther, we call into question Hegel's teleological reading of history and, more fundamentally, the continuity between his Trinitarian theology and the doctrinal tradition he wishes to claim. Luther, for all his real differences from Augustine, is nevertheless closer in his theology to the bishop of Hippo than to Hegel. From the Augustinian reformer, then, we can more easily move to Augustine himself.

Next, we turn to Hegel's use of soul and body imagery for the community. Because for Hegel the spiritual community is the point at which the divine renders itself actual in the world and in history, we analyze the structure of this community against the theoretical backdrop of Hegelian Trinitarian theology as well as the historical backdrop of his interpretation of medieval Catholicism, the Reformation, and the emergence of the modern European state. Here we rely largely on the *Enc.*, where Hegel presents his clearest discussion of the soul and its relation to the body, and on *LPH*, where he traces the drastic religious, social, and political changes that occur between the late medieval period and the early nineteenth century.

Finally, we consider how the organic Trinitarian structure of Hegel's spiritual community communicates or witnesses to Spirit. Here we see most concretely how Hegel's concept of the spiritual community and its worship closes off modes of discourse and practice that are essential to Christian life, because truer to the reality and variety of human experience, and hence to the church's ability to witness to God's love for the human beings in those experiences. By analyzing the form and content of practical religious aspects of Hegel's spiritual community, including the interpretation of scripture, the formulation of doctrine, and the celebration of the Eucharist, we can assess their capacity to accommodate modes of linguistic praxis which are vital, according to Augustine, to the life of the church: lament and praise. Here we avail ourselves primarily of *LPR*, where Hegel discusses religious worship and its relation to philosophy, as well as *Enc.* and *PR*, because it is there that Hegel displaces older ecclesiological concepts with a broader pneumatological conception of society and the state.

Spiritual Community: Hegel's Lutheran Claim

In his later works Hegel seldom speaks explicitly of the "church." His preference in *LPR* is for the "spiritual community" (*Gemeinde*). Hegel's purpose, Olson argues, is to avoid confusing pneumatology with ecclesiology or vice versa. Like early Pietism, Hegel sought to discover the work of Spirit beyond traditional theological and ecclesial confines.[5] Nevertheless, this pneumatological focus does not prevent him from validating the visible church. While in his early writings Hegel readily opts for the invisible over the visible church as the site of the kingdom of God, the notion of community in *LPR* encompasses both without conflating them or setting one in fundamental opposition to the other.[6]

So what exactly is this community, this kingdom of the Spirit? By the time of *The Spirit of Christianity* (1799), Hegel had moved beyond an early adherence to the Kantian rational kingdom to one of love. This concept of love already contained the structural roots of Hegel's mature concept of Spirit, which emerged as he gained greater clarity concerning the movement of love qua Logos. With the discovery of the concept of Spirit, the mature Hegel's thinking about the community becomes more religious, incarnational, and ultimately universalistic. In the section of *PS* on revealed religion the community (albeit one not yet fully reconciled with the world) is described as "the universal divine Man."[7] The communal divine man is rational, but his reason is ultimately not *Verstand* but *Vernunft*, which for Hegel includes feeling and intuition, modes of consciousness more appropriate to the sphere of religion. Moreover, Hegel becomes increasingly attuned to the way in which human beings develop over time; the community, he recognizes, has a history. The community and its development are understood as universally valid and all-encompassing. They constitute a totality, a coherent, unified system in which the multiplicity and distinctiveness of constituent individuals are maintained, but understood in their relation to each other and the whole. Hegel conceives of this developing communal system organically. Hence he frequently uses the image of the social or corporate body.[8]

The definitive form of the community, Hegel claims from *PS* onward, is Christian. In *LPR* it is interpreted according to a tripartite developmental schema that corresponds formally to the broader Trinitarian narrative which shapes Hegel's system as a whole and into which the community is situated as that narrative's third moment. Within the Christian community, Hegel demarcates three stages that operate both diachronically in history and synchronically in his exposition: (1) the *emerging* (*entstehende*) community, marked by the immediate feeling of the Spirit's presence and hence identifiable with Pentecost proper; (2) the *subsisting* (*bestehende*) community, in which the immediacy of feeling is articulated in the more rational form of doctrine and the worship of the cultus; and (3) the *realization* of the community through which, in the practical or real sphere, the distinctively religious community is sublated in the ethical life of the state and, in the ideal realm, the religious consciousness of the truth articulated representationally attains its end in philosophy.[9]

Ultimately, the form of community that is fully commensurate to its concept, hence in which Spirit is self-consciously present, is a post-Enlightenment version of society that Hegel clearly considers to be Lutheran Protestant. Yet despite Hegel's frequent appeals to the reformer, the strength of his ties to Luther both historically and systematically remains unclear. Scholars such as Olson and Ulrich Asendorf see enough essential continuity between the two thinkers to deem legitimate Hegel's claim of Lutheran pedigree.[10] However, other commentators point out stark differences between the two figures.[11] Here we will follow this latter group in questioning Hegel's Lutheran lineage. That requires, though, that we identify the kind of Lutheranism Hegel does in fact espouse. We will first consider attempts to establish a legitimate connection between Hegel and Luther, focusing primarily on Olson's account while also giving some attention to Asendorf. Then we will consider the problems with these accounts.

Olson contends that Hegel's insight into the process of Spirit, one that links and transcends subjective devotion and objective cultic practice "in rational belief and ethical life in the state," derives from his youthful habituation into the performative religious dialectic contained in Luther's explanation of the third article on the Holy Spirit in his *Small Catechism*: "I believe that I cannot, by way of reason or power, believe in Jesus Christ, my Lord, or come to him; but the Holy Spirit has called me through the Gospel."[12] In this catechetical formulation, Olson finds the seeds of Hegel's dialectic of Spirit:

> Viewed from a transcendental standpoint, Luther's formulation implies that the awareness of an Absolute-Unconditioned is also somehow present in the knowledge of nonknowledge as a datum of consciousness. What we have in Luther, then, is nothing less than an incipient dialectic of consciousness informing the manner in and through which faith and life in the Spirit are to be understood both formally and existentially.[13]

Asendorf also discovers parallels at the level of depth grammar. Luther's doctrine of justification, he argues, contains an inherent dialectical movement that anticipates Hegel's philosophy of Spirit.[14] And Asendorf claims that Luther's main doctrines of divine promise, Christ's two natures, the Eucharist, the cross, and the Trinity establish the concrete character of divine Spirit. The same concrete Spirit reemerges, he thinks, in Hegel's philosophy, with its all-encompassing, christologically grounded inclusion of history and the ethico-political sphere.[15]

For his part, Olson thinks that Hegel's claim to be more Lutheran than his orthodox Lutheran contemporaries rests on his deeper insight into the spiritual dynamism of Luther's pneumatology than that evidenced by the dry forensic character of later Lutheran doctrine. Olson sees the spiritual power of Luther's pneumatology firmly grounded in two traditions: (1) that of late medieval Rhineland mysticism, which in taking the dialectical *via negativa*, the knowledge of the nonknowledge of the divine, sought a deeper union with God, and (2) biblical traditions of Spirit, including the

Old Testament *ru'ah* ordering the waters of chaos and the New Testament advocate who shall comfort and enlighten the Christian faithful. "Hegel," Olson concludes, "is as firmly convinced as Luther, I think, of the general validity of these assertions—the fundamental difference being that Hegel goes on to demonstrate *how* and *why* it is the case that a complete cognitional theory can and should be developed through the category of Spirit, a category central to the otherwise sparse philosophical reflections found in scripture."[16]

Olson argues, furthermore, that Luther's doctrine of the priesthood of all believers, along with a pneumatology in which the Spirit is known primarily through his illuminating gifts to each member of the community of saints, lies at the root of Hegel's own restructuring of the relationship between pneumatology, church, and society. This social reconfiguration, Olson insists, is in accord with what Hegel labels the Protestant principle, the tenet that humans are destined to be free: "[The] shape of society, its conception of authority and its system of governance, could no longer be viewed as given a priori in religion or the pneumatology deemed proper to it. Such structural actualities must rather develop from within and be consistent with the process of Spirit's self-actualization in the consciousness of the individual subject."[17] Olson thus strives to situate the "spiritual community" within Hegel's broader philosophical system. He argues that Hegel's *Enzyklopädie* (1817) ought to be interpreted as a speculative pneumatology, an effort to follow Luther's dialectical pneumatology through to its conclusion without, however, falling into the contradictions of a representational account of the Trinity based on a precritical substance ontology. The *Philosophy of Right* (1821), written immediately after the 1817 *Enc.*, serves then as Hegel's analysis of society and government emerging from concrete Spirit conscious of itself as absolute and free. Human society must henceforth be built around this principle of self-conscious freedom. *PR* is, in this sense, Hegel's "ecclesiological" counterproposal.[18] In this practical sphere, both Olson and Asendorf argue that Hegelian pneumatology represents an advance over abstract Enlightenment, particularly Kantian, ethical thought, because its concrete, dialectical character is better able to account for the particular historical religious, social, and political contexts in which all thought and ethical action are realized. Hegelian Spirit is thus, they insist, more grounded in reality than the abstractly utopian, yet ultimately irrationally destructive, spirit of the *Schwärmer*, in Luther's case, or the Terror issuing from the rationalist-inspired French Revolution, in Hegel's.[19]

The Enlightenment Luther?
Eckhartian and Joachimite Redescription

Both Hegel's claim to be the rightful heir to Luther's spiritual legacy and Olson's and Asendorf's efforts to legitimate it turn especially on an assumed content identity between the philosopher's and the Reformer's uses of two related concepts: Spirit and freedom. Olson attempts to find this identity in a shared mystical method and content. The negative spiritual dialectic evidenced in Luther's *I believe that I cannot believe*—which Olson traces back to Rhineland mysticism—culminates, he thinks, in Hegel's dialectic of Spirit. The line, however, that Olson would trace from Rhineland mysticism through Luther to Hegel is tenuous. In his work *Homo Spiritualis*, Steven Ozment demonstrates how the theological movement of the young Luther toward his Reformation breakthrough is one away from the thought of mystical figures like Tauler and Gerson.[20] For the latter two figures, postlapsarian human beings possess soteriological capacities which enable them in this life to achieve ever greater likeness to, even a substantial (*weselich*) unity with, God. Luther, on the other hand, finds the human being devoid of any ability to save him- or herself. Only God saves. The life of faith, according to Luther, remains marked by the difference between the human and God, by the *simul* of sinfulness and grace.[21] Hegel's dialectic, contrariwise, resolves itself in humankind's this-worldly likeness to and union with God. In effect, Hegel appears much closer to the Rhineland mystics than he does to the historical Luther.

Furthermore, Hegel's positive anthropology is related to an understanding of freedom different from Luther's. In that regard

Merold Westphal observes an ambiguity in Hegel's articulations of the Protestant principle. Hegel actually formulates two principles: the "Principle of Subjectivity" and the "Principle of Autonomy."[22] While on the one hand Hegel emphasizes the need for each individual to judge and appropriate the truth—which he, Hegel, regards as continuous with Luther's insistence on faith—at other times he equates the Protestant principle with reason's freedom from any authority apart from itself. In other words, Hegel conflates Lutheran subjectivity with Enlightenment rationality without attending to the important differences between them: "For Luther, liberty of conscience is anything but the protest against all authority. It is freedom from human authority in order to be subject to divine authority as expressed in the teachings of Scripture."[23]

Hegel adopts certain elements of Luther's theology—the doctrine of *sola fide* and the priesthood of all believers—at the expense of others—*sola scriptura* and *sola gratia*.[24] By marginalizing the latter two doctrines, Hegel can more easily align faith with reason and align the priesthood of all believers with universal rationality and freedom qua self-determination. The Reformation and Enlightenment can then be more easily inscribed into a coherent, teleological reading of history and society that has Hegel's philosophy of Spirit at its end. This inscription has surprising consequences. On the one hand, Luther is set in the same camp as the adherents of rational autonomy. On the other hand, the Enlightenment is incorporated, to the chagrin of many of its exponents, into a normatively Christian narrative of history.

In identifying Luther and the Enlightenment as defining moments in the emergence of the spiritual community—which in *LPR* stands as his normative articulation of Christianity—Hegel is practicing what Cyril O'Regan calls "immanent subversion," whereby "Hegel tends to undermine a historically dominant tradition or tradition of interpretation not by appeal to his own singular authority, but rather by appeal to a minority or repressed tradition of interpretation."[25] The minority tradition to which Hegel appeals is a brand of Reformation and, in particular, Lutheran Christianity shaped by the Trinitarian-historical thought of the medieval theologian Joachim of Fiore.²⁶ We have more to say about the theological effects this Joachimite tradition has upon Hegel's spiritual community below. In the meantime it is enough to show the distance this tradition sets between the historical Luther and Hegel and how it enables the latter to incorporate the Enlightenment and its aftermath into his Christian narrative of history.

We can delineate Joachim's Trinitarian exegesis of history as follows: the age of the Father stretches from Adam to Christ, the age of the Son from Christ to St. Benedict, and the age of the Spirit from St. Benedict to the culmination of history.²⁷ In various ways, the earliest generation of Protestant reformers understood the import of their work in Joachimite eschatological terms.²⁸ They saw the Reformation as either anticipating or marking the advent of the Spirit and liberation from the mechanistic sacramentality of medieval Catholicism. But where Luther was reserved about making any definitive claims concerning the meaning of history and restricted his eschatological musings to the exegesis of the canonical texts of Daniel and Revelation, second- and third-generation reformers took over from Joachim a more intense interest in discovering the divine plan in history. The apocalyptic precedent of the Joachimite Reformers—apocalyptic in the sense of the unveiling of knowledge—permitted them to claim more definitive knowledge concerning the meaning of history and to extend that interpretation beyond biblical sources to the general course of history and politics. Following Joachim, they erased the distinction between sacred and secular history by extending soteriological import to all of human history and social affairs.²⁹ In a highly significant parallel to Hegel's *LPH*, O'Regan points out how second- and third-generation Lutherans employed the book of Daniel's division of history into four empires to interpret their own time: the era of Rome, the third empire, was now giving way to the final age, that of Germany.³⁰

With the emergence of Lutheran Orthodoxy in the sixteenth and seventeenth centuries, apocalyptic Lutheranism moved to the margins. It remained alive in the thought of figures like Jakob Böhme (1575–1624), only to resurface in the eighteenth century as a live option in Lutheranism, where Hegel is concerned, in the form of Württemberg Pietism. We have already discussed the young Hegel's religious context in chapter 3, but a few elements bear repeating here. In line with the Joachimite tradition, Württemberg Pietists understood their effort to complete the Reformation through concrete social reform in eschatological terms. Their positive sense of human potential was the fruit of a more universal understanding of the scope of salvation history, in which the line between church piety and action in the world had vanished.[31]

This socially oriented and eschatological Reformation tradition—which, as we recall, Dickey characterizes as Pelagian—presented Hegel with the interpretive means to make sense of the Enlightenment and the French Revolution in Christian terms. Rather than marking a radical break with what preceded them, these events became, in Hegel's interpretation, an extension, if not the fulfillment, of what Luther had begun in the Reformation.[32] That fulfillment, Hegel argues, is ultimately attained in the self-conscious freedom of the spiritual community.

Thus, although Olson is correct to insist that any proper understanding of Hegel's mature thought must take account of his Pietist background, his desire to trace Hegelian Spirit back to Luther's pneumatology seems a stretch. Hegelian pneumatology has its roots less in Luther's doctrine of the Holy Spirit, and more in the mystical thought of Böhme and Württemberg Pietism's Joachimite-eschatological focus on sanctification and deification. And while Asendorf distinguishes between the future orientation of Luther's eschatology and the realized present orientation of Hegel's, he attributes this to the difference between Luther's theological and Hegel's philosophical modes of speaking. In so doing he assumes a content identity between the two thinkers. This interpretation is problematic for a number of reasons: (1) It exaggerates the eschatological coloration of Luther's own theology, for the historical Luther's reforming efforts were as much animated by the goal of repristination—of returning to Christianity's purer origins—as by the goal of eschatological fulfillment. The more thoroughly Joachimite, eschatological self-interpretation of the Reformation, which comes to influence Hegel, only comes on the scene with the second and third generation of reformers.[33] Conversely, Asendorf (2) underemphasizes the all-consuming eschatological character of Hegel's philosophy. For Hegel, the difference between religion and philosophy is not simply a matter of two equivalent, yet different ways of talking about the same thing. Rather, religion has its true end in philosophy; philosophical discourse is the eschatological fulfillment of religious discourse.

Therefore, it is not at all obvious that Hegel's insistence on the content identity between philosophy and religion translates into a content identity between his philosophy and Luther's religion. The presence of the kingdom and fullness of vision that Hegel finds in his *Gemeinde* is very different from Luther's sense of the church still on its way and living according to faith in the Word.[34] This latter characteristic indicates much deeper-seated differences at the level of Trinitarian-ecclesial structure. In contrast to Hegel's spiritual community, Luther's concept of the Christian community is much more christologically determined. The dependence of the church upon the Word of God, understood primarily in terms of Christ and secondarily in terms of the scriptural witness, remains a central feature of Luther's ecclesiology throughout his career.[35] Asendorf's attempt to link Luther and Hegel through the concept of concrete Spirit falters on this point. Luther's primarily christological insistence on the visible marks of the church—the preaching of the Word and the sacraments—against the exaggerated pneumaticism of the radical Reformers differs from Hegel's pneumatologically inflected conception of community and history, with which he at once combats and sublates the empty formalism of Enlightenment rationalism. Luther's marks of the church are grounded in a Trinitarian dialectic of faith through which the Holy Spirit liberates believers from human authorities by setting them in radical dependence on the Word of God.[36] This is precisely not Hegel's dialectic of Spirit, which moves beyond the christological moment of dependence to the mystical identity of divine and human, to rational autonomy and freedom as self-determination. Whereas Luther's Trinitarian dialectic of faith is animated by the sustained interpersonal relationship between Christ and the Spirit in the life of the believer and the church, Hegel's Trinitarian dialectic is teleological and eschatological: the words of scripture give way to reason; religion has its end in the ethical life of the state and philosophy; faith in Christ is sublated in the fullness of spiritual vision.

Thus, by critically examining the narratives of Alan Olson and Ulrich Asendorf, we have gained historical and systematic leverage by which to bring Augustine's pneumatology to bear critically upon Hegel's normative and totalizing Trinitarian claims. Olson's and Asendorf's efforts to legitimate Hegel's claim to be the rightful heir of Luther's spiritual legacy are dubious given the vast differences between the two thinkers and Hegel's Pelagian and Joachimite theological pedigree. Because these features of Hegel's thought also distance him from Augustine, there then opens the space from which to mount a systematic theological critique of Hegel's Trinitarian-communal program. Indeed, the rest of this chapter shows how Hegel's pneumatological reconfiguration of the community, despite its explicit aim to make language transparent to the reality of the divine, effectively silences those who, at one extreme, experience tragedy and Godforsakenness, and at the other, wonder at the majesty of God's grace and love. Hegel's application of oral linguistic imagery to the immanent Trinity does not result in greater understanding of the divine. Rather, the fading of the eternal Word into Spirit results in a loss of language at those moments when it might be needed most.

Spirit's Decapitated Body

Hegel's and Augustine's theories of church and society are grounded in their distinct Trinitarian paradigms. To show this link, it will help to examine a form of communal imagery employed by both Hegel and Augustine: that of the body with a soul. Soul-body imagery serves better than other images used by Hegel or Augustine for several reasons. Both thinkers use the image frequently in a variety of contexts. More importantly, given that the body-soul relationship is important in both thinkers' work and has been explored in the secondary literature, the image itself and, as a consequence, its Trinitarian referents and ecclesiological implications can be determined rather specifically. This level of determination then allows the body-soul imagery to function in turn as a lens through which to interpret other important ecclesiological images, for example, "kingdom" in Hegel. Finally, the image has explicit biblical and traditional warrant, including a place of prominence in Augustine's ecclesiology, which makes it an important resource for determining Hegel's relationship to Augustine and to a long line of traditional ecclesiology.

Of course there is the important qualification that for Hegel no image or representation could exhaustively explain the reality of the spiritual community. What is more, it does not seem that Hegel explicitly uses the image of body and soul with regard to the church. This latter caveat, however, is not as damning as it might seem, because the image is explicit in some of Hegel's discussions of the Eucharist, which he considers to be determinative of the character of different church communities. Finally, the image is also explicit in Hegel's discussion of the modern state, which in his philosophy displaces the church as the spiritual community.

If we look at corporate imagery for the church from the Pauline and deutero-Pauline epistles, we find a distinction that is helpful in specifying not only Hegel's understanding of the church community, but also his understanding of its relationship to Christ and the Holy Spirit. We can start by citing a passage from Colossians:

> [Christ] is the head of the body, the church.
> He is the beginning, the firstborn from the dead.
> (Col 1.18 NRSV; square brackets mine)

Both Col 1.18 and Eph 1.22–23 offer one ecclesiological image: the church as a body with Christ as its head. This depiction differs slightly if not insignificantly from two other important sources of corporate ecclesiological imagery found in 1 Cor 12.12–27 and Rom 12.4–8, where Christ is identified with the body of believers, but is not mentioned as that body's head. Whether or not Hegel was aware of this distinction in the corporate imagery of the Pauline and deutero-Pauline epistles, a grasp of the distinction nevertheless seems implicit in his theoretical treatments of the ecclesiastical and secular communities. That is, Hegel appears to reject the type of ecclesiology in which Christ is the explicit or monarchical head of his ecclesial body, while advocating a form of church in which Christ is identified with the body of believers purely through a nonindividual, spiritual presence.

As we observed in previous chapters, Hegel views the Crusades as a historical turning point of central christological and pneumatological import, for when the European knights searching for the physical body of Christ instead find only an empty tomb, the entire sensuously bound mediational framework governing medieval Catholic spirituality comes subjectively—if not yet objectively in history—crashing down:

> In the negation of that *definite and present embodiment* [*Dieses*]—i.e. of the Sensuous—it is that the turning-point [*Umkehrung*] in question is found, and those words have an application: "Thou wouldst not suffer thy Holy One to see corruption" [Ps 16.10; Acts 2.27, 31; 13.35]. Christendom was not to find its ultimatum of truth in the grave. At this sepulchre the Christian world received a second time the response there: "*Why seek ye the living among the dead? He is not here, but is risen.*" You must not look for the principle of your religion in the Sensuous, in the grave among the dead, but in the living Spirit in yourselves."[37]

Whereas for Augustine Christ as head of his body the church is Christ risen and ascended with his own glorified body, Hegel thinks that the empty tomb reveals two errors in such a conception of Christ as "head": (1) What is seen as the locus of incorruptible life, Christ's glorified body, is in fact "das Tote des Geistes,"[38] what is dead and spiritless in itself, namely, fleeting sensuous externality. The notion (2) of the resurrected Christ's existence somewhere beyond the world [*Jenseits*] is abandoned as well.[39] These two mistakes exemplify, for Hegel, the unresolved contradiction at the heart of Catholicism: a simultaneous striving for the spiritual beyond the world and an uncritical overidentification of holiness with particular worldly things. Hence, there is an irony and pneumatic shift of reference in Hegel's prophetic use of Ps 16.10. The Holy One here is not the historical individual Jesus or his bodily remains. Those, Hegel insists, have decomposed as all natural bodies do. Indeed, for Hegel such corruption is essential, in order to rid Christ's followers of their vain attachment to external things and convert [*umkehren*] them to the immanent universal reality of Spirit. The Holy One is the incorruptible Spirit present in and unifying Christ's followers, indeed all human beings, as they become conscious of their infinite rationality.

Thus, although Hegel affirms the implicit incarnational truth of the traditional christological doctrine concerning the unity of the divine and human, he thinks that a mistaken insistence on that unity in the resurrected and ascended Christ, or, by extension, in the immediate presence of any particular thing—rather than in spiritual presence—results in a form of church community, both in its ecclesiological articulation and in actual practice, that systematically facilitates the enslavement, that is, spiritual determination *ab extra*, of rational human beings.[40]

In order to gain further insight into Hegel's rejection of this understanding of the church, we turn first to some of Hegel's comments on Catholic Eucharistic theology. Hegel himself argues in *LPR* 3 that "the Lord's Supper is . . . the midpoint of Christian doctrine, and from this point all the differences within the Christian church receive their coloration and definition."[41] Because Christ has withdrawn as a historically present individual, the Catholic church therefore sought to make Christ present through the Eucharist at Mass. The problem with the Catholic Eucharist is that "the Host, this *Thing*, is set up to be adored as God."[42] And once God is understood to be repeatably manifest in delimited spatiotemporal phenomena, Hegel thinks, the floodgates are opened to an obsession with external mediation of the divine, be it through Marian devotion, the saints, miracles, pilgrimage sites, or most perniciously, the church hierarchy.[43] Because all of these so-called spiritual means of mediation function in such mechanical, external fashion, through such acts as repeated prayers, the lighting of candles, or monetary donations, or sacramentally through the principle of *ex opere operato*, they are divorced from any requirement of truly subjective involvement on the part of the believers. That is, they do not require any real ethical thought and transformation. Accordingly, Hegel explains how the medieval church hierarchy could indulge the basest of worldly passions under the mantle of spiritual legitimacy and how the Catholic Mass, "an imposing sensuous spectacle," lacks ethical force and demands "no exertion of thought."[44] Hegel concludes:

> Since God is thus known as something external in the Lord's Supper—this midpoint of doctrine—this externality is the foundation of the whole Catholic religion. Thus arises the servitude of knowledge and activity [in this religion]; this externality pervades all further characteristics [of it] since the true is represented as something fixed and external. As something existing outside the subject, it can pass into the control of others; the church is in possession of it as well as of all the means of grace. In every respect the subject is a passive, receptive subject that knows not what is the true, right, and good, but has only to accept the standard from others.[45]

Hegel's understanding of the relationship between Christ and the church is clearly not a traditional understanding of the risen and ascended Christ as head of his communal body, nor for that matter of Christ as king, if such kingship means the legitimation of a corrupt sacerdotal aristocracy, who reduce the laity "to the severest bondage."[46] It is not inconsistent, then, that when Hegel does speak explicitly of the "head" [*Haupt*] of Christianity, he is referring to the pope.[47] The pope stands at the pinnacle of an authoritative priestly and magisterial hierarchy distinct from and in control over the laity. To be sure, the introduction of organizational structure and a teaching authority is part of what Hegel considers the inevitable development of the church community from the spiritual immediacy of

Pentecost to a more concrete institutional structure in which Spirit is mediated through the more rational form of doctrine.[48] But while the Christian church, for Hegel, is implicitly the kingdom of God, a spiritual [*geistig*] kingdom in which all are essentially equal and, in principle, "slavery is impossible," practically speaking the establishment of a separate authoritative body in the church gives rise historically to an ecclesiastical [*geistlich*] kingdom.[49] The clerical authorities, who have received spiritual revelation, mediate that Spirit to the laity through the sacraments and church teaching. The laity are not yet really free, because they do not know themselves as rationally self-determining; for matters both religious and secular, they still depend upon the clergy's instruction.[50]

Other comments Hegel makes about the Catholic Eucharist give further insight into the character of his communal thinking. In this regard, his reading of medieval Catholicism is not entirely tragic. Even when Christian freedom has been transmuted into its very opposite, abject servitude, the "infinite elasticity" of Christianity's spiritual principle does not give way. For Hegel, the negative moment of the divine on the cross, the externality of christological distinction—with Christ as head of his ecclesial body, we could say—persists until the crusaders discover that the resurrection of Spirit is in them. Thereafter the pope would never again be able to command the whole of Western Christendom toward a common end. Analogously, the crude incarnational principle readily evidenced in the Catholic Eucharist ultimately transcends itself. The end of the Middle Ages is marked by a flourishing of artistic production, from which the church, sensing art's continuity with its principle of externality, feels no immediate threat to its authority. Yet Hegel points out that works of art are different from mere objects like a stick, rock, or even the eucharistic host. When an observer looks upon a work of art, she sees not just a foreign object allegedly manifesting the divine, but something with which she can identify affectively and cognitively, that is, in Spirit. Hegel's description of this spiritual recognition is telling in ways that yield ecclesiological significance:

Art spiritualizes—animates the mere outward and material object of adoration with a form which expresses soul, sentiment, Spirit; so that piety has not a bare sensuous embodiment of the Infinite to contemplate, and does not lavish devotion on a mere *Thing*, but on the higher element with which the material object is imbued—the expressive form with which *Spirit* has invested it.... [In contemplating] a painting, rich in thought and sentiment, or a beautiful work of sculpture ... soul holds converse with soul and Spirit with Spirit.... [In art] the sensuous object is a beautiful one, and the Spiritual Form with which it is endued, gives it a soul and contains truth in itself.[51]

The distinction Hegel sets up here appears to be one in which infinite truth, on the one hand, is practically identified with its phenomenal appearance as immediately given and, on the other, is found in the self-recognition of soul or Spirit which gives form to the artistic medium. We can gain a clearer sense of the relationship between "soul" and matter if we turn to Hegel's explicit comments on the soul-body relation in *Enc.* §389 and §389 *Zu*. There he argues: "The question of the immateriality of the soul has no interest, except where, on the one hand, matter is regarded as something *true*, and mind [*Geist*] conceived as a *thing*, on the other.... [However,] Mind [*Geist*] is the existent truth of matter—the truth that matter itself has no truth."[52] In §389 and its corresponding *Zusatz* Hegel is calling into question the very need for the metaphysical investigations of the seventeenth and eighteenth centuries into the immateriality of the soul as well as the attendant issue of its *communio* with the body. Such inquiries assume that the body and soul are two distinct substances with their own characteristics, effectively investing matter with independent truth value and thereby reducing the soul to a thing that exists "for itself" apart from the material world and that is merely linked to the body extrinsically. Hegel likewise rejects a materialistic position in which the soul is reduced to mere physico-chemical processes, whereby, again, matter is regarded as something true in itself.[53]

The errors manifest in these interpretations parallel those Hegel discerns in Catholic theology: an overly monarchic Christology—as he would consider Augustine's theology of Christ as head of his ecclesial body—is linked with a merely subjective reconciliation in the heart and full reconciliation and freedom in an otherworldly eschatological beyond (soul as thing) as well as an identification of the divine with sensuous immediacy (matter as true). Furthermore, in terms of ecclesiological imagery, there also appears to be a correlation between what Hegel views as an errant dualistic understanding of the soul and the body and the traditional representation of Christ and the Holy Spirit as unique Trinitarian persons at work in the church. Hegel critically observes how, in its truncated form under the control of the clerical hierarchy, "the Spirit is, as it were, the 'third person.'"[54] What from the perspective of Trinitarian theology is a subordination of Spirit to Christ translates, from an ecclesiological standpoint, into a clerical "soul" intrinsically disconnected from, yet extrinsically and mechanically in charge of, the passive "body" of the laity.

In investigating Hegel's understanding of the body-soul relationship, we must remember that our interest is not primarily anthropological, but ecclesiological. We need to determine how Hegel's conception of the soul and body in the individual human being informs his use of soul-body imagery for corporate humanity.

Hegel understands the relationship between soul and body to be one of dialectical identity. As Michael Wolff points out, the goal of the second part of Hegel's *Enc.*, *The Philosophy of Nature*, is to show how material nature cannot be conceived on its own, but rather issues in contradictions that are sublated only through *Empfindung* and *Gefühl*, which Hegel equates with soul.[55] Hence, by the time he has reached §389, Hegel thinks himself to have demonstrated the untruth of matter as something viewed independently. What is more, for Hegel soul and spirit are not coterminous. In §389 Hegel is dealing with the soul in a general sense, as common to both nonrational animals and human beings. The soul is, roughly put, the "stuff" out of which self-conscious spirit develops. Soul is "not yet" spirit, but spirit "is" soul, in the sense that a clay pot "is" clay.[56]

Hegel's solution to the so-called body-soul problem will become clearer as he works this relationship out. As that solution becomes clearer, so too will the relative roles played by Christ and the Spirit in his ecclesial thinking as well as their practical ramifications.

Hegel writes, "Soul is the *substance* or 'absolute' basis of all the particularizing and individualizing of mind."[57] There are two important aspects of Hegel's understanding of soul as substance. The first has to do with the soul as form or concept of the living organism; the second with soul as the foundation or basis of spirit. With regard to the former, Hegel claims that soul is the substance of corporeity, by which he means not some kind of underlying material substrate to which bodily characteristics attach, but rather the form that persists throughout material flux.[58] Another way Hegel speaks about this first aspect of the soul is as the concept [*Begriff*] of the living organism.[59] Both terms, "form" and "concept," are related to the notion of end or telos. Unlike, say, a tool which is designed and assembled for the achievement of an extrinsic end, Hegel thinks that organic things have an intrinsic end. This intrinsic end, which is soul *qua* the organism's concept or form, is neither the matter out of which the organism is made, nor some form abstracted from matter, nor any static combination of the two, but rather the organizational activity realized in the living thing's development and reproduction. As activity, soul is not reducible to matter, nor is it any thing.

In a rather telling parallel, Hegel here follows Aristotle, who uses the term λόγος as an alternate means of speaking about the soul as form.[60] Aristotle makes this connection insofar as he thinks one's ability to speak (λέγειν) about an object as a particular thing requires the determination of its form, beyond any mere reference to its constituent matter.[61] In this we see reflected Hegel's own use of the term *logos* according to both its central meanings: concept and word. This suggests that for Hegel the relationship between soul and body is conceived along the same lines of dialectical self-expression as the relationship between the immanent Trinitarian moment of the Father and the particularizing moment of the divine fall into evil as the Son. It is not surprising, then, that at this its abstract stage prior to the emergence of *Geist*, soul remains "*verfallen*," or left at the mercy of matter's self-externality.⁶² This reference thus recalls Hegel's reading of the fall, wherein the human being in her natural immediacy exists as *imago Dei*, that is, is according to her concept or telos, only implicitly. For Hegel, the unity of soul and body, realized teleologically through the absolute negation of matter in the freedom of spirit⁶³ or, in another sense, through the sublation of the word (logos) in the actualized concept (logos), anticipates not only figuratively but in a very real way the actualization of the *imago Dei* in a linguistically mediated, albeit thoroughly pneumatologically conditioned, communal "body."

We gain further insight into the contours of Hegel's ecclesiology if we turn to the second aspect of soul: soul as substance. It has to do with the soul as a foundation or basis—not, to be sure, in the sense of a material substrate, but rather as the basis of all determinations of mind or spirit. Accordingly, just as soul for Hegel is the substance of corporeity, so consciousness—the lowest level of spirit—can be regarded as the substance, form, or inner purpose of soul. This analogy, however, does not mean that Hegel falls back into a multiplicity or hierarchy of different substances. Rather, he avoids such substantial fragmentation by distinguishing between the actual soul and the soul in itself, that is, according to its implicit concept.⁶⁴

Hegel's discussion of soul in *Enc.* §389 remains at a general level prior to the distinction between human and lower animal life. The discussion concerning the intrinsic teleology of organic life in Hegel's philosophy thus requires some qualification. Although Hegel thinks that animals have souls, talk of their intrinsic telos in their organizational development and reproduction is only partially accurate within the context of his broader system. The goal of Hegel's philosophy of nature is to prove that nature is not self-sufficient. Natural organisms only appear to be ends in themselves; Hegel's discussion of the antagonisms of natural life in *Enc.* §§367–76, encompassing struggle, gender distinction, sickness, and natural death, indicates natural life's thoroughgoing dependency upon external conditions.⁶⁵ The intrinsic telos of natural life, or natural soul, turns out to be a merely *subjective end*.⁶⁶ When Hegel speaks of the soul as the foundation or basis of spirit in §389, then, he is referring to the animal's immediate feeling of self, in which there is as yet no conscious distinction between feeling as such and the content of that feeling as disparate perceptions, inner needs, or their satisfaction.[67] Because the animal seeks mere satisfaction of internal desires without knowing that what it does externally aims at its development and reproduction, and because what the animal does thus has no objective, communicative function, the natural soul is not, in Hegel's view, actual [*wirklich*].[68] Like Hegel's immanent Trinity or moment of the Father—an unreal, impersonal, and unconscious play of love with itself—the natural soul is epitomized by its character of lack or need, an unfulfilled inner striving ending only in natural death.[69] But in that fatal end, the natural soul is also like the fallen divine in the "creation" of external nature, divine fallenness reversed only with Christ's natural death on the cross.

Consistent, then, with Hegel's inherently incarnational Trinitarian theology, which ascribes a necessarily expressive character to rational λόγος, the natural soul becomes actual, and thereafter spiritual, only when the body is no longer just a body, mere externality, but rather becomes a "sign" of the soul, "in which [the soul] *feels itself* and makes *itself felt*."[70] The actual soul can now distinguish between its feeling and that which is felt. Accordingly, its content assumes a propositional structure, one in which the actual soul is able to express itself through the body:[71]

> In order to become adequate to . . . its Notion, the soul must . . . transform its identity with its body into an identity brought about or mediated by mind [*Geist*], must take possession of its body, must form it into a pliant and skilful instrument of its activity, so transform it that in it soul relates itself to itself and its body becomes an accident brought into harmony with its substance, with freedom.[72]

Whereas the natural soul, which has its unity with the body in immediate self-feeling, escapes its fallenness—the unfulfilled back and forth of needs and their fleeting satisfaction—only through natural death, spirit is able to transcend immediate self-feeling without succumbing to bodily disintegration: "The death of merely immediate and individual vitality is the 'procession' of spirit."[73]

Considered ecclesiologically, the discovery of the empty tomb during the Crusades, the death of otherworldly striving and the fixation on sensuous immediacy, opened the way for the transfiguration of what we might call the ecclesial soul and body into spirit. Already this process of transformation was under way when the principle of sensuous presence, epitomized by Catholic eucharistic theology and practice, began to undo itself in the art of the late Middle Ages. The immediate unity of an otherworldly God in the eucharistic body is transcended as soul or spirit expresses itself in art. The passages in the *The Philosophy of History* where Hegel contends that in art "soul holds converse with soul and Spirit with Spirit" and the "Spiritual Form . . . gives [the artistic medium] a soul and contains truth in itself"[74] gain clarity when considered in light of Hegel's thoughts on the spiritually mediated unity of soul and body. In such mediated unity, the body is not only the soul's "instrument," but also its "work of art."[75]

By emphasizing this spiritually mediated unity, Hegel tries to avoid both reductive and dualistic solutions to the soul-body "problem." In denying independent substantiality to matter, he is by no means denying embodiment, but rather the reduction of soul to mere material causation. At the same time, the difference between soul and body is not absolute. In this way Hegel shows that the "soul-body problem" is merely apparent, for soul and body are dialectically identified.[76] In differentiating itself from the body, soul comes to know itself as the concept, form, or telos of body. But as form of the body it cannot be realized apart from the body. This unifying realization is the activity of self-knowledge or spirit. Human soul and body thus attain their end through transfiguration into spirit.

What Hegel seeks here is an all-encompassing, yet rationally comprehensible, unity that can nevertheless preserve difference—what he calls a totality. Through the dialectical unity of soul and body, whereby the body is the soul's work of art, spirit comes to know itself as active in the world: "Body is the middle term by which

I come together with the external world as such. Consequently, if I want to realize my aims, I must make my body capable of carrying over this subjectivity into the external objective world."[77] In the immediate context, Hegel is discussing the transition from natural soul to actual soul and then spirit through a process of habituation. The issue of habituation as the means whereby the soul comes to know itself as free in its body in the world has social implications that are pertinent to our discussion. Recall that one of the major problems with Catholicism, in Hegel's view, is the ethical inefficacy of its practices, manifest in overly subjective pious actions wielding no moral control over outward bodily action. The church as ecclesial body combines an otherwordly hope for complete reconciliation—encapsulated in the risen and ascended Christ as head—with the existence of the church as an institution in the world. The result, on Hegel's analysis, is a corporate "practice" of unreconciled internal division, the heteronomy of the clergy over the laity, that then further inhibits reconciliation with and free exercise in the world. Similar to what we saw in his critique of martyrdom, Hegel thinks the preeminent Catholic virtues of poverty, chastity, and obedience are too subjective, hence too selfish and antisocial in their renunciation of the world. Yet, Hegel suggests, this allegedly dualistic view of spirit and body permits others—most egregiously the medieval clerical elite invested with spiritually sanctioned worldly power and privilege—to treat the body as if it were ethically meaningless, such that the corporate body becomes the site of the most sordid and, again, antisocial vice. Greed and corruption thus mark an ecclesial body that asserts its spiritual superiority in an utterly unspiritual effort to gain control over secular authority.

According to Hegel, the spiritual unity of soul and body begins to realize itself both individually and communally when Lutheranism transcends the Catholic division of the world into the sacred and the profane. The body-suppressing and world-renouncing virtues of chastity, poverty, and blind obedience to the church are replaced in the Reformation with the socially constructive values of marriage, industry, and the rational obedience to the laws of the state.[78] Indeed, this last virtue is important with regard to the ultimate telos of Hegel's corporate ecclesial imagery. He lauds Lutheranism for its teaching of inclusive holiness, in which the secular realm is also treated as sacred.[79]

Toward the beginning of his analysis of the German world in the *The Philosophy of History*, Hegel discusses state formation among the early medieval Germanic peoples. The state is formed, according to Hegel, at the nexus of individual freedom and the bond formed in community, where duties and rights lose their subjective and arbitrary character through the establishment of concrete legal norms governing the relationships between individuals and groups. This process of normalizing individual rights and duties entails the "condition that the state should be the soul of the whole ... and remain its sovereign."[80] Without going too deeply into Hegel's very complex concept of the state, we can sufficiently identify the state in this context not with any specific institutions or historical laws, but rather with the organizational form of the communal totality.

At this early stage in the development of the Germanic nations, the state is still characterized by its overly subjective character, by a focus on "*private* rights and *private* obligations."[81] Hegel, we have seen, argued that it is the Germanic peoples who were to pass on and realize the Christian principle—the equality and freedom of all human beings. Yet that principle remains merely implicit at this early medieval period: "The True is present only as an unsolved problem, for [the Germans'] Soul is not yet purified. A long process is required to complete this purification so as to realize concrete Spirit."[82] At a communal level, the Germans' soul has yet to shed its natural immediacy, its orientation toward particular, subjective interests. Hegel casts the intervening centuries prior to his own time as a long period of training and struggle—that is, of communal habituation—through which the Christian principle implicit in the Germans' soul strives to gain mastery over the "bodily" material in which it is to become Spirit: "The Spirit of God lives in the Church; it is the inward impelling Spirit. But it is in the World that Spirit is to be realized—in a material not yet brought into harmony with it."[83]

Although the church succeeds during the Middle Ages at leading a great number of individuals to master their passions through ascetic renunciation, the next task, if spirit is to attain to truly universal rationality, is to harness one's passions within the worldly context itself: "In the World, secular business cannot be thus repudiated; it demands accomplishment ... the discovery is made, that Spirit finds the goal of its struggle and its harmonization, in that very sphere which it made the object of its resistance—it finds that *secular pursuits are a spiritual occupation.*"[84] The full unity and transfiguration of soul and body into spirit is possible only once the church passes beyond itself in the state. It is no coincidence that the dialectical unity of the soul and the body is one of the most dominant metaphors in Hegel's *Philosophy of Right*, where he elucidates his theory of the modern state. For example:

> The concept [of right] and its existence [*Existenz*] are two aspects [of the same thing], separate and united, like soul and body. The body is the same life as the soul, and yet the two can be said to lie outside one another. A soul without a body would not be a living thing, and vice versa. Thus the existence [*Dasein*] of the concept is its body, just as the latter obeys the soul which produced it. ... If the body does not correspond to the soul, it is a wretched thing indeed. The unity of existence [*Dasein*] and the concept, of body and soul, is the Idea. It is not just a harmony, but a complete interpenetration. Nothing lives which is not in some way Idea. The Idea of right is freedom, and in order to be truly apprehended, it must be recognizable in its concept and in the concept's existence.[85]

Every particular right of the modern rational state is something "*utterly sacred*" insofar as it gives shape to, and is the existence [*Dasein*] of, self-conscious freedom.[86] In the sphere of human relations, "Reason and the Divine commands are now synonymous."[87] Because God is now understood as absolute reason, knowable to humans as rational creatures themselves, the rules according to which humans act and structure their societies are no longer understood to come from on high and demand compliance simply on the basis of their divine authority. Rather, insofar as humans gain insight into the rationality of the concrete laws of the state, into the necessity of particular laws, they understand them to be divinely given and yet in accordance with the principle of rational self-determination.

Thus, if we recall the two biblical images of the church as Christ's body, one where Christ is identified with the community of believers and another where he is explicitly described as its head, it appears that Hegel's ecclesial body resembles the former. He is in several places quite explicit: "The Holy Spirit is in [the Christians]; they are, they constitute, the universal Christian church, the communion of saints. Spirit is the infinite return into itself, infinite subjectivity, not represented but actual divinity, the *presence* of God, not the substantial in-itself of the Father or of the Son and of Christ, who is the truth in the shape of objectivity."[88] The objective, individual person of Christ passes away and is supplanted by Spirit. Again we see the communal upshot of Hegel's use of oral linguistic imagery to illustrate his fundamental Trinitarian logic. Christ does not remain as head alongside the Holy Spirit present in his body. Rather, "in the expressions 'with you,' 'in you,' he is the Holy Spirit."[89] In the sense that the spiritual community now gives actual shape to the divine concept, they can indeed be called the "body of Christ,"[90] because for Hegel there is no other body. But they are thus also a *headless* body. Insofar as their communal soul and communal body are ultimately transfigured into *Geist*, the community is perhaps better labeled the "body of Spirit."

In a startling way, Hegel's spiritual body represents a transfer of the resurrection body into the present world. Indeed, Hegel's language of the soul's control over the body in the freedom of spirit sounds a great deal like Augustine's understanding of the resurrection body. But it differs insofar as it is one in which humans always retain aspects of their natural fallenness. Wolff argues that even at the level of the "Denken Gottes," Hegel's philosophy retains this anthropological determination. There is no escaping corporeal necessity or the need to train one's affects. To the contrary, Hegel insists that when understood correctly—that is, when the body, its needs, and its desires are not understood as ends in themselves or as some external force to be quelled and vanquished, but rather as forces that are to be harnessed and trained toward a rational, spiritual end—then these affects are rational and spiritual. Lest, however, Hegel's language of the soul's need to "take possession" of the body give the impression of anthropological dualism, Wolff argues that an adequate interpretation of Hegel's anthropology ought not to personify the soul. In that regard, we can think back to Staudenmaier's fear concerning Hegelian ecclesiology, namely, that the loss of a personal, Trinitarian ground reduces the church to a mere aggregate of people. Staudenmaier's concern seems to have warrant considering how for Hegel any understanding of church articulated representationally constitutes a corporate body whose impersonal soul awaits full transfiguration as Spirit; in such transfiguration, spiritual personality is ultimately mediated objectively through the state.

In any case, just as we saw concerning Hegelian theodicy in relation to the cross, the universal spiritual telos of Hegel's Trinitarian-communal thought requires us to ask whether he does not risk losing sight of the individual and especially of the Christian message of God's love to each person who suffers. That is to say, without a christological referent as its head—and the attendant distinction from the state—does the church maintain its ability to speak to and for someone in his or her particularity, to speak to and for those in need? Does it not thereby lose the ability to witness to God's Word of love? Which types of Christian language and practice are supported or suppressed by Hegel's Trinitarian logic of the spoken word and overly pneumatological rendering of the Christian social body?

Hegelian Mystery: The Sacramental Body

How, if at all, for Hegel, is the religious community a sacrament of divine love in the world? Recall that in Hegel's thought, "Spirit" redescribes the Christian theologoumenon of love. In his philosophy of religion Hegel continues to use his notion of love to interpret Spirit or at least to serve as its representational equivalent. Yet the theological assumptions underlying his philosophical redescription of Trinitarian Christianity restrict communal Christian life and practice.

Although Hegel's spiritual community does through its practices witness to Spirit qua absolute love, those practices are not compatible with two modes of biblically grounded discourse, lament and praise, which exemplify the range of Christian experience. Ultimately, the ways in which the practices of Hegel's spiritual community announce the message of divine love prevent (1) those who suffer from crying out to God for help, (2) those in the community from comforting them with the message of God's love, and (3) those who experience God's grace in a way that defies rational explanation from offering God thanks and praise.

First we must further define "sacramental body." The Latin *sacramentum* is a translation of the Greek μυστήριον, a term Hegel employs in *LPR* when explaining the inherently revelatory character of the divine. He first considers the conventional meaning of "mystery," that is, a secret or something that cannot be understood, and attributes partial truth to this definition. As long as God is described according to the categories of sense perception or the understanding (*Verstand*), his nature *is* incomprehensible. But by way of a telling example—the transcendence of the dialectic of organic self-feeling, of life's drives and their satisfaction, through thought—Hegel shows that God as mystery gives himself to be known or, more accurately, comes to know himself as reason (*Vernunft*) or Spirit. This, indeed, is for Hegel the truth revealed distinctively in Christianity: "μυστήριον is what the rational is. . . . The nature of God is not a secret in the ordinary sense, least of all in the Christian religion. In it God has made known what he is; there he is manifest."[91]

In Christianity God reveals himself as the living God, and life, Hegel thinks, is a process marked by drives and needs. *Verstand*, unable to explain the connections between its categories, finds only a contradiction in a God beset by the needs of life. But when the living being has raised itself to thought, when it is able to distinguish between itself and its feeling, it has already transcended the limit imposed upon it by its need and is, qua Spirit, able to comprehend their unity as precisely what it means to be a living being. For Hegel, the living God revealed in Christianity needs his creation, nature and finite spirit, to realize, that is, to know what he truly is as living and life-giving Spirit. Hegel sees this mystery of divine life, of self-differentiation and its overcoming through Spirit, anticipated in the doctrine of the Holy Trinity, albeit still represented insufficiently by the categories of understanding, which cannot advance beyond the contradiction of one-and-three. It is only in philosophy that God is truly a totality, absolute Spirit, that nature and finite spirit are raised up and united with him, inasmuch as God knows himself in and through them:

> Merely as the Father, God is not yet the truth (he is known in this way, without the Son, in the Jewish religion). Rather, he is both beginning and end; he is his own presupposition, he constitutes himself as presupposition ... he is the eternal process. The fact that this is the truth, and the absolute truth, may have the form of something given [as doctrine]. But that this should be *known* as the truth in and for itself is the task of philosophy and the entire content of philosophy. In it is seen how all the content of nature and spirit presses forward dialectically to this central point as its absolute truth. Here we are not concerned to prove that this dogma [of the Trinity], this tranquil mystery, is the eternal truth; this comes to pass ... in the whole of philosophy.[92]

What, then, are fundamental elements of Hegel's understanding of God as mystery, as sacrament? Vital to this concept is that (1) the living God, as absolute truth, is inherently dynamic and revelatory; it is pointless calling God the truth if he cannot be known. As an inherently revelatory idea, God is the Father. In giving himself to be known, (2) God must define himself, must posit a distinction in himself, and show himself to an other who can know him. This is God the Son, the creation of the world and the incarnation. Yet (3) God cannot know himself, nor can he be known, as God, if he is not known fully, as absolute truth. Thus, the distinction, necessarily drawn, is also necessarily overcome; God and the world—nature and humankind—are known as one rational totality. God knows himself in and through human beings knowing and recognizing themselves through him. This process is the process of knowledge, which Hegel calls Spirit. Spirit is at once the result and the whole, and only as such is it mystery in its fullness.

This rehearsal of Hegel's Trinitarian logic underscores again how he at once claims traditional warrant while at the same time subverting the content of that tradition. By insisting on Christianity's uniquely mysterious or mystical character, Hegel aligns himself with a tradition that has its roots in Paul.[93] For the latter, the mystery of God means, at its core, the Spirit's revelation of God's hidden plan of salvation in Christ.[94] Stressing such revelatory character, Hegel uses the concept of Christian mystery to repudiate contemporaries like Jacobi, Schelling, or Schleiermacher, who, he thinks, follow Kant in situating the divine beyond the grasp of reason.[95] This preference for the cataphatic over the apophatic in Hegel would appear to parallel the transformation the notion of "mystical" or "mysterious" undergoes in Paul, where it has been drawn away from the sense of ritual secrecy it had possessed in the pagan mystery religions.[96]

However, upon further analysis this surface parallel with regard to the revelatory character of the Christian mystery fades for several reasons. For Hegel, divine mystery is primarily pneumatological, rational, and fully explicit. The early Christian understanding of mystery, by contrast, is much more christological, biblical, and, from the human perspective, qualified by its provisional and partial character. For early Christianity, God is a mystery because he sets himself in relationship with human beings through a gratuitous gift of love, a gift that is at once revelatory of who God is yet exceeds the ability of humans to fully grasp or express it.

For Hegel, on the other hand, God is a mystery, ultimately, because he sets himself in relationship to himself though a reflexive process of self-recognition. It is in this regard, then, that we especially need to think about what it means to call Hegel's communal body sacramental or mystical, to say that it reveals who God is and what he does. In Hegel's account of the Christian mystery, the members of the spiritual community come to know themselves insofar as they come to know that God comes to know himself through them. Above we characterized the Christian communal soul and body and its development toward Spirit as a process of communal habituation. Hegel's use of the organic imagery of the body elevated to spirit in the Trinitarian explication of divine mystery now enables us to contextualize that process of communal habituation more properly within the broader process of divine habituation on its way to the realization of Spirit in history. The universal focus of Hegel's philosophy of history as theodicy bears upon our investigation into the sacramental witness of the spiritual community. When the community and its practices witness ultimately to the justification of the divine through history, it becomes difficult to see what possibilities remain for the community of believers to give voice to those silenced by the injustices of history or to tell them that the message of the cross is that God loves them.

In other words, the very language through which Hegel thinks the modern Christian community can know and say that the God who is love is really present in the world in fact does not speak of God's love. In theological terms, this is because Hegel's christological moment, in particular the moment of death on the cross, is like a fleeting spoken word sublated into the predominant and eschatologically fulfilled moment of the Spirit. Because the moment of particularity is assimilated into a universal rational narrative, Hegel's Trinitarian God and the religious community in which he is fully immanent lose the continued ability to speak to particular individuals and groups suffering in the world. This is because the message they bring is of a God who satisfies his own need and has in fact already done so. The struggle is over, and it was never really about the world God loves as much as the world God needed for his own self-actualization.

We can begin to see how this bears out in the life of the community if for a moment we shift our frame of reference back to the particular, in this case to the relation of soul and body in its anthropological register. In so doing, we are able to follow how Hegel's Trinitarian narrative assimilates that moment of particularity into the universal narrative of Spirit. This process also demonstrates how Hegel, while claiming continuity with the Christian Trinitarian tradition, reconstructs it in radical ways.

The development we looked at in the previous section, the transfiguration and unification of soul and body in spirit, has as its broader conceptual context Hegel's understanding of the human being as the image of God. Hegel's interpretation of Gn 3 in *LPR*, as we saw above, seeks on the one hand to account for the radical evil of fallen humanity—perhaps under the influence of an Augustinian Lutheran theology of original sin—while on the other making room for and encouraging human striving toward the good by sublating that aboriginal evil in a rational dialectic of human becoming sustained by a more positive Pelagian anthropology and sense of human autonomy.[97] Original sin, linked by Hegel to humankind's merely natural state, is sublated in the course of human rational development. Human goodness, the *imago Dei*, which is merely implicit at the outset, becomes explicit at the end of that same development. Thus Hegel aligns himself with a traditional Christian doctrine, here original sin, only to transform it in an unconventional manner.

This is evident insofar as Hegel describes the achievement of goodness in terms that subvert any Augustinian pedigree even more drastically than just its linking with a Pelagian anthropology. Consider the following from *LPH*:

> It was then through the Christian Religion that the Absolute Idea of God, in its true conception, attained consciousness. Here Man, too, finds himself comprehended in his true nature, given in the specific conception of "the Son." Man, finite when regarded *for himself*, is yet at the same time the Image of God and a fountain of infinity *in himself*. He is the

object of his own existence—he has in himself an infinite value, an eternal destiny.⁹⁸

Hegel is here assimilating finite spirit into his universal Trinitarian narrative. His image theology corresponds predominantly with humanity in its infinitude. It is clear that for Hegel, unlike Augustine, human imaging of the divine has less to do with a likeness that always falls short of its original than with an identity between the human and the divine. But the radicality of what Hegel is up to far exceeds the tradition of deification mediated to Hegel through Württemberg Pietism. Hegel's study of the medieval Dominican mystic Meister Eckhart can partly account for this excess.⁹⁹ There is evidence that Hegel was engaged with Eckhart at some point during the years 1794–95 and 1823–24.¹⁰⁰ In the latter case, knowledge of Eckhart was mediated to Hegel through the work of Franz von Baader. Baader found in Eckhart an articulation of what he considered the truth of Christianity, an affirmation of the infinite worth of the individual through a divine-human identity founded by the infinite divine—in other words, by a God understood as *Geist*, the unity of infinite and finite. Eckhart, on Baader's reading, expresses that unity through his central concepts of the birth of God in the soul (*Gottesgeburt*) and the divine spark (*Fünklein*). For Baader, these concepts undergird Eckhart's radical theology of the *imago Dei* and divine sonship, in which consciousness of oneself as the divine image raises one to God's knowledge of himself.¹⁰¹

In a composite quotation of Eckhart most likely derived from Baader, Hegel discovers a taxonomic precedent for his own mystical articulation of Christianity: "Meister Eckhart, a Dominican monk of the fourteenth century, says in one of his sermons on the inner life, 'The eye with which God sees me is the eye with which I see him; my eye and his eye are one and the same.... If God did not exist nor would I; if I did not exist nor would he.'"¹⁰² This is the only explicit mention of Eckhart in the Hegelian corpus, but on the basis of this quotation alone it is nevertheless startling to observe the parallels on two interrelated fronts: (1) the gnoseological and (2) the ontological. Hegel is citing Eckhart as a historical witness against those who would restrict the ability of human reason to know the divine. When discussing the same theme in the *Enc.*, Hegel makes an argument similar to what he found in Eckhart: "To know what God is as spirit . . . requires careful and thorough speculation. It includes . . . the propositions: God is God only so far as he knows himself: his self-knowledge is, further, a self-consciousness in man and man's knowledge *of* God, which proceeds to man's self-knowledge *in* God."[103] Just a few paragraphs later, Hegel confirms his sense in which this dialectical unity of God and human as self-conscious spirit is not merely a unity of knowledge, but of being as well.[104]

Even if it functions only implicitly in Hegel, Eckhart's concept of the *Gottesgeburt* in the soul shares with Hegel's notion of mystical union and vision a radical erasure of the distinction between the eternal generation of the divine Logos and the act of creation.[105] The dialectical flip side of that erasure, moreover, is a running together of earthly and eternal life.[106] Eckhart provides Hegel with a historical Christian warrant for his post-Enlightenment reconceptualization of immortality, which is achieved in this life through the saving knowledge of one's unity with the divine: "Eternity is not mere duration. . . . On the contrary, it is *knowing*, and, thus understood, it is what spirit is in itself."[107]

Yet Meister Eckhart cannot exhaustively explain Hegel's mystical rendition of Christianity. Hegel does not account for the extreme apophatic dimension of Eckhartian thought, which would, if fully applied to Hegel, deconstruct not only representational language, but also his conceptual articulation of Spirit. Furthermore, Eckhartian mysticism cannot do justice to time and history, which is essential to Hegel's thought. For Hegel, the Christian truth of humanity's identity with God emerges explicitly and in its universal breadth only at the end of a continuous process of revelation. On Hegel's reading, the full truth of Christianity remains merely implicit from the pneumatic immediacy of the early church through the servitude imposed by medieval Catholicism. It is revealed fully only with the advent of a Lutheran Protestantism interpreted by Hegel in a distinct pneumatological register.

In this respect Hegel is heir to the Trinitarian-historical tradition going back to the medieval theologian Joachim of Fiore, whom we discussed briefly in the first section of this chapter.[108] We return to this tradition here for more conceptual determination of Hegel's rendition of Christianity. There are a number of morphological parallels between Joachim and Hegel. Both articulate a correlation between the development of history and the distinctions within the divine Trinity, though Hegel goes further in arguing for history's definitive role in divine self-realization than Joachim, for whom the divine *in se* remains more insulated from its personal manifestations *ad extra*. All the same, the Trinity's openness to history imbues temporality with soteriological value in terms of knowledge, freedom, and the relationship between humanity and the divine. Hegel follows Joachim in erasing the Augustinian-informed distinction between sacred and secular history. Indeed, their ability to interpret the truth revealed in and through history is facilitated by their shared conviction that the eschaton has arrived. From a Trinitarian perspective, the advent of Christ is fundamental in ushering in the kingdom of God, but it serves only as the kingdom's objective foundation. The Spirit, for both Joachim and Hegel, plays a more significant role in the kingdom's realization, a realization that brings with it a fullness of knowledge and freedom in the human community's transfigured relationship to the divine.[109]

Joachimized Lutheranism was mediated to Hegel historically through the radical Reformation, the sixteenth-century Lutheran mystic Jakob Böhme, and speculative Pietist theologians like Bengel and Oetinger.[110] The latter two were significant theologians who helped shape the practically oriented culture of Württemberg Pietism in which Hegel received his early religious and educational formation. Although the question of direct influence remains disputed, the works of Dickey and Ernst Benz nonetheless show the high likelihood of strong indirect influence upon Hegel's philosophical development.[111] Bengel and Oetinger, like Joachim, consider all of history to be salvation history. In words that anticipate Hegel, Bengel argues that an "Idea permeates everything," that the divine economy manifests itself "through all ages of the world, as a beautiful and gloriously coherent system," as a "whole [*Ganzes*]."[112] Moreover, for both Bengel and Oetinger, as for Hegel afterwards, divine revelation occurs developmentally, rather than once and for all. Indeed, Oetinger extends revelational authority to postbiblical mystics and visionaries like Böhme and Emanuel Swedenborg.[113] More radically still, he, like Hegel, follows Böhme in conceiving of God as essentially self-revelational and developmental.[114]

In the precarious political climate of late-eighteenth-century Württemberg, Bengel's interest in history was no mere curiosity; it was eschatological (concerned with the final age of history and its meaning) and apocalyptic (convinced that the *Endzeit* was at hand and that God's plan in history could now be grasped in its entirety). But Oetinger pushes Bengel's apocalyptic vision further. What in Bengel is an eschatological knowledge of God and his plan of salvation as it has been realized in history moves in Oetinger an incarnational step closer to Hegelian dialectical identity and absolute knowledge: it is eschatological knowledge of the God who is now all in all in human beings. Like Hegel, Oetinger describes this eschatological gnosis in pneumatological terms. It is an all-inclusive wisdom or intuition that, from its eschatological standpoint, grasps the unity of all diverse branches of knowledge. And as historically realized and all-encompassing, it is both theoretical and practical. Oetinger sets forth a concrete ethical, social, and political program of reform aimed at effecting the eschatological "güldene Zeit."[115]

The conceptual resonance of such figures as Bengel and Oetinger with Hegel distinguishes him from Kant in a number of respects. In the latter's *Dreams of a Spirit-Seer*, where he criticizes the same Swedenborg Oetinger considered an authoritative source of divine revelation, Kant denies the label of knowledge to spiritual or mystical vision.[116] His thought lacks the historical focus of apocalyptic Pietism or German Idealism, and his sociopolitical, eschatological vision could be characterized as utopian—Benz's term indicating a disconnectedness from the historical present—over against the more concrete social programs of an Oetinger or Hegel. The latter are concrete, in Benz's view, because they take into account historical development and the present state of affairs in creating their reform programs.[117]

The parallels between Joachim and Hegel underscore how for Hegel the realization of the *imago Dei* is not only an eschatological good, but an intrahistorical eschatological good. The unhappy consciousness of the *Phenomenology*, found in a Catholicism which places its faith in Christ as an incarnate beyond and does not possess the reality of resurrection unity of mind with its embodied willing and working in the world, is overcome decisively and unsurpassably in a concretely eschatological Lutheranism.[118] There the subjective appropriation of faith through the Holy Spirit enables the individual to know him- or herself in truth and freedom:

> In the Lutheran Church the subjective feeling and the conviction of the individual is regarded as equally necessary with the objective side of Truth. Truth with Lutherans is not a finished and completed thing; the subject himself must be imbued with Truth, surrendering his particular being in exchange for the substantial Truth, and making that Truth his own. Thus subjective Spirit gains emancipation in the Truth, abnegates its particularity and comes to itself in realizing the truth of its being. Thus Christian Freedom is actualized.[119]

The elevation, the resurrection, of the subject to knowledge of the infinite truth of his or her being thus entails not only the vertical, gnoseological trajectory, the realization of absolute Spirit, but also the horizontal, practical one in Free Spirit, the spiritualization of the actual world.[120]

The achievement of divine-human identity on both these trajectories is understood by Hegel more communally than individually.[121] On the practical level he considers an essential feature of Lutheranism its inclusive sense of holiness, which upends the Catholic distinction between the sacred and the secular.[122] Free Spirit is realized beyond the confines of the Christian community in the modern state. Through the process of education or culture [*Bildung*], the soul or form of the corporate body is raised to the universality of Spirit.[123] Despite Catholicism's claims to universality, its self-contained morality, which views the actual world as a still-fallen force of resistance, means it has no real Spirit, no truly universal soul to animate a real corporate body. In Hegel's view, Catholicism offers only a retrograde form of education and culture sundered from science, and cannot serve as the ground of the state.[124] By contrast, the inclusively holy *Gemeinde* founded upon Lutheran Protestantism effectively represents the spiritual resurrection body:

> The development ... of Spirit from the time of the Reformation onwards consists in this, that Spirit, having now gained consciousness of its Freedom, through that process of mediation which takes place between man and God ... now takes it up and follows it out in building up [*Weiterbildung*] the edifice of secular relations. That harmony [of Objective and Subjective Will] which has resulted from the painful struggles of History, involves the recognition of the Secular as capable of being an embodiment of Truth [*daß das Weltliche fähig ist, das Wahre in ihm zu haben*]; whereas it had been formerly regarded as evil only, as incapable of Good—the latter being considered essentially ultramundane. It is now perceived that Morality and Justice in the State are also divine and commanded by God, and that in point of substance there is nothing higher or more sacred.[125]

Humanity knows its essential goodness, its unity with the divine, and its free will no longer burdened by a conscience guilty on account of its action in the world.[126] Hegel's is a realized eschatology: "Secular life is the positive and definite embodiment of the Spiritual Kingdom [*Die Weltlichkeit ist das geistige Reich im Dasein*]."[127]

This has important consequences for the way Hegel conceives of divine love and its manifestation in the world. From the perspective of the historical Luther, Hegel's Joachimite Lutheranism has transmuted the theology of the cross into a theology of glory.[128]

The cruciform moment of difference has definitively given way to the resurrection moment of Spirit. Thus, contrary to Hegel's own intentions perhaps, his necessarily incarnational Trinitarian paradigm, illustrated through the image of the transient spoken word, does not enable a cruciform message of divine love, one that addresses and bespeaks a world different from God and still struggling with evil. Rather, Hegel's Trinitarian message of love is expressed through the proclamation of Spirit's full presence, of humanity's resurrection and participation in the divine: "Now the principle of absolute Freedom in God makes its appearance. Man now no longer sustains the relationship of Dependence, but of Love—in the consciousness that he is a partaker in the Divine existence."[129]

What is more, the same Trinitarian dynamic that gives Hegel's version of Christian love less a cruciform and more a pneumatological determination results, ultimately, in the sublation of love in divine reason. Practically speaking, this occurs in the necessary movement from the Christian community to the ethical state. In his *Philosophy of Right*, Hegel argues that it was necessary for the unified medieval Catholic church, which made universal claims to authority over against the state—in a reactionary rather than reforming capacity—to be broken up in order that the secular state might come to "fulfill its destiny [*Bestimmung*] as self-conscious rationality and ethical life."[130] The modern state must come to know itself as a "moral totality," as self-determining, concrete universality that nevertheless preserves particular subjectivity.[131] In one sense, then, Hegel fears too close an identification of religion and state. Because religion for Hegel has a universal object, God, but is situated anthropologically in the subjective, cognitively indeterminate sphere of feeling, it can neither account for individual particularity nor offer an objective, rational—that is, spiritual—justification for any particular laws it might impose.[132] Any effort to establish theocratic government is, for Hegel, sheer fanaticism, "the refusal to admit particular differences."[133] In *LPH* Hegel expounds further: "*Fanaticism* . . . is . . . an enthusiasm for something abstract—for an abstract thought which sustains a negative position towards the established order of things. It is the essence of fanaticism to bear only a desolating destructive relation to the concrete."[134]

Hegel strives here to take rational, that is, spiritual, account of particularity. He separates religion from the state in order to legitimate and strengthen secular authority. The result, Hegel thinks, is in fact more freedom for religion and thought, inasmuch as a state confident in its own rational legitimacy is able to tolerate different churches, including even sects which abstain from civic duties.[135] But, in fact, the overarching thrust is a domestication of religious particularity through a program of (Protestant-inspired) ethical training or habituation aimed at forming rational citizens of the state. While religion, as Hegel conceives it, has its freedom vis-à-vis the state insofar as the sphere of love is the merely inward, subjective realm of conscience, church and state are unified in their joint affirmation of individual subjectivity as infinite truth and their affirmation of religion's practical purpose in cultivating its members' intuitions of love, of the unity of the subject with the infinite divine. That religious task nevertheless finds its broader end as it is sublated in the task of cultivating the rational will toward the ethical life of the state:

> It is a common notion and saying, in reference to the power of Religion, abstractly considered, over the hearts of men, that if Christian love were universal, private and political life would both be perfect, and the state of mankind would be thoroughly righteous and moral. Such representations may be a pious *wish*, but do not possess truth; for religion is something internal, having to do with conscience alone. To it all the passions and desires are opposed, and in order that heart, will, intelligence may become true, they must be *thoroughly educated*; Right must become Custom—Habit; practical activity must be elevated to rational action; the State must have a rational organization, and then at length does the will of individuals become a truly righteous one. Light shining in darkness may perhaps give color, but not a picture animated by Spirit.[136]

Religion, in Hegel's view, cannot redress injustice. It can promise a balancing of the scales only in an eschatological judgment. For all that religion might thereby assuage grieving souls during times of calamity or political oppression, the reality, Hegel points out, is that religion has served just as often as a means of restraining human freedom, and thus "that we instead require a power to rescue us from it in some of the shapes it assumes and to champion the rights of reason and self-consciousness."[137] Justice can be really achieved only in a rationally constituted state.[138]

Hegelian eschatology, then, is prescriptive in at least two fundamental ways. First, it demands the conceptual restriction of religion's scope to the inward realm of feeling and conscience as well as its teleological orientation toward the achievement of self-conscious reason and self-determining freedom in the world. The latter, moreover, requires the structures of a rationally constituted state if it is to be at all real. Both elements are necessary in Hegel's view. Without the subjective transformation of the populace wrought by a religion now aware of the infinite value of the subject, the introduction of a rational political constitution comes to naught.[139] But without the rational objective structures of the state, religious love remains an inward and otherworldly hope or, if it expresses itself in the world, it does so with fanatical and annihilating force, an arbitrariness of the particular will that need not justify its actions to others.

This normative flattening of Christianity is part of the broader flattening of the world's resistance and particularity at the level of the Trinitarian divine. It is ultimately part of Hegel's normative articulation of Trinitarian doctrine, in which the world, as the moment of the Son, has been transfigured by the immanent presence of Spirit. Humanity's eschatological consciousness of its divinity is a moment in God's knowledge of himself: "It was then through the Christian Religion that the Absolute Idea of God, in its true conception, attained consciousness."[140] Again Hegel's integration of oral linguistic imagery into his articulation of the immanent Trinity is decisive. His goal is the rational transparency of language to the divine, an affirmation of humanity and indeed the whole world as necessarily expressive of and describable in terms of universal rational truth. Yet Hegel's effort to make the divine speakable in the world paradoxically evacuates certain types of linguistic expression of that possibility. The shift from the particular moment of the Son to the universal and all-encompassing plane of Spirit obviates two modes of biblically based religious discourse: lament and praise. We can begin to understand why this is theologically problematic if we turn to the first mode of discourse—lament as a form of individual and communal prayer.

The Sacramental Body: Lament and Praise

Lament is exemplified by Job's outcries, the book of Lamentations, the psalms of lament, and the crucified Christ's cry of dereliction in the words of Ps 22.1: "My God, my God, why have you forsaken me?"(NRSV).[141] There are three essential structural moments of lament: (1) a subject who laments, (2) the act of lamentation, and (3) the addressee of the lament. Martin Wendte expounds: "In order to be the one who laments, one must be perceived in one's relatively autonomous, historical particularity.... The receiver [of the lament] must have the power and goodness to turn to the lamenter, and he must also have previously shown his ability to do so.... Third, the content of the lament must be taken seriously in its full character of resistance."[142] In Hegel's realized eschatology, evil and suffering have been conquered and sublated in Spirit. In other words, there is nothing to lament, nothing that radically opposes the realization of good in the world.[143] Discussing the subsistence of the religious community, Hegel insists: "The battle is now over, and the consciousness arises that there is no longer a struggle, as in ... Kantian philosophy, where evil is always sure to be overcome, yet it stands in and for itself over against the supreme good, so that ... there is nothing but an unending progression."[144] Yet, in overcoming Kantian dualism of good and evil and the idealistic utopianism he thinks it represents, Hegel collapses the difference between the divine and human in his realized eschatological state. God, the one to whom a sufferer would lament, loses his independence and power vis-à-vis the world and cannot come to the aid of those in need.[145] Conversely, the human being is assimilated into the divine. From one perspective, lament simply becomes the byproduct of ignorance concerning humanity's divine nature. From another, the sufferer loses the relative independence and historical particularity that enables her to lament in the first place. Theological delegitimation of lament silences the suffering.

Although Hegel does not address the phenomenon of lament explicitly in *LPR*, there are passages in *LPH* that confirm these conclusions.[146] In a move betraying elements of Marcionite, gnostic, or Manichaean biblical exegesis, all of which call into question the goodness of creation and thereby, implicitly or explicitly, the doctrine of resurrection founded upon it, Hegel declares that Old Testament psalmic lamentation should not have a place in Christian worship. He deems such discourse to be born of a human spirit unsure of the abiding presence of the divine within it. Such spiritual self-torment was manifest historically, he thinks, in the Protestant practice of spiritual introspection and autobiography aimed at discovering the inward work of grace as well as in the Jesuits' microscopic examinations of the will. These practices, Hegel thinks, betray the same kind of self-centered and potentially fanatical inwardness that we have seen in his analyses of the beautiful soul, that is, the judging conscience, and the Christian martyrs. The latter desire to escape the world, because it, the world, remains, in its secular form, a bastion of evil.[147]

Hegel attempts to rectify this otherworldly fanaticism through a univocal christological mediation that gives way to an intensified, immanent pneumatology. The immanent presence of Spirit affirms, in Hegel's view, the value of this world and enables action in it. Christ's cry of Godforsakenness is a past memory sanitized of its terrifying character in the peace of the spiritual kingdom. Christ's plea fades as a part of the transience of divine Word, now resurrected in Spirit. The pneumatic neutralization of that cry is structurally emblematic of Hegel's retrospective sanitizing of all the blood shed on the altar of history, the explaining away of unjust (particular) death and destruction at the hands of Caesar and Napoleon as the just (universal) work of God bringing about a new world of freedom.[148] In the face of the carnage of history, Hegel insists on God's essential goodness, but this is not the *benignitas* Augustine saw manifest in God's act of creation or the good use made of death by Christ on the cross.[149] Those are gratuitous acts of grace and love, emerging from the fullness of God's goodness. The goodness of Hegel's God, by contrast, is "the universal and divine *reason*, [which] has the *power* to fulfill its own purpose" in world history, and has in fact done so, insofar as the philosopher of history sees "that the actual world *is* as it *ought* to be."[150] In other words, God's reconciliation of the world with himself is not God in his goodness reaching out to a fallen world to restore it to its original goodness. The message of reconciliation preached by the philosopher of history is not one of consolation.[151] It is rather the reconciliation of universal reason with the particularity of history,[152] the knowledge, after the fact, that history is rational and not just a random collection of *res gestae*. It is God qua reason's reconciliation with himself in and through history.

It is in precisely that way that Hegel contends one can describe God, in representational language, as "eternal love, whose nature is to treat the other as its own."[153] That "other" is the finite world, and God's love and goodness are results, eschatological realities known insofar as God qua reason has shown his power in actualizing himself in and through all the death and destruction of world history. Like the heroes, men of action whose often violent deeds are known to be good and just from the standpoint of eschatological vision and freedom, so, on a broader scale, God is known to be good and just, inasmuch as history in its particularity is known as his work, as rational and thus elevated to the universal.[154] Unlike Augustine, for whom the message of the cross is a loving demonstration of and exhortation to seek justice before power, Hegel assimilates the cross, radical particularity, into the universal movement of the rational divine, such that divine love, goodness, and justice all follow upon divine power. Therefore, history is the means by which God rationalizes and justifies himself to himself. The "other" whom God loves is, on Hegel's account, God's other, his work, whereby he comes to love and ultimately know himself as absolute reason. History is the arena in which God establishes a relationship with himself, not with any genuine other.

Augustine would thus agree with the assessment of William Desmond that Hegel's concept of divine love is best described as autoerotic, and I think he would argue that no genuine relationship between God and human beings or human beings with each other is possible so long as power or the search for power precedes justice.[155] By eschatologically collapsing the difference between God and the world, the *is* and the *ought*, Hegel loses sight of the other as other and robs her of her ability to cry out to God, to appeal to his goodness, to point to the world's original goodness as his creation, and thus, in the face of suffering, to ask: God, where is your justice?[156]

At bottom, Hegel's affirmation of the real world just does not seem very realistic. It is in this regard that the Christian community needs a Trinitarian theology and Trinitarian ecclesiology that can, in more unresolved dialectical fashion, affirm the goodness of creation while simultaneously offering a more realistic assessment of the perdurance of evil in the world. We find such strengths in Augustine's concept of the *totus Christus*. We examine that concept in more detail in the next chapter, but it is worth introducing some of its essential features here as a point of contrast with Hegel. Augustine works out a notion of the whole Christ around the mutually informative relation of his scriptural exegesis and his christological doctrine of two natures in one person.[157] Significantly, Augustine's doctrine of the *totus Christus* articulates the unity of Christ and the church not in terms of speculative knowledge but as a dynamic expression of love.[158] As such the *totus Christus* is a Trinitarian doctrine of the Christian community that is both christological and pneumatological, but that, in contrast to Hegel, retains a dialectical, interpersonal relationship between Christ and the Spirit rather than the subsumption of the former by the latter. Christologically, Augustine's *totus Christus* further differs from Hegel's spiritual community qua

Totalität, in that a difference is maintained between Christ as head of his body and Christ present in the members of his body still struggling on earth. Within this space, divine love works to conform believers to Christ while at the same time respecting their otherness, their particularity in a world still marked by sin and death.

This openly dialectical character of divine love is evidenced by the central role lament plays in Augustine's doctrine of the *totus Christus*. Although Hegel attempts to avert the pitfalls of subjectivism by integrating the objective moment of the cross into the divine, his teleological reconfiguration of the Trinity ultimately leaves him with a (non)community that witnesses to a self-absorbed divine, because the moment of critical otherness has been assimilated to universal Spirit.[159] In contrast, Augustine's *totus Christus* legitimates lament, indeed shows how Christ gives his own voice to the suffering, while at the same time retaining a transcendent christological point of orientation (Christ as head). Augustine legitimates lamentation as an expression of the particularity and suffering of the world without legitimating it as such. The insistence upon Christ as transcendent head of the church grounds a genuine relationship with God as other, whereby humanity possesses a critical objective ground around which to orient its striving and hopes. By including psalmic lament in his understanding of the Christian community as *totus Christus*, Augustine enables lament while giving it pedagogical christological form—he affirms the *is* of the world in its goodness and particularity, but also makes clear that the world is not yet as it *ought* to be.[160] By rendering the divine radically immanent in the world, Hegel, by contrast, erases any forward-looking hope and, surprisingly, any objective model toward which that hope might look.

The theological strength of Augustine's doctrine of the *totus Christus* derives in large part from his christologically grounded struggle with difficult passages of scripture: "My God, my God, why have you forsaken me?" Inversely, the inability of Hegel's religious community to truly witness to the love of God stems in no small measure from the fact that the rough texture of the biblical text itself is pneumatologically surmounted in Hegelian philosophy. As a point of reference, compare the theological foundation of

Augustine's scriptural exegesis in *De doctrina Christiana*. Augustine grounds his understanding of scriptural revelation and the means of its interpretation upon an unresolvable dialectic between God and humanity. Contrary to Hegel, Augustine argues that the triune God is essentially inexpressible, yet that God graciously gives himself to be expressed by expressing himself in human terms.[161] This takes place preeminently in the incarnation of Christ, the entry of the eternal Word into human language, and secondarily in the witness to the incarnation in the human words of scripture.[162] Observe again Augustine's restriction of oral linguistic imagery to the incarnation of the Word. Unlike Hegel, he does not render the Trinity *in se* transparent to human language and thought. The incarnation and scripture are, in Augustine's view, at once an affirmation of creation, of humans in their humanity, and a radical relativization of them, for through a human being it is God who shows himself to be the one who creates and re-creates the world.[163] Just as we saw with regard to the incarnation, where it was for Augustine a misunderstanding of divine love to adhere to one side of the person of Christ at the expense of the other—that is, to believe Christ is only a divine spirit or only a human being—so too does Augustine maintain the tension of divine inspiration in human language.[164] If one gets too hung up on the mere words of scripture, especially the many potentially scandalous passages in the Old Testament, one might, like the Manichaeans, dismiss the Creator God and his creation, including human bodies, as evil. In effect, such a reading of scripture is too proud and ironically too "material" in practice to be able to see the spirit in and behind the lowly letter.[165] On the other hand, there are Christians who think their direct spiritual knowledge is so great that they do not need the linguistic mediation of scripture or other members of the church to teach them about it. Against these spiritual virtuosos, Augustine points out that all that humans have received is a gift from God. Such a gift is not reason for pride, but for humility and love: one ought to teach others what one knows and thereby build up the church as the body of Christ.[166]

The purpose of Augustine's exegetical strategy—to affirm the material letter of scripture through a spiritual reading—might look similar to that of Hegel's arguments concerning the relationship of soul to body: to affirm material creation by pointing out that its truth rests in knowing that it is not merely material. For his part, Hegel lauds early Christian theologians—by implication Origen, Ambrose, Augustine, and others—who, following in the tradition of the Jewish Platonist Philo, "idealized" the "bare shell" of scripture through figurative exegesis.[167] Yet Hegel's praise also distinguishes him from the likes of Augustine insofar as he shifts the ultimate locus of interpretive authority away from the narrative of scripture to the spiritual interpreter.[168] Put in Trinitarian terms, Hegel shifts from a christological to a predominantly pneumatological hermeneutic register. In Augustine's understanding of divine revelation, contrariwise, the divine mystery remains strongly incarnational in both content and form. That kenotic expression of divine humility and love both undergirds the divine authority of the scriptural text written in human language and serves as the text's substantive and hermeneutical core. The message and transformative power of scripture, for Augustine, is that of redeeming love more than of knowledge. The struggle to understand the obscurities of scripture, and the need to teach others what one has learned, aim at cultivating humility and reorienting one's love toward God.

In contrast to Augustine's more christologically centered understanding of revelation, in which spiritual transformation is part of a lifelong struggle with the flesh of scripture, biblical language for Hegel has its proximate end in the more rational, hence more spiritual, language of doctrinal teaching, and ultimate end in the conceptual language of philosophy. By no means is this to imply that Hegel's understanding of revelation lacks an objective christological foundation. Indeed, it is standard for Hegel to critique Romanticism and Pietism for their focus on the immediacy of religious feeling. Knowledge, he insists, is always mediated. But precisely as knowledge, and even more as absolute knowledge achieved in history, divine revelation elevates the particular media through which it has expressed itself to the spiritual, rational plane commensurate to its inherent universal concept. That is to say, Hegel's distinctive incarnational paradigm necessarily moves beyond itself—like a spoken word transcended in thought—beyond inadequate modes of religious discourse to the fully rational discourse of speculative philosophy, the latter of course being possible because Hegel conceives the Trinitarian logic of thought itself along the lines of spoken language.

Hegel praises Luther for liberating the Bible from the grasp of the Catholic hierarchy. The locus of authority was thereby transferred from an external body to "the *Bible* and the testimony of the Human Spirit."[169] The former, in Hegel's view, proved instrumental in the liberation of the latter. Luther's translation of the Bible not only encouraged literacy among the broader population, but, more importantly, put them in touch with a book proclaiming the kingdom of God, "a book in which the heart, the spirit, can find itself at home in the highest, infinite fashion."[170] The Bible is for Hegel the Word whereby the Spirit calls the believer to faith and instills in her heart the love of God. But this love, we should note, is not yet *real* love on Hegel's reading. As immediate, it recalls the maternal love of the Virgin Mary, a love not yet actual, hence not yet actually good, not yet absolute divine love.

The Bible in its positivity, its often incoherent episodic, poetic, and mythological language, stands over against the believer and the immediate certainty of her faith. Hegel was aware, as was Augustine, of the inconsistencies of scripture and of the fact that these intratextual contradictions stand in even more fundamental contradiction to the believing subject herself. Like Augustine, Hegel argues that these contradictions are evidence that the truth of scripture exceeds the mere letter of the text and hence serve paradoxically as an aid toward its own subjective appropriation and the formation of the community of faith. Yet for Augustine those contradictions aid in subjective appropriation and communal edification by helping beat back selfish pride—by confession of the God whose difference from the world grounds the latter's goodness and its capacity to be a revelatory medium of grace. For Hegel, by contrast, the contradictions of scripture stand as a necessary moment in the teleological emergence of free self-consciousness and the knowledge of divine-human identity. As part of the broader christological moment of divine fallenness, the contradictions found in the body of the scriptural text are more a function of knowledge than of love, in this case, of God's necessary self-distinction as he comes to know himself through human beings knowing themselves through him.

As such, the contradictions found in scripture do have an anthropological reference. But for Hegel they aim less at drawing the believer back to the scriptural text in order to form her character through listening and confession of God's love than at liberating her to form herself through recognition of a realizable identity with the divine. They are a necessary, but necessarily surpassable, part of human and, more inclusively, divine rational becoming. The christological moment of fallenness—when believers, like the Virgin Mary, must submit their immediate love to the contradictions of finite reality, must figuratively give birth to and feel their hearts pierced by pain of the cross—is but a moment passing over to resurrection in Spirit. In other words, reading the Bible emancipates thought:

> Just as soon as religion is no longer simply the reading and repetition of passages, as soon as what is called explanation or interpretation begins, as soon as an attempt to find out the meaning of the words in the Bible, then we embark on the process of reasoning, reflection, and thinking; and the question then becomes how we should exercise this process of thinking, whether our thinking is correct or not. It helps not at all to say that one's thoughts are based on the Bible. As soon as these thoughts are no longer simply words of the Bible, their content is given a form, more specifically a logical form. Or certain presuppositions are made with regard to this content, and with these one enters into the process of interpretation. These presuppositions are the permanent element in interpretation; one brings along representations and principles which guide the interpretation.[171]

Here Hegel makes two essential points: (1) thinking about the Bible means thinking about how one reads the Bible, what the presuppositions are that one brings to the task of interpretation; and

(2) this is in effect a reflexive process, ultimately a thinking about thinking. The pneumatic emphasis of Hegel's scriptural exegesis as well as its doctrinal exposition, as fleeting linguistic moments in the longer development of thought, is unavoidable: the consequence of the movement of thought, Spirit, is that thought is its own presupposition, that it has itself for its own object—hence it is absolute Spirit that knows itself and knows itself as infinite and free.[172] This is for Hegel none other than the resurrection consciousness, the finite consciousness elevated to knowledge of itself as its own ground, hence to rationality, to infinitude and divinity: "Only the *concept* on its own account liberates itself truly and thoroughly from the positive [= heteronomous, external]. For in philosophy and religion there is found this highest freedom, which is thinking itself as such."[173]

Conceptually inseparable from the theoretical knowledge of God, mediated representationally to believers through church doctrine, is its practical realization:

> At this point the practical relationship commences, in which I exist on my own account, I stand over against the object, and I now have to bring forth my own union with it. I have not only to know the object, to be filled, but to *know myself* as filled by this object, to know it as within me and likewise myself as within this object that is the truth—and so to know myself in the truth. To bring forth this unity is *action*, or the aspect of the cultus.[174]

The cultus, in which believers actively "partake" of the divine, is the final moment in Hegel's concept of religion. In contrast to other determinate religions, which have only cultic practices, hence only partial participation in the divine Spirit, the Christian community is a cultus.[175] Here Hegel has in view the sacraments, the Eucharist in particular. But with Christianity the stakes are higher than just the exposition of a particular religious rite. As Walter Jaeschke argues, Hegel is in effect articulating a sacramental principle underlying the whole of reality.[176]

The language and action of worship—which, according to William Desmond, entails some form of communication between humans and the divine—are thus bound up with ontology, in Hegel's case, a symmetrical relational ontology between the divine and human, such that each side requires the other to exist fully.[177] Hegel describes cultic worship accordingly:

> In the cultus . . . God is on one side, I am on the other, and the determination is *the including, within my own self, of myself with God*, the knowing of myself within God and God within me.
> The cultus involves giving oneself this supreme, absolute enjoyment. There is feeling bound up within it; I take part in it with my particular, subjective personality, knowing myself as this individual included in and with God, knowing myself within the truth (and I have my truth only in God), i.e., joining myself as myself in God together with myself.[178]

Worship, for Hegel, unfolds according to the moments of his scientific method—in Greek μέθοδος, best understood according to its root ὁδός, or way—which at its full breadth is the very Trinitarian movement of absolute Spirit. Hegel's way of Spirit, which I would distinguish from Augustine's understanding of Christ as way, is one of mediation proceeding through "mutual determinations that serve the generation of a more inclusive self-determination."[179] But when the eschatological goal is God's self-determination in and through humanity and the human subject's self-determination in and through God, one ends with a radical symmetry and immanence of divine and human spirit that renders pointless any talk about worship as a form of genuine communication across difference.

This radically reflexive understanding of worship leads Hegel to demote forms of religious language that bespeak any asymmetry in the divine-human relationship. Such demotion is evident in the first form of the cultus, which Hegel labels "*devotion* in general."[180] The German term he uses for devotion, *Andacht*, is etymologically related to the term for thought, *Denken*. Hegel exploits this link in support of his claim that devotion is a form of thought, albeit one inadequate to the self-expression of the divine concept. It is at this stage that Hegel situates the religious language of thanksgiving and, by extension, it would seem, Augustinian confession and praise of God.[181] Yet Hegel subverts and obviates such forms of prayer and worship through the reflexive identity he sees realized in the cultus. If the cultus is one of the important loci where Hegel seeks to reconcile divine grace with human freedom speculatively, then that reconciliation is ultimately one in which freedom, conceived as rational self-determination, trumps grace.[182] Subjective freedom is the telos of Hegel's all-encompassing Trinitarian vision, and the practice of Christian worship aims to cultivate the disposition toward such freedom, to arouse the desire to make freedom real ethically and politically.[183] As a result, the religious language of thanksgiving and praise is necessarily left behind.

It is perhaps ironic, then, that the Eucharist—the Greek εὐχαριστία translates literally as "thankfulness" or "gratitude"—features so centrally in Hegel's interpretation of Christianity. The Eucharist as a sacramental rite falls under the second moment in Hegel's elucidation of the cultus, where it is a matter of "the external forms through which the feeling of reconciliation is brought forth in an external and sensible manner."[184] Insofar as cultic actions in general and the Eucharist in particular are performed outwardly, Hegel thinks they contain a sacrificial element, one we can liken to the Father's kenotic sacrifice of abstract subjectivity through the incarnation of Christ.[185] In a public communication with others, each believer sacrifices something of him- or herself in order to share or "partake" in the universal Spirit shared by all. Yet many cultic sacrifices, preeminently the Christian Eucharist, culminate in the sharing and consumption of the sacrificial offering. This communal act of consumption corresponds to believers' spiritual internalization of the truth of Christ following his death and bodily dissolution. It is the "sensible enjoyment [of the sacrifice],"[186] the negation of the sacrificial elements' externality.

Consistent with the pneumatological displacement of grace by freedom is Hegel's further displacement of sacrifice by the enjoyment of reconciliation. Enjoyment indicates the Hegelian

Eucharist's function of furnishing the certainty of the presence of God within the human consciousness. While we might be tempted here to think also of Augustine's distinction between use and enjoyment and the attendant instruction that only God is to be enjoyed, it is worth recalling that Augustine's eschatological state of unimpeded enjoyment of God is characterized as an unending hymn of praise to God.[187] The enjoyment attained in Hegel's Eucharist, by contrast, signals a radical unity and equality between the human subject and the divine that renders doxological language otiose. For Hegel, praise and thanksgiving are linguistic indicators of passive forms of worship that effect no internal transformation, at least not until the worshiping subjects become aware of their own moral agency through conscience, on the one hand, and the sanctity of the world in which they act, on the other.[188]

Hegel thinks that his pneumatological rendition of the Eucharist based upon the joint principles of subjective agency and the real presence of the divine truth in the world is an effective means of training individuals to freely align their particular natural wills with the universal will, embodied in this case by the laws of the rationally constituted state. Thus Hegel's eucharistic practice is subordinated to the state's goal of cultivating the ethical life of its populace. On the same principle of rational self-determination, philosophy too is a "continual cultus," indeed, the truest form of *Gottesdienst* (worship), because its object is the rational truth, absolute Spirit.[189] Philosophy's service (*Dienst*) is to sacrifice particular concerns for the sake of objective reason, to discern the work of God qua reason in history (theodicy), and ultimately, to know Spirit through spirit, through the categories of pure thought shorn of all externality or representational language.[190]

As worship, philosophy, on Hegel's account, beats religion at its own game.[191] The Eucharist must thus be interpreted in a way that serves the end of rational self-determination and facilitates its own trumping and integration into ethics and philosophy. We have seen the broad strokes of this interpretation as they relate to Hegel's concept of worship generally speaking. In the next few pages, let us turn briefly to a more detailed account of Hegel's eucharistic theology, in order to make a final theological assessment before turning to Augustine.

CONSUMPTION OF THE BODY: EUCHARISTIC RESURRECTION

In *LPR* 3 (1824) Hegel declares that the sacrament of communion is the sensible representation "that Christ is eternally sacrificed and rises again in the heart."[192] Yet Hegel goes further; were Christ's death and resurrection to take place only in the heart, reconciliation would not yet be achieved. Hegel means something stronger than Christ's rising again merely "in the heart." This is Christ's resurrection precisely as the believer's resurrection, his or her conscious appropriation of the truth: "The eternal sacrifice is the process through which single individuals *make themselves their own*, the process by which their implicit being passes away."[193] The eucharistic context suggests that this taking ownership of oneself can be linked to the process of intrahistorical bodily resurrection traced out above, when implicit goodness becomes explicit as one emerges from the immediacy of self-feeling—when soul and body are transfigured in *Spirit*. Moreover, this eschatological realization is marked by its strong mystical character. In the Eucharist it is "a question ... of unity with God, the *unio mystica*, [one's] self-feeling of God, the feeling of God's immediate presence within the subject."[194]

This mystical union is ultimately a communal reality. The subject's immediate communion with God is mediated by the community's practice of worship, whereby the individual subject is united with the other members of the community in this communion of Spirit.[195] In this way, Hegel argues, the community is preserved, continually created anew through the resurrection of Christ in the reconciliation of each individual with the universal Spirit.[196] The individual's resurrection of body is a resurrection into the communal body, the sacramental body of Spirit, mediated through the community's teaching and practices.

Precisely because of its communal and eschatological implications, the practice of the Lord's Supper forms for Hegel the "midpoint of Christian doctrine" and distinguishes the various Christian churches from each other. Deficient understandings of the Eucharist intimate deeper deficiencies with regard to one's knowledge of and attitude toward reality as a whole. Hegel identifies two in particular: on the one hand, the consecration of the host in the Catholic Mass independent of the subject's act of faith epitomizes in Hegel's view the mechanistic externalism, heteronomy, and subjective passivity which characterize the Roman church and the social and political cultures under its influence. The Reformed tradition, on the other hand, treats the Eucharist as only a memorial of Christ's death. Whereas the former objectifies the divine presence in a particular sensuous thing, the latter, on Hegel's reading, has no sense of divine presence at all. It is a merely human act of recollection, in which the subject remains sundered from objective truth. In neither is there a real, living reconciliation of the subject with God. In neither, then, is a real reconciliation into the community of Spirit possible. In Hegel's view, these celebrations of the Eucharist would be the religious practices which in fact call forth lamentation, since God remains distant and distinct from the believing subject. Any praise and thanks expressed therein would be, at best, inadequate to the truth of the divine-human relation and, at worst, deceptive and hypocritical. They are sacraments in the weakest sense, for in them God remains a mystery, albeit the wrong kind of mystery, according to Hegel. By such mystery, which the individual cannot know, believers are enslaved either to their clerical masters or to the abstract madness of their subjective whims.

Lutheran eucharistic theology and practice stands between these two extremes, as the apogee of religion on "the threshold of rationality."[197] In it Hegel finds the principle whereby the individual believer is united to the universal truth. Just as he insists on the historical Christ's singular physical appearance, so he argues that in the sacrament of communion the believer confronts the sensible, the host: "The starting point is the consumption of God objectively present."[198] Hegel finds it apt that the believer's contact with the sensible world takes the form of eating and drinking. These activities, unlike breathing air, require conscious decision and involve each individual in his or her natural, sensible particularity.[199] The consumption of the host, the very sensation of its dissolution in one's body, is also necessary: as in the empty tomb, where there is sensation of the loss of Christ's individual natural body, so the individual host matters only inasmuch as it passes away in its natural immediacy and singularity.[200] It is in the believer's act of faith while eating that God is present: "The sensible is first spiritualized in the subject."[201] Apart from the subject's act of appropriation, the host is simply bread.

It is here, in Hegel's insistence upon and elucidation of physical consumption, that I think we discern very concretely the theological problems in Hegel's conception of the spiritual community and the Trinitarian theology that undergirds it. In this regard, Stepelevich offers a helpful summary of Hegel's interpretation of salvation history:

> With the Fall, the simple self-immediacy of the animal is sundered into the alienated human, who is broken into aspiring spirit and sinful body. The body is the alien "other" of emergent self-consciousness, set against mind as an inert and often hostile self. The history of man will end, in this mythic history, when the sinful body of Adam is transformed into the holy body—the Eucharistic body, the Host—of Christ and *is consumed*. The secular history of man, which is framed within the sacred history of God, is set between the body of Adam and the *Corpus Christi*. This is the Hegelian view of how actual, i.e., philosophic, world history is taken by the religious consciousness. The main truth of this religious narrative is found in its dialectical form: the passage of history from an immediate universal (God) through its particularization as self-alienation (God in Nature) to its synthesizing terminus in self-reconciliation, the true individuality of the Holy Spirit.[202]

Stepelevich therefore concludes that because, for Hegel, "the [Lutheran] Eucharist is the final *presentation* of the alien body before its consumption and return into spirit," it is not fully grasped without considering Hegel's view of the physical world, the fallen other of God.[203] As we have seen, Hegel articulates both the divine and human Trinitarian narratives not only in terms of oral linguistic production, but also in a parallel way in the organic terms of growth and development. His account of physical consumption and spiritualization of the Eucharist could, accordingly, be viewed as the place, practically speaking, where the divine and human Trinitarian histories flow together.

The Eucharist, then, as symbolic or spiritual consumption, aims to assimilate what is external to, what limits, the believing subject— the natural, selfish body in both its individual and social forms—to its spiritual, rational essence. The subject who partakes of Hegel's eucharistic practice resurrects himself, gives himself the resurrection body by transforming the fallen, natural body into that which nourishes and sustains spirit. Practically speaking, the Eucharist facilitates the resurrection, as conceived by Hegel, inasmuch as it affectively encourages and sustains a program of habituation, of subordinating the individual physical body to the commands of reason and the social body to the rational laws of the state. Yet such a program, Hegel thinks, is inconceivable unless the human knows herself as rational, in other words, unless through the Eucharist the human also assimilates the God who is reason itself. External to the believer, God is a limit who must be consumed and only thereby transformed into the infinite process of Spirit, in order that the believing subject might be within herself what she truly is. Yet if the subject is to assimilate God into herself, she must, Hegel thinks, see herself in God. Because the eucharistic subject is this process of spiritual consumption, so too is God.

As Spirit, God really is only insofar as he consumes his fallen other, the world and finite spirit. In the exposition of the Eucharist in *LPR* (1824) Hegel argues, "The Father is what exists insofar as it surrenders itself [into the finite world, the Son]; but it first exists as real spirit, spirit realized, in self-consciousness."[204] Both Father and Son have their existence in Spirit, more precisely in their negation in Spirit. Transfiguration, the resurrection of the sacramental body, of the concrete "divine man," is the movement in fact of a single divine substance toward its own eschatological realization, a movement into which all reality is included and "by which externality is annulled, so that the presence of God is utterly a spiritual presence."[205] Thus does the sacramental body of the community witness to divine love, where the subject's eschatological enjoyment of God is but a necessary moment in God's enjoyment of himself.

Yet does one worship such a God? Hegel's worship, wherein the recognition of oneself as the image of God is in fact the recognition of one's own divinity, and ultimately of God's recognition of himself as divine, differs radically from Augustine's own inward turn. For the latter, even the most penetrating investigation into the human mind ultimately gives one all the more reason to praise God, because in its original, and even more so in its re-created, state the mind is evidence of God's gratuitous love, a love that constitutively exceeds the bounds of human comprehension. Consequently, Augustine's eschatological vision is accompanied and perfected by songs of eternal thanksgiving and praise.[206]

The love to which Hegel's Christian community witnesses, by contrast, cannot be described as anything other than a sophisticated version of self-love, now consummated in the modern world. Alas, the eschatological eucharistic feast celebrated in Hegel's heavenly city does not seem so joyous. In fact, it seems quite lonely and silent. The voices of the city's inhabitants, whose erstwhile cries of lamentation should have been changed into shouts of joy, are muffled inside the belly of a God who has consumed the world.

HEGEL'S RECONSTRUCTED TRINITARIANISM issues in an understanding of the church that deviates rather starkly from the tradition in which he claims to reside and that is, furthermore, theologically problematic. Hegel's appeal to a Lutheran Protestant pedigree is shaky. Whereas Hegel stresses a radical identity between God and humankind which, in a strongly pneumatological register, is marked by the eschatological fullness of knowledge and rational self-determination, Luther underscores the difference between humans and God and the continued dependence of humans upon

God. For Luther, the Holy Spirit guides the church, which still awaits the kingdom, to listen in faith to the Word of God.

Hegel's deviations from Luther are owing to the imprint of mystical thinkers like Meister Eckhart and Joachim of Fiore. The influence of Joachimite Lutheranism helps account for Hegel's extension of soteriological value to all of human history and political affairs, for his realized eschatology, and for the strong pneumatological determination of his concept of Christian community. Significantly, it enables us to grasp how Hegel could inscribe the Enlightenment into a normatively Christian historical narrative in which the political enshrinement of freedom qua rational self-determination stood as the legitimate fruit of Lutheran Protestantism, when Luther himself would have rejected such a concept of freedom as born of a theology of glory.

From a more systematic and ecclesiological perspective, Hegel's Trinitarian paradigm and his theory of the unification and transfiguration of soul and body by human spirit lead to a shift away from Christ to the Spirit as the definitive ground of the Christian community. The trajectory of this Trinitarian movement results, ultimately, in the sublation of the church in the modern rational state, which for Hegel represents most concretely the objective body of Spirit in its resurrected and transfigured condition.

Practically speaking, the adoption of Hegel's Trinitarian dynamics severely restricts the theological resources available to the Hegelian spiritual community. In their scriptural exegesis and teaching and in their sacramental worship, members of the spiritual community no longer have any recourse to the scriptural language of lament, even in the face of suffering and death. Hegel's all-consuming pneumatology and realized eschatology obviate such language. The upshot of Hegel's understanding of history as theodicy, then, is a silencing of voices on both sides of the divine-human relationship: those who suffer no longer find the words with which to cry out to God, and God and the church that witnesses to him no longer preach the message, "God loves you," to a suffering world.

Hegel's interpretation of the Eucharist displays his erasure of the world's resistance. According to Hegel, the consumption and inward dissolution of the eucharistic host bring to sensible expression the death of bodily externality and its resurrection and transfiguration in Spirit. The result, on Hegel's account, is an intrahistorical eschatological enjoyment of divine-human identity. In the context of Hegel's all-encompassing Trinitarian paradigm, this enjoyment ultimately boils down to God's justification and enjoyment of himself, which leaves us to wonder what, in the end, the language of worship was supposed to mean for Hegel apart from self-worship. In any case, it underscores the inability of Hegelian conceptuality to assist in the theological articulation of what the Christian community is and what it is called to be and do in a still fallen world.

Chapter 6

AUGUSTINE AND A CATHOLIC CHURCH WITH SOUL?

At the beginning of chapter 5, we considered the claim by Peter Hodgson that Hegel is unaware that Augustine's pneumatologically rich concept of the Catholic church constitutes an alternative to the hierarchical, legalistic version of Catholicism which bears the brunt of Hegel's critique. Hodgson's observation regarding the role of the Holy Spirit in Augustine's ecclesiology gives good reason to bring Augustine forward as a thinker who offers a vibrant pneumatological conception of the Christian community. By underscoring the pneumatological side of Augustine's ecclesiology, Hodgson makes us wary of lumping the bishop of Hippo together too hastily with a desiccated and juridical vision of Catholicism. Yet because Hegel's historical account of Spirit, in which Catholicism is incorporated merely as an intermediate, negative step on the way toward Protestantism and the Enlightenment, is at the same time structurally determinative of the Hegelian spiritual community, Augustine's pneumatic Catholicism also undermines the systematic continuity Hodgson wishes to find between the two thinkers. Thus, Hegel's historical narrative having been problematized, including not only his portrayal of Catholicism but also his claimed Lutheran pedigree, the ground is clear, in both historical and systematic respects, for a retrieval of Augustine's Trinitarian theology. We thus break free of a teleological account of history that denies continued theological relevance to a figure like Augustine.

In contrast to Hegel's conceptions of the relationship of the Spirit to Christ, the church, and the status of lament and praise, Augustine offers us his concept of the *totus Christus*, the whole Christ. In keeping with Augustine's mature Christology, the *totus Christus* has both this-worldly and transcendent reference in the distinction between Christ as body and as head, between Christ as the way for this life and as the object of vision in the next. The maintenance of these distinctions is vital for comparing him with Hegel. Whereas Hegel realizes the eschatological state in a fully immanent totality and thereby loses the conceptual wherewithal to give voice to those still suffering under the weight of evil, Augustine is able through his understanding of Christ present in his communal body to give theological voice to those who lament their suffering. At the same time, Augustine invests the cries of lamentation with transformative pedagogical and soteriological value, because they have a critical transcendent reference in Christ as the body's head. In this way, lamentation qua prayer gives reason for and is itself transformed into thanksgiving and praise of the God who saves through it. By retaining the incarnate Trinitarian person of Christ and not collapsing God into the world, as Hegel does, Augustine is at once able to affirm the goodness of creation, acknowledge the reality of evil and suffering, and show how God works to console and transfigure a world still struggling to reach its eschatological goal. In other words, the theological advantage Augustine's concept of the *totus Christus* offers over Hegel's spiritual community is that it is better able to sustain difference within the unity of the *whole* Christ. This is possible because the *totus Christus* is a unitive, yet nonabsorptive, expression of the love of God and neighbor in both the subjective and objective genitive senses.

This communal manifestation of love suggests, moreover, the pneumatological depth of Augustine's ecclesiology. The church is the body of Christ, and, as Augustine says, the Holy Spirit is its soul. Thus, our purpose in this chapter is not merely to illumine the stronger christological determination of Augustinian ecclesiology vis-à-vis Hegel's spiritual community, but more importantly to show how Augustine's Christocentric conception of the church need not translate into pneumatological impoverishment. To take a hint from Staudenmaier, Augustine's ability to critically balance the work of both Christ and the Holy Spirit in the life of the church constitutes a relative theological strength over against Hegel's displacement of Christ by the Spirit. The christological structure of Augustine's ecclesiology imbues the church with an immanent and transcendent objective point of orientation that affords it potential for self-critique as well as a critical standpoint vis-à-vis the broader society.

In the terms explored above in Part I, Augustine's simultaneous application of oral linguistic imagery to the incarnation and refusal to extend that imagery to the Trinity *in se* in fact, contrary to Hegel's critique, enable a broader range of critical Christian language in the world. Augustine does not render the Trinity transparent to human language, but he does not silence Christians in the process. Rather, he prioritizes love and faith over direct knowledge; through the love of the Spirit, which forms Christians into the body of Christ and inspires their faith in the Son's unity with the Father, Christians remain connected in a real way to God and are empowered to speak of God more accurately, inasmuch as they do not idolatrously identify God with any part of his creation. Indeed, Augustine's pneumatology imbues the church with a dynamism and openness to the Trinitarian mystery that challenges the drawing of any clear-cut institutional boundaries or any purely mechanistic understanding of the church's sacramental life. Augustinian pneumatology thus avoids the deleterious features of the excessively christological Catholicism found in Hegel's account of the Spirit, where the reduction of the Spirit to the control of the visible church's clerical masters issues in the very opposite of freedom.

Against the backdrop of the complex and often elusive nature of the church as a simultaneously visible and mystical reality, the soul-body relationship in Augustine's thought reveals, albeit in a way limited by human theological language, the relative operation of Christ and the Holy Spirit in his understanding of the ecclesial body. The central text of *ep.* 137 is particularly helpful in that it signals a decisive conceptual and terminological advance in Augustine's anthropology and Christology. This mutually informative christological and anthropological analysis helps us grasp the incarnational substructure of Augustine's understanding of the church as *totus Christus*. The transformative dynamism of that incarnational structure is then illuminated by situating it into its broader pro-Nicene Trinitarian context. By considering the fluidity of Augustine's use of soul-body imagery in *ep. Jo.* and *Jo. ev. tr.*, we can see how he uses scriptural language to draw his congregation ever deeper into the Trinitarian mystery.

Accordingly, the *totus Christus* may then be seen, more concretely, as a sacrament of divine love in the world, both in itself and through the church's practices of scriptural exegesis and the Eucharist. The essential textual resources for analyzing this sacramental perspective are Augustine's *Enarrationes in Psalmos*, the vast collection of his homilies on the psalms where he develops his concept of the *totus Christus* most extensively; *civ. Dei* 10, where he most explicitly discusses his concept of worship; and *s.* 71, one of his most sustained treatments of the Holy Spirit and the church.

The Church: Soul and Body

If we are to make any sense of Augustine's concepts of the church as the body of Christ or the Holy Spirit as the church's soul, we need to understand in general how he conceives of the relationship between the human body and soul. Augustine is consistent throughout his career in affirming that the human being is a composite of soul and body. In *Trin.* he offers a standard definition: "Man is a rational substance consisting of soul and body."[1] The soul is different from the body, and Augustine thinks of the former as superior to the latter.[2] It is in the rational soul, we recall, that the human being is the image of God: "Man was not made to the image of God as regards the shape of his body, but as regards his rational mind. It is an idle and base kind of thinking which supposes that God is confined within the limits of a body with features and limbs."[3] Augustine himself reports having succumbed to such base thinking while a Manichee.[4] Through the Platonist books, however, he learned about spiritual substance and thereby abandoned such materialistic thinking. Thereafter the Platonic conception of the immateriality of the soul remains a stable feature of his anthropology. Bodies, according to Augustine, are extended three-dimensionally in space.[5] The soul, on the other hand, is "an independent, nonmaterial substance present to the body in a causal but not spatiotemporal way—the subject of knowledge and desire, the seat of self-consciousness, the unifying center of the human person."[6] It is consequently the soul's very immateriality and wholeness throughout the body that enables each human being to make sense of the multifarious physical world and grounds the value of an individual's action therein.[7]

This is not to imply that the body does not really matter, or that Augustine never really breaks free of his Manichaean past. Indeed, Augustine reports that Julian of Eclanum accused him of being a Manichee late into his theological career.[8] To be sure, in his early writings Augustine does talk of escape or flight (*fuga*) from the corruptible body to eternal things, thereby recalling Porphyry: *Corpus est omne fugiendum*.[9] The young Augustine also speaks of the body as a very heavy chain (*gravissimum vinculum*) and the need to flee the cave (*cavea*) of sensible things.[10]

However, Augustine's negatively hued emphasis is never upon the body *per se*, but upon its postlapsarian corruption.[11] Even in his early works, he affirms that the body is good because it is God's creation, and that the soul's well-being is tied up with the well-being of the body.[12] Yet it is only after he has studied Paul more intensively that Augustine gains a noticeably greater appreciation for the body.[13] He must then take account of Eph 5.29, where the deutero-Pauline author claims that no one hates his own flesh.[14] At the same time, Augustine develops a deeper awareness of the resurrection. In *f. et symb.* 10.24 (393), he had maintained that the resurrection body is spiritual, not fleshly. But in *retr.* 1.17, he corrects himself on that point. In fact, Augustine had already rejected a nonfleshly spiritual resurrection in *c. Faust.* 11.3 (ca. 402).[15] For Augustine, the spiritual transformation of the flesh, which remains an object of eschatological hope, is not the immanent transformative process of self-possession that we saw in Hegel. In the latter's thought, that process threatens to erase the world in its relative autonomy. Contrariwise, in Augustine's theology the resurrection is the re-creative act of the God who created the world as good at the very beginning.[16]

Rist argues that "blending," for all its limitations, is perhaps the most fitting word in English to describe the relationship between the soul and the body in Augustine's thought.[17] This relationship, a unity in difference, remains marked by a fundamental asymmetry: the body retains its integrity and identity as a body only through the soul.[18] Yet such asymmetry raises a question that Hegel, too, would probably ask: is the body merely accidental to the soul? Augustine's developing thought on the nature and work of Christ helps him gain clarity on the issue. Or perhaps better put, it helps him achieve insight into the miraculous and paradoxical character of the incarnation and, by extension, of human nature itself.[19] And when that christological insight is translated into linguistic terms, especially concerning the usefulness and limitations of the image of spoken language, Augustine comes to understand the transformative power of spiritually inspired, albeit thoroughly human, language, language intimately close to some of the most emotionally intense human experiences, grief and joy.

In *ep.* 137 to Volusianus, written in 411, Augustine articulates both Christ's subjective integrity and that of each human being. The teaching of the incarnation—and Augustine is explicit that the incarnation itself is that teaching—is lost on so many because they are unable to look at the created world with a sense of wonder.[20] Most miraculous, and yet so apparently ordinary, is the human being herself.[21] At the heart of that which happens every day—the birth of new human beings—Augustine discovers something astonishing: the inexplicable unity of an immaterial soul and a material body.[22] He then compares the everyday miracle of the human being to the utterly unique miracle of the incarnation: "For just as the soul is united to the body in the unity of the *person* in order that a human being might exist, so God is united to the man in the unity of the *person* in order that Christ might exist."²³

Here we encounter a new technical term in Augustine's anthropology and Christology: the unity of soul and body in one person (*persona*) and the parallel unity of divine Word and human being in the one person of Christ. In this context the term *persona* denotes the subjective unity of two distinct substances. Prior to 411, however, Augustine's use of the term, following a tradition of Latin usage in theatrical and legal contexts, had been more exegetical and dramatic.²⁴ It aimed at identifying the speaker of a biblical text as "playing a particular role" and identifying how the speaker played that role. For example, Christ sometimes is understood to speak in the person of one's old humanity (*personam . . . veteris hominis*) or the person of Adam (*ex persona Adam*).²⁵ At the same time, Christ is unique among human beings in that he does not merely participate in, but naturally impersonates (*personam*) divine Wisdom.²⁶ A number of scholars agree that the dramatic sense of "person" takes on a more metaphysical meaning of "acting subject" in Augustine's later writings.²⁷ (We will attend further to the development of Augustine's Christology in relation to his prosopological exegesis of the psalms when we investigate how Augustine interprets psalmic lament and praise as spiritually inspired paradigms of worship aimed at forming believers into the body of Christ.)

Throughout his theological career, Augustine resists any form of Apollinarianism. The person of Christ consists of the divine Word and a whole human being, soul and body. In fact, Augustine argues,

> The union of two incorporeal realities ought . . . to be believed with more ease than that of one incorporeal and one corporeal reality. For, if the soul is not mistaken about its nature, it grasps that it is incorporeal; much more is the Word of God incorporeal, and for this reason the union of the Word of God and the soul ought to be more believable than that of the soul and the

body. But we experience the latter in ourselves; the former we are commanded to believe in Christ.[28]

In Augustine's view there is something all too familiar in the incarnation, so familiar indeed that it is alienating to many, because humans are all too alienated by what is most familiar. Docetists, Augustine contends, would prefer see a miraculous show of divine power, rather than a savior who sleeps, eats, and experiences the full range of human emotions. But it is precisely through the full humanity of Christ that Augustine thinks God shows his mercy to, saves, and glorifies humankind.[29]

Any metaphysical developments in Augustine's Christology, then, are soteriological at their core. And Augustine cannot overemphasize either side of the divine-human relation without imperiling that salvation. Manichaeism, by positing a metaphysical identity between the divine Word and human souls, effectively robbed God of his ability to save humans from evil and suffering. In that regard there are similarities to Hegel's Christology, especially the latter's identification of Trinitarian linguistic logic with spoken human language, at least when the latter is expressed in fully rational form. On the other hand, docetic Christologies that deny the full humanity of Christ effectively say that God did not save human beings in their full integrity. Thus, in language that counteracts the divine assimilation or consumption of the world that we saw in Hegel's eucharistic theology, Augustine states explicitly that the divine Word does not consume but rather assumes humanity (*hominem . . . quem non consumpsit . . . sed adsumpsit*).[30] By not consuming humanity, by not demonstrating overwhelming divine power, but rather by humbly assuming humanity in its fullness, God is able to persuade human beings (*persuadet hominibus*) of his mercy, grace, and love.[31] Divine love is revealed in Augustine by a paradoxical "mixture" of Logos and human being in which neither substance loses its integrity.[32] The distinction within the subjective unity of Christ is essential to the miracle of the incarnation: "But now a mediator has appeared between God and human beings so that, *uniting both natures in the unity of his person*, he may raise up the ordinary to the extraordinary and temper the extraordinary to the ordinary."[33]

We need to keep the dynamics of Augustine's Christology in mind as we think not only about the relationship between the soul and the body at the anthropological level, but also about that relationship's symbolism at the ecclesial level. From an ecclesiological perspective, the soul's positive relation to the body is especially pertinent for at least two reasons: (1) like the images of the soul and body, so several of the figures Augustine uses to depict their relationship also crop up in his ecclesiology, including those of marriage and the body as a temple of the Spirit; (2) all of these images are subservient to Augustine's broader ecclesial vision of the *totus Christus*, a concept of corporate personality which is an extension of Augustine's Christology.

Thus Augustine's position toward the material world is one of relative affirmation. He rejects any view that would fall exclusively to one side or the other of the spirit-matter divide, be it in either a strictly spiritualist or strictly materialist vein.[34] Yet this dialectical balancing of soul and body is hierarchical, not egalitarian. The soul ought not to give itself over inordinately to sensual objects, but rather—in the language of the earlier Augustine, at least—to rule or use the body rightly. Recall that "use" for Augustine can be just or unjust. "Use" admits of the possibility of "exploitation," but their meanings are not coterminous. What Augustine is saying is rather that the body provides the means whereby the soul interacts with the material world. Yet the soul's relation to this means is not extrinsic, but intrinsic. From early in his career onward, Augustine describes this relationship of soul to body as intentional, as a natural and morally neutral orientation of the will toward governing the body.[35] In his *Literal Interpretation of Genesis* 12, Augustine is clear: "The mind has a natural appetite for ruling the body"—the soul loves its life; hence it loves its flesh.[36] Because "a man's body is no mere adornment, or external convenience; [because] it belongs to his very nature as a man," Augustine insists that Christians ought to bury the bodies of the dead.[37] At the resurrection, when the final enemy, death, no longer intervenes between soul and body, "my flesh will be for ever my friend."[38]

In *civ. Dei* 22 Augustine insists that the value of the body exceeds its mere utility. Because every part of the body has aesthetic value in addition to its function, and because God has even created parts of the body that increase its beauty while lacking any obvious function, "it can . . . readily be inferred that in the design of the human body dignity was a more important consideration than utility."[39] At the resurrection, when the different parts of the body will no longer handle the exigencies of temporal survival, the faithful will enjoy the beauty of each other's bodies in a nonlustful and nonexploitative way. Such genuinely loving enjoyment of human bodies issues ultimately in the praise of God, who created the human body and will beautifully re-create it through the gift of grace.[40] Accordingly, as Augustine stresses several years earlier in *s.* 82 (408–9), one ought to avoid bodily sins already in this life, because the body, not just the mind, is the temple of the Holy Spirit.[41]

Frequently Augustine uses another image which fortuitously links anthropological and ecclesial corporate imagery: the marriage bond. We see this image used anthropologically in *On the Advantage of Fasting*.[42] There Augustine claims that the Manichaeans—adducing Gal 5.17, "The flesh lusts against the spirit, and the spirit against the flesh"[43]—conclude that the body is evil *in se* and consequently stems from a different deity than the spirit does. Against this radical dualism, Augustine appeals to Eph 5.29, "For nobody ever hates his own flesh."[44] Significantly, Augustine finds in that biblical passage "a kind of marriage between flesh and spirit."[45] The relationship manifest in this image has clear theological and ecclesial implications. The soul loves and cares for its flesh just as Christ loves and cares for the church. The same one God who created both soul and body is Father of Christ and of his church. There are not two gods, one of Christ and another of the church.[46] The body matters. As much as the unity of love between the spiritual soul and the material body points toward the goodness of the one God who created them, so much the more does the unity of Christ the Son with his body the church lead the members of that body toward the Father, hence toward the mystery of the one triune God.

Uncertain Imagery?
Between the Head and the Soul

The relationship between the soul and the body in Augustine's anthropology, then, serves as a conceptual background for his image of the Holy Spirit as the soul of Christ's body, the church. Augustine distinguishes between the soul and the body especially in terms of the role the soul plays as the center of human subjectivity. But when he describes the Holy Spirit as the soul of Christ's body, an ambiguity arises concerning the respective roles of Christ and the Holy Spirit in the life of the church. Some of this ambiguity disappears when we look at what Augustine says about Christ as the head and the Holy Spirit as the soul of the church body. Nonetheless, Augustine never entirely avoids ambiguity in his description of the Trinitarian persons and their economic operation. This is a consequence of his pro-Nicene Trinitarian theological commitments and need not be construed as theological weakness, especially when contrasted with Hegel's Trinitarian paradigm.

Augustine's ecclesiological image of Christ as head of the church contains distinctive elements that mark an important point of contrast with Hegel, who effectively excises that image from his radically pneumatological concept of Christian community. Whereas in Hegel the historical, human Christ is "das Tote des Geistes" ("the moment of Spirit which is dead"), for Augustine Christ is head of the church in his resurrected, living humanity. In *en. Ps.* 148 (ca. 405–11) Augustine makes this quite clear in relation to Christ's two natures:

> Here on earth [Christ] chose for himself a nuptial chamber, where bridegroom was joined to bride. *The Word was made flesh* (Jn 1:14) in order to become the head of the Church. In his own nature the Word is not part of the Church, but in order

to be the Church's head he took flesh. Something of ours is already on high, something he assumed as his own here, where he died, where he was crucified. The first-fruits of yourself has gone ahead already. Can you doubt that you will follow?[47]

For Hegel it is essential that the human Christ, of one spiritual nature with God, die and remain dead in order that divinity qua Spirit be mediated to the community of believers. That is, Christ in his external particularity dies and remains dead in order that believers may possess resurrection life now through the autonomous recognition of their own divinity. Augustine, by contrast, is convinced that humanity cannot give itself life, either as natural or self-consciously rational. It is the eternal fullness of Christ's divinity that mediates life to the humanity he has assumed. But it is in that humanity, in which Christ was born, suffered, died, rose, and ascended, that believers have already, in the form of hope if not yet in their own bodies, risen and ascended to heaven.

Augustine emphasizes in *en. Ps.* 148.8 that the incarnation expresses God's love for humanity. The church continues to witness to that love, because the church is grounded and animated by the incarnate unity—soon Augustine would use the term *persona*—of Christ as divine Word and complete human being. To call Christ head of the church is to profess faith in his death and resurrection, in Christ's living, glorified humanity, and in God's promise to restore humans to their complete integrity, soul and body, on the last day. To call Christ head of the church is to insist on the church's explicit christological structure, but, pace Hegel, not necessarily at the expense of the Spirit. In *en. Ps.* 148.8, to be sure, Augustine does not mention the Spirit explicitly, but pneumatological resonances are not absent. Christ is head of the church in his glorified humanity, as the firstfruits of the resurrection from the dead. This christological affirmation of God's love for humanity comes in terms that Augustine elsewhere attributes to the Holy Spirit:

> Do you think that God sets little store by human beings, when he willed that his only Son should die for them? Let us fix our

eyes on the proof of his love that he has already given. We have received peerless pledges [*arrhas*] of God's promise: we hold Christ's death, we hold Christ's blood. Who died? God's only Son. For whom did he die? ... If he made a gift of his death to the wicked, what can he be reserving for the righteous, except his life?[48]

Here, as at *en. Ps.* 122.5 (ca. 406–7/412), the pledge is Christ's blood. At *en. Ps.* 127.8 (ca. 406–7/412), though, Augustine includes the Holy Spirit as the means of unity between the bride on earth, the church, and Christ, her ascended bridegroom: "The bridegroom to whom we have been wedded is absent.... *He gave us his Holy Spirit as his pledge* [*arrha*], but he is absent himself; he redeemed us with his blood, but now he has gone away."[49]

When we turn, then, to the work of the Holy Spirit within Christ's body, the church, we find that the image of the soul helps Augustine describe the body's unity. For example, in *s.* 268, preached on the Feast of Pentecost, possibly in 405, Augustine takes up the issue of unity against Donatist schismatics. He argues that the miracle of tongues which took place at Pentecost was intended to show the presence of the Holy Spirit in the one church spread throughout all lands and speaking all languages. Drawing a parallel between the Holy Spirit and the human soul, Augustine next illustrates the church's unity with an image from scripture, "one body and one spirit" (Eph 4.4):

> Consider our own bodies and their parts. The body consists of many parts, and one spirit quickens all the parts. Look here, by the human spirit, *by which I am myself this human being*, I bind together all parts of my body; I command the limbs to move, I direct the eyes to see, the ears to hear, the tongue to talk, the hands to work, the feet to walk. The functions of the different parts vary, but the unity of the spirit coordinates them all. Many things are commanded, many things are done; but it's just one who commands, and one who is served. What our spirit, that is our soul, is to the parts or members of our body,

that the Holy Spirit is to the members of Christ, to the body of Christ.[50]

There are different members within the one body. Diversity is not stifled, but affirmed in the unity of the church. This is precisely because it is by no single part of the body, but by the soul that "I am myself *this human being*." At the level of the communal body, then, no individual human being can define the community as a whole. Only God, through the Holy Spirit, constitutes and defines the church as Christ's body.

Moreover, Augustine stresses that the Spirit gives life to the communal body. Otherwise, there is merely an aggregate of human individuals, no better than a corpse. In a living body, the one spirit senses and works through the various parts; thus it is that the human subject sees and not just the eye. At the level of the communal body, then, this unity of the Spirit enables different members to share in each other's distinct gifts, but also in each other's pain: "If one member is hurt in any way, all the other members sympathize with it."[51] However, that grief, made possible by the unity of feeling in the Spirit, has a more ominous implication. Those who separate themselves from the body and thus lose the Spirit become like dead, insensate limbs. By restricting the scope of their love, so it appears on Augustine's account, they lose the ability to feel with and for others at all.

Augustine confirms this conclusion in *ep. Jo.* 6.10 (407). As in *s.* 268, there is a discussion of the miracle of tongues at Pentecost. In this case, the problem concerns the fact that believers no longer speak in tongues. So, the question is asked, how do they know that they possess the Holy Spirit? In chapter 4 we saw one way Augustine solves the dilemma: it does not matter that Christians no longer speak in tongues, because the church, spread throughout the world, speaks all languages and is united by the one spiritual language of the heart. In *ep. Jo.* 6.10, Augustine solves the problem with another image: the spirit that unites diverse parts of the body.

At stake in the question concerning the cessation of glossolalia is the determination of the Spirit's presence or absence in the Donatist and Catholic churches. Notice Augustine's emphasis upon sight and the eyes. In chapter 4 we saw how Augustine sought to train the faithful in a new way of speaking by showing them how the Holy Spirit mediated sacramentally between the diversity of vocal languages spoken in the universal church and the unifying language of the heart. In parallel fashion we can here interpret Augustine to be training his congregation to see in a new way, to strive to see the way God sees. We have already encountered Augustine's answer: "If he loves his brother, the Spirit of God abides in him. Let him see [*videat*]; let him prove himself before the eyes of God [*oculis dei*]; let him see [*videat*] if there is in him the love of peace and unity, the love of the Church spread throughout the whole world."[52] This entails the Holy Spirit transformatively mediating between sensible, here visible, parts of the communal body and its deeper spiritual, hence invisible, reality.

Augustine accuses the Donatists of a shortsightedness tantamount, in the end, to lovelessness. By circumscribing the geographic extent of the church to North Africa—and there, to an allegedly pure remnant at that—they in effect "love" only those whom they can see, thereby sundering the body of Christ. Augustine advises: "Let him not take care to love only that brother of whom he takes notice before his own eyes, for we do not see many brothers of ours, and yet, we are joined to them in the unity of the Spirit. . . . We are in one body, we have one Head in heaven."[53] Augustine has in mind the analogy of the human soul or spirit, which, as an immaterial and nonspatial substance, is present equally and fully to all parts of the human body at once. By limiting one's vision, one's love, geographically, one misunderstands spiritual substance generally and the Holy Spirit in particular, who is able to unite believers across great distances.

To limit one's love means to lose a grasp on who and what one truly is. Following a Stoic theory of vision, in which the eyes direct some form of ray outward toward the object of sight, Augustine seeks to show that the eyes are truly what they are meant to be, and know themselves as such, only as part of the larger communal body:

> Can it be that they [the eyes] do not know themselves in the love of the bodily structure? For, that you may know that they know themselves in the conjoining of love, when both are open, it is not permitted for the right eye to take notice of anything that the left one does not take notice of. Direct the ray of the right eye without the other if you can. They converge at the same time, they are directed at the same time. Their focusing is one; their locations are different.[54]

It is essential in this example that the diverse parts of the body not simply be joined physically or in some other external, worldly fashion—to that extent, they might as well be a corpse—but that they be animated by the Spirit and as such united in the love of God: "If, then, all who love God with you have one focusing with you, take no care that you are separated in place by the body; you have together fixed the sight of your heart on the light of truth."[55]

Augustine has shifted the visual metaphor from the sight of the eyes to the sight of the heart. But he has done so in a way that does not disparage or dismiss material creation but rather affirms its essential value as a part of God's creation. The Donatists, on Augustine's account, look only at what is visibly closest, at the brothers (and sisters) they can see. As a consequence, they lose what is in fact the closest and most inward, the Holy Spirit. By restricting their love and seeking to establish a separate, perfect church, they end up losing their ability to love altogether, and their faction is rendered a dead limb. Looking only at what one can see results in a loss of love and life. What one sees is then just a dead body or a dead part of one. But by "looking at" those brothers and sisters they cannot see, that is, by cultivating the humility necessary to remain in unity with the universal church, despite its countless flaws and imperfect members, they open themselves up to the Spirit's help for growing in a love that binds them to a greater living—spiritually and materially—body than they could have otherwise imagined. In this way, Augustine thinks, believers begin to learn to see the way God sees: spiritually, universally, and with mercy, looking creatively beyond the flaws of fallen human beings toward what they ought to become.

In *ep. Jo.* 6 Augustine makes quite clear that the Holy Spirit trains the eyes of believers to see God, that is, focuses their love on God, by focusing on the way in which God shows his love for human beings: through the incarnate Christ. Thus, in *ep. Jo.* 6.11–14, sections immediately following the one we just analyzed, Augustine asks how to determine whether the spirit that speaks of Christ is the Spirit of truth. Although we examined these sections at length in chapter 4, Augustine's answer is worth reiterating. He derives it from 1 Jn 4.2: "Every spirit that confesses that Jesus Christ has come in the flesh is of God." Why, Augustine asks, has Christ come in the flesh? He came in order to give human beings hope in the resurrection. Only as human could Christ die; only as human could he rise. But as always for Augustine, what matters is the *how* of the deed. Scripture is again the determinant. Citing Jn 15.13, "Greater love than this no one has than that he lay down his life for his friends,"[56] Augustine concludes that because Christ became incarnate out of love, those who do not love others in effect deny the incarnation and, by extension, their own salvation.[57] How does Augustine define love in this case? Specifically, the way they act vis-à-vis the Christian community illustrates what they really believe about Christ's incarnation. Augustine's Latin text of 1 Jn 4.3 and the Vulgate both contain language that gives him traction in this interpretation: "Every spirit ... who *dissolves* [*solvit*] Christ ... is not of God."[58] Augustine accordingly argues that those who create division in the church, which is the body of Christ, effectively deny the incarnation, through which Christ sought to draw human beings together.[59]

The Holy Spirit, according to Augustine, directs the inward eyes of faith outward toward the flesh of Christ, his cross and resurrection, in order to know the love of God. Christ's death and resurrection in the flesh mediate that love as a sacrifice for his friends, for fallen human beings, who are thereby joined by that love into Christ's communal body, where they await their full reintegration as human beings at the final resurrection. Working backward, we could put it as follows: according to Augustine, there is no Holy Spirit where there is no affirmation of love in the church community, where in that community there is no affirmation of and hope for the complete reintegration of the complete human being, soul and body, or where that faith and hope are not affirmed and guaranteed by Christ as the community's head in his own glorified humanity. In this relation between the Holy Spirit and the incarnate Christ, then, we see a very real affirmation of human beings in their full integrity both as individuals composed of souls and bodies and as beings who can flourish together only in a peaceful social environment.

What I mean by this Trinitarian relation between the Holy Spirit and the incarnate Christ can be made clearer, I think, by first identifying and assessing ambiguities in Augustine's Trinitarian ecclesiology and by then setting that ecclesiology into contrast with Hegel's more extreme pneumatological conception of community. The ambiguity is evident enough if we compare the aforementioned texts, in which Augustine describes the Holy Spirit as the soul of Christ's body the church, to *ep. Jo.* 10.3, where Augustine describes the unity of Christ with his church. At *ep. Jo.* 10.3 Augustine explicitly characterizes that unity as one of love, but surprisingly never mentions the Holy Spirit. The issue at stake is genuine faith and its relationship to love. Linking 1 Jn 5.1 and Gal 5.6, Augustine argues that every person who believes that Jesus is the Christ and loves him as the way to the Father is a true Christian. But Augustine is then stumped, rhetorically at least, by what follows in 1 Jn 5.2: "In this we know that we love the sons of God." In his interpretation of 1 Jn 5.1, he has established that those who love the Father, those who wish to be near to the Father, love the Son Jesus as the way to God the Father. But how, Augustine asks, do we get from love of the Son of God to love of the sons?

His answer is not unlike what we have seen before, but is for our purposes notable on account of the Spirit's absence: "What sons of God? The members of the Son of God. And by loving he [a believer] also himself becomes a member and by love comes to be situated in the structure of the Body of Christ, and there will be one Christ loving himself. For when the members love one another, the Body loves itself."[60] In what sounds very much like a description of the immateriality of the soul, Augustine proceeds to argue that "Love . . . cannot be split into parts."⁶¹ Thus, when one loves the members of Christ, one loves Christ, the Son of God. And if one loves the Son of God, then one loves the Father. Augustine here insists on the indissolubility of love between the church, Christ, and the Father without ever mentioning the Holy Spirit.⁶²

Lewis Ayres has pointed out in an article devoted to the Spirit as the soul of Christ's body that Augustine's fluid Trinitarian attribution makes it difficult to identify with any precision the respective roles of Christ and the Holy Spirit in the church. He suggests that Augustine's Nicene Trinitarian theology, which includes the mysterious unity of action between the three divine persons, is the reason why Augustine is able to move so easily between Christ and the Spirit in his homilies.⁶³ But this fluid Trinitarian attribution should not be misconstrued as theological incoherence. Rather, it is a component of an important rhetorical strategy on Augustine's part. Ayres puts this in question form: "how does the particular account of perichoresis that Augustine espouses allow *and intentionally prevent* clear separation of the work of Son and Spirit?"⁶⁴ Augustine thus strives to model his theological language—and in this process note that the language's very representational character is essential—on the mystery of the incarnation. In the incarnation God reveals himself as triune, makes himself speakable—hence the applicability of the image of the spoken word for the incarnation—but in so doing God shows how infinitely he exceeds the human capacity to grasp and describe the unity of the Godhead, on the one hand, and the unity of the divine and human in the person of Christ, on the other. In the latter especially, we see the transformative tension between Augustine's use of spoken linguistic imagery for the incarnate Christ and the breakdown of that same imagery when it comes to speaking of the simplicity and equality of the Son, Father, and Holy Spirit. Within the one person of Christ theological language is thus both legitimated, on the one hand, and transcended and transformed, on the other. What holds the two sides together is the proper orientation of love. Christologically we saw this especially in Augustine's discussion of the Holy Spirit's role in binding the divine Word to the man Jesus. Linguistically we see it at work in Augustine's theology of Pentecost, when the diversity of human languages is overcome in the one body of Christ, which speaks the one language of the heart.

Ayres accordingly draws out the implications of Augustine's use of soul imagery for the Holy Spirit. In the first place, he argues that any conception of Christian community aimed at conforming itself to the general Trinitarian dynamics of scripture needs to underscore the Spirit's role of witnessing to and perpetuating the saving work of Christ, such that "through a meditation on the *totus Christus* and the *corpus Christi*, Augustine draws us into a complex reflection on the interplay between Son and Spirit without succumbing to a ... narrative separation into two distinct 'ages.'"[65] Furthermore, Augustine's ecclesiological imagery needs to be understood in its Nicene context. The theological import of Augustine's description of the Holy Spirit as the soul of Christ's body accordingly lies not only in its capacity as a means of distinguishing between the Son and the Spirit, but also in its ability to lead believers deeper into the mystery of the Son and Spirit's inseparable operation.

It is perhaps helpful to contrast these features of Augustine's Trinitarian ecclesiology with those of Hegel's spiritual community. In that regard it is telling that Ayres highlights the "complex ... interplay between Son and Spirit" in Augustine's *totus Christus* over against a distinction between an "age of the Son" and an "age of the Spirit." We saw in the last chapter how Hegel offers one of the most radical articulations of the Joachimite tradition of Trinitarian "ages." Hegel's Trinitarian distinction into ages or kingdoms, set on a trajectory of growth toward divine self-realization, results in an eschatological Christian community that seems woefully unrealistic on account of its inability to make sense of a fundamental tension characterizing the present Christian experience of the world. On the one hand, the radical divine immanence of Hegel's spiritual kingdom cannot account for the positive Christian experience of transcendence, of the love of God that draws individuals and communities beyond themselves and arouses hope for full eschatological communion with God and each other. On the other hand, the fully immanent and realized character of Hegel's eschatology is unable to give voice to the experience of suffering, to the continued resistance of the fallen body and a fallen world, which testifies day in and day out to the fact that eschatological reintegration and communion have not yet been achieved. Hegel's Trinitarian paradigm and its attendant conception of spiritual community, in other words, seem unable to make sense of the Christian tension between eschatological optimism and a rather realistic anthropological and social pessimism.

In this regard Augustine's *totus Christus* possesses distinct theological advantages, which manifest themselves across two interconnected, yet distinct axes. First, the christological axis is marked by two essential elements: (1) the ascended Christ as head and (2) the church, his body composed of many members. Hegel, by sublating the christological moment of differentiation into the moment of Spirit, excises both of these elements from his concept of the community or *Gemeinde*. As we have seen, he thinks both elements, a distinct, glorified mediator in heaven and a sacrally demarcated church body, result in individual and social alienation. However, Augustine's understanding of the person of the whole Christ offers a more complex and comprehensive ecclesial vision than Hegel's juridical Catholicism without sacrificing as much theologically as the latter does in his concept of the spiritual community. Christ the mediator as head, the divine Word with his glorified humanity, anchors the church transcendently—such that it is not merely a human body—by beginning already to raise and transfigure believers spiritually and by guaranteeing their hope in complete restoration at the end of time. Simultaneously and inextricably linked to Christ's role as head is, furthermore, his spiritual presence in the body; by guaranteeing his members' eschatological hope, he is always and already with them in their present suffering. In the personal unity of the *totus Christus*, the one Christ transcendent to and immanent in his body gives voice to the suffering and ensures that their cries have been and are still heard through the certainty of their faith and hope in the resurrection from the dead and establishment of peace in the city of God.

Second, there is the Trinitarian axis, where we see the interplay of the Son and the Spirit. This relationship grounds and sustains a church as at once holy and unblemished and yet still in and open to the world. Hegel, in his historical and social thought, appears to have in his sights something like Augustine's distinction between the city of God and the city of humankind when he deconstructs what he considers to be the Catholic dichotomy between the sacred and the profane.[66] Yet Augustine's ecclesiology eludes any simple characterization. The church, as a sacrament of God's love for the world in the world, is distinctly visible and yet mysteriously transcends institutional bounds. As a jointly christological and pneumatological reality, the church on Augustine's account is neither a pure sect apart from the world nor so radically diluted into the broader society or identified with the state that it loses its distinctiveness altogether.[67]

This critical tension evidenced on the practical plane is paralleled on the theoretical level by the fact that scriptural and theological language are not, for Augustine, subsumed and completed by philosophical discourse, but rather anchor it objectively and resist its dominance in fundamental respects. John Cavadini and Lewis Ayres both point out how, for Augustine, scriptural language aims at interrupting thought without stifling it.[68] This is evidenced concretely inasmuch as the biblical imagery in his preaching aims to draw believers into the mysterious difference-in-unity of the Trinitarian persons. This means, though, that we encounter in Augustine a concept of mystery different from that of Hegel. Like the distinction between spiritual soul and material body, God remains, in Augustine's view, fundamentally other than humanity. Yet just as the reality of the soul manifests itself through the body, so God reveals himself through the incarnate Christ and then through the language of scripture that witnesses to Christ and shapes the church into his communal body. The images Augustine draws from scripture offer glimpses of the divine mystery, but never tell the whole story. The Christian life is defined by the continued struggle with language that offers only partial vision. Through this struggle, in which the particular—the body of scripture informing the communal body of Christ—is not consumed, but rather gradually reformed and transfigured, believers are led deeper into relationship with the triune God. These contrasts with Hegel form a helpful background for a more concrete examination of Augustine's understanding of divine mystery, the role the Holy Spirit plays therein, and the ways in which Augustine thinks that that mystery affirms and transfigures humankind through the communal linguistic practices of lament and praise.

SACRAMENTAL (TRANS)FIGURATION

There has been fruitful discussion of the mutually informative developments in Augustine's figurative exegesis of scripture and Christology that enable him to generate and employ the concept of the *totus Christus* in defense of the Catholic church during the Donatist controversy.[69] In Augustine's figurative exegesis, a tension is apparent: on the one hand, he shows a spiritualizing tendency, whereby temporal images of scripture share a likeness with eternal realities. This can be labeled the anagogic sense of figurative exegesis, which raises the soul upward from the temporal sign to the spiritual *res*.[70] On the other hand, he evidences a horizontal form of figurative exegesis, which moves from the sign to the thing signified along a temporal axis. In this mode of signification, which Cameron illuminatingly calls dramatic, a present or past sign points toward its future fulfillment.[71]

Just as the early Augustine prioritized the soul over the body, so his early figurative exegesis favored the anagogic sense. He never abandons the anagogic sense of scripture entirely, but just as he gradually comes to a greater appreciation for the embodied, historical character of the human person, so does he increasingly come to favor the dramatic sense of scripture. Furthermore, Cameron shows that within Augustine's dramatic exegesis, the bishop comes to emphasize a conjunctive relation of *signum* and *res*—in which the *res* is present in the sign, if not yet fully disclosed—over a disjunctive relation, in which the sign is expendable once the *res* is known.[72]

The shift toward a more dramatic understanding of figurative exegesis is linked to developments in Augustine's Christology. In his early works Christ serves largely as a teacher of virtue. But by 394 and his *Expositio Epistulae ad Galatas*, Augustine evidences a more complex understanding of Christ's role as mediator between God and humankind. There, Augustine follows, yet exceeds, Paul's example of integrating Old Testament narratives into Christian history by means of figurative exegesis. Using 1 Tm 2.5—where Paul writes that the mediator between God and humans is one, just as God is one—as warrant to refer the image of the "mediator" of the law in Gal 3.19 to Christ, rather than Moses, Augustine argues that Christ is mediator between the Old and New Testaments. This leads Augustine to stress the unity of salvation history, that is, the dramatic perspective, in and through the presence of Christ's eternal divinity. Then, connecting the notion of mediator to the hymn of kenosis in Phil 2, Augustine describes the "exchange" between weak humanity and the power of divinity in the one Christ.[73] The incarnate Christ now not only teaches or exemplifies virtue, but also imparts it to believers.

After 394 Augustine articulates this "exchange" especially with the help of the term *transfiguratio* and its related forms. In a general sense the word indicates a change in external form. But it was also used in a metaphorical sense whereby an individual or group of persons or things were represented by or borne under "the figure" of someone or something else.[74] In *en. Ps.* 32(2).2 (403), we see how this metaphorical sense of transfiguration helps Augustine bring together Christology, scriptural exegesis, soteriology, and ecclesiology:

> In his human will [Christ] embodied [*figuravit*] ours in advance, since he is our Head and we all belong to him as his members.... *Father*, he said, *if it is possible, let this cup pass*

from me. It was his human will speaking here, wanting something individual and private, as it were. But he wanted the rest of us to be right of heart, and whatever might be even slightly warped in us to be aligned with him who is always straight, and therefore he added, *Yet not what I will, but what you will be done, Father* (Mt 26:39).... Could [Christ], in the end, will anything other than what the Father willed?

They are one in godhead, so there can be no disparity of will. But in his manhood, he identified his members with himself [*ex persona hominis transfigurans in se suos*], just as he did when he said, *I was hungry, and you fed me* (Mt 25:35), and as he identified us with himself when he called from heaven to the rampaging Saul who was persecuting God's holy people, *Saul, Saul, why are you persecuting me?* (Acts 9:4).... So too in displaying the will proper to a human being he displayed your nature, and straightened you out. "See yourself reflected in me [*ecce vide... te in me*]," Christ says.[75]

Christ figuratively represents (*figuravit*) the bent human wills of all human beings in his own human will, drawing them (*trans...*) to himself (*in se*), and thereby reshaping their warped wills, that is, straightening and realigning them with that of God, from which Christ, qua Son, does not deviate. Augustine's concept of transfiguration rests upon an objective, ontological change wrought in humanity by the incarnation, a change which therefore stands as the very real precondition for any subjective appropriation by faith.[76]

Given the inextricable relationship between Augustine's Christology and his language theory, it is perhaps not entirely surprising that in *en. Ps.* 32(2).2 he understands Christ to effect this transfiguration through speech. It is, however, worth noting that in this passage the form of language is prayer to the Father. And this prayer is not just that of the historical Christ. Augustine understands Christ to be giving his followers an example of how to pray, but even more so the strength and the ability to follow his example of prayer. The typical Augustinian images of language and vision flow together. Augustine puts these words in Christ's mouth: *See yourself in me.*

By seeing themselves in Christ's humanity, believers attain deeper knowledge of themselves and God—he the creator, they his creatures.

Yet it is especially the language of prayer that Augustine thinks enables each believer to join him- or herself subjectively to Christ and thus begin the gradual conversion of will. If the incarnate Christ's prayer sets the objective condition for human transfiguration, the fact that it is a prayer that Christians are themselves to speak shows that Augustine has in no way neglected subjective spiritual appropriation. *Yet not what I will, but what you will be done, Father.* It is natural for fallen human beings to will their own private good, Augustine observes. Conversion of will is gradual, then, and Augustine suggests that prayer—indeed, repeated, continual prayer ("But when [selfishness] happens... think of God... and say...")—is an essential component of that transformative process.[77] What is more, Augustine indicates how this prayer to God cannot be separated theoretically or practically from care for the most basic needs of other human beings. Augustine's notion of the body of Christ thus eludes Hegel's critique of Catholicism, namely, that its practices of piety remain sundered from any true ethical transformation. For the same Christ who identifies human beings with himself (*transfigurans in se suos*) through his prayer to the Father identifies the hungry, sick, and homeless with himself in Augustine's interpretation of Mt 25.35–36.

In this way, Augustine illustrates how one begins the gradual advance of mind and heart toward the Trinitarian mystery. The fact that it is the incarnate Christ's prayer and that it is a prayer are both significant in this regard. Inherent in the form of a prayer, and even more in a prayer that Christ addresses explicitly to the Father, is the difference between Father and Son. That is, the Son can pray to the Father only if they are distinct.[78] At the same time, the transformative power of Christ's prayer rests in the unity of divine substance, and the consequent singleness of will, shared by the Father and the Son. His prayer is not a gift of grace to human beings if it is not a gift of God's very self which he himself is qua divine Logos.

For human beings, then, prayer enables them to join with Christ, who transfigures them into himself, who gradually straightens their bent wills and thereby joins them to the Father: "How can you ... be separated from God, when you now will what God wills?" Thus, by praying the prayer of Christ—the prayer by which Christ shows his difference from and unity with the Father—humans too are slowly drawn into the mystery of the divine Trinity. Yet it is telling that, on Augustine's account, the transfiguration of the human will is accompanied by a transfiguration of language; prayer is transformed into praise as the will is aligned with that of God.[79] This is not the radical identity with the divine that characterizes Hegel's account of the resurrection and transfiguration of believers. It is rather a unity that sustains a genuine relationship between God and humankind, a relationship already in evidence by the fact that Christ the Son himself prays to the Father during his passion. Hegel's paradigm of Trinitarian ages, in which the Son succeeds the Father, cannot account for Christ's prayer. Consequently, Augustine would likely maintain, it cannot accommodate the prayers of Christ's followers either.

For our purposes, *en. Ps.* 32(2).2 is an illuminating text. It helps establish the Christoformic character of Augustine's communal vision, a character that at once affirms believers' continued existence in a fallen world and yet begins, in and through that world, to draw them deeper into the Trinitarian mystery. This happens through prayer as a subjective means of joining oneself spiritually to the church's objective ground in Christ. But how does Augustine's vision differ from Hegel's, since the latter also identifies Christ as the objective foundation of the Christian community? A significant part of that difference lies in the role that Hegel reserves for the Spirit, as contrasted with Christ. In *en. Ps.* 32(2).2, discussed above, the Holy Spirit goes unmentioned. But other texts shed further light on Augustine's concept of Trinitarian mystery and its relation to the church as the body of Christ, and thus show more concretely the way in which Augustine's Trinitarian theology and ecclesiology can more adequately account for a broader range of Christian experience and practice, especially with regard to suffering and eschatological hope.

In *ep.* 55, written around 400, Augustine presents a relatively concrete explication of the term "sacrament" or "mystery." He distinguishes a sacrament from a mere memorial of a past event: "But there is a sacrament in a celebration when the commemoration of the event is carried out in such a way that it is understood also to signify something that must be received in a holy manner."[80] At issue is the sacramentality of Easter, the church's celebration of Christ's passion, death, and resurrection. Augustine argues that Easter indeed recalls a past event, but one that is still present in the sign as something for the believing subject to receive. Moreover, this reception is not purely mechanistic, for what is received is received in a holy manner. What, then, is the reality that is received at Easter? It is "a certain passage from death to life [that] is marked off as holy in that passion and resurrection of the Lord."[81] Augustine argues that the word Christians use for Easter, "pasch," derives not from the Greek term for suffering, *paschein*, as is often supposed, but from the Hebrew *pascha*, which means "passage" (*transitus* in Augustine's Latin). This distinction is important for our comparison with Hegel, especially when we recall his criticism of the martyrs. Augustine's understanding of the mystery of Christ, rightly understood, cannot issue in a glorification of suffering simply for suffering's sake. The Easter mystery entails not just the cross, but rather the passage from death to life.

In *ep.* 55 Augustine articulates further than in *en. Ps.* 32(2) the Trinitarian character of this transformation through his discussion of the paschal *transitus*. He is adamant that the resurrection—by which he means the resurrection of the body, the outer person—has not yet taken place. Hope remains for Augustine, as for Paul, an essential component of Christian life. What does Paul mean, then, when he says that believers have died with Christ (Rom 6.6) and that they have been raised with him up to heaven (Eph 2.6)? Augustine argues that "our present passage from death to life ... takes place through faith [and] is accomplished in the hope of the future resurrection and glory in the end *when this corruptible body*, that is, this flesh in which we now groan, *puts on incorruptibility and this mortal body puts on immortality*" (1 Cor 15:53).[82] The passage from death to life takes place now *inwardly* "through faith that leads to the remission of sins in the hope of eternal life for us who love God and the neighbor."[83]

Augustine situates the reception of the virtues of faith, hope, and love at baptism, when believers first die with Christ and rise with him in grace in the hope of complete reintegration at the end of time. Especially interesting here is Augustine's intense interaction with Paul and its Trinitarian implications. With faith, hope, and love believers have the firstfruits of the Spirit (Rom 8.23), but the resistance and corruption of their bodies cause them still to groan as they await the final resurrection from the dead. Groaning, as we have seen, seems to be a particularly apt pneumatic expression marking the travails of eschatological distention, of the tension between gradual inward renovation and a body that marches ever forward toward dissolution. That groaning is not a sign of otherworldly dualism, but rather of the unity of spirit and body. Quoting Rom 8.10–11, Augustine underscores the Holy Spirit's past operation in the resurrection of Christ and future operation in the resurrection of the members of Christ's ecclesial body. Those pneumatological passages from scripture in turn enable Augustine to draw a christological-ecclesiological conclusion: "The universal Church, then, which is now found on the pilgrimage of mortality, awaits at the end of the world what has already been revealed in the body of Christ, who is the firstborn from the dead, because his body, of which he is the head, is also none other than the Church."[84] The Spirit, in effecting and binding together the past and future transfiguration in one Christ, head and body, affirms the historical existence of believers while orienting and drawing them toward their eternal Trinitarian ground. Contrary to Hegel, who effectively denies the resurrection by identifying it with the community's spiritual appropriation, Augustine affirms the reality of the resurrection and the Holy Spirit's role in bringing it about.

This is in evidence when Augustine compares the present life of toil with the life of rest in heaven. Believers are now "living in exile in faith and hope, and what we are striving to attain by love is a certain holy and perpetual rest from all the toil of all our troubles."[85] Augustine shows here that the first two virtues characterize the present life of exile and will consequently pass away, while love is what remains and establishes continuity between the current striving and its end goal. Indeed, the continuity of love is further supported by Augustine's description of eschatological rest: "In that rest . . . there is not a lazy idleness, but a certain ineffable tranquility of leisurely action. After all, we shall in the end rest from the works of this life so that we rejoice in the action of the next life. . . . Such action is carried out by the praise of God without the labor of our limbs and the worry of cares."[86] According to Augustine, boredom is simply not a possibility in heaven. But for those not yet there, it takes creativity to begin to wrap one's mind around that "ineffable tranquility of leisurely action." The figurative reading of the Sabbath that Augustine uses to link the eschatological rest of those sanctified by the love of the Holy Spirit (Rom 5.5), on the one hand, and the creation account ending in the day of rest (Gen 1.31 and 2.2), on the other, suggests that only the grace of God offers the re-creative possibility of thinking and acting beyond the alternating miseries of toil and boredom that characterize this life.[87] Augustine readily claims that the human being—and he emphasizes the whole human being composed of soul and body—strives after rest. But boredom would be the ironic and fruitless result, the restlessness, of uncreatively seeking rest in that which cannot provide it, including material things or, most egregiously, one's own soul. These are created realities marked by flux. Any rest they could provide would be fleeting.[88] Thus, paradoxically perhaps—especially in the face of Hegel's critique of the unhappy consciousness in search of an unchanging beyond—only the God who is unchanging and eternal can grant the eternal rest with which one does not, indeed cannot, become bored, the eternally restful activity which keeps going while creatively and decisively breaking free of struggle, including the struggle to divert oneself from the reality of struggle.

Thus, according to Augustine, the very possibility of rest entails a structural asymmetry in the relationship between God and humankind. In *ep.* 55 Augustine describes this re-creative relation of grace in the pneumatological language of Rom 5.5. He links the Holy Spirit's present sanctifying work of love, which prepares believers for future eschatological rest, with the Sabbath rest ordained by God at the creation of the world:

> Because, then, *the love of God is poured out in our hearts through the Holy Spirit who has been given to us* (Rom 5:5), our sanctification is commemorated on the seventh day on which rest is commended to us. But because we cannot do good works unless helped by his gift … we shall not be able to rest after all our good works that we do in this life unless we have been made holy and perfect for eternity by his gift. Hence, scripture says of God himself that, after he had made *all things very good, he rested on the seventh day from all the works which he made* (Gn 1:31 and 2:2). For that day signified the future rest that he was going to give us human beings after our good works. After all, just as when we do good works, he by whose gift we do good works is said to work within us, so when we rest, he by whose gift we rest is said to rest.[89]

Augustine's figurative interpretation of the Sabbath underscores the gracious character of creation as an expression of divine love. However, the interpretation can convey this meaning only if the figure is not left behind in the interpretation, if a part of that creation itself continues to mediate that love.

In Augustine, then, Christ and the Spirit are at work in the world in a vastly different way from that which we find in Hegel. In the latter the Son is sublated and retained only as a moment of the broader reality of Spirit; correlatively, the representational modes of biblical and theological language are transfigured into the philosophical language of absolute Spirit. The less adequate imagery of scripture and the creeds is set aside once one has articulated their content in the rational language of philosophy. Or, translated back into the elements of the paschal mystery for the sake of comparison with Augustine, the cross as the moment of particularity, of creation's resistance to rational articulation through suffering and death, is overcome and left behind as the community rises to the knowledge that the God who was separate from them has died and now lives in them as the Spirit. The world, a necessary, but necessarily fleeting part of the spoken divine Word, has faded away in its otherness, because it is now understood. The major theological problem we detected in Hegel's Trinitarian paradigm, however, is that the eschatological immanence achieved by Spirit too radically delimits adequate Christian discourse to a philosophical narrative of universal rational self-actualization. The vicissitudes of history and those who suffer under its weight—all those who stand under the sign of the cross—become a part of the story of God's reconciliation with himself rather than with them. Once evil is explained as part of an all-encompassing philosophical system, the voices of those who cry out need no longer be heard. To make the experience of evil transparent to language and, more problematically, to language commensurate to rational self-comprehension—for that is the upshot of Hegel's use of not only linguistic, but oral linguistic imagery in his articulation of the Trinitarian logic at the root of all reality—is to lose a sense of those experiences as they really are.

Augustine's Trinitarian paradigm offers a different theological and communal vision. To be sure, it remains grounded in the language of scripture—hence, from Hegel's perspective, in the sphere of representation—but this is in many ways precisely the point. We saw above how Augustine's insistence on the Spirit's role in the goodness of creation goes hand in hand with the revelatory function of scripture in both the Old and New Testaments. Conversely, Augustine's effort to find God's love revealed in the whole of scripture is an affirmation of the goodness of creation. It is no surprise, then, that Hegel's linking of creation with a divine fall issues in an eschatological reconciliation that transcends scriptural language and thereby calls into question the ultimate value of the created world in his overarching spiritual vision. Yet Augustine's struggle to find the love of God manifest in and through the world is by no means a naive donning of rose-tinted glasses. His pneumatological references, we recall, are always ultimately christologically oriented. *Ep.* 55 bears this out. From his discussion of Sabbath rest as a pneumatically inspired adumbration of eschatological rest Augustine proceeds to survey other Old Testament prophecies of Christ's passion. This in turn leads him again to consider the full sacramentality of the Easter Pasch, namely, that it is a passage believers make in and through Christ. This *transitus* is marked by eschatological tension: "Consider," Augustine writes, "the most sacred three days of the crucified, buried, and risen Lord. Of these three the cross signifies what we are doing in the present life, but what the burial and resurrection signify we have only in faith and hope."[90] He insists that "it is the time of the cross."[91]

Building on Paul, Augustine fleshes out his claim: "As long, therefore, as our works strive to destroy the body of sin, as long as our exterior self is being corrupted in order that our interior self may be renewed from day to day, it is the time of the cross."[92] Whereas Hegel would diagnose in this text a classic example of the alienation that besets the unhappy consciousness—reconciliation in the heart but not in the world—Augustine would respond that what he is describing here is in fact the very process of reintegration through the sanctification of the Holy Spirit. That process is not at all a negation of the external world for the sake of the spirit, precisely because the renewal of the interior self takes place in and through the toil of the body. The cross is God's affirmation of the world as the expression of his love for it. But it is precisely here that we see concretely how Augustine differs from Hegel. For Hegel, the corruption of the external world, the moment of the Son, gives way to its assimilation into Spirit, which now knows itself in and through the world. But the God who is caught up explaining himself to himself through the world seems distracted from it and concerned, ultimately, with himself alone. This is different from the God who reaches out to the world in the cross and says, "I love you, broken world, and I will make you whole again." It is the latter that Augustine believes God is saying. Furthermore, Augustine is here articulating that divine love for the world in a Trinitarian way. In *ep.* 55 he continues:

> These [struggles of the present life] are, of course, also good works, but they are, nonetheless, still full of toil, though their

> reward is rest. But scripture says, *Rejoicing in hope* (Rom 12:12), in order that, when we think of our future rest, we may work at our labor with joy. The breadth of the cross in the transverse beam, to which the hands are nailed, symbolizes this joy. For we understand the works in the hands and the joy of the worker in the breadth, because sadness causes narrowness.[93]

The joy of hope anticipating the rest of the resurrection, which Augustine linked with the Holy Spirit a few paragraphs beforehand, is now shown to be present in the midst of the time of the cross. We see here the operation of Christ and the Holy Spirit in the church in a way that clearly acknowledges the reality of toil and suffering in the world and begins to transfigure it at the same time. The movement of grace brings joy through the creative broadening of horizons, as symbolized by the breadth of the transverse beam of the cross itself. If we think back to chapter 1, we could say we are nearer here to Luther's *simul* of death and life on the cross than to Hegel's punctuation between the death of Christ and the spiritual resurrection of the community.

Augustine goes on to interpret the sacramental meaning of the various dimensions of the cross. The last one he mentions is the depth of the cross buried in the ground, which "symbolizes the secret of the mystery [*secretum sacramenti*]."[94] The mystery Augustine has most proximately in mind is the mystery of the cross, especially those stages of the *transitus* that are still outstanding. But as Augustine makes clear a few paragraphs further in the letter, the mystery of Christ's passion has as its context the divine life of the Trinity, into which the Holy Spirit has already begun to lead believers even in this time of the cross: "Where there is rest, there is also sanctification. Hence, we have now received the pledge [of the Holy Spirit] in order that we may love and desire it. But *in the name of the Father and of the Son and of the Holy Spirit* (Mt 28:19) all are called to the rest of the next life to which we pass from this life, and this is what the Pasch signifies."[95]

Transfiguration of the Body: Lament and Praise

According to Augustine, believers are now in the time of the cross. It is a time of groaning or lament. In one sense, groaning does indeed indicate a condition of alienation—of the soul, ascended with Christ to heaven, from its corruptible body and of a church body from the surrounding world, in the Johannine sense of the word. But in another sense, as we have begun to see, believers are already united with the divine reality that the communal body signifies, albeit in a way that allows for growth through that very groaning. The church is united to God in love, but in a love that must grow and thus still hopes for its eschatological perfection. Augustine's notion of Christian community eludes both the simple label of alienation, on the one hand, and the myth of eschatological fulfillment, on the other. Because their business remains unfinished, Christians have reason to work lovingly, mercifully, and humbly not only within their community, but in the broader society around them. This is a function of Augustine's Trinitarian theology. To be sure, he endorses a stronger notion of the church as Christ's body than Hegel does. At the same time, though, the sacramentality of that body precisely as a suffering body and the charitable and pneumatological thrust of its growth (not just geographically or numerically, either) in and through that suffering ensure that no one can ever pin down the full range of the Holy Spirit's operation in the world.

Toward the end of discerning this sacramental growth or transfiguration, it is helpful to recall the elements of biblical lament with which we assessed Hegel's Trinitarian narrative. Lament entails a relatively autonomous subject who laments something to someone. Based on what we have seen thus far, we can safely say that for Augustine that definition holds, insofar as the members of Christ's body lament to God their continued struggle with concupiscence and the general unhappiness and insecurity of life in the hope of full reintegration and peace at the final resurrection. As we saw in the last chapter, Hegel's philosophy of Trinitarian moments or ages obviates the Christian language of lament by sublating the christological moment into that of Spirit, where the peace of God has been achieved in the full rational self-consciousness of the spiritual community.[96] Augustine's pro-Nicene Trinitarian theology, by contrast, legitimates and encourages the Christian practice of lament as a central means whereby the community of believers comes to know and love the triune God. This becomes clear when the respective roles of Christ and the Holy Spirit are identified in the practice of lament. However, just as we discovered Augustine's ability to apply the functions of the "soul" of the communal body either to Christ or to the Spirit depending upon rhetorical exigencies, so we find that he can also attribute lament to both Christ and the Spirit. Are there, nonetheless, certain distinctive features of each Trinitarian person in this practice?

The answer begins with some background regarding Augustine's christological reading of the Old Testament in general and the psalms in particular.[97] Christians had long understood the Old Testament as prophetic. With regard to the psalms, Hilary of Poitier articulates a general rule of patristic commentary: "All prophecy of the psalms must be applied to Christ."[98] Augustine's earliest *Enarrationes* evidence, furthermore, the application of an exegetical principle set forth by the Donatist commentator Tyconius, according to which the psalms refer prophetically either to Christ as head or to his body the church. This rule helps Augustine resolve the problem posed by an insistence on the universal christological reference of the psalms, on the one hand, and the textual witness of psalmic verses that seem inappropriate to Christ in his divinity, especially those that express deep human emotions and suffering, on the other.[99]

Augustine develops the principle further in a couple ways. Tyconius's concern is with the subject of the text, with whom or what it speaks about. In line with his practice of prosopological exegesis, however, Augustine is interested in the issue of scriptural voice, in who is speaking the psalmic verse.[100] Augustine's earliest psalm commentaries apply Tyconius's principle in an either-or fashion: either Christ the head or his body is speaking.[101] But the development of Augustine's incarnational paradigm, to use Cameron's term, leads to a gradual melding of the voices into one. Augustine comes to hear in the language of the psalms the *vox totius Christi*, the voice of the whole Christ.[102] As McCarthy writes: "Such an exchange of words, rooted in the divine Word's appropriation of human flesh, allows Augustine to emphasize the singularity of the psalms' subject. The 'I' who speaks in the psalms is always Christ, the 'person' in whom God has definitively joined with all humanity."[103]

Augustine thinks he stands on strong scriptural ground when he unites the voices of Christ and suffering humankind. In *ep.* 140, for example, he responds to a question posed by one Honoratus, a catechumen in Carthage, concerning the lament of Ps 21.2(22.1). Augustine devotes a good portion of the letter to an interpretation of Psalm 21(22) itself, but he integrates that exposition into a broader treatment of the letter's main theme: the grace of the New Testament. Because Christ cries out on the cross in the words of Ps 21.2(22.1), the text serves as an ideal resource for Augustine's Christian appropriation of Old Testament forms of religious language and worship practices.

When Christ cries out the words of the psalm, "God, my God, why have you abandoned me?" he indicates, according to Augustine, that the psalms find their full meaning in the message of grace proclaimed by the New Testament.[104] That grace assumes christological shape in Augustine's theology. Augustine attributes Ps 21.2(22.1) to Christ in *forma servi*, in his human weakness. Christ, the head, speaks this lament on behalf of his body, the church. The suffering of the members of Christ's body is very real, as is their sense of Godforsakenness, for, Augustine claims, God does *not* answer their prayers. That is, God does not answer their prayers with regard to temporal blessings. In this case, the blessing sought is a longer life, the postponement of an inevitable death. Augustine considers this a universal trait of fallen humanity, the fear of death (*timor mortis*) that affects even the noblest martyrs and other believers who nonetheless have faith in the resurrection: "So great a power does the sweet companionship [*dulce consortium*] of the flesh and soul have! *For no one ever hates his own flesh* (Eph 5:29), and for this reason the soul also does not want to leave its weakness even for a time, though it trusts that it will receive its flesh for eternity without weakness."[105] For Augustine, fallen humanity's fear of death evidences the unnatural character of death and the natural bond of love between the soul and the body. We can begin to understand the transformative christological character of lament for Augustine:

> In the cry, then, of this weakness of ours, which our head applied to himself, the psalmist says in this psalm, *God, my God, look at me; why have you abandoned me?* (Ps 22:2). He is, of course, abandoned in prayer insofar as he is not heard. Jesus applied this cry to himself, that is, the cry of his body, that is, of his Church, which was to be formed anew from the old man into the new man, that is, the cry of our weakness, to which the blessings of the Old Testament were going to be denied in order that it would learn to desire and to hope for the blessings of the New Testament.[106]

At first glance, it might appear as though Christ's love is world denying and, as such, rather cold: God denies pleas for help in this temporal life in order to turn the eyes of believers toward eternity. For Augustine, however, transformation and growth occur in the cry of lament itself. Augustine is able to account theologically for the depths of suffering in a fallen world and that world's transfiguration through the grace of God. To be sure, he says that God does not answer some prayers for temporal blessings. But precisely by legitimating and even encouraging the form in which those prayers are made to God—that of lament—Augustine does acknowledge the reality of evil and suffering in the world and provide a means of expressing the reality of that experience to God.

According to Augustine, Christ himself, through his lament on the cross, gives the suffering a voice and, in so doing, a means of transforming that suffering through the love that builds up the Christian community. The christological articulation of lament in *ep.* 140 could not be any further from the individualistic, world-denying monkishness that Hegel identifies with Catholicism. Weaving together bodily and marital imagery from scripture, Augustine shows how Christ establishes a relationship of love with his church and thereby makes possible a communal witness to the divine mystery revealed in Christ:

> Christ speaks these words [of lament] in the person of his body, which is the Church; he speaks these words in the person of the weakness of sinful flesh ... The bridegroom speaks these words in the person of his bride because he united her to himself in a certain way.... But *they will be two in one flesh, a great mystery*, the apostle says, *in Christ and in the Church* (Eph 5:31–32); *therefore they are no longer two, but one flesh* (Mt 19:6). If, then, there is one flesh, there is certainly also fittingly one voice.[107]

Like the soul that loves its body, so Christ binds to himself the community of believers as his corporate body. He gives the faithful a voice, a voice that is genuinely theirs in their humanity, but one that simultaneously has transcendent reference, precisely because it is Christ's gift. Paradoxically, on Augustine's account, the asymmetrical character of this gift—which Hegel fears results in alienation and an otherworldly religious orientation—drives believers into this world, urges them to listen to others in their suffering and therein to hear Christ. In *ep.* 140 Augustine makes it especially clear that, to see God, one must first have the humility to hear the divine Word in suffering humanity.[108] Augustine provides us in this letter with two of his favorite scriptural warrants for his theology of the *totus Christus*: Ps 21.2(22.1) and Acts 9.4. What is significant therein is that the divine mystery—Christoformic, incarnational, communal—is manifest in the cries of lamentation. God is present in a form of language that is born of the experience of evil and suffering, but that nevertheless sustains a relationship in difference by not identifying God and humankind as radically as Hegel does. Augustine's simultaneously this-worldly and transcendent orientation is seen in a question he asks in *ep.* 140: "Why, then, do we disdain to hear the voice of the body from the lips of the head?"[109]

In *en. Ps.* 30(2), possibly preached in 411, we find a vivid example of Augustine's sense of the transfigurative power of lamentation. As is common in his psalm commentary, Augustine begins here with an investigation into the possible meanings of the enigmatic psalm title: "To the end, a psalm for David himself, an ecstasy." With the assistance of Rom 10.4, "Christ is the end of the law," Augustine identifies the "end" of the psalm title with Christ, albeit with the qualification that "end" here means not finishing something but bringing it to perfection.

Proceeding to the term "ecstasy," Augustine notes that it is a Greek term meaning a state of being out of one's mind or "next to oneself." He points to two possible causes of such ecstasy: (1) fear or (2) an intense mystical experience such as Paul experienced.[110] But Augustine's next move is telling. He cites 2 Cor 5.13–14, "Whether we are beside ourselves, for God, or in our right mind, for you, the charity of Christ constrains us," and then provides a paraphrase for his congregation. Paul, Augustine insists, would have been acting uncharitably if he had concerned himself simply with contemplation of inexpressible divine mysteries while failing to carry out the more mundane task of serving those who were not yet prepared to contemplate heavenly realities. Augustine then points out that Paul, in accommodating himself to those who could not yet ascend to the heights of contemplation, was following Christ's example set forth in Phil 2.6–8, according to which the latter humbled himself and took the form of a slave (*forma servi*). Through his homiletic exegesis of the psalm—itself an act of love aimed at teaching the "little ones"—Augustine articulates his principle of "ascent" through humility, through charity forged in community with others in the body of Christ.

Based upon this incarnational foundation, Augustine turns then to consider the other possible reason for an ecstatic condition: fear. As divine, Christ himself did not fear death. But, Augustine argues, Christ humbly came in the flesh, speaking words born of human fear, in order to transfigure fearful humans into his body. Augustine views the depth of Christ's suffering, manifest in the latter's lament, as evidence of the reality of the incarnation. It is also evidence of the continued unity of humankind with its savior. Their voice is one, but this unity is not an assimilation tantamount to the silencing of human voices. Here we see one of the practical advantages of Augustine's application of the imagery of spoken language to the incarnation, but insistence that such imagery not be applied to the immanent Trinity. The unity of humanity and Christ in one voice—itself grounded in the personal unity of the divine and human in Christ—is in fact the basis upon which humans can cry out in the first place: so that they might speak in the words of Christ. Through Christ's initiative, through his sacramental words and example, human language and indeed the whole social body—one voice and one flesh—are transfigured according to the objective, incarnate form of love: "In him we too are Christ."[111]

Augustine links a property of the bond of love between Christ and his body, described elsewhere in relation to the Holy Spirit, with the transfiguration of believers. How, Augustine asks, can Christ, seated in heaven, claim that he is being persecuted by Paul? His answer: "The Head was crying out on behalf of the members, and the Head was transfiguring the members into himself. It is like the tongue speaking in the foot's name. It may happen that someone's foot is trodden on in a crowd, and it hurts: the tongue cries out, 'You're treading on me!' It does not say, 'You are treading on my foot'; it says it is being trodden on."[112] We have seen elsewhere how Augustine argues that the love (or the soul) within the body unites its members affectively across geographic distance, so that they learn to sense each other's suffering and pain. Here, though, we have a concrete example of how Augustine's ecclesial vision differs from that of Hegel. For both thinkers, the Spirit is a unifying and universalizing force. But only in Augustine are the individual members bound together in a genuinely *personal* unity with God in Christ.[113] In contrast to Hegel's fully immanent, rational Spirit, Augustine's ecclesiology of the *totus Christus* grounds the universal church to its transcendent, yet at the same time really incarnate head, whereby believers gain not just any voice to express their pain, but the sacramental example of Christ's own lament, to which they strive to conform their words of lament so that they may thus be gradually transfigured.

Next Augustine links his theology of the *totus Christus* to martyrdom in a way that establishes concretely the thoroughly communal context and shape of transformational witness to Christ. The unity of head and body in the whole Christ, Augustine argues, can help us understand what he means by the ecstasy of fear. Adducing the example of Peter, he reminds his hearers that even the greatest martyrs feared death:

> If the apostle Peter was so perfect that he willingly went where he did not want to (I mean he did not want to die, but he did want to win his crown), why wonder if there is some fear when the righteous suffer . . . ? Fear springs from human weakness, hope from the divine promise. Your fear is your own, your hope is God's gift in you. In your fear you know yourself better, so that once you are set free you may glorify him who made you. Let human weakness be afraid, then, for divine mercy does not desert us in our fear.
>
> So it is a frightened person who begins the psalm: *In you, O Lord, have I put my trust; let me not be shamed for ever.* He or she is both afraid and trustful, you see; and you see too that the fear is not devoid of hope. Even if there is some turmoil in the human heart, divine comfort has not left it alone.[114]

A frightened person is speaking, Augustine claims. Just a few lines later, he tells us that Christ speaks in the words of the psalmic prophet; "no," he then says, "I would dare go further and say simply, Christ is speaking."[115] Finally, after establishing the scriptural basis of the *totus Christus*, he declares that the church's voice is to be heard in Christ's words and vice versa.[116]

Only on account of the grace of Christ, who, as God's Word become expressible, speaks for suffering humankind, does Peter's martyrdom bear any semantic value. Otherwise Peter simply has fear, but no hope. What is more, only in the communal body of Christ is Peter's witness possible; only there does he find the bond of charity with Christ that gives him the hope and thus the ability to die for Christ, hence in Christ for others. Augustine has, then, in the first paragraphs of this homily, given us an example of transfiguration through lament. The world in itself, in its resistance to God, is acknowledged—*your fear is your own*—but it is at the same time being transfigured through the grace of Christ, which draws fearful individuals together into a community of love and hope. The whole community is grounded on the grace of Christ; it is otherwise inconceivable. It is bound together by the grace that empowers its members to love others, to teach the truth like Paul, even to die for them like Peter. Individuals are thereby being transfigured into something greater than they are on their own, for through the humble love of Christ, each member of the body comes to share in what the other members have—both their pain and their hope and joy—that is, each member starts to share again in the whole that is being remade, the whole Christ, a whole they had lost when they greedily tried to seize it for themselves rather than share it with others in God.[117]

One clear theological consequence of an ecclesiology in which Christ is head, then, is that those who witness to him are able to do so in their suffering and in their caring for others who suffer, just as Christ did and continues to do. Furthermore, in the body of Christ believers are linked together with voices from the past in the ongoing prayer of lament. Present believers are linked sacramentally with Paul, Peter, and all others who cry out. The laments of those who cry out are remembered and, indeed, made present when they are remembered in Christ, who cries out with them in the church's continued prayer of the psalms. In Augustine's concept of the *totus Christus*, then, space is opened for the witness of love to a world that still awaits the establishment of God's justice, but which in hope is empowered to work for that just society through humble self-sacrifice. Such witness, however, does not seem possible in the eschatological presence of Spirit in Hegel's *Gemeinde*, where humanity has attained consciousness of its divinity.[118] In Hegel's reading of history, the true witnesses to Spirit are those whose action helps establish the rational state, those who in making Spirit a reality often trampled many an innocent flower. And in the

Erinnerung of Hegel's spiritual community, the voices of witness that are not heard are those of the flowers who were trampled in the forward march of history.

Augustine's ability to ensure the transfigurative witness of lament rests, then, perhaps paradoxically, upon his theological insistence that

> Christ and the Church together are one person, but the Word and flesh do not form one nature [*Christus et ecclesia utrumque unus; sed Verbum et caro non utrumque unum*]. The Father and the Word together are one nature; but Christ and the Church together are one person, one perfect man growing towards his fullness *until we all meet in unity of faith, in knowledge of the Son of God, to form a perfect man, and attain to the mature stature of the fullness of Christ* (Eph 4:13). But until that meeting poverty is our lot, and our business here is still hard work and groaning. Thanks be to his mercy.[119]

We have seen how believers in Hegel's spiritual community—or at least those who have attained consciousness of what they are doing when they worship—have no need for such lamentation, because in their self-consciousness they claim divinity and answer their own prayers. For Augustine, however, it is not simply a matter of struggling with oneself in the formation of virtue. One must first learn how to speak the language of the incarnation in the humility of faith before one can ever hope for even a glimpse of the mysterious unity of the Father and his eternally begotten Word in the Holy Spirit. Augustine's groaning requires someone else who hears it and has the ability to answer. In the growth of the "one perfect man" toward his fullness, then, the creator is never collapsed into creation.

Note the distinction between the type of unity found between the Father and the Word, on the one hand, and that between the Word and humanity, on the other. One is a relationship of nature, the other of grace. In the latter regard, it is telling that Augustine can, in the same breath, admit that the human lot on earth is "hard work and groaning" and yet say, "Thanks be to his mercy." These are the words of someone who knows he is loved, who has experienced God's grace and thus has hope. Here again we witness the practical strength of Augustine's insistence on the linguistic inexhaustibility of the Trinitarian mystery. The distance between the divine Word and the spoken human word, whose unity is nevertheless preserved through love in the incarnation, is what enables language on account of the possibility of its sacramental transfiguration.

This is extremely important to keep in mind when thinking about the kind of unity we find in the *totus Christus*.[120] We can identify three inextricably related "layers" of the unity of love in Augustine's concept of the *totus Christus*: (1) the unity of God and humanity in the incarnate person of Christ; (2) the unity of human beings with one another through Christ; (3) a special unity with those who suffer.[121] Furthermore, we can discover, in various Augustinian texts, the work of the Holy Spirit at each of these layers. In so doing, we then also begin to grasp more deeply the distinction Augustine draws above between the unity of the divine persons according to nature and the unity of God and humankind by grace. In chapter 2 we explored how, during the Pelagian controversy, Augustine stresses the role of the Holy Spirit in the incarnation as the paradigmatic evidence of unmerited grace. With regard to the second layer of unity, several of the texts examined in this chapter have shown just how interrelated the incarnation of the divine Logos in the man Jesus and the formation of the communal body of the church are in Augustine's eyes.[122] Augustine indicates elsewhere—more explicitly, perhaps, than the examples we surveyed in chapter 4—the relationship between Pentecost and the *totus Christus*:

> At that time [Pentecost] a single person by receiving the Holy Spirit spoke in the tongues of all; today it is our unity which achieves the same thing—it speaks in all languages. And today it is still one person who speaks in all nations and all tongues, one man, Head and body, one person who is Christ and the

Church, a perfect man, he the bridegroom, she the bride. But, says scripture, *they will be two in one flesh* (Gn 2:24).[123]

Again we see that for Augustine the individual is (re-)formed, has her identity, outside herself. To receive the Holy Spirit is to be formed into something larger than oneself, into a community that takes the objective shape of Christ.

Like Paul, Augustine is fully aware that spiritual gifts, as gifts, cannot be grounds for self-exaltation.[124] At their root they all derive from the gift of God himself. Augustine insists in *Trin.* 15 that "all have the gift by which their special gifts are distributed to each, that is the Holy Spirit," and that "the gift of the Holy Spirit is nothing but the Holy Spirit."[125] And yet, by linking Eph 4.7 and Ps 68.18, which Augustine understands to refer, respectively, to Christ giving and receiving gifts, he concludes:

> [Christ] has given [the Holy Spirit] to men as the head to its members; he in turn of course received [the Holy Spirit] among men his members, the members on whose account he cried out from heaven, *Saul, Saul, why are you persecuting me* (Acts 9:4)?; the members of whom he said, *When you did it to one of the least of mine, you did it to me* (Mt 25:40). So this Christ both gave from heaven and received on earth.[126]

Once again Augustine is clear that the shape, as it were, of the giving of the Holy Spirit is Christoformic, communal, and particularly manifest in the human cry of dereliction and the love that seeks to comfort those who suffer.

Augustine accordingly speaks of the Holy Spirit's role in the groaning of believers as well. Indeed, we saw this already in chapter 4, in *ep. Jo.* 6.8. We need not revisit that text in detail, except to underscore a few important points. Augustine there links Rom 8.26–27, in which Paul speaks of the Spirit's unutterable groans, with Rom 5.5 and the love of God poured into human hearts by the Holy Spirit. Therefore, he concludes, "Love itself moans, love itself prays; against it he who gave it cannot close his ears. Be free of anxiety; let love ask, and God's ears are there. What you wish does not happen; but what is advantageous does happen."[127] We find here characteristics similar to those evidenced in the laments of the person of the whole Christ. The wayward reality of the created world is affirmed in its relative autonomy, inasmuch as the struggle with the selfish will is acknowledged by divine love itself, which enters into the depths of the individual's groaning. Yet at the same time, the Holy Spirit begins to transform that will by teaching trust in divine love's efficacy, in the promise that the prayer of love will be heard by the one who is love itself. Finally, this last point again underscores the gradual integration of the believer into the Trinitarian mystery, into the relation of love that gives itself yet does not ever diminish.

In *en. Ps.* 26(2).1, Augustine underscores the fundamental eschatological tension characterizing the Christian life and the special way in which the psalms graciously embody and thus give expression to that tension. In the singing of the psalm, Augustine suggests, the church remembers and participates in salvation history. The psalm, in itself and in its repeated recitation in the prayer life of the church, witnesses to the abundant measure of God's grace in creation and its continued preservation even in the midst of just toil: the psalm first comes about through God's initiative, through the inspiration of the Holy Spirit, and through its repeated singing, church members know that God dwells in them. But they learn this through the groaning taught to them by scripture, through the fact that scripture inspired by the Holy Spirit speaks words that are more properly their own than God's, but that could not be or be said without God's initiative or continued sustenance. Psalmic lament brings humans back to themselves—these words speak truthfully about the reality of human misery—but, even more, lament draws human beings beyond themselves into deeper relationship with God, who is with them in and through their groaning. Through the Holy Spirit, present in the church's groaning, believers therefore learn and experience who God is: God is merciful.[128]

Augustine also underscores how that mercy takes the communal form of Christ, for Christians have all been anointed (χριστός), like David once was, into the body of Christ: "This anointing will make us spiritually perfect in the life which is promised to us." Hence, the "psalm is the cry of one who longs for that life, who longs for that grace of God which will be perfected in us at the end."[129] Through the groaning of the Holy Spirit in the body of Christ, the God who created human beings makes known his continued presence in the midst of their suffering and grounds their hope for the fullness of the life to come.

Augustine offers further insight into the Holy Spirit's role in transformative lament in *en. Ps.* 93. After discussing the fairness of divine judgments and the future punishment of the proud, Augustine stops and asks the obvious question: But when? The world is full of evil people who enjoy all manner of good fortune while the upright groan in misery. "Does this upset you?" Augustine asks his congregation. He knows well that it does. Yet he repeats the question:

> Does it upset you? The psalm grieves with you, and asks questions with you, but not because it does not know. Rather does it ask with you the question to which it knows the answer, so that in it you may find what you did not know. Anyone who wants to console someone else acts like this: unless he grieves with the other, he cannot lift him up. First of all he grieves with him, and then he strengthens him with a consoling word.... So too the psalm, indeed the Spirit of God, though knowing everything, asks questions with you, as though putting your own thoughts into words.[130]

Augustine considers praying the psalms to be a means of training the affections. Here the divine mercy and consolation manifest in the psalm is not for God's benefit, but rather for those who wish to pray rightly. In the psalm, the Spirit teaches the believers the way to bring their questions before God, in order that they might be opened to his instruction.

This time of groaning is the time of instruction. Augustine's further exposition of Ps 93 shows that opening oneself to divine teaching entails paying attention to the economy of God's mercy, first through the patriarchs and prophets who foretold the coming of Christ, then through the incarnation of the divine Logos himself. Now, in the church spread throughout the nations, Christ remains present in the world: "[God] sent his only Son; and he sent the servants of his Son, and in those servants he sent the Son himself."[131] Christ's servants call sinners to humble themselves before God, a message that is incarnational in form and content.[132] It is a message aimed at those both in and outside the church, for the process of growth does not cease in this life. Augustine enumerates several interrelated steps: (1) the confession of sins; (2) the striving to grow in virtue, the main component of which is thanksgiving to God, who is the source of any good one is able to do; (3) finally, never judging oneself better than those who are less virtuous, "for [it is not as though] God's grace is ... used up on us, leaving none to reach those other folk."[133] Pride seeks to limit the scope of divine grace; hence it seeks to limit God. God is merciful; for Augustine, there is no God beyond this God of mercy.[134]

This is also the essential message of one of Augustine's most sustained pneumatological treatments, *s.* 71 on the unforgivable sin against the Holy Spirit. There Augustine admits that Mt 12.31–32 poses a confusing problem: "Whoever speaks a word against the Son of man will be forgiven; but whoever speaks against the Holy Spirit will not be forgiven. . . ." A cursory reading of Augustine's solution to the dilemma could be read, from our contemporary perspective, as simply another example of Catholic ecclesiocentrism. That reading goes something like this: the sin against the Holy Spirit is the resolute and final rejection of forgiveness offered by Christ through his Holy Spirit. Since Christ has given the Spirit to his church, definitive and ultimate rejection of unity with the Catholic church is tantamount to a rejection of the possibility of forgiveness and salvation. Hegel would certainly view this as evidence of the confinement of Spirit within the walls of the institutional church.

In basic outline, that is Augustine's argument.[135] We may be better served theologically, however, if we read *s.* 71 in light of his understanding of sacramentality. The main point of the sermon is divine mercy and love. The incarnation is an expression of God's grace—a point we have seen Augustine elsewhere link explicitly with the Holy Spirit.[136] What is clear here is that the Holy Spirit's presence in the church, the body of Christ, is a continuation of the Spirit's presence in Christ. Put another way, if we take seriously the incarnation of Christ, we must also take seriously (1) the embodied character of the community that is bound to Christ by that grace, as well as (2) the presence of the Spirit in that body formed by the same grace.

Augustine's investigation into the question "what is this word against the Holy Spirit?" leads him to realize that the answer can be found only in the Trinitarian mystery professed and believed by the Catholic church: the Father is properly called the origin or principle of the Son and the Spirit; the Son is eternally begotten of the Father; the Holy Spirit is properly "the communion of Father and Son"; what is distinctive to all three, Father, Son, and Spirit, is their equality as one God, not three. Augustine then expounds on the property of the Holy Spirit:

> So by what is common to them both the Father and the Son wished us to have communion both with them and among ourselves; by this gift which they both possess as one they wished to gather us together and make us one, that is to say, by the Holy Spirit who is God and the gift of God. By this gift we are reconciled to the godhead, and by this gift we enjoy the godhead.... Thus *charity has been poured into our hearts through the Holy Spirit which has been given to us* (Rom 5:5). And because it is by sins that we were barred from possession of those things that are really and truly good, charity has covered a multitude of sins.[137]

What is unique to the Holy Spirit, then, is that he is shared in common by the Father and the Son and that he draws human beings into (1) a community that begins (2) to share in common with God the life of love that the three divine persons share with each other. This communion with God is established through forgiveness, which has a communal shape. While proper to the Holy Spirit, it is a Trinitarian act: based on the Johannine Pentecost of Jn 20.22–23, Augustine argues that just as Christ casts out demons by the Spirit, so too does he forgive sins by the Holy Spirit. Faith in the incarnation is faith in the forgiveness of sins by the Holy Spirit. But Augustine is clear that this is not just a one-time booster shot. He distinguishes between initial rebirth and subsequent nourishment by the Spirit.[138] And at the eschaton, "perfect love or charity is the final, perfect gift of the Holy Spirit."[139] Augustine thus concludes that the unforgivable word spoken against the Holy Spirit is the word of a hardened, utterly unrepentant heart, a word that definitively denies to God who he is as God: mercy and love.[140]

Augustine is pushing his listeners to look beyond the body to the heart, since what really matters is how one loves. Here I want to push Augustine's image of the body even further—and I think there is warrant in the text for such a move—by suggesting that, at the level of the ecclesial body, we see how the Holy Spirit operates in ways that do not align perfectly with the bounds of the visible body. But what, then, of Augustine's frequent insistence in this sermon that forgiveness of sins can be had only in the one, true church? Augustine's shift from a spiritualist paradigm to an incarnational paradigm in his Christology reminds us that the visible, groaning body has been made a part of God's plan of salvation. The communal body itself, Christ's body the church, forms the way to the eschatological vision of Christ in *forma Dei* by tempering spiritual pride and cultivating humility as the means of ascent. In a particularly suggestive passage of *s. 71*, Augustine suggests how, in the lowliest members of the church body, one comes to an awareness of the presence of the Spirit, whose operation exceeds the bounds of human knowing:

> So those who are fully in the Church as little ones in Christ have this Spirit, but still being sensual and carnal they are not equipped to perceive that they have him, that is, to understand and know it. I mean, how could they be little ones in Christ unless they had been born again of the Holy Spirit? Nor should it strike you as odd that someone should have something and

be ignorant of what they have. To say nothing of the power of the Almighty and the unity of the unchangeable Trinity, who can easily grasp by knowledge what the soul is? And who doesn't have a soul?[141]

Augustine is arguing against Donatist separatism and elitism. This text seems aimed at the claim to have a perspicacious knowledge of the Spirit's presence and thus the temptation to look judgingly upon the "carnal," flawed members of the Catholic church. Augustine's argument rests on the conviction that human beings have some knowledge of the soul in other people.[142] But Augustine goes further by suggesting that even the nature of the soul, in its greatest depths, is slippery and difficult to grasp. How much more, then, does the mystery of the divine Trinity, with which believers are properly brought into communion by the Holy Spirit, exceed human cognitive abilities. And yet it is in the unity of the visible, groaning body of Christ, with its flawed, unworthy members, that Augustine thinks that human minds are not nullified in some obscurantist fashion, but rather fulfilled by the gift of love, which draws them beyond themselves into the knowledge of the Trinitarian mystery, that graciously gives itself to be known and loved by, yet at the same time always—even in the beatific vision—exceeds them.[143]

What our reading of *s.* 71 helps show us is the mutually informative relationship between the Son and the Holy Spirit in the present life of the church. This differs from what we have seen in Hegel. For Augustine, Spirit does not consume or sublate the christological moment of the particular. In Hegel's system, such an exacerbated pneumatology issues, practically, in the state effectively displacing the church as the body of Spirit and, theoretically, in philosophy's supplanting representational religion as its eschatological end. The major problem we discerned in such a pneumatology, however, was the loss of the Christian church's ability to witness to and identify with the continued suffering of the world. By contrast, Augustine's Trinitarian articulation offers us a theological grounding for the life of the church that enables that community to operate positively and constructively in the world while at the same time preserving enough distance from worldly structures that its critical biblical witness to the love of God and neighbor is not lost or compromised.

Social and Political Implications

The scope of this work allows only for a brief gesture toward the more practical social and political implications of Augustine's Trinitarian and ecclesiological visions. The views of a few interpreters will establish what is at stake. The work of Robert Markus, *Saeculum: History and Society in the Theology of St. Augustine*, has achieved the status of a classic in the secondary literature. Markus traces development in Augustine's theology of politics and history. From an early Eusebius-like glorification of the Christianized Roman Empire as a part of the divine plan of salvation, Augustine moved toward a more critical, theologically indifferent stance vis-à-vis any secular political institutions. On this reading, political institutions are necessary for the attainment of worldly goods. Insofar as Christians also value such finite goods as peace, security, and the other resources needed for survival in this world, they should not reject secular political institutions. Because all human societies fall short of divine justice, however, they must be regarded as neutral with regard to the plan of eternal salvation. In this age, when the church exists, quite rightly, as part of societies seeking the achievement of relative goods, no definitive theological interpretation of history, society, or political institutions can or should be made. Augustine, on Markus's reading, lays the groundwork for a neutral secular sphere in which Christians and non-Christians cooperate for the attainment of relative goods. What distinguishes Christians is their ultimate orientation or love, which governs the way they seek and use those finite things.

Rowan Williams, however, has sought to qualify what he sees as a privatizing and flattening tendency in Markus's account. That is, Markus aims to defend Augustine from accusations of Donatist-like otherworldliness, perfectionism, and separatism to such an extent that he, Markus, loses sight of the church's distinctiveness in Augustine's eyes. Williams, for his part, does not think Augustine really offers a systematic account of something like "church-state relations" in the *City of God*, but does believe that, alongside his often radical deconstruction of Roman religious and civic values, Augustine offers a constructive "scheme for reflecting on the nature of social virtue."[144] According to Williams, what Augustine does is show that classical society, grounded upon the love of praise and glory, is inherently not public, but rather individualistic and divisive at its core. Christianity, by contrast, offers the only truly public vision and common project by seeking to orient individuals toward the one truly common good, God himself. In the totality of Christ, there is a continuum between the order one strives to establish in one's soul and the order of the social sphere, and if called to do so, the Christian should extend the "private" discipline she exerts over herself and her family to the broader social sphere as well. Nevertheless, such a Christian who exercises political power always faces the dilemma of the duty to pursue the ends of justice and love in the world while never being able to identify any worldly structures or processes with those of the City of God, because the justice and love of any human society are always imperfect. This, Williams argues, evidences the surprising inversion Augustine has wrought: it is not Augustine who seeks to escape from the reality of human temporality, but those who set up some kind of sphere of human perfection insulated from the real marks of time, from groaning and death. Platonic ascent to the One, Donatist pretensions to a pure church, or Pelagian claims to perfectibility—these are worldviews that effectively deny the reality of death and thereby relinquish the most transfigurative of hopes, the hope in the God who is justice and love itself.[145]

Grace thus has important social and political implications, according to Augustine. The sacramentality of the church, the City of God—its outward, visible witness of love in the world—rests upon the perfect justice and love of its founder and ruler, the incarnate Christ, and his gift of the Spirit who forms imperfect human beings into Christ's body.[146] Human claims to justice or perfectibility only stand in the way of true service or worship of God. This is not Hegel's worship which consumes the other into oneself. Augustine makes clear in *civ. Dei* 10 that true worship or service is due only to the one God shared in common by all, not to any other intermediary (e.g., pure Donatist bishop) or to oneself (e.g., Platonist philosopher, Pelagian perfect saint). Indeed, worship itself is God's gift, itself Trinitarian and communal, as Augustine, blending pneumatological and christological references, shows us: "To this God we owe our service—what in Greek is called *latreia*.... For we are his temple, collectively and as individuals. For he condescends to dwell in the union of all and in each person."[147]

As God's gift of himself to human beings, true worship or service cannot be anything other than what God is. Thus Augustine insists: "Mercy is, in fact, the true sacrifice."[148] One with the love that unites the different members of the body of Christ together across the greatest distances, "the true sacrifice is offered in every act which is designed to unite us to God in a holy fellowship, every act, that is, which is directed to that final Good which makes possible our true felicity."[149] It encompasses sacrifices of the body and the soul. A Christoformic totality,

> the whole redeemed community ... is offered to God as a universal sacrifice, through the great Priest who offered himself in his suffering for us—so that we might be the body of so great a head—under "the form of a servant." For it was this form he offered, and in this form he was offered, because it is under this form that he is Mediator, in this form that he is the Priest, in this form that he is the Sacrifice. Thus the Apostle first exhorts us to offer our bodies as a living sacrifice ... not to be "con-formed" to this age but to be "re-formed" in newness of mind to prove what is the will of God ... because we ourselves are that whole sacrifice.[150]

Through the mediation of Christ, the body, even in its imperfection and groaning, begins to "prove what is the will of God" as

Augustine and a Catholic Church with Soul? 293

that toward which it strives. In the liturgical practice of that visible body, believers are reminded not of their divinity, but that they are a sacrificial community dependent always upon the love of God: "This is the sacrifice which the Church continually celebrates in the sacrament of the altar, a sacrament well-known to the faithful where it is shown to the Church that she herself is offered in the offering which she presents to God."[151]

In all that it does, the church, as the body of Christ, is a eucharistic body, striving ever to give thanks to God for the gift of his mercy. The City of God, for Augustine, is a penitential community, a community of confession. Forgiveness of sins through Christ is never just a private affair. Christ teaches the faithful how to confess their sins to God, and in so doing he teaches them how to build up his body.[152] But this is not the mechanistic and individualistic devotion Hegel finds in simple Catholic piety. In the *totus Christus*, one learns that forgiveness is a social phenomenon to which one must bring one's own voice: "Say it with all your heart, with faith and unwavering trust, say it with certainty of being heard: *Forgive us as we forgive*. What you imply is, 'Do not forgive us unless we forgive.'"[153] The community is formed through reconciliation with God and neighbor. It is thus formed around God's gift of himself in the Holy Spirit.[154]

The sacramental, eucharistic body of Christ is built up, furthermore, by the extension of mercy to those who suffer. Through his use of Mt 25.40, Augustine shows that one has not truly received Christ's grace unless one offers the same love toward all those in whom Christ dwells. Indeed, the extent of Christ's unity with the visibly suffering is universal in a way that eludes and exceeds the bounds of the visible church.[155] Especially telling is the way Augustine interprets Christ's double gift of the Holy Spirit not only as a manifestation of the double love commandment, but also as evidence of the practical priority of the love of neighbor as the means to the love of God:

> So while love of God is the great commandment that first has to be impressed on us, love of neighbor the second, one begins

all the same from the second in order to attain to the first: *For if you do not love the brother whom you can see, how will you be able to love God, whom you cannot see?* (1 Jn 4:20). And that's why, perhaps, in order to activate or mold us to the love of neighbor, it was while he was still visible on earth and very much neighbor to neighbors, that he gave the Holy Spirit by breathing in their faces; and then from this supreme charity which is in heaven, he sent the Holy Spirit from heaven. Receive the Holy Spirit on earth, and you love your brother; receive the Holy Spirit from heaven, and you love God. Christ gave it on earth, but what he gave is from heaven. The one who gave it, after all, is the one who came down from heaven.[156]

Through the gift of the Holy Spirit, believers are drawn into the unity of the whole Christ. By loving their visible neighbors with the help of the invisible Spirit, they love Christ who became their neighbor in *forma servi*. By loving their neighbors, then, they are led by the Spirit in and on Christ the way toward greater love of God.

The visible sacrament of the Eucharist, one with all acts of mercy, manifests and nourishes believers in the ongoing struggle to bind themselves to others in the body of Christ.[157] What is thereby manifest in the sacramental body is not the realization of one's own self-determination, but rather that who one is can be received, can be known, only in a community founded upon a love that always and forever exceeds finite knowing and loving. In this life this excess is met with groaning and lamentation. Yet through God's love that very groaning becomes the site and means of salvation inasmuch as it is conformed to Christ's own words of lament. And we can see in that process how, for Augustine, the Holy Spirit can be understood to bridge the gap between the expressibility of Christ in *forma servi*—an expressibility described by Augustine in terms of the spoken word—and the inexpressibility of the eternal Trinity *in se*—the logic of which, as we have seen throughout, Augustine refuses to articulate according to the dynamics of oral word production. Thus, the *unutterable* or *ineffable* groans that the Spirit (Rom 8.26) enables humans to make reflect not only Augustine's sense of the incomprehensible depths of evil and suffering in the world, but also, and indeed even more, the ineffable mystery of the triune God who reveals his mercy and love through the gift of that groaning.

Through the grace of Christ and the Spirit, those ineffable groans are being transfigured even now into joy and praise of God. In the *totus Christus*, unified by the one Holy Spirit, these groans, which are a form of confession, are distinct from, yet of a piece with, the other form of confession, the praise of God's glory: "But does this too not redound God's glory, when you confess your sins? Yes, indeed, it is very much part of the praise you give to God. Why is that? Because the more desperate was the patient's case, the more credit is due to the healer.... When we recognize our sins, we acknowledge God's glory."[158] In this praise of the triune God who exceeds all words, believers already have a foretaste of heaven, where they remain active, but no longer toil, where they gaze upon God, but their eyes never falter, where, as Augustine prays at the end of his *de Trinitate*, "there will be an end to these many things which we say and do not attain, and you [God] will remain one, yet all in all, and we shall say one thing praising you in unison, even ourselves being also made one in you."[159]

THE ECCLESIAL RESULT of Augustine's articulation of Trinitarian mystery is a theological notion of Christian community better equipped than Hegel's concept of spiritual community to address the reality of evil and suffering while at the same time cultivating an openness to transformative grace and deeper participation in God's triune life. We found this exemplified in Augustine's interpretations of the church's praying of the psalms. There Augustine discovers theological legitimation of lament as a form of Christian prayer and worship. Because, unlike Hegel, he retains Christ as head of the church whose own words are heard in the psalms, the suffering are at once given christological voice with which to express their pain and the objective transcendent form to which they are to conform their cries. Furthermore, through the gift of the Holy Spirit, they are given the grace whereby their striving toward that transcendent form is first possible. The groaning, suffering body—the visible body of Christ the church—is affirmed in its struggles, and that body and its cries of lament have become the very locus of grace and means of transformation. In that transformative process, the love of the Holy Spirit draws members of the church beyond themselves and the bounds of the discrete communal body through love of God and neighbor. Those who lament are thereby granted a foretaste of the eschatological community of the City of God, where the cries of the suffering body are transfigured into the songs of praise and thanksgiving to God. That praise, the flipside of the language of lament incompatible with the life of Hegel's spiritual community, is the ultimate expression of the perfection of relationships of humans with each other and with their creator. It is the most fitting form of discourse for the human community redeemed by and re-created in the image of that inexpressible font of perfect loving relationship: the mysterious triune God whom Christians shall then see face-to-face, but can never know so fully that their songs of praise ever cease.

CONCLUSION

There has been much talk of a renaissance of Trinitarian theology in recent decades, and this work has attempted to contribute to that conversation by retrieving the Trinitarian thought of Augustine of Hippo, who played a foundational and influential role in the theology and philosophy of the Latin West. What is more, this study has looked afresh at Augustine's theology of the Holy Spirit, that divine person deemed by some the orphan child of classical Trinitarian doctrine and judged especially deficient in Augustine's theology.

These negative assessments are frequently couched in historical narratives bearing, in one way or another, the conceptual marks of a defining thinker of the modern period: G. W. F. Hegel. Hegel saw himself as the great defender of Trinitarian doctrine against the rationalist philosophical and theological forces of his day. He argued, however, that the defensibility of the doctrine in the modern age required its philosophical reconstruction, a reconstruction that he did not think he arbitrarily imposed upon Christian doctrine, but that rather emerged of itself from that teaching. Hegel insisted that his philosophical Trinitarianism was not only in continuity with, but indeed the very fulfillment of, Christian Trinitarian doctrine and its implicit rationality.

Inherent to Hegel's Trinitarian paradigm, then, are both a critique of the apparent contradictions found in premodern Trinitarian doctrinal formulations and the claim to have preserved their content while overcoming any rational difficulties in form. This has rendered Hegel's thought attractive to theologians seeking to articulate Christianity's Trinitarian identity in a way more accessible to the modern mind. And the conceptual dynamics of Hegel's Trinitarian paradigm have indeed been and continue to be influential in Trinitarian theology.[1] In that way Hegelian thought, with its intrinsic and definitive historical claims, has also informed the narrative told by modern Trinitarian theologians concerning the development of the history of Trinitarian doctrine, including the formative period into which Augustine falls.

These historical narratives have tended to take one of two general forms: teleological or archaeological. Teleological narratives, such as those of F. C. Baur in the nineteenth century or the much more recent iteration we saw in Alan Olson, have discovered the fulfillment of biblical and premodern doctrines in their reconstruction according to post-Enlightenment categories of thought. For our purposes, Baur's account proved especially pertinent, because in it Augustine features prominently in an explicitly teleological Hegelian narrative of the history of Trinitarian doctrine. Baur argued that Augustine's alleged point of departure in the structure of human consciousness is an advance over earlier Trinitarian doctrine, but he, Baur, thought Augustine ultimately fell short by insisting upon a distinction between the divine and human minds. After Baur, further Idealist interpretations of *Trin.* in the nineteenth century tended to argue for a necessary movement from the Trinitarian structure of the human to the divine mind and accordingly cast the Augustinian Trinity along the lines of divine self-consciousness.

The accusation later leveled at Augustine's Trinitarian theology by some twentieth-century systematic theologians (e.g., Gunton, LaCugna) of an overly intellectual and individualistic focus appears to be informed by an Augustine read in light of thought systems under Idealist influence or in reaction to it, such as neo-scholasticism. With regard to the Holy Spirit in particular, Colin Gunton exemplifies the archaeological tendencies of the narratives told by such theologians: narratives of doctrinal fall from the golden age of biblical pneumatology and the consequent loss of that pneumatology's transcendent eschatological horizon and communal focus. However, recent patristic scholars (e.g., Barnes, Ayres, Cavadini) have stressed the need to read beyond the inward Trinitarian speculations of *Trin.* 8–15 in Augustine's works and without the hermeneutic constraints of Enlightenment and post-Enlightenment views of subjectivity. They thus strive to achieve a more comprehensive sense of Augustine's Trinitarian theology and its relation to his practical concerns with soteriology, ethics, ecclesiology, and history.

Against that background of the theological reception of Hegel and his influence upon the interpretation of classical Trinitarian doctrine, this book has heeded the call of the latter group of scholars and offered a reading of Augustine's doctrine of the Holy Spirit. The pneumatological comparison between Hegel and Augustine offered here has, accordingly, served several ends. First, in light of Hegel's strong influence upon Trinitarian theology and especially in light of his own claim to set forth a Trinitarian paradigm identical in content with the preceding tradition, it has been worthwhile to assess just how conceptually continuous his paradigm is with the longer "representational" doctrinal tradition. Importantly, the comparison has been theological, not philosophical. Nor has it been a purely historical attempt to establish any direct influence of Augustine upon Hegel. My concern with regard to Hegel has been rather with the possibility and consequences of appropriating him theologically. I have taken seriously the metaphysical implications of his philosophy, not only because I am convinced that the strong presence of religious language in his works cannot simply be wished away, but also because my question is whether Hegel offers conceptual resources for articulating what Christians believe and experience in their community and its worship.

For this reason a theologian like F. A. Staudenmaier merited several pages,[2] as a Catholic thinker who, in Hegel's immediate wake, grappled with the possibility of the latter's theological appropriation. Despite some initial optimism concerning the ability of Hegelian philosophy to revitalize Catholic teaching on the Holy Spirit, Staudenmaier soon found the obstacles to the appropriation of Hegel to be systemic and insuperable. At the level of fundamental

Trinitarian grammar, Staudenmaier argued, Hegel's radically inclusive, developmental Trinity reduces the world to divine fodder, a necessary means to the end of divine self-fulfillment. Any love that God has for the world in such a system is effectively an erotic self-love marked by a fundamental exploitation of creation.

Staudenmaier's analysis shows that, when it comes to the question of the possibility of theological appropriation, it is not enough to describe what Hegel says in his philosophy of religion simply on its own terms. The conceptual moves he makes need to be identified according to the type of Christianity they constitute. Toward that end his Trinitarian narrative must be compared with others—in this case, with a voice from that tradition he claims as his own lineage and which those who would appropriate him trust he is correcting and fulfilling. Figures from that tradition other than Augustine, such as Aquinas or Luther, could have served this purpose, but the fact that from Baur onward Augustine and Hegel have been viewed by scholars as conceptually similar or as part of the same Western tradition of interiority only gave me further reason to choose Augustine as the point of comparison. Thus I have tried to determine whether Hegel and Augustine are as similar as Baur or Hodgson has thought. If not, then perhaps the alleged similarity is rather a function of Hegelian Trinitarian grammar serving as the standard according to which members of the tradition are judged.

Consequently, Hegel's argumentation and categories have not set the terms of the comparison. Rather, I have organized my investigation of Hegel's thought around certain biblical and creedal theologoumena that play prominent roles in Augustine's Trinitarian theology. Yet this was not the unfair imposition of Augustinian thought categories upon Hegel that it might seem. All of these theologoumena appear in Hegel's mature work to a greater or lesser extent, and where I supplemented my analysis with material from his earlier period, mainly from *The Spirit of Christianity and Its Fate*, I did so only if that earlier material already bore the form of his later thought. What this enabled me to do was see how the fundamental dynamics of Hegel's Trinitarian paradigm, in which the christological moment of differentiation is transfigured into the all-encompassing moment of Spirit, results in the sublation of those theological images and indeed all Christian sacramental religious language in the universal rationality of philosophical discourse. That in turn helped me assess what elements of Christian worship and communal witness are lost in the adoption of Hegel's Trinitarian grammar.

This comparative method served the further, more constructive end of illustrating how Augustine's pneumatology has greater breadth than some twentieth-century commentators have given him credit for. Whereas Gunton accuses Augustine of having an impoverished pneumatology that is overly rational and individualistic, the contrasting of Augustine with Hegel showed that the latter's exacerbated pneumatology is far more radical in its identification of the divine and human minds than anything Augustine ever attempts in *Trin.* 8–15. Following the advice of Barnes and Ayres, moreover, we drew from a wider array of Augustinian sources in order to highlight the deep scriptural roots, communal focus, and transcendent eschatological horizon of his pneumatology above and beyond the inward mental speculation of the latter books of *De Trinitate*.

In addition to the three points of our comparison—Christ, Pentecostal witness, and the church—more surely could be done with such complex, prolific, and influential thinkers as Hegel and Augustine. The discussion of the church and its relation to Trinitarian theology could be extended, as suggested in chapter 6, to a more concrete exploration of the effect of different Trinitarian theologies upon the relationship between the church and the broader society, particularly civil and government institutions.[3] Tracing the civic implications of Trinitarian theology would then segue well into a comparison of Hegel's and Augustine's theologies of history. In the latter respect, it would be important to investigate in greater detail the role Joachim of Fiore played in transforming the Augustinian theology of history and how he thereby came to inform Hegel's views via the Radical Reformers and Württemberg Pietism. The issue of history leads naturally into eschatology and the question of the postponement of the eschaton or its intrahistorical realization. The topic of eschatology would include each thinker's view of time and eternity and the role the Spirit plays in the past, present, and future temporal modes with regard to the sacramental mediation of eschatological reality. Furthermore, it would entail characterizing and contrasting each thinker's position in relation to Christian apocalyptic. Finally, against the backdrop of these economically oriented pneumatological investigations, one could carry out a more contextualized comparison of Hegel's and Augustine's Trinitarian ontologies "in se" in terms of both knowledge and love.[4]

The present comparison has, nonetheless, brought us a good deal closer to understanding the differences between Hegel's and Augustine's Trinitarian paradigms. In spite of efforts to set the two thinkers in continuity, they each offer conceptual narratives operative according to such divergent grammars that, when it comes to the question of theological appropriation, one is compelled to choose between them. Hegel continues to dominate the landscape of contemporary Trinitarian theology. In this capacity, his philosophical reconstruction of central Christian doctrines sets the terms for the reception and critique of traditional Trinitarian articulations like that of Augustine. In response, the purpose of this work has been to bring Augustine's Trinitarian theology and pneumatology to bear on the challenge Hegel poses on two different fronts. On the one hand, I have sought to indicate that Hegel's theological sources lie in fact outside the tradition he claims to complete; on the other, I have undertaken a more direct thematic comparison with the conviction that Hegel's challenges are met through Augustine's robust, comprehensive Trinitarian theology and pneumatology, which, from the perspective of Christian narrative grammar, is more theologically adequate, rhetorically powerful, and existentially persuasive than Hegel's philosophy of Spirit.

In the light of modernity, Hegel tried valiantly and with great sophistication to account for the Trinitarian belief of Christians, to take seriously the implications of the incarnation and Christ's death on the cross, and to articulate the Spirit's presence in the Christian community and the church's constructive role in the modern state. Hegel insisted that the Christian God, precisely as the God who reveals himself as love, is knowable and describable, not just indirectly through his outward actions in history, but in his very essence. Decisive in that regard is Hegel's blurring, if not erasure, of the line between God and the world by incorporating oral linguistic imagery into his fundamental Trinitarian grammar. One side of that move is perhaps quite appealing: the Trinitarian God is rendered fully accessible—and that by means of God's identification with the most human of vulnerabilities, the awareness and experience of one's own mortality—because God is necessarily self-revealing, necessarily creative and incarnational, and as a result of that process, self-knowing and free.

But it is the other side of that move where, from a theological standpoint, problems crop up. The divine Word that is spoken, that creates and identifies with the world up to the point of death, also necessarily passes away as an external reality and is resurrected and transfigured in the minds of its hearers, who now understand it and therefore fully possess it as their own. In Trinitarian terms, the Son passes away as the Son and is risen as Spirit, now fully and immanently present in the community which knows itself as one with the divine, that is, as self-consciously rational and self-determining. The kingdom of God is then realized on earth in the modern state, where self-consciously rational human beings can actually be such, where, like the self-revealing and self-actualizing God, they can determine their own lives and actualize themselves. Such autonomy comes at a steep price, though, for any dialogical understanding of the God-world relation is flattened into a monologue of divine becoming, revelatory ultimately of nothing but God's love for himself. Depending upon how one looks at the result, either God or the world is lost. Lost, then, too are those voices born of particularity and difference, voices that paradoxically, perhaps, span the extremes of human experience and often strain rational explanation. They are the voices that, on the one hand, protest against any premature claim to eschatological fulfillment by viscerally expressing the continued reality of injustice, suffering, and death, and that joyfully praise God, on the other, for the goodness of his creation and hope for its re-creation on the basis of Christ's death and resurrection. Hegel's necessarily fleeting divine Word does not give voice to those who would lament the very real evil of the world or those who would give God praise and thanksgiving for the miracle of their existence and the gift of their salvation.

Augustine, by contrast, insists on the paradoxical character of any speech about God. The divine Trinity is essentially incomprehensible and indescribable, yet by grace God has made it possible for humans to say something about who he is. He has done this through the incarnation of his Word, whereby the divine enters into the realm of humanly cognizable and utterable signs. The tension between the divine Word's entry into human language and the inexhaustibility of the divine essence by any finite words or concepts is epitomized by Augustine's use of linguistic imagery when speaking about the person of Christ. Augustine applies imagery of the spoken word to the incarnation of the Logos, but not to the eternal generation of the Word. What holds the divine and the human together without ever erasing their difference is the love of the Holy Spirit. Thus theological language for Augustine is marked throughout by its Trinitarian character, hence its character as relational, as gracious, loving, and free. Augustine describes the work of the Holy Spirit in the divine works *ad extra*, from creation to the incarnation to the establishment of the church to eschatological renewal. The inwardly working Spirit invests external material and embodied creation with its value, a value grounded in the abundance of divine goodness and love.

Augustine's affirmation of the created world rests on a mutually informative, albeit ultimately mysterious relationship between the Son and the Holy Spirit. That mysterious Trinitarian relationship at once makes human language about God possible—through grace—and frustrates such speech inasmuch as the Trinity explodes finite linguistic bounds, hence inasmuch as it teaches the humility of faith in the light of divine mercy. It is here that Augustine's Trinitarian theology legitimates a wider scope of human language and experience than Hegelian conceptuality. For Augustine, the believer does not only meet God in the rarefied language of philosophic rationality, but also in the most unphilosophical of places, in the broken bodies of those who struggle and suffer, in the mixed body of believers still beset by temptation and sin, in those who witness to love with their bodies even unto death, and in the language born of these individual and communal experiences. There, according to Augustine, in those places notable for their philosophical inadequacy, indeed precisely on account of their inadequacy, believers can meet God. This greater breadth of potentially theological and salutary language is guaranteed by the fact that the divine Word does not necessarily pass over into Spirit, but remains in relation to the Spirit as a constant expression of love.

In that way Augustine understands both Christ and the Spirit to be operative in establishing the sacramentality of the church: the visible, embodied character of the church as an incarnate reality is respected and affirmed, but the church is at the same time drawn beyond itself in love toward other human beings and toward the Trinitarian mystery. The laments of those who suffer in the world are conformed through the grace of the Holy Spirit to Christ's objective example, to Christ's prayers of lamentation. The incarnate Christ thus forms, for Augustine, the way along which believers now journey, fired by the love of the Holy Spirit, who gives them already a foretaste of the joy and peace of the City of God in its eschatological completion. Already in this life, then, Christ and the Holy Spirit begin to transfigure the laments of Christ's body—transfigurable only in the reality of its human frailty—into thanksgiving and praise of God. Already in this life of very real suffering, then, Augustine believes that Christ and the Holy Spirit are drawing believers into mysterious communion with the one Trinitarian God of mercy and love.

NOTES

Introduction

1. Adolf von Harnack, *History of Dogma*, trans. Neil Buchanan, 7 vols. (New York: Dover, 1961), 4:111. On early Christians' awareness of pneumatology's unique dependence upon scripture, see Robert Wilken, "Is Pentecost a Peer of Easter? Scripture, Liturgy, and the Proprium of the Holy Spirit," in *Trinity, Time, and the Church: A Response to the Theology of Robert Jenson*, ed. Colin Gunton (Grand Rapids, MI: Eerdmans, 2000), 158–77.

2. See von Harnack, *History of Dogma*, 4:108–19.

3. This teleological approach to early Christian pneumatology in general is assumed by Alan M. Olson, *Hegel and the Spirit: Philosophy as Pneumatology* (Princeton, NJ: Princeton University Press, 1992), esp. 14–35, and John E. Smith, "Hegel's Reinterpretation of the Doctrine of Spirit and the Religious Community," in *Hegel and the Philosophy of Religion: The Wofford Symposium*, ed. Darrel E. Christensen (The Hague: Martinus Nijhoff, 1970), 157–77. More recently, an interpretation of Augustine that views Hegel as the corrective fulfillment of the former's theology of history is offered by Floy Doull and David Peddle, "Augustine and Hegel on the History of Rome," in *Augustine and History*, ed. Christopher T. Daley, John Doody, and Kim Paffenroth (Landham, MD: Lexington Books, 2008), 169–96.

4. See Doug Finn, "Hegel," in *The Oxford Guide to the Historical Reception of Augustine*, ed. Karla Pollman and Willemien Otten, 3 vols. (Oxford: Oxford University Press, 2013), 2:1106–10.

5. Ferdinand Christian Baur, *Die christliche Lehre von der Dreieinigkeit und Menschwerdung Gottes in ihrer geschichtlichen Entwicklung*, 3 vols. (Tübingen: C. F. Osiander, 1841–43), esp. 1:826–88.

6. Baur, *Die christliche Lehre*, 1:xix.

7. Baur, *Die christliche Lehre*, 1:iii.

8. Baur, *Die christliche Lehre*, 1:868.

9. Baur, *Die christliche Lehre*, 1:827. Augustine's pro-Nicene theological commitments prevent him from ever drawing together too closely, let alone identifying, the divine and human minds. This has been a point of contention in historical Augustinian scholarship. Olivier du Roy (*L'Intelligence de la foi en la Trinité selon Saint Augustin: Genèse de sa théologie Trinitaire jusqu'en 391* [Paris: Études Augustiniennes, 1966]) had argued that in his earliest works Augustine identifies the Holy Spirit with the human soul. However, in recent years Chad Tyler Gerber and Lewis Ayres have shown Du Roy to be mistaken on that point. See Chad Tyler Gerber, *The Spirit of Augustine's Early Theology: Contextualizing Augustine's Pneumatology* (Farnham, Surrey, England: Ashgate, 2012), esp. 57–122, and Lewis Ayres, *Augustine and the Trinity* (Cambridge: Cambridge University Press, 2010), esp. 13–41.

10. Baur, *Die christliche Lehre*, 1:829 and 836. By "mediating," Baur means between substantial and accidental differences. Roland Kany finds here a situation in which Baur's reading of Augustine loses sight of the latter's actual argument, in this case, what Augustine means by introducing the concept of relation in books 5–7. Baur, Kany claims, has abstracted the issue into a discussion of Aristotelian categories (*Augustins Trinitätsdenken: Bilanz, Kritik und Weiterführung der modernen Forschung zu "De trinitate"* [Tübingen: Mohr Siebeck, 2007], 313n1323).

11. Baur, *Die christliche Lehre*, 1:838.

12. For the essentiality of the distinctions between persons, see Baur, *Die christliche Lehre*, 1:839, 835. On the singularity of divine personhood, see Baur, *Die christliche Lehre*, 1:841–44. Baur credits Augustine with driving the traditional formulation of three persons in one God to the point of ultimate contradiction. But his questions as to why Augustine cannot speak of one divine person suggest that this would be the solution to the dilemma if thought along Hegelian rather than dualistic "Arian" lines.

13. Baur, *Die christliche Lehre*, 1:855.

14. Baur, *Die christliche Lehre*, 1:877.

15. Baur, *Die christliche Lehre*, 1:878.

16. Baur, *Die christliche Lehre*, 1:878n47: "Wie nahe Augustinus immer daran ist, die Trinitäts-Idee als das Wesen des Geistes zu begreifen, sich aber doch die Sache nie recht klar machen kann." The overarching category for the entire Trinitarian problematic is that of *Geist*.

17. Baur, *Die christliche Lehre*, 1:886.

18. Baur, *Die christliche Lehre*, 1:878–80, esp. 880n47.

19. Baur, *Die christliche Lehre*, 1:879n47.

20. *Civ. Dei* 11.24.
21. Baur, *Die christliche Lehre*, 1:880n47.
22. Baur, *Die christliche Lehre*, 1:865.
23. Baur, *Die christliche Lehre*, 1:880.
24. Baur, *Die christliche Lehre*, 1:xix.
25. Genealogically, Hegel's religious imagery and language implies certain theological commitments that cause his philosophy to deviate from Augustine and the Augustinian tradition. Cyril O'Regan has already pointed in this direction in *The Heterodox Hegel* (Albany, NY: SUNY Press, 1994), tracing out the "heterodox" mystical sources that determine the shape of Hegel's philosophy of religion. Following O'Regan, this monograph falls squarely into that line of Hegel interpretation which argues that one cannot make sense of his philosophy without taking account of the motley collection of religious influences upon it. Throughout our investigation, therefore, we will remain in conversation with other recent, theologically informed readings of Hegel, including those of Peter C. Hodgson (*Hegel and Christian Theology: A Reading of the "Lectures on the Philosophy of Religion"* [Oxford: Oxford University Press, 2005]), Alan M. Olson (*Hegel and the Spirit: Philosophy as Pneumatology* [Princeton: Princeton University Press, 1992]), and William Desmond (*Hegel's God: A Counterfeit Double?* [Aldershot: Ashgate, 2003]). However, the interpretation here will differ from those of Hodgson and Olson significantly. Against Hodgson, I argue that Augustine's Trinitarian theology is distinct from Hegel's philosophy of Spirit in fundamental ways. These differences point to deeper-seated discontinuities between Hegel's philosophy and the longer tradition of Trinitarian theology that he claims to fulfill. Hodgson tries to avert this difficulty by extending the boundaries of such categories as "tradition" and "orthodoxy," but his revisionist move cannot easily solve the dilemma posed by Hegel's insistence on a content identity between Christian theology and his philosophy. For his part, Alan Olson takes such content identity seriously, arguing two points rather ambitiously, albeit in an oversimplified way: (1) that Hegel's philosophy must be understood, at its core, as pneumatology, or religiously informed doctrine of Spirit, and (2) that, in fact, it is only with Hegel's concept of *Geist* that Christian Trinitarian theology achieves a rationally adequate teaching on the Holy Spirit. By driving a wedge between Augustine (as well as the subsequent Augustinian tradition, including Luther) and Hegel, however, I call into question Olson's reading of Hegel as the telos or goal of all prior Christian pneumatology.

The argument here thus falls much closer to that of Desmond, in whose view Hegel's philosophical God is a "counterfeit double" of the personal God of Judaism and Christianity. O'Regan and Desmond—the former more genealogically, the latter more systematically—both deny that Hegel's Spirit shares much, if anything, with the Christian God. Accordingly, both also argue that Hegel's philosophy cannot serve as a resource for constructive Christian theology. This book will make that point as well, but will make it, in contrast to O'Regan and Desmond, through a sustained comparison of Hegel and Augustine, so as to offer not simply a theological critique of the former but also a fresh perspective on the latter's Trinitarian theology, and to highlight its continued relevance to current theological and philosophical discussions on ethics, culture, and politics.

This project overlaps, in a negative sense, with the recent work of Hegel scholar Thomas Lewis (*Freedom and Tradition in Hegel* [Notre Dame, IN: University of Notre Dame Press, 2005] and *Religion, Modernity, and Politics in Hegel* [Oxford: Oxford University Press, 2011]). Like O'Regan and Desmond, Lewis seeks to distance Hegel's concept of Spirit from any Jewish or Christian notion of a transcendent personal God; however, Lewis's goal in so doing is expressly *not* to insulate a particular theological tradition from Hegel's allegedly corrupting influence. Rather, he attempts to situate Hegel's philosophy of religion into a strand of interpretation set forth by such scholars as Robert Pippin and Terry Pinkard, who argue for a greater continuity between Kant and Hegel than commentators historically have found. On this reading, Hegel's *Geist* is nothing but human self-consciousness, and what Lewis finds in Hegel's philosophy of religion, then, is a way to describe rationally what humans do at a more emotive level when they practice their faith. What is more, Lewis argues that Hegel's interpretation of religious faith and its relationship to philosophy and politics continues to offer a compelling account of the role religion can and does indeed play in modern liberal democracy. Lewis is careful in his scholarship; nonetheless, his desire to find in Hegel a means of conceiving the current relationship between religion and democracy leads him to an inadequate account of Hegel's philosophy of religion. Lewis cannot sufficiently account for the presence of overtly theological language in Hegel's philosophy, particularly that of nontraditional mystical provenance. Furthermore, his effort at retrieving Hegel for the contemporary discussion concerning liberal democracy and its handling of religion overlooks Hegel's very real sense of eschatological closure and the attendant supersession of religion practically by the modern state and theoretically by philosophy.

26. For Hegel's influence on contemporary Trinitarian theology, see Samuel M. Powell, *The Trinity in German Thought* (Cambridge: Cambridge University Press, 2001), and Martin Wendte, *Gottmenschliche Einheit bei Hegel: Eine logische und theologische Untersuchung* (Berlin: De Gruyter, 2007).

27. In addition to the article by Doull and Peddle mentioned above, other contemporary literature bringing Augustine and Hegel together explicitly includes Edward Booth, "Hegel's Conception of Self-Knowledge Seen in Conjunction with Augustine's," *Augustiniana* 30 (1980): 221–50; Marcello Caleo, "Sant' Agostino e Hegel a Confronto," *Sapienza: Rivista di Filosofia e di Teologia* 44, no. 1 (1991): 57–76; Enrico de Negri, "L'elaborazione hegeliana di temi agostiniani," *Revue internationale de Philosophie* 6, no. 1 (1952): 62–78; Massimo Donà, *Sull' Assoluto: Per una reinterpretazione dell idealismo hegeliano* (Turin: Einaudi, 1992), 105–56; Klaus Hedwig, "Trinität und Triplizität: Eine Untersuchung zur Methode der Augustinischen und Hegelschen Metaphysik" (PhD diss., University of Freiburg, 1968); Bernhard Lakebrink, "Hegel und Augustin vor dem Rätsel der Geschichte," in *Studien zur Metaphysik Hegels* (Freiburg: Verlag Rombach, 1969), 163–81.

28. *Nicaea and Its Legacy: An Approach to Fourth-Century Trinitarian Theology* (Oxford: Oxford University Press, 2004), 404–5.

29. Here I follow Roland Kany, "Typen und Tendenzen der De Trinitate-Forschung seit Ferdinand Christian Baur," in *Gott und sein Bild—Augustins "De Trinitate" im Spiegel gegenwärtiger Forschung*, ed. Johannes Brachtendorf (Paderborn: Ferdinand Schöningh, 2000), 13–28.

30. Theodor Gangauf, *Des heiligen Augustinus spekulative Lehre von Gott dem Dreieinigen: Ein wissenschaftlicher Nachweis der objektiven Begründetheit dieses christlichen Glaubensgegenstandes, aus den Schriften des genannten großen Kirchenlehrers gegen den unter dem Scheine der Wissenschaft dieses christliche Grunddogma bekämpfenden Unglauben zusammengestellt* (Augsburg: B. Schmid, 1865).

31. Wilhelm Dilthey, *Introduction to the Human Sciences: An Attempt to Lay a Foundation for the Study of Society and History*, trans. Ramon J. Betanzos (Detroit: Wayne State University Press, 1988), 231–39; Charles Taylor, *Sources of the Self: The Making of the Modern Identity* (Cambridge, MA: Harvard University Press, 1989); Wilhelm Windelband,

A History of Philosophy, trans. James A. Tufts (1901; repr., New York: Harper, 1958).

32. Kany, "Typen und Tendenzen," 14–15.
33. Kany, "Typen und Tendenzen," 15.
34. Kany, "Typen und Tendenzen," 15.
35. Kany, "Typen und Tendenzen," 16.
36. Colin Gunton, "God the Holy Spirit: Augustine and His Successors," in *Theology through the Theologians: Selected Essays, 1972–1995* (Edinburgh: T&T Clark, 1996), 124.
37. Karl Rahner, *The Trinity*, trans. Joseph Donceel (1970; repr., New York: Crossroad, 2003), 17–19.
38. Gunton, "God the Holy Spirit," 124–26.
39. See Denise Souches-Dagues, "Thinking *Logos* in Hegelianism," *Philosophical Forum* 31, nos. 3–4 (2000): 216–32; and John H. Smith, "Hegel: *Logos* as Spirit (*Geist*)," in *Dialogues between Faith and Reason: The Death and Return of God in Modern German Thought* (Ithaca, NY: Cornell University Press, 2011), 95–119.

Part I

WORD AND SPIRIT

1. Richard Kroner argues: "It is not difficult to recognize the link between the early theological speculation and Hegel's mature philosophy. What Hegel rejected in framing the Pantheism of Love, he never reaffirmed later on. He found a new logic, a new rationalism to solve the problem insoluble by the rationalism he had overcome in his earlier years" (introduction to Georg Wilhelm Friedrich Hegel, *Early Theological Writings*, trans. T. M. Knox, with an Introduction and Fragments trans. Richard Kroner [Chicago: University of Chicago Press, 1948], 12). For the development to which Kroner is alluding, one in which the dominant category alternates—(1) reason (Kantian); (2) love or divine life (under the influence of Hölderlin's identity theory); (3) reason (Hegelian *Vernunft* in contrast to *Verstand*)—see H. S. Harris, "Hegel's Intellectual Development to 1807," in *The Cambridge Companion Guide to Hegel*, ed. Frederick C. Beiser (Cambridge: Cambridge University Press, 1993), 25–51. Because sublation (*Aufhebung*), according to Hegel, does not destroy its objects, but rather negates them as unconnected, in that it elevates them into a larger spiritual whole, some commentators contend that love remains

present in the philosophical culmination of Spirit in Hegel's mature philosophy. In diverse ways, this seems to be the point of such works as Werner Schultz, "Die Bedeutung der Idee der Liebe für Hegels Philosophie," *Zeitschrift für deutsche Kulturphilosophie* 9 (1943): 217–38; Vinzenz Rüfner, "Die zentrale Bedeutung der Liebe für das Werden des Hegelschen Systems," in *Erkenntnis und Verantwortung: Festschrift für Theodor Litt*, ed. Josef Derbolav and Friedhelm Nicolin (Düsseldorf: Pädagogischer Verlag Schwann, 1960), 346–55; Alice Ormiston, *Love and Politics: Reinterpreting Hegel* (Albany, NY: SUNY Press, 2004); A. R. Bjerke, "Hegel and the Love of the Concept," *Heythrop Journal* 52, no. 1 (2011): 76–89; and Ferdinand Ulrich, "*Gnosis* und *Agape*: Ein Beitrag zum Verhältnis von Philosophie und Religion bei Hegel," *Kairos* 15 (1973): 280–310. Ulrich assumes too hastily that one can label Hegel's religious concept of love ἀγάπη without further qualification. In that regard, Schultz is better, though his identification of Hegelian love is limited by his dependence upon the taxonomy of Anders Nygren. For her part, Ormiston's focus is practical, but with little concern for the theological implications of Hegel's ethical and political thought. She does not adequately grasp the personal character of divine grace. My view comes closer to the interpretation set forth by Walter Kern, S.J., "Das Verhältnis von Erkenntnis und Liebe als philosophisches Grundproblem bei Hegel und Thomas von Aquin," *Scholastik* 34 (1959): 394–427. The governing category of Hegel's philosophical Trinitarianism remains knowledge rather than love in a way that cannot sufficiently account for the other as other.

Chapter 1
THE LOGIC OF CHRIST: HEGEL'S CHRISTOLOGY

1. O'Regan, *Heterodox Hegel*, 68 and elsewhere.
2. On Hegel's interpretation of the Delphic injunction, see *PR* §343 (Nisbet, 372–73) and *Enc.* §377 *Zusatze* (hereafter *Zu.*) (*Mind*, 1–2).
3. *LPR* (1824) 3:192–94.
4. *LPR* (1827) 3:275–90. See also *LPR* (1831) 3:274n67: "According to the first [determination of the idea as divine self-revelation], God is [present] for finite spirit purely and solely as thinking. This is the theoretical consciousness in which the thinking subject has an attitude of full composure and is not yet posited in this relationship itself, is not yet posited in the process [of reconciliation], but remains in the wholly undisturbed

calm of thinking spirit. Here God is thought for thinking spirit, the latter's thought consisting in the simple conclusion that God brings himself into harmony with himself, is immediately present to himself, by means of his differentiation—which, however, is still [found] here in the form of pure ideality and has not yet reached the form of externality. This is the first relationship, which is only for the thinking subject, and is occupied only with pure content. This is *the kingdom of the Father.*"

5. In addition to the relevant chapters in works on Hegel's philosophy of religion as a whole, a number of works focus explicitly on his Christology. In particular see Emilio Brito, *La christologie de Hegel:* Verbum Crucis, trans. B. Pottier (Paris: Beauchesne, 1983). But see also Emilio Brito, *Hegel et la tâche actuelle de la christologie*, trans. Th. Dejond (Paris: Lethielleux, 1979); Hayo Gerdes, *Das Christusbild Søren Kierkegaards, verglichen mit der Christologie Hegels und Schleiermachers* (Düsseldorf: E. Diederichs, 1960); Hans Küng, *The Incarnation of God: An Introduction to Hegel's Theological Thought as a Prolegomena to a Future Christology*, trans. J. R. Stephenson (New York: Crossroad, 1987); Wendte, *Gottmenschliche Einheit bei Hegel*; James Yerkes, *The Christology of Hegel* (Missoula, MT: Scholars Press, 1978; Albany, NY: SUNY Press, 1983).

6. *PS* §770 (Miller, 465).

7. See James E. Griffiss, "Hegel's *Logos* Christology," in Lux in lumine: *Essays to Honor W. Norman Pittinger*, ed. Richard A. Norris (New York: Seabury Press, 1966), 80–92.

8. *Science of Logic*, 825.

9. Daniel J. Cook, *Language in the Philosophy of Hegel* (The Hague: Mouton, 1973), 125.

10. *PS* §770 (Miller, 465); italics mine.

11. *LPR* (1827) 3:276.

12. *LPR* (ms) 3:86. Augustine ponders the ambiguous attribution of the title "love" to both the Holy Spirit and the Trinity as a whole at *Trin.* 15.17.27.

13. *LPR* (ms) 3:86.

14. *LPR* (1824) 3:195; italics and first set of square brackets mine.

15. *LPR* (1827) 3:276.

16. "God is the beginning, he acts in this way; but he is likewise simply the end, the totality, and it is as totality that God is the Spirit. Merely as the Father, God is not yet the truth. . . . Rather he is both beginning and end; he is his own presupposition . . . he is the eternal process" (*LPR* [1831] 3:284n93).

17. *LPR* (1827) 1:176.
18. *LPR* (ms) 3:86.
19. *LPR* (ms) 3:87, including n. 79; (1827) 3:290–94.
20. *LPR* (1827) 3:293; first and third italics mine.
21. *LPR* (1827) 3:293.
22. *LPR* (1827) 3:293.
23. Hodgson, *Hegel and Christian Theology*, 142–43.
24. O'Regan, *Heterodox Hegel*, 146–47.
25. *LPR* (1827) 3:306–7.
26. *LPR* (1827) 3:292.
27. *LPR* (1827) 3:293.
28. *LPR* (1827) 3:295–300.
29. *Trin.* 12.7.
30. *LPR* (ms) 3:100.
31. *LPR* (ms) 3:101.
32. *LPR* (ms) 3:102–3. Cf. Immanuel Kant, *Religion within the Boundaries of Mere Reason, and Other Writings*, trans. and ed. Allen Wood and George di Giovanni, Cambridge Texts in the History of Philosophy (Cambridge: Cambridge University Press, 1998), 58.
33. *LPR* (1827) 3:301.
34. *LPR* (1827) 3:297–300.
35. *LPR* (ms) 3:106; (1827) 3:302.
36. *LPR* (1824) 3:221.
37. *LPH*, 325–26.
38. E.g., *LPR* (ms) 3:146–50.
39. "For the appearance of God art provides to the contemplative consciousness the special presence of an actual individual shape, a concrete picture too of the external features of the events in which Christ's birth, life and sufferings, death, Resurrection, and Ascension to the right hand of God are displayed, so that, in general the actual appearance of God, which has passed away, is repeatedly and perpetually renewed in art alone" (*Aes.*, 535).
40. *Aes.*, 540.
41. *Aes.*, 541.
42. *Aes.*, 539.
43. *Aes.*, 533.
44. *Aes.*, 534–39.
45. *Aes.*, 536.
46. *Aes.*, 541.
47. *Aes.*, 536.

48. *Aes.*, 541.

49. "In such a beautiful way maternal love, the picture as it were of the Spirit, enters romantic art in place of the Spirit itself because only in the form of feeling is the Spirit made prehensible by art, and the feeling of the unity between the individual and God is present in the most original, real, and living way only in the Madonna's maternal love. This love must enter art necessarily if, in the portrayal of this sphere, the Ideal, the affirmative satisfied reconciliation is not to be lacking" (*Aes.*, 542).

50. *Aes.*, 542.

51. *Aes.*, 542.

52. Mary has not suffered "the infinite battle against sins, or . . . the agony and pain brought about by the self" (*Aes.*, 542).

53. *Aes.*, 540.

54. *Aes.*, 540.

55. *PS* §787 (Miller, 478).

56. *Aes.*, 542–43.

57. See *ETW*, 274n97, where the editor finds Hegel's exegesis "dubious and perplexing."

58. *ETW*, 274.

59. *ETW*, 274–75; square brackets mine.

60. *ETW*, 276.

61. *LPH*, 328.

62. Brito, *La christologie de Hegel*, 353.

63. *ETW*, 277–78.

64. *LPH*, 327–28; *LPR* (1827) 3:318–21.

65. *ETW*, 285.

66. *ETW*, 282–83, 287–92.

67. *LPH*, 327.

68. *LPH*, 327; *LPR* (1827) 3:319.

69. *LPH*, 328; *LPR* (1827) 3:216; cf. Brito, *La christologie de Hegel*, 352–53.

70. *Enc.* §459; §464 *Zu*.

71. Brito, *La christologie de Hegel*, 353.

72. *ETW*, 276; square brackets mine.

73. *Enc.* §350; Brito, *La christologie de Hegel*, 427.

74. Brito, *La christologie de Hegel*, 427–28.

75. Hodgson, *Hegel and Christian Theology*, 173–74; O'Regan, *Heterodox Hegel*, 212–13.

76. *LPR* (Strauss 1831) 3:370.
77. *Enc.* §§90–91; cf. Brito, *La christologie de Hegel*, 428.
78. Brito, *La christologie de Hegel*, 428–29; "This is . . . to posit God's negation; in death the moment of negation is envisaged" (*LPR* [1824] 3:219).
79. *LPR* (Strauss 1831) 3:370; "what it means is . . . that God has died, that God himself is dead" (*LPR* [1824] 3:219).
80. *Enc.* §376; Brito, *La christologie de Hegel*, 430.
81. *LPR* (1827) 3:326.
82. *LPR* (1824) 3:220.
83. *LPR* (1824) 3:220.
84. *LPR* (Strauss 1831) 3:370.
85. At the heart of the inclusive Trinity, that is. Because the moment of the Father remains abstract, one cannot say that Hegel integrates the cross into the immanent Trinity.
86. *LPR* (Strauss 1831) 3:370.
87. Benedetto Croce, *What Is Living and What Is Dead in Hegel's Philosophy*, trans. Douglas Ainslee (New York: Russell and Russell, 1969), 59; italics original.
88. "The individual may well be treated unjustly; but this is a matter of indifference to world history, which uses individuals only as instruments to further its own progress" (*Reason*, 65).
89. O'Regan, *Heterodox Hegel*, 317. On the character of Hegel's theodicy, see Pierre Chételat, "Hegel's Philosophy of World History as Theodicy: On Evil and Freedom," in *Hegel and History*, ed. Will Dudley (Albany, NY: SUNY Press, 2009), 215–30; Vittorio Hösle, "Theodicy Strategies in Leibniz, Hegel, Jonas," *Philotheos* 5 (2005): 68–86; Sean J. McGrath, "Boehme, Hegel, Schelling, and the Hermetic Theology of Evil," *Philosophy & Theology* 18, no. 2 (2006): 257–86. For further discussion of the problems with Hegel's theodicy, see Part III below, especially the literature mentioned at chapter 6, n. 118.
90. "A mighty figure must trample many an innocent flower underfoot, and destroy much that lies in its path" (*Reason*, 89).
91. E.g., *civ. Dei* 19 and 22.22.
92. *Civ. Dei* 13.11.
93. See esp. Brito, *La christologie de Hegel*, 431n539 and the literature mentioned there. More recently, O'Regan, *Heterodox Hegel*, 209–31.
94. Werner Schultz, "Die Transformierung der *theologia crucis* bei Hegel und Schleiermacher," in *Theologie und Wirklichkeit: Ausgewählte*

Aufsätze von Werner Schultz, aus Anlass seines 75. Geburtstages mit einem Geleitwort, ed. Hans-Georg Pust (Kiel: Lutherische Verlagsgesellschaft, 1969), 77–79.

95. Cf. *LPR* (1827) 3:315–16.

96. E.g., Stephen Houlgate, "Religion, Morality and Forgiveness in Hegel's Philosophy," in *Philosophy and Religion in German Idealism*, ed. William Desmond, Ernst Otto-Onnasch, Paul Cruysberghs (Dordrecht: Kluwer Academic, 2004), 81–110. Houlgate points out that for Hegel this gift of forgiveness is not given by a personal God.

97. *LPR* (1827) 3:322.

98. O'Regan, *Heterodox Hegel*, 214.

99. Hodgson, *Hegel and Christian Theology*, 175.

100. *LPR* (1827) 3:326. See the even stronger evidence of the transfer of the resurrection to the spiritual community in *LPR* (1827?) 3:330n220, if we can assume that text's authenticity: "This conversion, which already begins with the resurrection and ascension, is what we call the origin of the community."

101. It appears that Hegel is here exploiting John's own ambiguity between Christ's death and ascension.

102. *LPR* (Strauss 1831) 3:369: "It is always faith resting on the witness of the Holy Spirit that gives to the appearance of Christ its full meaning."

103. See *Logic*, 153–56, 160–63.

104. Brito, *La christologie de Hegel*, 460.

105. Brito, *La christologie de Hegel*, 462.

106. Brito, *La christologie de Hegel*, 463.

107. *LPR* (1824) 3:220.

108. *LPR* (1827) 3:327–28.

109. For this concept with regard to Hegel, see Daniel P. Jamros, S.J., *The Human Shape of God: Religion in Hegel's Phenomenology of Spirit* (New York: Paragon House, 1994), 217.

110. *LPR* (ms) 3:128.

111. *LPR* (1827) 3:332.

112. O'Regan, *Heterodox Hegel*, 241.

113. *LPR* (ms) 3:140.

114. *LPR* (1827) 3:331.

115. Brito, *La christologie de Hegel*, 463.

116. *PS* §784 (Miller, 475). The German is taken from G. W. F. Hegel, *Phänomenologie des Geistes*, ed. Johannes Hoffmeister (Hamburg: Meiner, 1952), 545.

117. *LPR* (Fragments) 3:387.
118. *LPR* (ms) 3:137–38.
119. *LPR* (ms) 3:130–31.
120. *LPR* (ms) 3:138.

Chapter 2
THE RHETORIC OF CHRIST: AUGUSTINE'S CHRISTOLOGY

1. Cited in *Trin.* 15.2 (WSA I/5:395). Where possible, scriptural texts are quoted from the referenced English translation of Augustine's work, in order to adhere as closely as possible to the wording that he was reading in his Old Latin version. In the event that Augustine alludes to, but does not directly cite a scriptural text, a modern translation from the New Revised Standard Version (NRSV) has sometimes been adduced, as long as its wording does not distort the interpretation of Augustine's thought.
2. *Trin.* 15.2 (WSA I/5:395–96).
3. *Trin.* 15.44 (WSA I/5:429).
4. Cited in *Trin.* 15.14 (WSA I/5:405).
5. Cited in *Trin.* 1.17 (WSA I/5:77).
6. John Cavadini, "Pride," in *Augustine through the Ages*, 679.
7. Cited at *Trin.* 14.25 (WSA I/5:390).
8. *Trin.* 15.14.
9. *Trin.* 15.2, where Augustine adduces Is 7.9 (LXX), "Unless you believe you shall not understand."
10. *Trin.* 15.32.
11. *Trin.* 15.13 (WSA I/5:405).
12. Wis 2.1; Mt 9.2; 15.11–18; Lk 5.21; 12.17 (*Trin.* 15.17).
13. *Trin.* 15.17 (WSA I/5:408).
14. Michel René Barnes, "The Visible Christ and the Invisible Trinity: Mt 5:8 in Augustine's Trinitarian Theology of 400," *Modern Theology* 19, no. 3 (July 2003): 343.
15. *Trin.* 15.18 (WSA I/5:409).
16. *Trin.* 15.20 (CCL 50A:486; WSA I/5:409); see Johannes Brachtendorf: "Gegenstand der Sprachbetrachtung ist nicht mehr primär die Einheit von Klang und Bedeutung, sondern der Gedanke als mentales Ereignis" (*Die Struktur des menschlichen Geistes nach Augustinus: Selbstreflexion und Erkenntnis Gottes in "De Trinitate"* [Hamburg: F. Meiner, 2000], 267).
17. See Brachtendorf, *Die Struktur*, 267–69.

18. *Trin.* 15.20 (WSA I/5:410).
19. *Trin.* 15.20 (WSA I/5:410).
20. Brachtendorf, *Die Struktur*, 272.
21. See *Trin.* 15.23: "And the reason this Word is truly truth is that whatever is in the knowledge of which it was begotten is also in it; and anything that is not in that knowledge is not in it. And this Word can never have anything false in it because it unchangeably finds itself exactly as he from whom it is finds himself. For, *The Son cannot do anything of himself except what he sees the Father doing* (Jn 5:19). He is powerfully unable to do this, nor is this weakness, but the strength by which truth cannot be false" (WSA I/5:415).
22. *Trin.* 15.21–22.
23. *Trin.* 15.25.
24. See Brachtendorf, *Die Struktur*, 279.
25. *Trin.* 15.22.
26. *Trin.* 15.25 (WSA I/5:417).
27. *Trin.* 15.25: "For this reason it is called God's Word without also being called God's thought, to avoid the assumption that there might be in God anything like a chopping and changing element, which will now receive, now regain a form in order to be a word, and which can lose it too and so somehow roll formlessly around" (WSA I/5:417).
28. See *conf.* 13.23.34–24.37.
29. *Trin.* 15.26 (WSA I/5:417–18).
30. *Trin.* 15.26 (WSA I/5:417).
31. *Trin.* 15.26.
32. *Trin.* 15.19.
33. John Cavadini, "The Quest for Truth in Augustine's *De Trinitate*," *Theological Studies* 58, no. 3 (1997): 434. Markus, too, finds freedom in the act of judgment: "The mind's judging manifests a dimension of freedom it has over its self-identification with the material images which solicit its care and threaten to engulf it. Judgment is the mind's return to itself from such 'estrangement' incurred by its captivity to the sphere of its practical engagements." (Robert Markus, "St. Augustine on Signs," *Phronesis* 2, no. 1 [1957]: 81).
34. *Trin.* 9.12; Markus, "St. Augustine on Signs," 84.
35. Markus, "St. Augustine on Signs," 82.
36. *Trin.* 9.13 (WSA I/5:278).
37. Markus, "St. Augustine on Signs," 85.
38. *Trin.* 15.20 (WSA I/5:411).

39. *Trin.* 15.20 (WSA I/5:411).
40. *Trin.* 15.20 (WSA I/5:411).
41. Hegel's rational account is illustrated well in condensed form in the three syllogisms of revealed religion found at *Mind* §§567–70. The first moment of universality (§567) contains the abstract idea of God, in which the self-differentiation of the "Son" has not yet attained the status of a real separation. Hegel then distributes the different elements of the moment of the Son, that is, creation and incarnation, under the syllogisms of particularity (§568) and individuality (§§569–70).
42. Cf. *conf.* 13.4.5.
43. *Civ. Dei* 13.11.
44. *Trin.* 15.20 (WSA I/5:411).
45. Cavadini, "Quest for Truth," 439n39.
46. *Trin.* 15.20 (WSA I/5:409–10).
47. *Trin.* 9.13 (WSA I/5:278).
48. Cited in *Trin.* 15.32 (WSA I/5:421).
49. *Gn. adv. Man.* 2.5 (FC 84:99). This internal source of spiritual nourishment is for Augustine symbolized by the spring that waters the entire earth in Gn 2.6 (*Gn. adv. Man.* 2.6). Cf. Ulrich Duchrow, "Signum und Superbia beim jungen Augustin," *Revue des études augustiniennes* 7 (1961): 369–72. In many texts Augustine links the image of a spring or flowing water with the Holy Spirit, typically by warrant of Jn 4.10–14 or 7.37–39. For example, in a sermon from the year 397 (*s.* Dolbeau 9/28A), Augustine comments upon Ps 116 and Prv 23. The beginning of the sermon is pertinent: "The apostle says, But having the same spirit of faith, according to what is written: 'I believed; for which reason I spoke,' we too believe; for which reason we also speak (2 Cor 4:13; Ps 116:10). If you want to speak when you don't believe, you are wanting to pour out from a jug you haven't filled. It has to be filled, for you to pour out. But it must be poured out for others in such a way that you are not left empty yourself. That's why the Lord, when promising believers an abundance of his Holy Spirit, said, *It will become in him a fountain leaping up to eternal life* (Jn 4:14). It's in the nature of fountains, you see, to pour out their water without getting empty. And if God grants us this, what shall we pay back to the Lord for all the things he has paid back to us?" (*s.* 28A.1/*s.* Dolbeau 9.1 [*Revue Benedictine* 101 {1991}: 251; WSA III/11:48]). Fountain imagery, here drawing upon Jn 4.14, is linked directly with the Holy Spirit, and even more specifically with the Holy Spirit's inspiration of speech uttered in and through faith. Noteworthy as well for our purposes is how Augustine proceeds in

the remainder of *s.* 28A to identify believers' sharing in Christ's sufferings as the most appropriate means of repaying the Lord.

50. *Gn. adv. Man.* 2.6 (FC 84:99; square brackets mine).
51. Cited in *Gn. adv. Man.* 2.5 (FC 84:98).
52. *Gn. adv. Man.* 2.6 (FC 84:100).
53. Cited in *Gn. adv. Man.* 2.6 (FC 84:100).
54. Luigi Alici, "Sign and Language," introduction to Augustine, *Teaching Christianity: De doctrina Christiana,* ed. John E. Rotelle, O.S.A., trans. Edmund Hill, O.P., WSA I/11 (Hyde Park, NY: New City Press, 1996), 35. Luigi suggests in this article that Augustine's treatment of the role of pride in the genesis of language has its turning point here in *Gn. adv. Man.*
55. *Sol.* 1.2.7.
56. E.g., *doc. Chr.* P.5.
57. Cavadini, "Quest for Truth," 432–33. Cf. John Cavadini, "The Sweetness of the Word: Salvation and Rhetoric in Augustine's *De doctrina christiana,*" in De doctrina christiana: *A Classic of Western Culture,* ed. Duane W. H. Arnold and Pamela Bright (Notre Dame, IN: University of Notre Dame Press, 1995), 164–81.
58. See Augustine's criticism of his earlier desire to succeed in the art of rhetoric, since his "motive was the damnable proud desire to gratify [his] human vanity" (*conf.* 3.4.7 [WSA I/1:79; square brackets mine]).
59. As in the case of Nimrod at Babel, according to Augustine's reading of the story in *civ. Dei* 16.4.
60. *Jo. ev. tr.* 25.17: "Not without, outside you [God], but within, with you, there is the fountain of life" (FC 79:254–55; square brackets mine).
61. *Jo. ev. tr.* 25.16: "In order that the cause of all diseases, that is, pride, might be healed, he came down and the Son of God became humble.... You are instructed to be humble.... All your humility is this, that you know yourself" (FC 79:254); cf. *mus.* 6.13.40; M.-F. Berrouard, "Orgueil et extériorité," supplementary note 48, BA 72, pp. 793–96; M.-F. Berrouard, "Incarnation et guérison de l'orgueil," BA 72, pp. 796–97.
62. "Orguiel et extériorité," supplementary note 48, BA 72, p. 795; translation mine.
63. *Mus.* 6.13.40 (PL 32:1185; translation mine).
64. *Mus.* 6.13.40 (PL 32:1184).
65. *En. Ps.* 32(1).9 (WSA III/15:389); cf. *en. Ps.* 148.7. Note that Augustine's numeration differed from the modern numeration from Ps 9

to Ps 146. Here and in subsequent references to Psalms, the first psalm number is Augustine's and is followed by the modern psalm number in parentheses.

66. *Vera rel.* 55.113: "Neither would all things come to be from the Father through the Son, nor would they be safe within their limits, were not God good in the highest degree. God has not begrudged any nature which could take its goodness from him, and he has granted [*dedit*] that his creation remain in the good either as much as it wills or as much as it can. For this reason it is fitting that we worship and hold the Gift of God to be equally unchangeable with the Father and the Son. . . . He is the God who said, 'Let it be' (Gn 1.2), the Word, through whom everything was made . . . and the Gift of his benevolence, through whom it pleased him that whatever was made through the Word be reconciled to its creator in order that it might not perish" (CCL 32:260; translation mine).

67. E.g., *conf.* 12.8.8.

68. *Reason*, 66; cf. O'Regan, *Heterodox Hegel*, 314.

69. Cavadini, "Pride," in *Augustine through the Ages*, 679.

70. Here Cavadini is perceptive: "The usefulness and importance of the doctrine of the inner word is that it enables Augustine to show how human beings cannot simply transmit pure knowledge independent of value judgments. . . . The problem in the communication and signification of knowledge is not primarily the difficulty of representing what is 'inner' in what is 'outer' (a problem more characteristically emphasized by the earlier Augustine), but rather the difficulty that knowledge cannot be represented at all until it is 'spoken' within, 'conceived' by a love which binds it to the understanding as a word 'begotten.' And because the image of God within is distorted by original sin, by a primal preference for power over justice, our sign systems will inevitably be marked by and inevitably transmit this preference encoded into them, and so fail to 'image' God effectively" ("Quest for Truth," 437–38n35).

71. *Trin.* 9.15.

72. Cavadini, "Quest for Truth," 436.

73. *Doc. Chr.* 2.20.30; cf. Robert Markus, "Augustine on Magic: A Neglected Semiotic Theory," *Revue des études augustiniennes* 40 (1994): 375–88.

74. *Doc. Chr.* 2.38.57 (WSA I/11:158). For an analysis of Augustine's developing views on the liberal arts, see Ayres, *Augustine and the Trinity*, 121–33, and the literature cited there.

75. *Trin.* 4.20; cf. Cavadini, "Quest for Truth," 438.

76. *Trin.* 12.14.
77. *Conf.* 1.17.27.
78. *Conf.* 1.16.25.
79. *Conf.* 1.16.26.
80. *Conf.* 1.16.26.
81. *Jo. ev. tr.* 25.16 (FC 79:254).
82. *Jo. ev. tr.* 25.16 (FC 79:254).
83. *Jo. ev. tr.* 25.16 (CCL 36:257; FC 79:254).
84. *F. et symb.* 4.8 (CSEL 41:11).
85. *F. et symb.* 4.8 (CSEL 41:11; translation mine).
86. *Ench.* 11.36–37.
87. E. P. Meijering, *Augustine: "De Fide et Symbolo": Introduction, Translation, Commentary* (Amsterdam: J. C. Gieben, 1987), 68.
88. *Ench.* 11.37 (Augustine, *The Augustine Catechism: The Enchiridion on Faith, Hope, and Love*, trans. Bruce Harbert [Hyde Park, NY: New City Press, 1999], 67).
89. *Ench.* 12.40 (Harbert, 70).
90. *Trin.* 13.22–23 (WSA I/5:361).
91. Jacques Verhees, "Heiliger Geist und Inkarnation in der Theologie des Augustinus von Hippo," *Revue des études augustiniennes* 22 (1976): 241.
92. See *c. Jul. imp.* 1.140; Verhees, "Heiliger Geist und Inkarnation," 241.
93. *Trin.* 13.23: "What was born," Augustine argues, "was a man who had not and never would have any sin at all, a man by whom would be reborn those who were to be set free from sin, who could not themselves be born without sin" (WSA I/5:362).
94. *Trin.* 13.22, citing Phil 2.8; cf. *Gn. adv. Man.* 2.24.37; Verhees, "Heiliger Geist und Inkarnation," 242.
95. *Trin.* 13.21–22 (WSA I/5:361).
96. See Brian Daley, S.J., "A Humble Mediator: The Distinctive Elements in St. Augustine's Christology," in *Word and Spirit* 9 (1987): 100–117.
97. *Jo. ev. tr.* 74.3 (CCL 36:514; translation mine).
98. *Jo. ev. tr.* 74.3 (CCL 36:514; translation mine).
99. *Trin.* 13.23 (WSA I/5:361).
100. *Trin.* 15.31–32.
101. *Trin.* 15.46: "How then can he who gives the Holy Spirit not be God? Indeed, how much must he who gives God be God!" (WSA I/5:431),

referring to Jn 20.22 and Acts 2. In the same section of *Trin.*, Augustine affirms that Christ receives the Spirit in his humanity.

102. *Trin.* 15.46.

103. *Jo. ev. tr.* 74.3, citing Jn 3.34.

104. Jacques Verhees, *God in Beweging: Een onderzoek naar de Pneumatologie van Augustinus* (Wageningen: H. Veenman & Zoonan N.V., 1968), 32. Cf. *Trin.* 15.46.

105. *S.* 215.4 (WSA III/6:162).

106. *Trin.* 15.46 (WSA I/5:431), nonscriptural emphasis mine.

107. *Trin.* 15.31–32.

108. Douglas W. Johnson, "'Verbum' in the Early Augustine (386–397)," *Recherches augustiniennes* 8 (1972): 49.

109. Cited in *doc. Chr.* 1.34.38 (WSA I/11:123).

110. *Doc. Chr.* 1.34.38 (WSA I/11:123).

111. *Doc. Chr.* 1.34.38 (WSA I/11:123).

112. Recall that this conveyance was by the grace of the Holy Spirit.

113. *Civ. Dei* 11.3 (Augustine, *Concerning the City of God against the Pagans*, trans. Henry Bettenson [Harmondsworth, Middlesex, UK: Penguin, 1972], 431).

114. *Trin.* 4.2 (WSA I/5:153).

115. *Trin.* 13.7–9.

116. *Trin.* 4.3.

117. *Trin.* 4.4 (WSA I/5:155).

118. *Trin.* 4.4 (WSA I/5:155).

119. *Trin.* 4.2 (WSA I/5:153).

120. *Trin.* 4.2 (WSA I/5:153).

121. *Trin.* 4.2.

122. See Robert Dodaro, O.S.A., "Justice," in *Augustine through the Ages*, 481–83, for a brief treatment of the topic and bibliography. Integral to Augustine's concept of divine justice is the free gift of grace by which God renders human beings just. Through the blood of Christ, the justice of God is manifest as mercy, as the will that humans be saved. The result, at the individual, ecclesial, and broader social levels, is a self-critical understanding of the imperfection of human justice and forward-looking striving to conform the individual and community to God's perfect justice, that is, the striving toward properly ordered love of God and neighbor. This, as will become further evident below, especially in chapters 5 and 6, contrasts sharply with Hegel's reconceptualization of the cross, whereby

the justification of human beings becomes merely a moment in a broader process of divine self-justification. The result, at the level of the community, is a backward-looking affirmation of God's justice in past events and their present consequences, rather than a forward-looking critique of past and present events and relations as falling short of perfect justice.

123. *Trin.* 13.17 (WSA I/5:356).
124. *Trin.* 13.17 (WSA I/5:357).
125. *Trin.* 13.17.
126. *Trin.* 13.18 (WSA I/5:357).
127. *Trin.* 13.18 (WSA I/5:357–58).
128. See *Trin.* 13.25.
129. *Trin.* 4.4: "[The consonant proportion of the single to the double] is found extensively in us, and is so naturally ingrained in us (and who by, if not by him who created us?), that even the unskilled feel it whether singing themselves or listening to others. It is what makes concord between high-pitched and deep voices, and if anyone strays discordantly away from it, it is not our knowledge, which many lack, but our very sense of hearing that is painfully offended" (WSA I/5:155).
130. *Trin.* 4.4 (WSA I/5:155).
131. *Trin.* 4.5.
132. *En. Ps.* 108.26 (WSA III/19:257). In this passage Augustine suggests that the same Holy Spirit operates in the resurrection of Christ and in the gift of grace to believers at Pentecost.
133. *Trin.* 4.6 (WSA I/5:156).
134. WSA I/5:178n18.
135. *Trin.* 4.6 (WSA I/5:156).
136. *Trin.* 4.6 (WSA I/5:157).
137. Mt 10.28: "not to fear those who kill the body but cannot kill the soul." Col 1.24: "That I may make up what is wanting from Christ's afflictions in my flesh" (as trans. in WSA I/5:157).
138. *Trin.* 4.6 (WSA I/5:157).
139. *Trin.* 4.11.
140. *Trin.* 4.12.
141. *Trin.* 4.15 (WSA I/5:163; brackets mine).
142. *Trin.* 4.13 (WSA I/5:162).
143. *Trin.* 4.17 (WSA I/5:164).
144. *LPR* (1827) 3:293.
145. *LPR* (1827) 3:302.
146. *Civ. Dei* 11.15.

147. *Civ. Dei* 14.11.
148. *Civ. Dei* 14.13.
149. *Trin.* 4.17 (WSA I/5:164).
150. *Trin.* 4.18.
151. *Trin.* 4.17.
152. See *Trin.* 13.22.
153. *Trin.* 4.17.
154. *Trin.* 4.20 (WSA I/5:167).

155. *Trin.* 4.21–23. In his work *De catechizandis rudibus*, which is roughly contemporary with the first books of *Trin.*, Augustine explicitly attributes to the Holy Spirit the revelation of Christ's future advent to the saints of the Old Testament. See, e.g., *cat. rud.* 19.33.

156. *Trin.* 13.5 (WSA I/5:345).

157. For Augustine's comments on the beauty of world history as a whole, see *civ. Dei* 11.18 and 11.23. My rejection of any governing tendency toward theodicy in Augustine runs counter to the evaluation of Gillian R. Evans, *Augustine on Evil* (Cambridge: Cambridge University Press, 1982).

Part II
Pentecost

1. *ETW*, 281–95.

Chapter 3
Hegel's Language of Spirit and Its Social Realization

1. *LPR* (1827) 3:325, 328–30; *LPH*, 325.

2. Peter Hünermann, "Die Hegel-Rezeption Franz Anton Staudenmaiers," in *Kirche und Theologie im 19. Jahrhundert: Referate und Berichte des Arbeitskreises Katholische Theologie*, ed. Georg Schwaiger (Goettingen: Vandenhoeck & Ruprecht, 1975), 147–55; Albert Franz, *Glauben und Denken: Franz Anton Staudenmaiers Hegelkritik als Anfrage an das Selbstverständnis heutiger Theologie* (Regensburg: Verlag Friedrich Pustet, 1983), esp. 51–74; Cyril O'Regan, "Hegel as Roman Catholic Opportunity and Challenge in the Nineteenth Century: The Emblematic Case of Franz Anton Staudenmaier (1800–1856)," unpublished manuscript, 1995.

3. Franz, *Glauben und Denken*, 56; O'Regan, "Hegel as Roman Catholic Opportunity and Challenge," 10–12.

4. O'Regan, "Hegel as Roman Catholic Opportunity and Challenge," 13.

5. Hünermann, "Die Hegel-Rezeption," 148.

6. O'Regan, "Hegel as Roman Catholic Opportunity and Challenge," 14–16.

7. Portions of the text were originally published in the *Theologische Quartalschrift* 10 (1828): 389–432, 608–40. For Staudenmaier's discussion of the text's origin and eventual publication, see *Pragmatismus der Geistesgaben. oder, Das Wirken des göttlichen Geistes in Menschen und in der Menschheit* (1835; repr., Frankfurt: Minerva, 1975), viii–xi.

8. Staudenmaier, *Pragmatismus der Geistesgaben*, 1.

9. Staudenmaier, *Pragmatismus der Geistesgaben*, 6.

10. Staudenmaier, *Pragmatismus der Geistesgaben*, 132, 176.

11. Staudenmaier, *Pragmatismus der Geistesgaben*, 193.

12. Staudenmaier, *Pragmatismus der Geistesgaben*, 195.

13. Staudenmaier, *Pragmatismus der Geistesgaben*, 16.

14. Staudenmaier, *Pragmatismus der Geistesgaben*, 165.

15. Staudenmaier, *Pragmatismus der Geistesgaben*, 59: "Im Christentume dagegen erscheinen die individuellen Unterschiede als immanente Bestimmtheiten, als Momente der Idee, und alle zusammen machen die Eine, systematische Totalität des Geistes der Menschheit aus" (translation mine).

16. Staudenmaier, *Pragmatismus der Geistesgaben*, 16–17.

17. Staudenmaier, *Pragmatismus der Geistesgaben*, 139.

18. Staudenmaier, *Pragmatismus der Geistesgaben*, 144.

19. Staudenmaier, *Pragmatismus der Geistesgaben*, 194.

20. Staudenmaier, *Pragmatismus der Geistesgaben*, 193.

21. Franz, *Glauben und Denken*, 73.

22. Franz, *Glauben und Denken*, 56.

23. O'Regan, "Hegel as Roman Catholic Opportunity and Challenge," 20, 23.

24. Staudenmaier, *Darstellung und Kritik des Hegelschen Systems: Aus dem Standpunkte der christlichen Philosophie* (Mainz: F. Kupferberg, 1844), 755–57.

25. Staudenmaier, *Darstellung und Kritik*, 772.

26. Staudenmaier, *Darstellung und Kritik*, 653.

27. O'Regan, "Hegel as Roman Catholic Opportunity and Challenge," 21.

28. Staudenmaier, *Darstellung und Kritik*, 461.

29. Staudenmaier, *Darstellung und Kritik*, 756.

30. "Babylonische Verwirrung der Begriffe und des Lebens" (Staudenmaier, *Pragmatismus der Geistesgaben*, 166; translation mine). Disciples of modernity might find in the later Staudenmaier a conservative agenda fundamentally opposed to the freedoms sought by the more revolutionary or progressive of his day. Should such critique be directed toward Augustine, Hegel's primary interlocutor here, a strong case could be made that Augustine's Trinitarian paradigm grounds an understanding of Christian freedom that is consistent with the longer biblical and theological tradition, distinct from the notion of autonomy upheld by secular modernity, and yet not at complete odds with existence in the modern world.

31. Staudenmaier, *Die Philosophie des Christentums; oder, Metaphysik der Heiligen Schrift als Lehre von den göttlichen Ideen und ihre Entwicklung in Natur, Geist, und Geschichte* (1840; repr., Frankfurt: Minerva, 1966), 238–44, 800–802.

32. See Johannes Wallmann, "Geisterfahrung und Kirche im frühen Pietismus," in *Charisma und Institution*, ed. Trutz Rendtorff (Gütersloh: Gütersloher Verlagshaus Gerd Mohn, 1985), 134.

33. "Es ist kein Widerspruch, wenn sich aus dieser Ausdehnung des Handlungsspielraums des Heiligen Geistes über das kirchliche Amt hinaus faktisch eine Verengung des Wirkungsfeldes des Heiligen Geistes ergibt" (Wallmann, "Geisterfahrung und Kirche," 137).

34. Wallmann, "Geisterfahrung und Kirche," 137.

35. Olson, *Hegel and the Spirit*, 26–27.

36. Laurence Dickey, *Hegel: Religion, Economics, and the Politics of Spirit, 1770–1807* (Cambridge: Cambridge University Press, 1987).

37. Dickey, *Hegel*, 16–17; square brackets mine.

38. Robert Markus, *Saeculum: History and Society in the Theology of St. Augustine* (Cambridge: Cambridge University Press, 1988).

39. Kant, *Religion within the Boundaries*, 72.

40. Kant, *Religion within the Boundaries*, 71.

41. Kant, *Religion within the Boundaries*, 71.

42. Kant, *Religion within the Boundaries*, 65–66, 72.

43. Kant, *Religion within the Boundaries*, 72.

44. Dickey, *Hegel*, 168.

45. Indeed, "Kant offers us a philosophical millenarianism in which the eschatological notion of the coming of the Kingdom of God (i.e., as an 'ethical commonwealth') acts as an incentive to this-worldly ethical activism (i.e., to the idea of virtue as the pursuit of holiness)" (Dickey, *Hegel*, 170).

46. Dickey, *Hegel*, 170.

47. Dickey, *Hegel*, 171–72.

48. Olson, *Hegel and the Spirit*, 38–39.

49. Olson, *Hegel and the Spirit*, 39.

50. Olson, *Hegel and the Spirit*, 42.

51. Dickey, *Hegel*, 136–37.

52. Dickey, *Hegel*, 144; square brackets mine. Dickey is citing J. G. A. Pocock, *The Machiavellian Moment: Florentine Political Thought and the Atlantic Republican Tradition* (Princeton, NJ: Princeton University Press, 1975), 7, 85, 135–37, and 462; and Ernst Kantorowicz, *The King's Two Bodies: A Study in Mediaeval Political Thought* (Princeton, NJ: Princeton University Press, 1957), 234–35, 248.

53. *ETW*, 301.

54. *ETW*, 247.

55. Hegel comments, "A doctrine pure and simple can be preached, and supported by the testimony of events, without being itself possessed by the Holy Spirit. But teaching of that kind is no consecration, not a baptism of the spirit" (*ETW*, 277).

56. *ETW*, 277–78.

57. *ETW*, 293–94.

58. *ETW*, 301.

59. *ETW*, 301.

60. Jamros, *Human Shape*, 36, 42.

61. O'Regan, *Heterodox Hegel*, 240.

62. See *PS* §787 (Miller, 477–78) and *LPR* (1824) 3:221–22.

63. See *PS* §787 (Miller, 477–78) and *LPR* (1824) 3:221–22.

64. *LPR* (1824) 3:222.

65. See *PS* §217 (Miller, 131–32).

66. *PS* §787 (Miller, 477–78).

67. *LPR* (ms) 3:154–55. Both Hodgson (*LPR* [ms] 3:155n241) and Lawrence S. Stepelevich ("Hegel and Roman Catholicism," *Journal of the American Academy of Religion* 60, no. 4 [Winter 1992]: 686) point out

Hegel's deliberate play on the double meaning of "Messe" in German. It means both "market" and "mass" and suggests that the church distributes grace as a vendor exhibits and sells his or her wares. The rational criticism of "grace" here shares much with that of Kant in *Religion within the Boundaries*.

68. *LPH*, 84; Stepelevich, "Roman Catholicism," 687–88.
69. *ETW*, 281.
70. See further *ETW*, 288n, and *PR* §5.
71. See Robert E. Norton, *The Beautiful Soul: Aesthetic Morality in the Eighteenth Century* (Ithaca, NY: Cornell University Press, 1995).
72. *PS* §658 (Miller, 400).
73. Jeanette Bicknell, "The Individuality in the Deed: Hegel on Forgiveness and Reconciliation," *Bulletin of the Hegel Society of Great Britain* 37/38 (1998): 76.
74. The conceptual and verbal parallels with the act of judgment (*Urteil*) by which the abstract Father "creates" the finite world (Son) in *LPR* 3 are not mere coincidence. See, e.g., *LPR* (ms) 3:86.
75. *PS* §666 (Miller, 405).
76. *PS* §666 (Miller, 405).
77. Spirit can be really universal only when it is known and enacted as such, universally, by all in the existent community.
78. *PS* §667 (Miller, 406).
79. *PS* §658 (Miller, 399).
80. *PS* §668 (Miller, 406–7); cf. Olson, *Hegel and the Spirit*, 84–106, where he argues for the possibility that Hegel's fear of madness, as witnessed in his friend Hölderlin, led him to the discovery of a dialectic that issued not in the indiscriminateness of mere being, but rather in the concrete being of Spirit.
81. "Just as the [one who first confessed] has to surrender its one-sided, unacknowledged existence of its particular being-for-self, so too must this other set aside its one-sided, unacknowledged judgment. And just as the former exhibits the power of Spirit over its actual existence, so does this other exhibit the power of Spirit over the specific Notion of itself" (*PS* §669 [Miller, 407]; square brackets mine).
82. *PS* §670 (Miller, 408).
83. *PS* §671 (Miller, 409).
84. *LPH*, 326.
85. *LPH*, 326–28.

86. *LPH*, 329.
87. *Aes.*, 544.
88. *Aes.*, 544, 548; italics mine.
89. *Aes.*, 545.
90. *Aes.*, 545.
91. "Now given his still unfulfilled inner life, the first thing that can be negatived in the martyr, with a view to his sanctification and his release from the world, is his natural being" (*Aes.*, 545).
92. *Aes.*, 546; square brackets mine.
93. *Aes.*, 546–47; square brackets mine.
94. *Aes.*, 547.
95. Such confidence, we will see in the upcoming chapter, contrasts with the confidence Augustine believes is given to Christians by the Holy Spirit. Augustine's pneumatological concept of confidence bears a positive, world-affirming side, while still not being so thoroughly aligned with any particular culture's system of values that it cannot speak against them if need be.
96. *Aes.*, 548; square brackets mine.
97. *Aes.*, 547.
98. *LPR* (ms) 3:121.
99. Although in *LPR* 3 Hegel explicitly refers this analysis to Muslims in Africa, it is consistent with his statements regarding martyrdom and Catholicism's tendency toward political and social disunity.
100. *LPH*, 329, 336.
101. *Reason*, 85.
102. *Reason*, 84.
103. *Reason*, 83, 86.
104. One does wonder, then, why Hegel is so intent on diagnosing the thoroughgoing selfishness of the martyr. Is he, too, something of a valet? The main distinction between the two groups is the direction of their passions: one group, in Hegel's view, effectively flees or even destroys the world, while the other group builds it. Empire builders, it seems, fall into a different category from terrorists. Their victims would appear to as well.
105. *Reason*, 88.
106. *Reason*, 87.
107. *Reason*, 89; bold emphasis Hegel's.
108. *Reason*, 45, 52.
109. *Reason*, 94; square brackets mine.

Chapter 4
Augustine: The Holy Spirit and the Transformation of Language

1. *Civ. Dei* 12.22–23.

2. In this respect, Augustine also employs the Pauline distinction of flesh and spirit. However, noting the fluidity with which scripture uses the word "flesh," he points out that, because bodily flesh endures corruption only as a consequence of sin, which originates in a distorted will, one ought to equate love of flesh with love of self, or with the desire to live according to human rules, rather than those of God. Thereby affirming the innate goodness of creation, Augustine argues that in this regard "flesh" functions synecdochically and is not to be restricted to the stuff from which the human body is made (*civ. Dei* 14.2–3).

3. That is not to say, however, that possession of a common language indemnifies a society against sin, as Augustine himself readily admits: "Just as when all men had one language, that did not mean that the 'sons of pestilence' were not to be found—for there was only one language before the Flood, and yet all men deserved to be wiped out by the Flood, except for the one family of the righteous Noah" (*civ. Dei* 16.11 [Bettenson, 667]).

4. *Civ. Dei* 16.4 (Bettenson, 658).

5. *Civ. Dei* 16.4 (Bettenson, 657).

6. *Civ. Dei* 19.7.

7. *Trin.* 10.2 (WSA I/5:287).

8. *Trin.* 10.2.

9. Cited in *Jo. ev. tr.* 27.5 (FC 79:280).

10. *Jo. ev. tr.* 27.5 (FC 79:280–81).

11. *En. Ps.* 8.8 (WSA III/15:133).

12. Against Donatist claims of persecution by governmental authorities, Augustine declares: "They truly persecute the Church who persecute by deceits; they strike the heart more gravely who strike with the sword of the tongue; they pour out blood more bitterly who, as far as it is possible for them, kill Christ in a man." A deceitful will can rob another Christian of salvation and Christ's spiritual presence (*Jo. ev. tr.* 5.12 [FC 78:118]).

13. Cited in *en. Ps.* 54.11 (WSA III/17:65).

14. *En. Ps.* 54.11 (WSA III/17:65).

15. *En. Ps.* 54.11.

16. *En. Ps.* 54.11 (CCL 39:665; WSA III/17:65); square brackets mine.

17. *LPR* (1824) 3:230; square brackets mine.

18. See William H. Marrevee, *The Ascension of Christ in the Works of St. Augustine* (Ottawa: University of Ottawa Press, 1967).

19. *Trin.* 4.6.

20. *Trin.* 4.24 (WSA I/5:170).

21. "Because I have spoken these things to you sadness has filled your hearts. But I tell you the truth, it is expedient for you that I go; for if I do not go away, the advocate will not come to you" (cited in *Trin.* 1.18 [WSA I/5:78]).

22. *Trin.* 1.18 (WSA I/5:78).

23. Verhees, *God in Beweging*, 35.

24. "Do not touch me, for I have not yet ascended to the Father" (cited in *Trin.* 1.18 [WSA I/5:78]).

25. *Trin.* 1.18 (WSA I/5:78); square brackets mine.

26. Verhees, *God in Beweging*, 39; *Trin.* 15.46.

27. Verhees, *God in Beweging*, 39–40. Additionally, it could very well relate to the Spirit's gift of love, which, according to Augustine, perfects that knowledge. In that respect, *capax* has the related meaning of spaciousness, a meaning that resonates particularly with Augustine's frequent use of Rom 5.5, according to which the Holy Spirit pours the love of God into the hearts of believers. This love, as Augustine eloquently maintains in an early commentary on Ps 4, enlarges the believer's heart and bestows upon him or her a wide freedom (*en. Ps.* 4.2, 6).

28. Cited in *Jo. ev. tr.* 100.1 (FC 90:229); square brackets mine.

29. *Jo. ev. tr.* 100.1 (FC 90:229).

30. Verhees, *God in Beweging*, 40–42.

31. *Jo. ev. tr.* 100.1 (FC 90:229).

32. Augustine enumerates three different types of praise, the falsity of which depends upon the degree and locus of deception. In the first case, one honors a person on account of an evil act he or she performs, such that the deception lies in the act (*res*), but not in the person him- or herself. Conversely, a person can act justly, but not for the sake of justice, that is, for the sake of God, but for his or her own glory. In this case those who praise this individual are deceived not in the act but in the person. Finally, people could believe that an evil act—Augustine proposes magic arts—is good, and they could mistakenly praise someone for executing it when in fact that person does not know how to perform it. In this last case those who give glory are deceived in both the goodness of the person and the act (*Jo. ev. tr.* 100.2).

33. *Jo. ev. tr.* 100.2 (FC 90:231).

34. *Jo. ev. tr.* 100.2.

35. In his early text *The Spirit of Christianity*, Hegel criticizes an Augustinian-Lutheran concept of grace. His critique, inasmuch as he senses that such a notion of grace contradicts the Enlightenment understanding of freedom as self-determination, is one in spirit with that of Kant. For Hegel, it is the angst of a bad conscience that leads the individual to plea for divine grace. In an attempt to avert the law and justice, the sinner makes an appeal to the "administrator of abstract justice in order to experience his goodness." But to Hegel's mind this is nothing but sheer hypocrisy: "It is not that [the sinner] denies his transgression, but he has the dishonest wish that his transgression may be denied by goodness itself, and he finds consolation in the . . . untrue idea, which another being may frame of him." No genuine reconciliation can obtain through dishonesty, because the individual denies the truth, the truth of his or her own particularity as a sinner, in the self-deceptive hope that universal, immutable justice could show mercy toward the transgressor, when in fact the abstract justice of God, qua abstract, can do nothing of the sort, can in no way bridge the gap and give the sinner a share in its goodness (*ETW*, 227–28; square brackets mine).

36. Cf. Mk 1.10; Mt 3.16; Lk 3.22.
37. *Jo. ev. tr.* 6.1.
38. Cited in *Jo. ev. tr.* 6.2 (FC 78:129).
39. *Jo. ev. tr.* 6.2 (FC 78:130).
40. *Jo. ev. tr.* 6.2 (CCL 36:53–54; FC 78:130); square brackets mine.
41. *Jo. ev. tr.* 6.2.
42. *Jo. ev. tr.* 6.3 (FC 78:131).
43. *Jo. ev. tr.* 6.3.
44. *Jo. ev. tr.* 6.3 (FC 78:131); square brackets mine.
45. *Jo. ev. tr.* 6.3 (FC 78:132); square brackets mine.
46. Cited in *ep. Jo.* 2.2 (FC 92:144).
47. *Ep. Jo.* 2.2 (FC 92:144–45).
48. *Ep. Jo.* 2.2.
49. *Ep. Jo.* 2.1.
50. *Ep. Jo.* 2.3.

51. Augustine notes that Christians must strive for this understanding, which is conveyed to them by scripture. In fact, in *ep. Jo.* 2.2 Augustine points out two moments in which the despondent disciples, through the opening of scriptures following Christ's resurrection and at Pentecost, come to recognize Christ's body with all its sacramental and

ecclesial import. The first moment takes place when Christ breaks bread with the two disciples whom he had accompanied to Emmaus. By sharing the Eucharist with him, the disciples are able to recognize the risen Christ and thus to become part of his body. Then Augustine links Christ's death and resurrection to believers' understanding of it through the universal dissemination of the gospel. In this way Augustine highlights the dual action of Christ and the Holy Spirit in the subjective appropriation of salvation through Christ's death and resurrection and in the foundation of the community of believers.

52. See FC 92:145n13.
53. *Ep. Jo.* 2.3.
54. *Ep. Jo.* 2.3 (FC 92:145).
55. *Ep. Jo.* 2.2–3.
56. *Jo. ev. tr.* 6.10 (FC 78:138).
57. See FC 78:132n11.
58. *Jo. ev. tr.* 6.10 (FC 78:139).
59. *Jo. ev. tr.* 32.7 (FC 88:46).
60. *Jo. ev. tr.* 32.7 (FC 88:46–47).
61. *Jo. ev. tr.* 32.7 (FC 88:47).
62. "Have love, and you have everything, because without it, whatever you could have profits you nothing" (*Jo. ev. tr.* 32.8 [FC 88:49]).
63. *Ep. Jo.* 6.10.
64. Cited in *ep. Jo.* 6.12 (FC 92:212).
65. *Ep. Jo.* 6.12.
66. Cited in *ep. Jo.* 6.12 (FC 92:213).
67. *Ep. Jo.* 6.13 (FC 92:214); square brackets mine.
68. *Ep. Jo.* 6.13.
69. *Ep. Jo.* 6.12.
70. *Trin.* 15.46 (WSA I/5:431).
71. *Trin.* 15.46.
72. See *Trin.* 15.45–46.
73. *Jo. ev. tr.* 74.1 (FC 90:89); square brackets mine.
74. *Jo. ev. tr.* 74.2 (FC 90:90). On the topic of grace in Augustine's theology of Pentecost, see Anthony Dupont, "Augustine's Preaching on Grace at Pentecost," in *Studia Patristica* 61, ed. Markus Vinzent and Jonathan P. Yates (Leuven: Peeters, 2013), 3–14.
75. *Trin.* 15.46.
76. *Jo. ev. tr.* 74.3.
77. *Jo. ev. tr.* 74.2 (FC 90:90).

78. Assuming it is authentic. To its credit, Augustine's use of the distinction between a pledge and an earnest (*pignus* and *arrha*) is attested also in *s.* 23.8 and 156.16.

79. *S.* 378.1 (WSA III/10:353).

80. *S.* 378.1 (WSA III/10:353–54).

81. See, for instance, *div. qu.* 62; *Trin.* 4.29; *Jo. ev. tr.* 52.8. Later (419) confirmation of both the openness and universality of the Spirit's coming at Pentecost can be seen also in *Jo. ev. tr.* 74.2, where Augustine claims that before Pentecost the apostles had the love of the Holy Spirit, but to a lesser degree and in a hidden way. After Christ's glorification, that love was to be increased and manifest openly, so that the apostles might come to know what they had already been given. Moreover, in *Jo. ev. tr.* 95.1 Augustine points out that at Pentecost the apostles were sent to convict not one nation, but the whole world.

82. Verhees, *God in Beweging*, 49; see esp. *Jo. ev. tr.* 52.8.

83. Verhees argues that this contrast appears above all between 411 and 420, though he notes that the contrast is already found in *ep.* 55.29 from 401 (*God in Beweging*, 49).

84. The reference also to scripture in this process is clear: the preachers are "all preachers of the gospel [*euangelistae*], for through them the Lord travels among all peoples" (*en. Ps.* 90[2].8 [CCL 39:1275; WSA III/18:340]).

85. *En. Ps.* 90(2).8.

86. *S.* 156.13 (WSA III/5:104).

87. "As many as are led by the Spirit of God, these are God's sons" (cited in *s.* 156.13 [WSA III/5:104]).

88. "And you like living stones are being built together into the temple of God" (cited in *s.* 156.13 [WSA III/5:104]).

89. *S.* 156.14 (WSA III/5:105).

90. "This is a cry of the heart, not of the mouth, not of the lips; it makes itself heard inside, it makes itself heard in God's ears" (*s.* 156.15 [WSA III/5:105]).

91. *S.* 156.15 (WSA III/5:106).

92. *Ep. Jo.* 8.10 (FC 92:241).

93. Verhees, *God in Beweging*, 42–48.

94. *Jo. ev. tr.* 95.1 (CCL 36:565).

95. *Ep. Jo.* 8.13.

96. *Ep. Jo.* 1.9; 8.10.

97. *Ep. Jo.* 8.13.

98. *Ep. Jo.* 8.12.

99. "'No one has ever seen God.' See, most beloved: 'If we love one another, God abides in us and his love will be perfected.' Begin to love; you will be perfected. Have you begun to love? God has begun to dwell in you; love him who has begun to dwell in you that by indwelling more perfectly he may make you perfected" (*Ep. Jo.* 8.12 [FC 92:243]).

100. "For indeed, it would have been insufficient to encourage them by his own example if he were not to fill [them] with his Spirit" (*Jo. ev. tr.* 93.1 [FC 90:173]; square brackets mine).

101. Carole Straw, "Martyrdom," *Augustine through the Ages*, 539.

102. *Ep.* 89.2; cf. *Cresc.* 3.47.51; *en. Ps.* 34(2).1; 68(1).9; *s.* 275.1; 327.2.

103. *Jo. ev. tr.* 6.23 (FC 78:150).

104. *En. Ps.* 118(21).8; cf. *en. Ps.* 118(30).7. 1 Cor 13.3 is cited in *Jo. ev. tr.* 6.23 (FC 78:150).

105. *En. Ps.* 118(21).8.

106. *Jo. ev. tr.* 6.10.

107. *Jo. ev. tr.* 6.23.

108. *S.* 299.7 (PL 38:1372); cf. *s.* 299B.1.

109. *S.* 299B.1 (WSA III/8:245).

110. On the martyrs' fear of death in Augustine's anti-Pelagian period, see especially Robert Dodaro, O.S.A., "'Christus Iustus' and Fear of Death in Augustine's Dispute with the Pelagians," in Signum Pietatis: *Festgabe für Cornelius Petrus Mayer OSA zum 60. Geburtstag*, ed. Adolar Zumkeller, O.S.A., Cassiciacum 40 (Würzburg: Augustinus-Verlag, 1989), 341–61.

111. *En. Ps.* 30(2).3.

112. *En. Ps.* 68(1).3; incorrectly cited as *en. Ps.* 68(1).1 by Straw, "Martyrdom," 540; *s.* 299.8–9.

113. *En. Ps.* 68(1).3.

114. *Civ. Dei* 13.4; see Basil Studer, "'Sacramentum et exemplum' chez Saint Augustin," in *Dominus Salvator: Studien zur Christologie und Exegese der Kirchenväter*, Studia Anselmiana 107 (Rome: Pontificeo Ateneo S. Anselmo, 1992), 141–212, esp. 189–208, for the possible reinterpretation of the sacramentum-exemplum pair during the Pelagian controversy.

115. *S.* 299.8; cf. *en. Ps.* 68(1).3, where Peter goes to death unwillingly, but willingly for the crown.

116. *Civ. Dei* 13.4, citing Heb 11.1.

117. The upshot of *Jo. ev. tr.* 94, for instance, is basically that if Christ does not go away, the apostles will not be capable of receiving the Spirit, and

that if Christ does not send his Holy Spirit, the disciples will neither know Christ truly, that is, spiritually, nor be able to endure suffering in his name.

118. Straw, "Martyrdom," 539.

119. Straw, "Martyrdom," 541. Straw then distinguishes between Augustine and the Eastern tradition of deification in martyrdom, exemplified by Eusebius and Origen, wherein, she argues, the ontological line between Christ and the martyr begins to blur. This is interesting given Augustine's sense of the Spirit's role in making the martyr and the common Eastern Christian critique that Augustine's pneumatology denies the personality of the Holy Spirit apart from Christ and that Augustine's dependent Holy Spirit thus absorbs the individual believer into the body of Christ. Perhaps the way Augustine understands the operation of the Holy Spirit actually preserves the integrity of the individual believer over against the person of Christ even within the mysterious unity of Christ's body the church.

120. Straw, "Martyrdom," 541. On the concept of "deification" in Augustine, see David Vincent Meconi, *The One Christ: St. Augustine's Theology of Deification* (Washington, DC: Catholic University of America Press, 2013).

121. *Jo. ev. tr.* 84.2 (FC 90:135). Similarly—and reminiscent of aspects of Christ as *sacramentum* and *exemplum* highlighted by Studer: Christ as transformative foundation and way—Dodaro avails himself of the work of Karl Morrison (*The Mimetic Tradition of Reform in the West* [Princeton: Princeton University Press, 1982], 54–97), where he finds the concept of "mediated asymmetry": "Imitation required mediation, and the mimetic image always fell short of its archetype to which it was related 'per analogiam'" (Dodaro, "'Christus Iustus,'" 351, citing Morrison, *Mimetic Tradition*, 70–71).

122. *Jo. ev. tr.* 92.2 (FC 90:171).

123. *Jo. ev. tr.* 92.2 (FC 90:171).

124. *Jo. ev. tr.* 93.1.

125. *Jo. ev. tr.* 92.2 (FC 90:172).

126. *S.* 299.7 (WSA III/8:234).

127. *En. Ps.* 40.1 (CCL 38:448; WSA III/16:225). The date of the homily is contested; it was probably preached before 410.

128. *Jo. ev. tr.* 92.2 (FC 90:171–72). On the theme of sweetness and delight in Augustine's theory and practice of preaching, see John Cavadini, "Sweetness of the Word."

129. *S.* 315.1.

130. *S.* 315.5 (WSA III/9:131).

131. *S.* 316.3.
132. *S.* 316.3–4.
133. Cornelius Mayer, O.S.A., "'Attende Stephanum conservum tuum' (Serm. 317,2,3): Sinn und Wert der Märtyrerverehrung nach den Stephanuspredigten Augustins," in Fructus Centesimus: *Mélanges offerts à Gerard J. M. Bartelink à l'occasion de son soixante-cinqième anniversaire*, ed. A. A. R. Bastiaensen, A. Hilhorst, and C. H. Kneepkens, Instrumenta Patristica 19 (Dordrecht: Kluwer Academic, 1989), 236.

Chapter 5
HEGEL'S SPIRITUAL COMMUNITY

1. Hodgson, *Hegel and Christian Theology*, 184n10; emphasis mine. Hodgson argues at greater length, albeit unconvincingly, for parallels between Augustine's and Hegel's Trinitarian theologies in his *God in History: Shapes of Freedom* (Nashville: Abingdon Press, 1989), 55–70.
2. Olson, *Hegel and the Spirit*, 143.
3. Olson, *Hegel and the Spirit*, 143.
4. Olson, *Hegel and the Spirit*, 143.
5. Olson, *Hegel and the Spirit*, 161.
6. O'Regan, *Heterodox Hegel*, 238; H. S. Harris, *Hegel's Development: Toward the Sunlight, 1770–1801* (Oxford: Clarendon, 1972), 110–25.
7. *PS* §787 (Miller, 478).
8. O'Regan, *Heterodox Hegel*, 238–39.
9. *LPR* (1827) 3:327–48; Dale Schlitt, *Hegel's Trinitarian Claim: A Critical Reflection* (Leiden: Brill, 1984), 212–26; Hodgson, *Hegel and Christian Theology*, 181–204.
10. Ulrich Asendorf, *Luther und Hegel: Untersuchungen zur Grundlegung einer neuen systematischen Theologie* (Wiesbaden: Franz Steiner Verlag, 1982).
11. E.g., Schultz, "Die Transformierung der *theologia crucis*," 77–79; O'Regan, *Heterodox Hegel*, 209–31.
12. Quoted in Olson, *Hegel and the Spirit*, 28; see Olson, *Hegel and the Spirit*, 28–29, 161, and *Enc.* §555 (*Mind*, 292–93).
13. Olson, *Hegel and the Spirit*, 29.
14. E.g., Asendorf, *Luther und Hegel*, 159, 517.
15. E.g., Asendorf, *Luther und Hegel*, 162–63.

16. Olson, *Hegel and the Spirit*, 155.

17. Olson, *Hegel and the Spirit*, 143; square brackets mine.

18. Olson, *Hegel and the Spirit*, 142–43.

19. See Olson, *Hegel and the Spirit*, 107–28, and Asendorf, *Luther und Hegel*, 418–59, esp. 450–56.

20. Steven E. Ozment, Homo Spiritualis*: A Comparative Study of the Anthropology of Johannes Tauler, Jean Gerson and Martin Luther (1509–16) in the Context of Their Theological Thought* (Leiden: Brill, 1969), esp. 87–216.

21. Ozment, Homo Spiritualis, 214–16.

22. Merold Westphal, "Hegel and the Reformation," in *History and System: Hegel's Philosophy of History; Proceedings of the 1982 Sessions of the Hegel Society of America*, ed. Robert L. Perkins (Albany, NY: SUNY Press, 1984), 77.

23. Westphal, "Hegel and the Reformation," 80.

24. Westphal, "Hegel and the Reformation," 80.

25. Cyril O'Regan, "The Religious and Theological Relevance of the French Revolution," in *Hegel and the Modern World*, ed. Ardis B. Collins (Albany, NY: SUNY Press, 1995), 44.

26. O'Regan, "Religious and Theological Relevance," 44–45.

27. Cf. O'Regan, *Heterodox Hegel*, 265.

28. Robin Bruce Barnes, *Prophecy and Gnosis: Apocalypticism in the Wake of the Lutheran Reformation* (Stanford: Stanford University Press, 1988), 22–23.

29. O'Regan, "Religious and Theological Relevance," 45.

30. O'Regan, "Religious and Theological Relevance," 45, citing Barnes, 48.

31. O'Regan, "Religious and Theological Relevance," 46–47.

32. O'Regan, "Religious and Theological Relevance," 47.

33. O'Regan, *Heterodox Hegel*, 276.

34. Marc Lienhard, *L'évangile et l'église chez Luther* (Paris: Éditions du Cerf, 1989), 122–23.

35. In addition to Lienhard, 107–30, see Hans-Jürgen Prien, "Grundgedanken der Ekklesiologie beim jungen Luther," *Archiv für Reformationsgeschichte* 76 (1985): 96–119; Scott H. Hendrix, "The Kingdom of Promise: Disappointment and Hope in Luther's Later Ecclesiology," *Lutherjahrbuch* 71 (2004): 37–60; and the more extensive literature cited in Hendrix's notes.

36. See Walter Mostert, "Hinweise zu Luthers Lehre vom Heiligen Geist," in *Der Heilige Geist im Verständnis Luthers und der lutherischen Theologie*, ed. Joachim Heubach (Erlangen: Martin-Luther-Verlag, 1990), 15–45, here esp. 22.

37. *LPH*, 393; square brackets mine. German from G. W. F. Hegel, *Vorlesungen über die Philosophie der Geschichte*, ed. Eva Moldenhauer and Karl Markus Michel, Theorie-Werkausgabe 12 (Frankfurt: Suhrkamp, 1970), 471.

38. *Vorlesungen über die Philosophie*, 488. Sibree's rendering of "das Tote des Geistes" as "that *caput mortuum* of Spirit" (*LPH*, 408) is suggestive, inasmuch as *caput* means "head" in Latin, but perhaps too liberal with the German.

39. *LPH*, 408.

40. *LPH*, 389–90.

41. *LPR* (1831) 3:338n240.

42. *LPH*, 390.

43. *LPH*, 390.

44. *LPH*, 344, 422.

45. *LPR* (1831) 3:338n243.

46. *LPH* 333, 344.

47. *Vorlesungen über die Philosophie*, 468; *LPH*, 390.

48. *LPH*, 332; *LPR* (1827) 3:333.

49. *Vorlesungen über die Philosophie*, 402–3; *LPH*, 328, 334.

50. *LPH*, 332–33.

51. *LPH*, 408; square brackets mine.

52. *Enc.* §389 (*Mind*, 29–30). German from G. W. F. Hegel, *Enzyklopädie der philosophischen Wissenschaften III: Die Philosophie des Geistes*, ed. Eva Moldenhauer and Karl Markus Michel, Theorie-Werkausgabe 10 (Frankfurt: Suhrkamp, 1970), 43–44.

53. For a detailed treatment of Hegel's solution to the body-soul problem, see Michael Wolff, *Das Körper-Seele-Problem: Kommentar zu Hegel, Enzyklopädie (1830), §389* (Frankfurt: Vittorio Klostermann, 1992).

54. *LPR* (1824) 3:231n183.

55. Wolff, *Das Körper-Seele-Problem*, 28, 49, 74; cf. *Enc.* §389: "The fact is that in the Idea of Life the self-externalism of nature is implicitly at an end: subjectivity is the very substance and conception of life—with this proviso, however, that its existence or objectivity is still at the same time forfeited to the sway of self-externalism" (*Mind*, 30).

56. *Enc.* §388; Wolff, *Das Körper-Seele-Problem*, 118–19.

57. *Enc.* §389.

58. *Enc.* §409, referring to §389. See Wolff, *Das Körper-Seele-Problem*, 127, where he notes that Hegel here follows Aristotle's distinction of οὐσία as ὑποκείμενον or ὕλη, on the one hand, and εἶδος, on the other.

59. *Enc.* §216, §403 A.

60. E.g., *De anima* 2.4, 415b 14–15; cf. Wolff, *Das Körper-Seele-Problem*, 128.

61. Wolff, *Das Körper-Seele-Problem*, 128.

62. *Enc.* §389 (*Enzyklopädie der philosophischen Wissenschaften III*, 44; *Mind*, 30).

63. So Hegel, already in §389: "There [in spirit], in the intelligible unity which exists as freedom, as absolute negativity, and not as the immediate or natural individual, the object or the reality of the intelligible unity is the unity itself; and so the self-externalism, which is a fundamental feature of matter, has been completely dissipated and transmuted into universality, or the subjective ideality of the conceptual unity. Mind [*Geist* (spirit)] is the existent truth of matter—the truth that matter itself has no truth" (*Mind*, 30; square brackets mine).

64. Wolff, *Das Körper-Seele-Problem*, 131–32.

65. Wolff, *Das Körper-Seele-Problem*, 133–34.

66. Wolff, *Das Körper-Seele-Problem*, 136.

67. Wolff, *Das Körper-Seele-Problem*, 140.

68. Wolff, *Das Körper-Seele-Problem*, 140–41. Wolff points out that Hegel here deviates from important figures in the philosophical tradition. In Hegel's denial of actuality to the soul conceived as the inner telos of an animal, Wolff discovers implicit criticism of Aristotle. And in the reduction of any nonexpressive, hence purely subjective, soul to mere nature, he finds Hegelian critique of Kant (142). German from *Enzyklopädie der philosophischen Wissenschaften III*, 192.

69. Cf. Wolff, *Das Körper-Seele-Problem*, 140n60.

70. *Enc.* §411 (*Enzyklopädie der philosophischen Wissenschaften III*, 190; *Mind*, 147); square brackets mine.

71. Wolff, *Das Körper-Seele-Problem*, 142–43.

72. *Enc.* §410 Zu. (*Mind*, 146).

73. *Enc.* §222 (*Logic*, 282).

74. *LPH*, 408, here faithful to the German: "wo sich Seele zu Seele und Geist zu Geist verhält" and "ist ... die geistige Form das in ihm Beseelende und ein in sich selbst Wahres" (*Vorlesungen über die Philosophie*, 488–89; square brackets mine).

75. *Enc.* §411 (*Mind*, 147).
76. Wolff, *Das Körper-Seele-Problem*, 154–55.
77. *Enc.* §410 Zu. (*Mind*, 146).
78. *LPH*, 422–23.
79. *LPH*, 445, 456.
80. *LPH*, 354.
81. *LPH*, 354.
82. *LPH*, 354; square brackets mine.
83. *LPH*, 354–55.
84. *LPH*, 355.
85. *PR* §1 A. (Nisbet, 25).
86. *PR* §30 (Nisbet, 59).
87. *LPH*, 423.
88. *LPR* (ms) 3:140; square brackets mine, italics Hegel's.
89. *LPR* (ms) 3:140.
90. O'Regan, *Heterodox Hegel*, 238–49.
91. *LPR* (1827) 3:280.
92. *LPR* (1831) 3:284n93; square brackets mine, italics Hegel's.
93. Hegel's use of the term "mystical" (*mystisch*) bears the same meaning of "revelatory" as his use of the word "mystery": "For the mystical is not concealment of a secret, or ignorance, but consists in the self knowing itself to be one with the divine Being and that this, therefore, is revealed" (*PS* §722 [Miller, 437]). Concerning Paul, see, e.g., 1 Cor 2.1: "When I came to you, brothers, proclaiming the mystery of God . . ." Cf. Cyril O'Regan, "Hegelian Philosophy of Religion and Eckhartian Mysticism," in *New Perspectives on Hegel's Philosophy of Religion*, ed. David Kolb (Albany: SUNY Press, 1992), 121–22; more extensively, O'Regan, *Heterodox Hegel*, 29–80.
94. 1 Cor 2.1–10.
95. See *LPR* (ms) 1:86–88, including n. 15; *LPR* (1827) 1:162–63, including n. 33.
96. O'Regan, "Hegelian Philosophy of Religion," 121–22; Louis Bouyer, "Mysticism/An Essay on the History of the Word," in *Understanding Mysticism*, ed. Richard Woods (Garden City, NY: Image Books, 1980), 42–55.
97. For possible Augustinian Lutheran influence on the issue of original sin, see the editorial note at *LHP* (1825–26) 3:24n18.
98. *LPH*, 333.
99. O'Regan, "Hegelian Philosophy of Religion," 109–29; O'Regan, *Heterodox Hegel*, 250–63.

100. See the editorial comment at *LPR* (1824) 1:347n166.

101. O'Regan, *Heterodox Hegel*, 250–52.

102. *LPR* (1824) 1:347–48.

103. *Enc.* §564 (*Mind*, 298); Hegel is here drawing on Göschel.

104. The witness of spirit to Christ's divinity leads the believer "to know himself made one with the essential Being. Thus the Being of Beings . . . through this mediation brings about its own indwelling in self-consciousness, and is the actual presence of the essential and self-subsisting spirit who is all in all" (*Enc.* §570 [*Mind*, 301]).

105. O'Regan, *Heterodox Hegel*, 254; with regard to Hegel, see ch. 1 above.

106. O'Regan, *Heterodox Hegel*, 255.

107. *LPR* 3:387 frag. 3.

108. For the historical transmission of Joachimite concepts to Hegel, see O'Regan, *Heterodox Hegel*, 275–78. See also Henri de Lubac, *La postérité spirituelle de Joachim de Fiore* (Paris: Lethielleux, 1979), and Peter Henrici, "Die Säkularisierung der Apokalyptik in der neueren deutschen Philosophie," in *Hegel für Theologen: Gesammelte Aufsätze* (Fribourg: Academic Press Fribourg, 2009), 133–55.

109. O'Regan, *Heterodox Hegel*, 263–78, esp. 270.

110. O'Regan, *Heterodox Hegel*, 275–79.

111. On the dispute concerning influence, see Peggy Cosmann, "Der Einfluß Friedrich Christoph Oetingers auf Hegels Abrechnung mit Spinoza," *Zeitschrift für Religions- und Geistesgeschichte* 50, no. 2 (1998): 115–36, esp. 115n2. See also Dickey, *Hegel*, 77–112, and Ernst Benz, "Johann Albrecht Bengel und die Philosophie des deutschen Idealismus," *Deutsche Vierteljahrsschrift für Literaturwissenschaft und Geistesgeschichte* 27 (1953): 528–54.

112. Quoted in Benz, "Johann Albrecht Bengel," 533; translation mine.

113. Benz, "Johann Albrecht Bengel," 534–35.

114. Benz, "Johann Albrecht Bengel," 547. Compare Oetinger, "God's essence consists in the *manifestatio sui*, in revelation of his very self" (quoted in Benz, "Johann Albrecht Bengel," 547; translation mine), with Hegel, "It is the essence of God as spirit to be for an other, i.e., to reveal himself" (*LPR* [1824] 3:170). Concerning Oetinger's possible influence upon Hegel's interpretation of Leibniz, Cosmann argues, "Hegel dürfte kaum entgangen sein, daß die bei Böhme erst avant la lettre beschriebene und dann von Oetinger dafür geprägte 'Selbstbewegung Gottes' mindestens so spekulativ ist wie die 'causa sui' von Spinoza" (115).

115. Benz, "Johann Albrecht Bengel," 545–54.

116. See Gregory R. Johnson, ed., *Kant on Swedenborg: Dreams of a Spirit-Seer and Other Writings*, tr. Gregory R. Johnson and Glenn Alexander Magee (West Chester, PA: Swedenborg Foundation Publishers, 2002), 5–66; see also Ernst Benz, *Swedenborg in Deutschland: F. C. Oetingers und Immanuel Kants Auseinandersetzung mit der Person und Lehre Emanuel Swedenborgs* (Frankfurt: Vittorio Klostermann, 1947).

117. Benz, "Johann Albrecht Bengel," 550.

118. *PS* §212.

119. *LPH*, 416.

120. *LPH*, 416–17.

121. O'Regan, *Heterodox Hegel*, 270. In this regard he is again similar to Joachim, though Hegel radically ontologizes what for Joachim remains a transformed existential relation between the human community and the divine.

122. *LPH*, 445.

123. *LPH*, 417.

124. *Enc.* §552; *LPH*, 419, 449.

125. *Vorlesungen über die Philosophie*, 502; *LPH*, 422; square brackets containing German mine.

126. "The path of torturous discipline [found in Catholicism] is . . . dispensed with . . . for the waking up of consciousness finds man surrounded by the element of a moral state of society. The phase of negation is, indeed, a necessary element in human development, but it has now assumed the tranquil form of education, so that all the terrible characteristics of that inward struggle vanish. Humanity has now attained the consciousness of a real internal harmonization of Spirit, and a good conscience in regard to actuality—to secular existence. The Human Spirit has come to stand on its own basis. . . . There is no revolt against the Divine, but a manifestation of that better subjectivity, which recognizes the Divine in its own being" (*LPH*, 407–8; square brackets mine).

127. *Vorlesungen über die Philosophie*, 524; *LPH*, 442; square brackets mine.

128. Hegel's pneumatic and eschatological interpretation of Lutheranism, as shaped by concepts of Eckhartian and Joachimite provenance, entails a number of significant transformations of later Lutheran Orthodoxy as well. The Pietistic shift of focus from justification to sanctification and deification leads in Hegel to a parity between the divine and human that violates what for the orthodox is essentially a relationship of human dependence

upon God. The investing of time with revelatory and soteriological weight is also problematic. It undermines the historical uniqueness and sufficiency of revelation in Christ and prematurely unites faith and knowledge, whose intrahistorical attainment, along with that of freedom, only gives greater occasion for pride and sin (O'Regan, *Heterodox Hegel*, 277–79).

129. *LPH*, 334.
130. *LPH*, 383; *PR* §270 (Nisbet, 302).
131. *LPH*, 382; *PR* §270 A. (Nisbet, 302).
132. *PR* §270 A. (Nisbet, 304); cf. *LPH*, 448.
133. *PR* §270 A. (Nisbet, 304).
134. *LPH*, 358.
135. *PR* §270 (Nisbet, 295n, 302).
136. *LPH*, 338.
137. *PR* §270 (Nisbet, 292).
138. In that regard, the thesis of Alice Ormiston's work on Hegel's political philosophy, *Love and Politics*, takes on especial interest for our comparison with Augustine and his Trinitarian ethical injunctions of love of love and love of justice (see *Trin.* 8). Ormiston argues that Hegel's early concept of love, of dialectical unity in the whole of reality, in fact remains the underlying animating force of his mature social and political thought. There is, in her view, no rational explanation for the reconciliation of judging and active conscience in the *Phenomenology of Spirit* apart from religious experience, from grace, a primordial experience of love or unity now actively willed by the individual (Ormiston, *Love and Politics*, 54). *The Philosophy of Right* then stands as the fully concrete willing of that love in the secular world, the ultimate reconciliation of love and reason (Ormiston, *Love and Politics*, 65–71). All the same, even if there is an implicit moment of grace or love underlying Hegel's mature thought, that love is ultimately and definitively articulated in terms of *Vernunft* and freedom qua self-determination, such that its gracious or gift character is ultimately subsumed or even subverted in a system of rational autonomy.
139. "For it is a false principle that the fetters which bind Right and Freedom can be broken without the emancipation of conscience—that there can be a Revolution without a Reformation" (*LPH*, 453).
140. *LPH*, 333.
141. Mk 15.34; Mt 27.46
142. Martin Wendte, "Lamentation between Contradiction and Obedience: Hegel and Barth as Diametrically Opposed Brothers in the

Spirit of Modernity," in *Evoking Lament: A Theological Discussion*, ed. Eva Harasta and Brian Brock (London: T&T Clark, 2009), 77–78; square brackets mine. Wendte is following in part Oswald Bayer, "Zur Theologie der Klage," in *Klage*, ed. Martin Ebner, Jahrbuch für biblische Theologie 16 (Neukirchen-Vluyn: Neukirchener Verlag, 2001), 289–301.

143. Wendte, "Lamentation between Contradiction and Obedience," 78.

144. *LPR* (1827) 3:337.

145. Wendte, "Lamentation between Contradiction and Obedience," 79.

146. Wendte, "Lamentation between Contradiction and Obedience," 80.

147. *LPH*, 424–26.

148. *Reason*, 69.

149. *Reason*, 66–67.

150. *Reason*, 66–67; square brackets and italics mine.

151. *Reason*, 67.

152. *LPH*, 457.

153. *Reason*, 51.

154. See Robert Gascoigne, *Religion, Rationality, and Community: Sacred and Secular in the Thought of Hegel and His Critics* (The Hague: M. Nijhoff, 1985), 59–64.

155. Desmond, *Hegel's God*, 40–41.

156. See Job 10, where Job's lament expresses the anguished experience of unresolved contradiction: how is it that God, who apparently fashioned Job as a part of his good creation, now seems to abuse that same creation in a manner inconsistent with its original dignity?

157. This relationship is investigated in Michael Cameron, "Augustine's Construction of Figurative Exegesis against the Donatists in the *Enarrationes in Psalmos*" (PhD diss., University of Chicago, 1996), and Michael Cameron, *Christ Meets Me Everywhere: Augustine's Early Figurative Exegesis*, Oxford Studies in Historical Theology (Oxford: Oxford University Press, 2012); see also Hubertus R. Drobner, *Person-Exegese und Christologie bei Augustinus: Zur Herkunft der Formel* Una Persona (Leiden: Brill, 1986).

158. Kimberly Baker, "Augustine's Doctrine of the *Totus Christus*: Reflecting on the Church as Sacrament of Unity," *Horizons* 37, no. 1 (Spring 2010): 11.

159. "The Spirit is the whole, and not just one or the other elements in isolation" (*Reason*, 51).

160. In somewhat other terminology, these characteristics of Augustine's theology of lament in the *Enarrationes in Psalmos* are treated summarily in Brian Brock, "Augustine's Incitement to Lament from the *Enarrationes in Psalmos*," in *Evoking Lament: A Theological Discussion*, ed. Eva Harasta and Brian Brock (London: T&T Clark, 2009), 183–203.

161. *Reason*, 38; *doc. Chr.* 1.5–7.

162. *Doc. Chr.* P.6, 1.12.

163. *Doc. Chr.* P.6, 1.11, 1.13, 1.33.

164. Cf. *doc. Chr.* 1.38.

165. For an account of how Augustine's figurative exegesis aims to deconstruct "materialistic" or "fleshly" readings of scripture through the very struggle with the matter or words of scripture, see David Dawson, "Sign Theory, Allegorical Reading, and the Motions of the Soul in *De doctrina christiana*," in *De doctrina christiana: A Classic of Western Culture*, ed. Duane W. H. Arnold and Pamela Bright (Notre Dame, IN: University of Notre Dame Press, 1995), 123–44.

166. *Doc. Chr.* P.1–9.

167. *LPH*, 330–31; see Cyril O'Regan, "Hegel's Retrieval of Philo: Constitution of a Christian Heretic," *Studia Philonica Annual* 20 (2008): 101–27.

168. See O'Regan, *Heterodox Hegel*, 149–50.

169. *LPH*, 417.

170. *LPR* (1831) 3:319n191.

171. *LPR* (1827) 3:258.

172. In Hegel's concept of religion, this elevation of thought passes through the intermediate stage of doctrinal exposition. Both Augustine (e.g., *doc. Chr.* P.6) and Hegel consider teaching to be an essential task of the church (e.g., *LPR* [1827] 3:334). But for Augustine, doctrine remains fundamentally christological and incarnational in form and content. It remains governed by what he considers to be the overarching narrative structure, if not always the explicit or particular letter, of scripture: i.e., the rule of faith. Contrariwise, scripture and its doctrinal exposition, in Hegel's view, have a christological form but pneumatological content. Their form is positive; they come to the subject from without, both in terms of the historical development of Christian doctrine and the community's existence prior to the individual subject's integration into it through baptism.

But the former developmental trajectory conditions the latter inasmuch as in Hegel's spiritual community the kingdom of God has dawned. It is the community as a whole that is conscious of the Spirit's presence: "By means of the Spirit, which is present in it, the community is the infinite power and authority needed for the development and progressive determination of its doctrine" (*LPR* [ms] 3:151n235). The immanence of Spirit in the communal body means that individual members need only be properly taught. In his analysis of the emergence of rational self-consciousness in the modern period, then, Hegel does not share with Augustine a sense of a still fundamentally disordered resistance of creation to reason. Any resistance Hegel does find is rationally explicable and hence superable, because the logic of divine reason itself encompasses the movement of human becoming. It is that reason, i.e. Spirit, which forms the content of the community's teaching. Now that thought has become conscious of itself, the only adequate standard by which to interpret scripture is by the categories of thought itself, that is, by infinite Spirit. It is likewise in the formation of doctrine. The positive form of doctrine is unavoidable, but it must now be formulated in accordance with the community's consciousness of its own freedom, of its share in the Holy Spirit. In that sense, the content of doctrine must be pneumatological, must render individual humans aware of their identity with Spirit, of their own activity in interpretation, learning, and the appropriation of the truth.

173. *LPR* (1827) 3:260; square brackets mine.
174. *LPR* (1827) 1:442.
175. Hodgson, *Hegel and Christian Theology*, 190.
176. Walter Jaeschke, *Reason in Religion: The Foundations of Hegel's Philosophy of Religion*, trans. J. Michael Stewart and Peter C. Hodgson (Berkeley: University of California Press, 1990), 325–35. This helps explain Hegel's surprising emphasis on eucharistic doctrine in *LPH*. It is a means of doctrinally grounding the reconciliation of Spirit with the secular world in Lutheran Protestantism.
177. Desmond, *Hegel's God*, 58.
178. *LPR* (1827) 1:443.
179. Desmond, *Hegel's God*, 60. Martin Wendte describes the process thus: "Hegel begins with outside perspectives, then turns to the consideration of their contradictions, thus integrating further perspectives and building up an all-encompassing perspective that becomes an inside perspective" (Wendte, "Lamentation between Contradiction and

Obedience," 78). The inside perspective that is attained by Hegel is, essentially, the eschatological vision of the triune God, no longer in a dark mirror but face-to-face.

180. *LPR* (1827) 1:445.

181. By "Augustinian confession" I mean a gesture not only of admitting guilt, but of praising God for his grace and mercy. The relationship marked by Augustinian confession remains constitutively asymmetrical, as opposed to Hegel's account of confession and forgiveness, which aims ultimately at self-reconciliation.

182. E.g., *LPR* (ms) 3:156–58; see also *LPR* (1827) 1:445; Jaeschke, *Reason in Religion*, 325.

183. "The Relationship of Religion to the State according to the Lectures of 1831," in *LPR* 1:452.

184. *LPR* (1827) 1:445.

185. *LPR* (1827) 1:445–46.

186. *LPR* (1827) 1:446.

187. *Trin.* 15.51.

188. For Hegel's discussion of the development of moral agency through conscience, see *PS* §§217–30. The discussion of conscience and forgiveness at *PS* §§632–71 is also pertinent here.

189. *LPR* (1827) 1:446.

190. *LPR* (1827) 1:446–47.

191. Cf. Desmond, *Hegel's God*, 56–57.

192. *LPR* (1824) 3:236.

193. *LPR* (1824) 3:236; italics mine.

194. *LPR* (1827) 3:337.

195. *LPR* (ms) 3:153.

196. *LPR* (ms) 3:152–53, esp. 53n237.

197. Lawrence S. Stepelevich, "Hegel and the Lutheran Eucharist," *Heythrop Journal* 27, no. 3 (1986): 267.

198. *LPR* (1824) 3:236.

199. *LPR* (ms) 3:154.

200. Hegel holds this position early in his career. See *ETW*, 248–53.

201. *LPR* (1824) 3:236.

202. Stepelevich, "Hegel and the Lutheran Eucharist," 267–68.

203. Stepelevich, "Hegel and the Lutheran Eucharist," 268; square brackets mine.

204. *LPR* (1824) 3:236; square brackets mine.

205. *LPR* (1827) 3:339.
206. *Trin.* 15.51.

Chapter 6
AUGUSTINE AND A CATHOLIC CHURCH WITH SOUL?

1. *Trin.* 15.11 (WSA I/5:403).
2. *Trin.* 15.11.
3. *Trin.* 12.12 (WSA I/5:328–29).
4. *Conf.* 7.2.3.
5. See *ep.* 18.2 and 166.4; Alan D. Fitzgerald, O.S.A., "Body," in *Augustine through the Ages*, 105.
6. Brian Daley, S.J., "Christology," in *Augustine through the Ages*, 165.
7. John Rist, *Augustine: Ancient Thought Baptized* (Cambridge: Cambridge University Press, 1994), 96.
8. *Nupt. et conc.* 2; see Paula Fredriksen, "Beyond the Body/Soul Dichotomy: Augustine on Paul against the Manichees and the Pelagians," *Recherches Augustiniennes* 23 (1988): 87–114.
9. *Ord.* 2.16.44; 2.19.50; 2.11.31. For biblical qualification of this flight imagery, see T. J. Van Bavel, O.S.A., "'No One Ever Hated His Own Flesh': Eph. 5:29 in Augustine," *Augustiniana* 45 (1995): 53–54, 54n41, and Fitzgerald, "Body," 106. The quotation from Porphyry stems from his lost text, *On the Return of the Soul*, which Augustine discusses in *s.* 241.7 as well as *civ. Dei* 10.29 and 22.26. On the meaning of the statement in Porphyry's thought, see Andrew Smith, *Porphyry's Place in the Neoplatonic Tradition: A Study in Post-Plotinian Neoplatonism* (The Hague: Martinus Nijhoff, 1974), 20–39. For Augustine's controversy with Porphyry, see Isabelle Bochet, "Résurrection et réincarnation: La polémique d'Augustin contre les platoniciens et contre Porphyre dans les *Sermons* 240–242," in Ministerium Sermonis: *Philological, Historical, and Theological Studies on Augustine's* Sermones ad populum, ed. Gert Partoens, Anthony Dupont, and Mathijs Lamberigts (Turnhout: Brepols, 2009), 267–98, and Isabelle Bochet, "The Role of Scripture in Augustine's Controversy with Porphyry," *Augustinian Studies* 41, no. 1 (2010): 7–52.
10. On the heavy chain, see *mor.* 22.40; Van Bavel, "'No One Ever Hated,'" 51–55 and 54n43. On flight from the cave, see *sol.* 1.14.24; Van Bavel, "'No One Ever Hated,'" 51–55 and 54n42.

11. Fitzgerald, "Body," 105.
12. *Sol.* 1.1.2; *quant.* 33.73; *mor.* 5.7–8; Fitzgerald, "Body," 105–6.
13. Fredriksen, "Beyond the Body/Soul Dichotomy," 87–114.
14. Van Bavel, "'No One Ever Hated,'" 45–93.
15. Rist summarizes Augustine's new view of the resurrection: "The resurrection body—necessarily the best possible 'body'—is undubitably fleshly. Instead of a Neoplatonic spiritualizing away of the flesh, the flesh itself will become spiritual" (*Augustine: Ancient Thought Baptized*, 99).
16. See *civ. Dei* 13.16–18 and 22.30. It would betray a lack of faith in the creator's power to re-create the world, if one insisted in principle on the need to escape the body.
17. Augustine uses a number of terms in Latin: *contemperatio* (*quant.* 30.59); *mixtura* (*ep.* 137.3.11); *coniunctum* (*civ. Dei* 13.24) (Rist, *Augustine: Ancient Thought Baptized*, 99).
18. *Imm. an.* 14.24; *Jo. ev. tr.* 26.13; *s.* 65.4; Rist, *Augustine: Ancient Thought Baptized*, 100.
19. Rist concludes, "It seems that Augustine's growing theological confidence—itself the result of a long and shifting process of thought—about the appropriate language to be used for the Incarnation encouraged him to think that he need not worry about the queerness or uniqueness of the relationship between the substances soul and body. If so, it is another example of his view that *only theological* explanations will enable certain philosophical problems to be solved, or at least admit of a rational solution (to be fully understood by God if not by us)" (*Augustine: Ancient Thought Baptized*, 100–101).
20. On the incarnation as intrinsically pedagogical, see *ep.* 137.12; on the wondrousness of creation, see *ep.* 137.10: "But what does God do in all the movements of creatures that would not be marvelous if it had not grown common by daily familiarity?" (WSA II/2:217). Cf. *civ. Dei* 10.12.
21. See *civ. Dei* 10.12.
22. *Ep.* 137.11 (WSA II/2:218).
23. *Ep.* 137.11 (WSA II/2:218); italics mine.
24. For Hegel's interpretation of the Roman legal "person," see *PS* §§477–83 and *LPH*, 318–36; in the latter he discusses its relation to early Christianity. See also Doull and Peddle, "Augustine and Hegel," 169–96, though from a theological standpoint I resist their teleological assumptions concerning Hegel's resolution and sublation of the apparent difficulties in Augustine's interpretation of history.
25. *En. Ps.* 21(1).1 (CCL 38:117); *en. Ps.* 21(1).7 (CCL 38:118).

26. *Ex. Gal.* 27 (CSEL 84:92); Daley, "Christology," 165.
27. Daley, "Christology," 165; Drobner, *Person-Exegese*, 241–70.
28. *Ep.* 137.11 (WSA II/2:218).
29. *Ep.* 137.9.
30. *Ep.* 137.9 (CSEL 44:117–18).
31. *Ep.* 137.9: "Look, it has happened in that way, and yet certain heretics who are wrongly amazed and who wrongly praise that power absolutely refuse to acknowledge in him a human nature in which there is the full proclamation of the grace by which he saves those who believe in him" (WSA II/2:217).
32. *Ep.* 137.11.
33. *Ep.* 137.9 (WSA II/2:217); italics mine.
34. Rist, *Augustine: Ancient Thought Baptized*, 101.
35. Rist, *Augustine: Ancient Thought Baptized*, 108–9, citing *mus.* 6.5.9 and *Gn. litt.* 7.25.36; 8.21.42.
36. *Gn. litt.* 12.35.68.
37. *Civ. Dei* 1.13 (Bettenson, 22); square brackets mine.
38. *S.* 155.15 (WSA III/5:93).
39. *Civ. Dei* 22.24 (Bettenson, 1074).
40. *Civ. Dei* 22.24, where Augustine quotes Ps 103.1 (LXX): "You have clothed yourself in praise and beauty" (104.1 LXX according to Bettenson; the verse Augustine cites is actually Ps 103.1 LXX).
41. *S.* 82.13, citing 1 Cor 3.16–17 and 6.19–20.
42. Rist, *Augustine: Ancient Thought Baptized*, 111.
43. Cited in *util. jejun.* 4 (WSA III/10:474).
44. Cited in *util. jejun.* 4 (WSA III/10:474).
45. *Util. jejun.* 5 (WSA III/10:474).
46. *Util. jejun.* 4–5; Van Bavel, "'No One Ever Hated,'" 73.
47. *En. Ps.* 148.8 (WSA III/20:482–83); square brackets mine.
48. *En. Ps.* 148.8 (CCL 40:2170; WSA III/20:481–82); square brackets mine.
49. *En. Ps.* 127.8 (CCL 40:1872; WSA III/20:104); square brackets and italics mine.
50. *S.* 268.2 (WSA III/7:278–79); italics mine.
51. *S.* 268.2 (WSA III/7:279).
52. *Ep. Jo.* 6.10 (PL 35:2025; FC 92:209); square brackets mine.
53. *Ep. Jo.* 6.10 (FC 92:209).
54. *Ep. Jo.* 6.10 (FC 92:209); square brackets mine. For Augustine's use of the Stoic theory of vision, see FC 92:209n46.

55. *Ep. Jo.* 6.10 (FC 92:209).
56. Cited in *ep. Jo.* 6.13 (FC 92:214).
57. *Ep. Jo.* 6.13 (FC 92:214).
58. Quoted in *ep. Jo.* 6.14 (FC 92:215); italics and square brackets mine. See FC 92:215n65.
59. *Ep. Jo.* 6.14 (FC 92:215).
60. *Ep. Jo.* 10.3 (FC 92:265).
61. *Ep. Jo.* 10.3 (FC 92:265).
62. "'In this we know that we love the sons of God, because we love God.' And how? Are not the sons of God one thing, God another? But he who loves God loves his precepts. And what are the precepts of God? 'A new commandment I give to you, that you love one another' [Jn 13.34]. Let no one excuse himself by one love in reference to another love. This love totally maintains itself thus: as it itself has been bound together into a single whole, so all who are connected with it make a single whole, and it is as though a fire melts them together. . . . But unless the heat of love should blaze up, there cannot occur a melting together of many into a single whole. 'Because we love God, from this we know that we love the sons of God'" (*Ep. Jo.* 10.3 [FC 92:266]; square brackets mine).
63. Lewis Ayres, "Augustine on the Spirit as the Soul of the Body; or, Fragments of a Trinitarian Ecclesiology," *Augustinian Studies* 41, no. 1 (2010): 171–72.
64. Ayres, "Augustine on the Spirit," 178.
65. Ayres, "Augustine on the Spirit," 182.
66. In the preface to his Italian translation of G. W. F. Hegel's *Elements of the Philosophy of Right*, provocatively entitled *Hegel, filosofo di Babilonia* (Naples: Alfredo Guida, 2001), Marcello Caleo ponders whether Hegel's political philosophy implicitly intends to call into question Augustine's distinction between the "City of God," prefigured by Jerusalem, and the "City of Humankind," prefigured by Babylon. See also Marcello Caleo, "Sant' Agostino e Hegel a Confronto."
67. This, in spite of Augustine's notorious support for the coercion of the Donatists by the Roman state. See John Bowlin, "Augustine on Justifying Coercion," *Annual of the Society of Christian Ethics* 17 (1997): 49–70, and Markus, *Saeculum*, 133–53. For a constructive attempt to read Augustine against himself with regard to religious coercion, see Eric Gregory, *Politics and the Order of Love: An Augustinian Ethic of Democratic Citizenship* (Chicago: University of Chicago Press, 2008), 298–318.

68. In addition to Ayres's article on the Holy Spirit as the soul of the church and Cavadini's article "Truth in Augustine's *De trinitate*," see Cavadini, "The Darkest Enigma: Reconsidering the Self in Augustine's Thought," *Augustinian Studies* 38, no. 1 (2007): 119–32.

69. See esp. Michael Cameron, *Augustine's Construction of Figurative Exegesis*, but also Cameron, *Christ Meets Me Everywhere*.

70. Cameron describes the relationship in a way similar to Augustine's early, but consistent, substantial distinction between the soul and the body: "The *signum* given in the world of sense points beyond itself in order to raise the soul to understanding in the world of spirit to which the senses can bear witness but of which they cannot partake. *Signum* and *res* stand related but separate by reason of their participation in mutually exclusive universes which, even when mingled as water and earth are mingled in mud, nevertheless remain distinguishable" (*Augustine's Construction of Figurative Exegesis*, 58).

71. This can happen in two different ways: (1) the *signum* possesses a disjunctive relationship to its *res*, such that it is surpassed and discarded upon full manifestation of the *res*, or (2) "the *res* itself by a conjunction appears fragmentarily within the *signum*, temporally anticipating its own full disclosure" (Cameron, *Augustine's Construction of Figurative Exegesis*, 58).

72. Cameron, *Augustine's Construction of Figurative Exegesis*, 58–59.

73. Cameron, *Augustine's Construction of Figurative Exegesis*, 97–99.

74. Cameron, *Augustine's Construction of Figurative Exegesis*, 100–101.

75. *En. Ps.* 32(2).2 (CCL 38:248; WSA III/15:393); square brackets mine.

76. Cameron, *Augustine's Construction of Figurative Exegesis*, 103–4.

77. *En. Ps.* 32(2).2 (WSA III/15:393); square brackets mine.

78. This was in fact one line of defense against modalism made by Latin Trinitarian theologians prior to Augustine. Considering Hegel's tendency toward a form of reverse modalism, this is not an unimportant theological point. See, e.g., Tertullian, *Against Praxeas* 23, and Novatian, *The Trinity* 26.

79. *En. Ps.* 32(2).1–2.

80. *Ep.* 55.1.2 (WSA II/1:216).

81. *Ep.* 55.1.2 (WSA II/1:216); square brackets mine.

82. *Ep.* 55.2.3 (WSA II/1:217); square brackets mine.

83. *Ep.* 55.2.3 (WSA II/1:217).

84. *Ep.* 55.2.3 (WSA II/1:217).
85. *Ep.* 55.9.17 (WSA II/1:224).
86. *Ep.* 55.9.17 (WSA II/1:224).
87. *Ep.* 55.10.19.
88. *Ep.* 55.10.18.
89. *Ep.* 55.10.19 (WSA II/1:225).
90. *Ep.* 55.14.24 (WSA II/1:227).
91. *Ep.* 55.14.24 (WSA II/1:228).
92. *Ep.* 55.14.24 (WSA II/1:228).
93. *Ep.* 55.14.25 (WSA II/1:228).
94. *Ep.* 55.14.25 (WSA II/1:228).
95. *Ep.* 55.16.30 (WSA II/1:232); square brackets mine.

96. Hegel pushes Paul here: "This reconciliation is the peace of God, which does not 'surpass all reason,' but is rather the peace that *through* reason is first known and thought and is recognized as what is true" (*LPR* [1827] 3:347). He is quoting the German translation of Phil 4.7, which contains *Vernunft* rather than *Verstand*, a crucial distinction in Hegel's philosophy. See *LPR* (1827) 3:347n266.

97. Here I primarily follow Michael C. McCarthy, S.J., "An Ecclesiology of Groaning: Augustine, the Psalms, and the Making of the Church," *Theological Studies* 66, no. 1 (2005): 23–48, in particular his section entitled "The Development of Augustine's Theology of the Psalms."

98. Hilary of Poitier, *Tractatus super psalmum* 1.2 (CCL 61:20): "Omnis ad eum prophetia est referenda psalmorum."

99. The psalmic witness to a wide rage of emotions thus played a role in the development of Augustine's Christology: "These texts of joy, anguish, anger and despair injected images of seething human passions into the neat christology of the spiritualist paradigm, and pressed Augustine to go beyond mere confession to understand more exactly the saving function of Christ's full humanity" (Cameron, *Augustine's Construction of Figurative Exegesis*, 96).

100. Kimberly Baker, "Augustine's Doctrine of the *Totus Christus*," 12.

101. For a lucid analysis of Augustine's theological development as evidenced in his earliest commentaries on the Psalms, see Cameron, *Christ Meets Me Everywhere*, 165–212.

102. See the exhaustive treatment in Michael Fiedrowicz, Psalmus vox totius Christi: *Studien zu Augustins "Enarrationes in Psalmos"* (Freiburg: Herder, 1997).

103. McCarthy, "An Ecclesiology of Groaning," 32.
104. *Ep.* 140.5.13–6.15.
105. *Ep.* 140.6.16 (CSEL 44:167; WSA II/2:252); square brackets mine.
106. *Ep.* 140.6.15 (WSA II/2:252). Augustine's quotation from the Psalms would have been at 21.2 in his Bible.
107. *Ep.* 140.6.18 (WSA II/2:253); square brackets mine.
108. *Ep.* 140.6.18 (WSA II/2:253).
109. *Ep.* 140.6.18 (WSA II/2:253).
110. See 2 Cor 12.2.
111. *En. Ps.* 30(2).3 (WSA III/15:322–23).
112. *En. Ps.* 30(2).3 (WSA III/15:323).
113. In the present text, Augustine makes this personal unity explicit: "I want you to understand that Head and body together are called one Christ. To make this quite clear he says, when speaking of marriage, *They will be two in one flesh; so they are two no longer, but one flesh* (Mt 19:5–6). But perhaps it might be thought that he only means this to apply to any ordinary marriage? No, because listen to what Paul tells us: *They will be two in one flesh*, he says. *This is a great mystery, but I am referring to Christ and the Church* (Eph 5:31–32). So out of two people one single person [*una quaedam persona*] comes to be, the single person that is Head and body, Bridegroom and bride" (*en. Ps.* 30(2).4 [CCL 38:193; WSA III/15:324]; square brackets mine).
114. *En. Ps.* 30(2).3 (WSA III/15:323–24).
115. *En. Ps.* 30(2).4 (WSA III/15:324).
116. *En. Ps.* 30(2).4 (WSA III/15:324).
117. "By following God's directions and being perfectly governed by his laws [the soul] could enjoy the whole universe of creation; but by the apostasy of pride which is called the beginning of sin it strives to grab something more than the whole and to govern it by its own laws; and because there is nothing more than the whole it is thrust back into anxiety over a part, and so by being greedy for more it gets less" (*Trin.* 12.14 [WSA I/5:330]; square brackets mine).
118. Following a number of postmodern critics of Hegelian theodicy, O'Regan emphasizes that Hegel's notion of *Erinnerung*, or recollection, of the christological moment of difference in the totality of Spirit is not the same as the Greek and later Christian concepts of anamnesis, in which what is remembered is made present again in the act of remembering: "Transfiguration donated by the realization of totality effects a transfiguration of evil, suffering, and the voice of protest raised against both. Transfiguration

effectively implies the nonbeing (*meon*) of evil and suffering. . . . The contrary—the thought is originally Benjamin's—is anamnetic solidarity with the victims who have lost everything, even the right to speak" (*Heterodox Hegel*, 314–15). See also Paul Ricoeur, "Freedom in the Light of Hope," in *Essays on Biblical Interpretation* (Philadelphia: Fortress, 1980), 155–81, and Paul Ricoeur, "Evil, a Challenge to Philosophy and Theology," *Journal of the American Academy of Religion* 53, no. 4 (1985): 631–48; Emmanuel Levinas, *Totality and Infinity: An Essay on Exteriority*, trans. Alphonso Lingis (Pittsburgh: Duquesne University Press, 1969), preface, 21–30; Theodor W. Adorno, *Negative Dialectics*, trans. E. B. Ashton (New York: Seabury Press, 1973), 300–360, esp. 334–60.

119. *En. Ps.* 101(1).2 (CCL 38:1427; WSA III/19:47). Augustine does not use the Latin term *persona* here, as he does explicitly at, for example, *en. Ps.* 30(2).4. What is clear by his distinction between the masculine and the neuter in *"unus/unum"* is that Christ and the church form a transhistorical subjective unity, albeit one in which each is a distinct substance. A single nature between the human and divine would nullify the language of lament and the hope of transfiguration. Brian Brock observes, "The Psalter is not a warrant for believers to claim divinity, but is a promise that their prayer will be heard" ("Augustine's Incitement to Lament," 193).

120. Kimberly Baker points out, "Rather than being speculative, Augustine's doctrine instead is the story of a profound relationship of love of Christ for the Church" ("Augustine's Doctrine of the *Totus Christus*," 11). Along the same lines, Brian Brock underscores Augustine's pastoral impetus: "The written words of the Psalter set believers' affections in the heavenly Christ, so that they are not wrenched loose by earthly buffeting. This account seems more determined by scripture and the demands of the moral life than a substance ontology; Christ in his glorious state sings and in his humbled state laments, so that in him the City of God may both hope and lament, both prefiguring and taking humanity into himself. Notice how apparent inconsistencies in the ontology here produce an entirely consistent account of lament: 'We are suffering willingly—at least patiently—because there is no other way for us to make our Passover [Pascha] and cleave to Christ.' 'Our' passion is undergone in the processes of detachment from this world, which Augustine expressly links to the concept of clinging to Christ" ("Augustine's Incitement to Lament," 193, citing *en. Ps.* 68[1].3).

121. Baker, "Augustine's Doctrine of the *Totus Christus*," 17–18.

122. See also *Jo. ev. tr.* 65.2.

123. *En. Ps.* 18(2).10 (WSA III/15:210–11); square brackets mine. For a contemporary appropriation of Augustine's interpretation of Pentecost against the backdrop of the doctrine of the *totus Christus*, see Emmanuel Durand, "La variété des langues dans le *Christus totus* selon saint Augustin: L'universalité chrétienne en voie d'accomplissement," *Ephemerides Theologiae Lovanienses* 86, no. 1 (2010): 1–25.

124. See, in the preface to *doc. Chr.*, Augustine's exhortation to those who claim spiritually inspired understanding of scripture to build up the church by teaching others.

125. *Trin.* 15.34, 36 (WSA I/5:422, 424).

126. *Trin.* 15.34 (WSA I/5:422); square brackets mine.

127. *Ep. Jo.* 6.8 (FC 92:207).

128. *En. Ps.* 26(2).1: "The Lord is merciful; we are miserable. But the merciful Lord has deigned to speak to the miserable, and he deigns also to use the voice of the miserable. In this sense both statements are true: that it is our voice here and not our voice, that it is the voice of the Spirit of God and not his voice. It is the voice of the Spirit of God, because we would not be speaking these words if he did not inspire us; but it is not his, because he is not wretched, nor is he toiling. Yet these are the groans of people who are wretched and do toil. On the other hand, they are ours, because these words give expression to our misery; yet not ours, because our entitlement even to groan is the gift of God" (WSA III/15:274).

129. *En. Ps.* 26(2).2 (WSA III/15:275).

130. *En. Ps.* 93.9 (WSA III/18:385–86).

131. *En. Ps.* 93.13 (WSA III/18:389).

132. *En. Ps.* 93.15 (WSA III/18:391).

133. *En. Ps.* 93.15 (WSA III/18:392); square brackets mine.

134. On this point, see John Cavadini, "Eucharistic Exegesis in Augustine's *Confessions*," *Augustinian Studies* 40, no. 1 (2010): 87–108, and Brian Daley, S.J., "The Law, the Whole Christ, and the Spirit of Love: Grace as a Trinitarian Gift in Augustine's Theology," *Augustinian Studies* 40, no. 1 (2010): 123–44.

135. Underscoring the dilemma, Augustine asks, "Are there any, I ask you, who cannot be convicted of having spoken a word against the Holy Spirit before they became Christians or Catholics?" So is the promise of forgiveness a lie? Pagans, Augustine points out, ridicule the sanctification of Christians. That is surely blasphemy against the Spirit. What, then, of all the pagans who have converted to Christianity? Next

Augustine examines the exchange in the gospel that Jesus has with some Pharisees immediately before speaking about the sin against the Holy Spirit. The Pharisees contend that Jesus casts out demons by the power of Beelzebul, rather than the Spirit of God. Augustine draws the conclusion that those Jews or heretics "who confess the Holy Spirit but deny he is present in the Body of Christ, which is his one and only Church . . . these are . . . like the Pharisees of that time, who even if they confessed that there is a Holy Spirit, nonetheless denied that he was present in Christ" (s. 71.5 [WSA III/3:249]). Augustine proceeds to argue that only full and utter unwillingness to repent, which entails a rejection of the one body of Christ in which the Spirit is present, constitutes the unforgivable sin against the Holy Spirit. Those who blasphemed against the Spirit but repented and joined into unity with the Catholic church are indeed forgiven.

136. Augustine stresses that holiness comes from Christ's grace, not one's own merit, at *s.* 71.3.

137. *S.* 71.18 (WSA III/3:256).

138. *S.* 71.19.

139. *S.* 71.19 (WSA III/3:258).

140. *S.* 71.20.

141. *S.* 71.31 (WSA III/3:265).

142. At *Trin.* 8.9 he shows how an inward turn toward the human soul or mind links us to others in a relationship of faith: "So we know anyone else's mind from our own and from our own we believe [*credimus*] any mind we do not know" (CCL 50:280; WSA I/5:249; square brackets mine).

143. "So by what is common to them both the Father and the Son wished us to have communion both with them and among ourselves; by this gift which they both possess as one they wished to gather us together and make us one, that is to say, by the Holy Spirit who is God and the gift of God. By this gift we are reconciled to the godhead, and by this gift we enjoy the godhead. After all, what use would it be for us to know any kind of good if we didn't also love it? Now just as truth is what we learn by, so charity is what we love by, and it enables us to know things more thoroughly and to enjoy them when known more happily" (*s.* 71.18 [WSA III/3:256]).

144. Rowan Williams, "Politics and the Soul: A Reading of the *City of God*," *Milltown Studies* 19–20 (1987): 57.

145. Williams, "Politics and the Soul," 68–69. Another more recent interpreter of Augustine, Eric Gregory, has done an admirable

job at describing the constructive character of the Christian's present life of tension in his work *Politics and the Order of Love*. Over against twentieth-century interpreters of Augustine's political theology who tend, in Gregory's view, to overemphasize Augustine's doctrine of sin at the expense of his doctrine of love, Gregory articulates a public Augustinian ethic intended to highlight not only the critical stance Christians must hold vis-à-vis all temporal political institutions, but also the positive, participatory and upbuilding work of love they are called to do in the public sphere. In the latter regard, Gregory engages in a critical dialogue with the political philosophy of Hannah Arendt, who for our purposes is notable for her analysis of evil following the Holocaust in addition to her extensive treatment of Augustine. Yet her ultimate evaluation of the bishop of Hippo is ambivalent. While on the one hand Arendt's contention that the banality of evil could be its most insidious feature approaches Augustine's own insights, on the other she argues that his elucidation of the double love commandment—love of God and neighbor—actually undermines a robust active involvement in the political arena. To her mind, the primacy of the love of God will always draw the loving agent out of this world. As a consequence, the lover will never be able to love the neighbor authentically, as one's neighbor in this world here and now (see Hannah Arendt, *Love and St. Augustine*, ed. and trans. Joanna Vecchiarelli Scott and Judith Chelius Stark [Chicago: University of Chicago Press, 1996]). It is in response to this critique from Arendt, then, that Gregory attempts a retrieval of Augustine's mature Christology as a means of affirming the this-worldly potential of the double love command. After 411 Augustine becomes increasingly explicit in his articulation of Christ as two natures—divine and human—in one person. Gregory gains critical leverage over Arendt by stressing Augustine's mature Christology: in loving Christ, we love both God and neighbor. Gregory concludes: "Rather than either being morally paralyzed by the infinite claims of the neighbor, or spiritually distracted by the infinite claims of God, the Augustinian self loves the neighbor in God who lovingly identifies with the neighbor as God's own" (*Politics and the Order of Love*, 240). Gregory here builds upon the argument of Thomas Breidenthal, "Jesus Is My Neighbor: Arendt, Augustine, and the Politics of Incarnation," *Modern Theology* 14, no. 4 (October 1998): 489–504.

146. See Robert Dodaro, *Christ and the Just Society in the Thought of Augustine* (Cambridge: Cambridge University Press, 2004), esp. ch. 3.

147. *Civ. Dei* 10.3 (Bettenson, 375).

148. *Civ. Dei* 10.5 (Bettenson, 379).

149. *Civ. Dei* 10.6 (Bettenson, 379).
150. *Civ. Dei* 10.6 (Bettenson, 380).
151. *Civ. Dei* 10.6 (Bettenson, 380).
152. *En. Ps.* 143.7 (WSA III/20:367).
153. *En. Ps.* 143.7 (WSA III/20:367).
154. *En. Ps.* 143.7.
155. *S.* 38.8 (WSA III/2:212).
156. *S.* 265.9 (WSA III/7:242).
157. *S.* 272 (WSA III/7:300–301).
158. *En. Ps.* 94.4 (WSA III/18:412–13).
159. *Trin.* 15.51 (WSA I/5:437).

CONCLUSION

1. In addition to various discussions above, see Powell, *Trinity in German Thought*, 173–259, and Wendte, *Gottmenschliche Einheit bei Hegel*, 327–41.
2. See ch. 3.
3. In this regard, we could understand this book to be a Trinitarian prolegomena to scholarly expositions or appropriations of Augustine's political thought, e.g., Gregory, *Politics and the Order of Love*, and Charles Mathewes, *The Republic of Grace: Augustinian Thoughts for Dark Times* (Grand Rapids, MI: Eerdmans, 2010). More could still be done to trace the ecclesiological and political implications of Augustine's Christology and pneumatology. For a survey of readings of Augustine's political theology over the past century or so, see Michael J. S. Bruno, *Political Augustinianism: Modern Interpretations of Augustine's Political Thought* (Minneapolis: Fortress, 2014). Finally, more directly relevant to our undertaking here is Geoffrey J. D. Holsclaw, "Transcending Subjects: Hegel after Augustine; An Essay on Political Theology" (PhD diss., Marquette University, 2013).
4. With regard to the ontological basis of Augustine's pneumatology, see especially the last chapter of Verhees, *God in Beweging*.

BIBLIOGRAPHY

Primary Sources

Augustine

The Augustine Catechism: The Enchiridion on Faith, Hope, and Love. Translated by Bruce Harbert. Hyde Park, NY: New City Press, 1999.
Concerning the City of God against the Pagans. Translated by Henry Bettenson. Harmondsworth, Middlesex, UK: Penguin, 1972.
The Confessions. Translated by Maria Boulding, O.S.B. Works of Saint Augustine I/1. Hyde Park, NY: New City Press, 1997.
Expositions on the Psalms. Translated by Maria Boulding, O.S.B. Works of Saint Augustine III/15–20. Hyde Park, NY: New City Press, 2000–2004.
Letters 1–99. Translated by Roland Teske. Works of Saint Augustine II/1. Hyde Park, NY: New City Press, 2001.
Sermons (1–19) on the Old Testament. Translated by Edmund Hill, O.P. Works of Saint Augustine III/1. Hyde Park, NY: New City Press, 1990.
Sermons (20–50) on the Old Testament. Translated by Edmund Hill, O.P. Works of Saint Augustine III/2. Hyde Park, NY: New City Press, 1990.
Sermons (51–94) on the Old Testament. Translated by Edmund Hill, O.P. Works of Saint Augustine III/3. Brooklyn, NY: New City Press, 1991.
Sermons (94A–147A) on the Old Testament. Translated by Edmund Hill, O.P. Works of Saint Augustine III/4. Brooklyn, NY: New City Press, 1992.
Sermons (148–183) on the New Testament. Translated by Edmund Hill, O.P. Works of Saint Augustine III/5. New Rochelle, NY: New City Press, 1992.
Sermons (184–229Z) on the Liturgical Seasons. Translated by Edmund Hill, O.P. Works of Saint Augustine III/6. New Rochelle, NY: New City Press, 1993.
Sermons (230–272B) on the Liturgical Seasons. Translated by Edmund Hill, O.P. Works of Saint Augustine III/7. New Rochelle, NY: New City Press, 1993.

Sermons (273–305A) on the Saints. Translated by Edmund Hill, O.P. Works of Saint Augustine III/8. Hyde Park, NY: New City Press, 1994.

Sermons (306–340A) on the Saints. Translated by Edmund Hill, O.P. Works of Saint Augustine III/9. Hyde Park, NY: New City Press, 1994.

Sermons (341–400) on Various Subjects. Translated by Edmund Hill, O.P. Works of Saint Augustine III/10. Hyde Park, NY: New City Press, 1995.

Teaching Christianity. Edited by John E. Rotelle, O.S.A. Translated by Edmund Hill, O.P. Works of Saint Augustine I/11. Hyde Park, NY: New City Press, 1996.

Tractates on the Gospel of John. Translated by John W. Rettig. Fathers of the Church 78, 79, 88, 90, and 92. Washington, DC: Catholic University of America Press, 1988–95.

The Trinity. Translated by Edmund Hill, O.P. Works of Saint Augustine I/5. Brooklyn, NY: New City Press, 1991.

Hegel

Aesthetics: Lectures on Fine Art. Translated by T. M. Knox. Oxford: Clarendon Press, 1975.

Early Theological Writings. Translated by T. M. Knox. With an Introduction and Fragments translated by Richard Kroner. Chicago: University of Chicago Press, 1948.

Elements of the Philosophy of Right. Edited by Allen W. Wood. Translated by H. B. Nisbet. Cambridge: Cambridge University Press, 1991.

Enzyklopädie der philosophischen Wissenschaften III: Die Philosophie des Geistes. Edited by Eva Moldenhauer and Karl Markus Michel. Theorie-Werkausgabe. Vol. 10. Frankfurt: Suhrkamp, 1970.

Hegel's Science of Logic. Translated by A. V. Miller. London: Allen & Unwin, 1969.

Lectures on the History of Philosophy: The Lectures of 1825–26. Edited by Robert F. Brown. Translated by R. F. Brown and J. M. Stewart. Berkeley: University of California Press, 1990.

Lectures on the Philosophy of Religion. Edited by Peter C. Hodgson. Translated by R. F. Brown, P. C. Hodgson, and J. M. Stewart. 3 vols. Berkeley: University of California Press, 1984–87.

Lectures on the Philosophy of World History: Introduction. Translated by H. B. Nisbet. Cambridge: Cambridge University Press, 1975.

Logic (Part I of the *Encyclopedia of the Philosophical Sciences*). Translated by William Wallace. Oxford: Clarendon Press, 1975.
Phänomenologie des Geistes. Edited by Johannes Hoffmeister. Hamburg: Felix Meiner, 1952.
Phenomenology of Spirit. Translated by A. V. Miller. Oxford: Clarendon Press, 1977.
The Philosophy of History. Translated by J. Sibree. New York: Dover Publications, 1956.
Philosophy of Mind (Part III of the *Encyclopedia of the Philosophical Sciences*). Translated by William Wallace. *Zusätze* in Boumann's 1845 ed. translated by A. V. Miller. Oxford: Clarendon Press, 1971.
The Philosophy of Nature (Part II of the *Encyclopedia of the Philosophical Sciences*). Translated by A. V. Miller. Oxford: Clarendon Press, 1970.
The Spirit of Christianity and Its Fate. In *Early Theological Writings*, translated by T. M. Knox, with an introduction and fragments translated by Richard Kroner, 182–301. Chicago: University of Chicago Press, 1948.
Vorlesungen über die Philosophie der Geschichte. Edited by Eva Moldenhauer and Karl Markus Michel. Theorie-Werkausgabe 12. Frankfurt: Suhrkamp, 1970.

SECONDARY SOURCES

Adorno, Theodor W. *Negative Dialectics*. Translated by E. B. Ashton. New York: Seabury Press, 1973.
Alici, Luigi. "Sign and Language." Introduction to Augustine, *Teaching Christianity: De doctrina Christiana*, translated by Edmund Hill, O.P., 28–53. Hyde Park, NY: New City Press, 1996.
Arendt, Hannah. *Love and St. Augustine*. Edited and translated by Joanna Vecchiarelli Scott and Judith Chelius Stark. Chicago: University of Chicago Press, 1996.
Arnold, Johannes. "Die göttlichen Sendungen in 'De Trinitate.'" *Recherches Augustiniennes* 25 (1991): 3–69.
Asendorf, Ulrich. *Luther und Hegel: Untersuchungen zur Grundlegung einer neuen systematischen Theologie*. Wiesbaden: Franz Steiner Verlag, 1982.

Aulen, Gustav. *Christus Victor: A Historical Study of the Three Main Types of the Idea of Atonement*. Translated by A. G. Herbert. New York: Macmillan, 1969.

Avineri, Shlomo. *Hegel's Theory of the Modern State*. Cambridge: Cambridge University Press, 1972.

Ayres, Lewis. *Augustine and the Trinity*. Cambridge: Cambridge University Press, 2010.

———. "Augustine, Christology and God as Love: An Introduction to the Homilies on 1 John." In *Nothing Greater, Nothing Better: Theological Essays on the Love of God*, edited by Kevin Vanhoozer, 67–93. Grand Rapids, MI: Eerdmans, 2001.

———. "Augustine on the Rule of Faith: Rhetoric, Christology, and the Foundation of Christian Thinking." *Augustinian Studies* 36, no. 1 (2005): 33–51.

———. "Augustine on the Spirit as the Soul of the Body; or, Fragments of a Trinitarian Ecclesiology." *Augustinian Studies* 41, no. 1 (2010): 165–82.

———. "The Christological Context of Augustine's *De trinitate* XIII: Toward Relocating Books VIII–XV." In *Studies in Patristic Christology*, edited by Thomas Finan and Vincent Twomey, 95–121. Dublin: Four Courts Press, 1998.

———. "The Discipline of Self-Knowledge in Augustine's *De trinitate* Book X." In *The Passionate Intellect*, edited by Lewis Ayres, Rutgers University Studies in the Classical Humanities 7, 261–96. Brunswick, NJ: Transaction, 1995.

———. "Innovation and Ressourcement in Pro-Nicene Pneumatology." *Augustinian Studies* 39, no. 2 (2008): 187–206.

———. *Nicaea and Its Legacy: An Approach to Fourth-Century Trinitarian Theology*. Oxford: Oxford University Press, 2004.

———. "'Remember That You Are Catholic' (*serm.* 52.2): Augustine on the Unity of the Triune God." *Journal of Early Christian Studies* 8 (2000): 39–82.

———. "*Spiritus Arborum*: Augustine and Pro-Nicene Pneumatology." *Augustinian Studies* 39, no. 2 (2008): 207–21.

Ayres, Lewis, and Michel René Barnes. "God." In *Augustine through the Ages: An Encyclopedia*, edited by A. Fitzgerald, 384–90. Grand Rapids, MI: Eerdmans, 1999.

Bailleux, E. "La sotériologie de Saint Augustin dans le 'De Trinitate.'" *Mélanges de Science Religieuse* 23 (1966): 149–73.

Baker, Kimberly. "Augustine's Doctrine of the *Totus Christus*: Reflecting on the Church as Sacrament of Unity." *Horizons* 37, no. 1 (Spring 2010): 7–24.

Barnes, Michel René. "The Arians of Book V, and the Genre of *De Trinitate*." *Theological Studies* 44 (1993): 185–95.

———. "Augustine in Contemporary Trinitarian Theology." *Theological Studies* 56 (1995): 237–50.

———. "Augustine's Last Pneumatology." *Augustinian Studies* 39, no. 2 (2008): 223–34.

———. "The Beginning and End of Early Christian Pneumatology." *Augustinian Studies* 39, no. 2 (2008): 169–86.

———. "De Régnon Reconsidered." *Augustinian Studies* 26 (1995): 51–79.

———. "Re-reading Augustine's Theology of the Trinity." In *The Trinity: An Interdisciplinary Symposium on the Doctrine of the Trinity*, edited by S. T. Davis, D. Kendall, and G. O'Collins, 145–76. Oxford: Oxford University Press, 1999.

———. "The Visible Christ and the Invisible Trinity: Mt 5:8 in Augustine's Trinitarian Theology of 400." *Modern Theology* 19, no. 3 (July 2003): 329–55.

Barnes, Robin. *Prophecy and Gnosis: Apocalypticism in the Wake of the Lutheran Reformation*. Stanford, CA: Stanford University Press, 1988.

Baur, Ferdinand Christian. *Die christliche Lehre von der Dreieinigkeit und Menschwerdung Gottes in ihrer geschichtlichen Entwicklung*. 3 vols. Tübingen: C. F. Osiander, 1841–43.

Bayer, Oswald. "Zur Theologie der Klage." In *Klage*, edited by Martin Ebner, Jahrbuch für biblische Theologie 16, 289–301. Neukirchen-Vluyn: Neukirchener Verlag, 2001.

Behr, John. *The Way to Nicaea*. The Formation of Christian Theology 1. Crestwood, NY: St. Vladimir's Seminary Press, 2001.

Beierwaltes, Werner. *Denken des Einen: Studien zur neuplatonischen Philosophie und ihrer Wirkungsgeschichte*. Frankfurt: Klostermann, 1985.

Benz, Ernst. "Johann Albrecht Bengel und die Philosophie des deutschen Idealismus." *Deutsche Vierteljahrsschrift für Literaturwissenschaft und Geistesgeschichte* 27 (1953): 528–54.

———. *Swedenborg in Deutschland: F. C. Oetingers und Immanuel Kants Auseinandersetzung mit der Person und Lehre Emanuel Swedenborgs*. Frankfurt: Vittorio Klostermann, 1947.

Berrouard, M.-F. "Incarnation et guérison de l'orgueil." In *Homélies sur l'évangile de saint Jean:* Tractatus in Ioannis evangelium *XVII–XXXIII*, translation, introduction, and notes by M.-F. Berrouard, 2nd ed., Bibliothèque Augustinienne 72, 796–97. Paris: Études Augustiniennes, 1988.

———. "Orgueil et extériorité." In *Homélies sur l'évangile de saint Jean:* Tractatus in Ioannis evangelium *XVII–XXXIII*, translation, introduction, and notes by M.-F. Berrouard, 2nd ed., Bibliothèque Augustinienne 72, 793–96. Paris: Études Augustiniennes, 1988.

Bicknell, Jeanette. "The Individuality in the Deed: Hegel on Forgiveness and Reconciliation." *Bulletin of the Hegel Society of Great Britain* 37/38 (1998): 73–84.

Bjerke, A. R. "Hegel and the Love of the Concept." *Heythrop Journal* 52, no. 1 (2011): 76–89.

Blowers, Paul M. "The *regula fidei* and the Narrative Character of Early Christian Faith." *Pro Ecclesia* 6 (1997): 199–228.

Bochet, Isabelle. *"Le firmament de l'Écriture": l'herméneutique augustinienne.* Paris: Institut d'études augustiniennes, 2004.

———. "Résurrection et réincarnation: La polémique d'Augustin contre les platoniciens et contre Porphyre dans les *Sermons 240–242*." In Ministerium Sermonis: *Philological, Historical, and Theological Studies on Augustine's* Sermones ad populum, edited by Gert Partoens, Anthony Dupont, and Mathijs Lamberigts, 267–98. Turnhout: Brepols, 2009.

———. "The Role of Scripture in Augustine's Controversy with Porphyry." *Augustinian Studies* 41, no. 1 (2010): 7–52.

Bonner, G. "Augustine's Conception of Deification." *Journal of Theological Studies* 37 (1986): 369–86.

Booth, Edward, O.P. "Hegel's Conception of Self-Knowledge Seen in Conjunction with Augustine's." *Augustiniana* 30 (1980): 221–50.

Bourassa, François. "Théologie trinitaire chez saint Augustin." *Gregorianum* 58 (1977): 675–725.

———. "Théologie trinitaire de saint Augustin, II." *Gregorianum* 59 (1978) : 375–432.

Bouton-Touboulic, Anne-Isabelle. "Consonance and Dissonance: The Unifying Action of the Holy Ghost in Saint Augustine." *Studia Patristica* 61 (2013): 31–52.

Bouyer, Louis. *The Christian Mystery: From Pagan Myth to Christian Mysticism.* Translated by Illtyd Trethowan. Edinburgh: T&T Clark, 1990.

———. "Mysticism/An Essay on the History of the Word." In *Understanding Mysticism*, edited by Richard Woods, 42–55. Garden City, NY: Image Books, 1980.

Bowlin, John. "Augustine on Justifying Coercion." *Annual of the Society of Christian Ethics* 17 (1997): 49–70.

Brachtendorf, Johannes. *Die Struktur des menschlichen Geistes nach Augustinus*. Paradeigmata 19. Hamburg: Felix Meiner Verlag, 2000.

Brechtken, Josef. *Augustinus* Doctor Caritatis*: sein Liebesbegriff im Widerspruch von Eigennutz und selbstloser Güte im Rahmen der antiken Glückseligkeits-Ethik*. Meisenheim am Glan: Hain, 1975.

Breidenthal, Thomas. "Jesus Is My Neighbor: Arendt, Augustine, and the Politics of Incarnation." *Modern Theology* 14, no. 4 (October 1998): 489–504.

Brito, Emilio. *La christologie de Hegel:* Verbum Crucis. Translated by B. Pottier. Paris: Beauchesne, 1983.

———. *Hegel et la tâche actuelle de la christologie*. Translated by Th. Dejond. Paris: Lethielleux, 1979.

Brock, Brian. "Augustine's Incitement to Lament from the *Enarrationes in Psalmos*." In *Evoking Lament: A Theological Discussion*, edited by Eva Harasta and Brian Brock, 183–203. London: T&T Clark, 2009.

Brown, Peter. *Augustine of Hippo: A Biography*. 2nd ed. Berkeley: University of California Press, 2000.

———. *Power and Persuasion in Late Antiquity: Towards a Christian Empire*. Madison: University of Wisconsin Press, 1992.

Bruaire, Claude. *Logique et religion chrétienne dans la philosophie de Hegel*. Paris: Éditions du Seuil, 1964.

Brunkhorst-Hasenclever, Annegrit. *Die Transformierung der theologischen Deutung des Todes bei G. W. F. Hegel: Ein Beitrag zur Formbestimmung von Paradox und Synthese*. Frankfurt: Peter Lang, 1970.

Bruno, Michael J. S. *Political Augustinianism: Modern Interpretations of Augustine's Political Thought*. Minneapolis: Fortress, 2014.

Burnaby, John. Amor Dei: *A Study in the Religion of St. Augustine*. London: Hodder & Stoughton, 1938.

Caleo, Marcello. *Hegel, filosofo di Babilonia*. Naples: Alfredo Guida, 2001.

———. "Sant' Agostino e Hegel a Confronto." *Sapienza: Rivista di Filosofia e di Teologia* 44, no. 1 (1991): 57–76.

Cameron, Averil. *Christianity and the Rhetoric of Empire: The Development of Christian Discourse*. Berkeley: University of California Press, 1991.

Cameron, Michael. "Augustine's Construction of Figurative Exegesis against the Donatists in the *Enarrationes in Psalmos*." PhD diss., University of Chicago, 1996.

———. *Christ Meets Me Everywhere: Augustine's Early Figurative Exegesis*. Oxford Studies in Historical Theology. Oxford: Oxford University Press, 2012.

———. "The Christological Substructure of Augustine's Figurative Exegesis." In *Augustine and the Bible*, edited by Pamela Bright, 74–103. Notre Dame, IN: University of Notre Dame Press, 1999.

Canning, Raymond. *The Unity of Love for God and Neighbour in St. Augustine*. Heverlee: Augustinian Historical Institute, 1993.

Capanaga, V. "La Deification en la soteriologia augustiniana." In *Augustinus Magister: Congrès International Augustinien, Paris 21–24 Septembre 1954*, 3 vols., 2:745–54. Paris: Études Augustiniennes, 1954.

Cavadini, John. "The Darkest Enigma: Reconsidering the Self in Augustine's Thought." *Augustinian Studies* 38, no. 1 (2007): 119–32.

———. "Eucharistic Exegesis in Augustine's *Confessions*." *Augustinian Studies* 40, no. 1 (2010): 87–108.

———. "Pride." In *Augustine through the Ages: An Encyclopedia*, edited by A. Fitzgerald, 679–84. Grand Rapids, MI: Eerdmans, 1999.

———. "The Quest for Truth in Augustine's *De Trinitate*." *Theological Studies* 58 (1997): 429–40.

———. "The Structure and Intention of Augustine's *De trinitate*." *Augustinian Studies* 29 (1998): 103–23.

———. "The Sweetness of the Word: Salvation and Rhetoric in Augustine's *De Doctrina Christiana*." In *De doctrina christiana: A Classic of Western Culture*, edited by Duane W. H. Arnold and Pamela Bright, 164–81. Notre Dame, IN: University of Notre Dame Press, 1995.

Chapelle, Albert. *Hegel et la religion*. 3 vols. Paris: Éditions Universitaires, 1964–71.

Chételat, Pierre. "Hegel's Philosophy of World History as Theodicy: On Evil and Freedom." In *Hegel and History*, ed. Will Dudley, 215–30. Albany, NY: SUNY Press, 2009.

Chevalier, Irenee. *S. Augustin et la pensée grecque: Les relations trinitaires*. Fribourg: Librairie de l'Université, 1940.

Childs, Brevard. "The *sensus literalis* of Scripture: An Ancient and Modern Problem." In *Beiträge zur Alttestamentlichen Theologie, Festschrift für Walter Zimmerli zum 70*, edited by H. Donner et al., 80–93. Göttingen: Vandenhoeck & Ruprecht, 1977.

Cipriani, N. "Le fonti cristiane della dottrina trinitaria nei primi Dialoghi di S. Agostino." *Augustinianum* 34 (1994): 253–312.

Clark, Malcolm. *Logic and System: A Study of the Transition from 'Vorstellung' to Thought in the Philosophy of Hegel*. The Hague: Martinus Nijhoff, 1971.

Cook, Daniel J. *Language in the Philosophy of Hegel*. The Hague: Mouton, 1973.

Cosmann, Peggy. "Der Einfluß Friedrich Christoph Oetingers auf Hegels Abrechnung mit Spinoza." *Zeitschrift für Religions- und Geistesgeschichte* 50, no. 2 (1998): 115–36.

Croce, Benedetto. *What Is Living and What Is Dead in Hegel's Philosophy*. Translated by Douglas Ainslee. New York: Russell and Russell, 1969.

Daley, Brian, S.J. "Christology." In *Augustine through the Ages: An Encyclopedia*, edited by A. Fitzgerald, 164–69. Grand Rapids, MI: Eerdmans, 1999.

———. "The Giant's Twin Substances: Ambrose and the Christology of Augustine's 'Contra Sermonem Arrianorum.'" In *Augustine: Presbyter Factus Sum*, edited by Joseph Lienhard, Earl Muller, and Roland Teske, Collectanea Augustiniana 2, 477–95. New York: Peter Lang, 1993.

———. "A Humble Mediator: The Distinctive Elements in St. Augustine's Christology." *Word and Spirit* 9 (1987): 100–117.

———. "The Law, the Whole Christ, and the Spirit of Love: Grace as a Trinitarian Gift in Augustine's Theology." *Augustinian Studies* 40, no. 1 (2010): 123–44.

Dawson, David. "Sign Theory, Allegorical Reading, and the Motions of the Soul in *De doctrina christiana*." In *De doctrina christiana: A Classic of Western Culture*, edited by Duane W. H. Arnold and Pamela Bright, 123–44. Notre Dame: University of Notre Dame Press, 1995.

Decleve, Henri. "Schöpfung, Trinität und Modernität bei Hegel." *Zeitschrift für katholische Theologie* 107, nos. 3–4 (1985): 187–98.

De Lubac, Henri. *La Postérité spirituelle de Joachim de Fiore*. Paris: Lethielleux, 1979.

De Negri, Enrico. "L'elaborazione hegeliana di temi agostiniani." *Revue internationale de Philosophie* 6, no. 1 (1952): 62–78.

De Régnon, Theodore. *Études de théologie positive sur la sainte Trinité*. Paris: Retaux, 1898.

Desmond, William. *Hegel's God: A Counterfeit Double?* Aldershot: Ashgate, 2003.

Dickey, Laurence. *Hegel: Religion, Economics, and the Politics of Spirit, 1770–1807.* Cambridge: Cambridge University Press, 1987.

Dilthey, Wilhelm. *Introduction to the Human Sciences: An Attempt to Lay a Foundation for the Study of Society and History.* Translated by Ramon J. Betanzos. Detroit: Wayne State University Press, 1988.

Dodaro, Robert, O.S.A. *Christ and the Just Society in the Thought of Augustine.* Cambridge: Cambridge University Press, 2004.

———. "'Christus Iustus' and Fear of Death in Augustine's Dispute with the Pelagians." In Signum Pietatis: *Festgabe für Cornelius Petrus Mayer OSA zum 60. Geburtstag,* edited by Adolar Zumkeller, O.S.A., Cassiciacum 40, 341–61. Würzburg: Augustinus-Verlag, 1989.

———. "Justice." In *Augustine through the Ages: An Encyclopedia,* edited by A. Fitzgerald, 481–83. Grand Rapids, MI: Eerdmans, 1999.

Donà, Massimo. *Sull' Assoluto: Per una reinterpretazione dell idealismo hegeliano.* Turin: Einaudi, 1992.

Doull, Floy, and David Peddle. "Augustine and Hegel on the History of Rome." In *Augustine and History,* edited by Christopher T. Daley, John Doody, and Kim Paffenroth, 169–96. Lanham, MD: Lexington Books, 2008.

Drobner, Hubertus R. "Grammatical Exegesis and Christology in St. Augustine." *Studia Patristica* 18 (1990): 49–63.

———. *Person-Exegese und Christologie bei Augustinus: Zur Herkunft der Formel* Una Persona. Leiden: Brill, 1986.

Duchrow, Ulrich. "Signum und Superbia beim jungen Augustin." *Revue des études augustiniennes* 7 (1961): 369–72.

Dupont, Anthony. "Augustine's Preaching on Grace at Pentecost." In *Studia Patristica* 61, edited by Markus Vinzent and Jonathan P. Yates, 3–14. Leuven: Peeters, 2013.

Dupre, Louis. "The Absolute Spirit and the Religious Legitimation of Modernity." In *Hegels Logik der Philosophie,* edited by Dieter Heinrich and Rolf-Peter Horstmann, 221–33. Stuttgart: Klett-Cottal, 1984.

———. "Hegel's Religion as Representation." In *A Dubious Heritage: Studies in the Philosophy of Religion after Kant,* 53–72. New York: Paulist Press, 1977.

Durand, Emmanuel. "La variété des langues dans le Christus totus selon saint Augustin: L'universalité chrétienne en voie d'accomplissement." *Ephemerides Theologiae Lovanienses* 86, no. 1 (2010): 1–25.

Du Roy, Olivier. *L'intelligence de la foi en la Trinité selon Saint Augustin: Genèse de sa théologie Trinitaire jusqu'en 391*. Paris: Études Augustiniennes, 1966.

Evans, Gillian R. *Augustine on Evil*. Cambridge: Cambridge University Press, 1982.

Fackenheim, Emil L. *The Religious Dimension in Hegel's Thought*. Bloomington: Indiana University Press, 1967.

Fiedrowitz, Michael. Psalmus vox totius Christi: *Studien zu Augustins "Enarrationes in Psalmos."* Freiburg: Herder, 1997.

Finn, Doug. "Hegel." In *Oxford Guide to the Historical Reception of Augustine*, edited by Karla Pollmann and Willimien Otten, 3 vols., 2:1106–10. Oxford: Oxford University Press, 2013.

Fiore, Joachim de. *Enchiridion super Apocalypsim*. Edited by Edward K. Burger. Toronto: Pontifical Institute of Medieval Studies, 1986.

———. *Liber de concordia Novi ac Veteris Testamenti*. Edited by E. Randolph Daniel. Philadelphia: American Philosophy Society, 1983.

Fitzgerald, Alan, O.S.A. "Body." In *Augustine through the Ages: An Encyclopedia*, edited by Alan Fitzgerald, 105–7. Grand Rapids, MI: Eerdmans, 1999.

Franz, Albert. *Glauben und Denken: Franz Anton Staudenmaiers Hegelkritik als Anfrage an das Selbstverständnis heutiger Theologie*. Regensburg: Verlag Friedrich Pustet, 1983.

Fredriksen, Paula. "Beyond the Body/Soul Dichotomy: Augustine on Paul against the Manichees and the Pelagians." *Recherches Augustiniennes* 23 (1988): 87–114.

Frei, Hans. *The Eclipse of Biblical Narrative: A Study in Eighteenth and Nineteenth Century Hermeneutics*. New Haven: Yale University Press, 1999.

Gadamer, Hans Georg. *Hegel's Dialectic*. Translated by P. Christopher Smith. New Haven: Yale University Press, 1976.

———. *Truth and Method*. London: Sheed & Ward, 1975.

Gangauf, Theodor. *Des heiligen Augustinus spekulative Lehre von Gott dem Dreieinigen: Ein wissenschaftlicher Nachweis der objektiven Begründetheit dieses christlichen Glaubensgegenstandes, aus den Schriften des genannten großen Kirchenlehrers gegen den unter dem Scheine der Wissenschaft dieses christliche Grunddogma bekämpfenden Unglauben zusammengestellt*. Augsburg: B. Schmid, 1865.

Gascoine, Robert. *Religion, Rationality and Community: Sacred and Secular in the Thought of Hegel and His Critics*. The Hague: Martinus Nijhoff, 1985.

Gaumer, Matthew Alan. "Against the Holy Spirit: Augustine of Hippo's Use of the Holy Spirit against the Donatists." *Studia Patristica* 61 (2013): 53–62.

Gerber, Chad Tyler. *The Spirit of Augustine's Early Theology: Contextualizing Augustine's Pneumatology*. Ashgate Studies in Philosophy and Theology in Late Antiquity. Farnham, Surrey, England: Ashgate, 2012.

Gerdes, Hayo. *Das Christusbild Søren Kierkegaards, verglichen mit der Christologie Hegels und Schleiermachers*. Düsseldorf: E. Diederichs, 1960.

Grabowski, Stanislaus. "The Holy Ghost in the Mystical Body of Christ according to St. Augustine." *Theological Studies* 5, no. 4 (1944): 453–83, and 6, no. 1 (1945): 62–84.

Gregory, Eric. *Politics and the Order of Love: An Augustinian Ethic of Democratic Citizenship*. Chicago: University of Chicago Press, 2008.

Griffiss, James E. "Hegel's *Logos* Christology." In Lux in lumine: *Essays to Honor W. Norman Pittinger*, edited by Richard A. Norris, 80–92. New York: Seabury Press, 1966.

Gunton, Colin. "God the Holy Spirit: Augustine and His Successors." In *Theology through the Theologians: Selected Essays, 1972–1995*, 105–28. Edinburgh: T&T Clark, 1996.

———. *The Promise of Trinitarian Theology*. Edinburgh: T&T Clark, 1991.

Hanson, Richard P. C. *The Search for the Christian Doctrine of God: The Arian Controversy, 318–381 AD*. Edinburgh: T&T Clark, 1988.

Harris, H. S. *Hegel's Development: Night Thoughts (Jena 1801–1806)*. Oxford: Clarendon Press, 1983.

———. *Hegel's Development: Toward the Sunlight, 1770–1801*. Oxford: Clarendon Press, 1972.

———. "Hegel's Intellectual Development to 1807." In *The Cambridge Companion to Hegel*, edited by Frederick Beiser, 25–51. Cambridge: Cambridge University Press, 1993.

Hedwig, Klaus. "Trinität und Triplizität: Eine Untersuchung zur Methode der Augustinischen und Hegelschen Metaphysik." PhD diss., University of Freiburg, 1968.

Hendrix, Scott H. "The Kingdom of Promise: Disappointment and Hope in Luther's Later Ecclesiology." *Lutherjahrbuch* 71 (2004): 37–60.

Henrici, Peter. "Die Säkularisierung der Apokalyptik in der neueren deutschen Philosophie." In *Hegel für Theologen: Gesammelte Aufsätze*, 133–55. Fribourg: Academic Press Fribourg, 2009.

Hodgson, Peter C. *The Formation of Historical Theology: A Study of Ferdinand Christian Baur*. New York: Harper & Row, 1966.

———. *God in History: Shapes of Freedom*. Nashville: Abingdon Press, 1989.

———. *Hegel and Christian Theology: A Reading of the "Lectures on the Philosophy of Religion."* Oxford: Oxford University Press, 2005.

———. "Hegel's Christology: Shifting Nuances in the Berlin Lectures." *Journal of the American Academy of Religion* 53 (1985): 23–40.

Holsclaw, Geoffrey. "Transcending Subjects: Hegel after Augustine; An Essay in Political Theology." PhD diss., Marquette University, 2013.

Houlgate, Stephen. "Religion, Morality and Forgiveness in Hegel's Philosophy." In *Philosophy and Religion in German Idealism*, edited by William Desmond, Ernst Otto-Onnasch, and Paul Cruysberghs, 81–110. Dordrecht: Kluwer Academic, 2004.

Hösle, Vittorio. "Theodicy Strategies in Leibniz, Hegel, Jonas." *Philotheos* 5 (2005): 68–86.

Hünermann, Peter. "Die Hegel-Rezeption Franz Anton Staudenmaiers." In *Kirche und Theologie im 19. Jahrhundert: Referate und Berichte des Arbeitskreises Katholische Theologie*, edited by Georg Schwaiger, 147–55. Goettingen: Vandenhoeck & Ruprecht, 1975.

Iljin, Iwan. *Die Philosophie Hegels als kontemplative Gotteslehre*. Bern: Francke, 1946.

Jaeschke, Walter. "Absolute Idee-absolute Subjektivität: Zum Problem der Persönlichkeit Gottes in der Logik und in der Religionsphilosophie." *Zeitschrift für philosophische Forschung* 35 (1981): 385–416.

———. "Christianity and Secularity in Hegel's Concept of the State." *The Journal of Religion* 61 (1981): 127–45.

———. *Reason in Religion: The Foundations of Hegel's Philosophy of Religion*. Translated by J. Michael Stewart and Peter C. Hodgson. Berkeley: University of California Press, 1990.

———. "Speculative and Anthropological Criticism of Religion: A Theological Orientation to Hegel and Feuerbach." *Journal of the American Academy of Religion* 48 (1980): 345–64.

Jamros, Daniel P., S.J. *The Human Shape of God: Religion in Hegel's "Phenomenology of Spirit."* New York: Paragon House, 1994.

Johnson, Douglas W. "'Verbum' in the Early Augustine (386–397)." *Recherches Augustiniennes* 8 (1972): 23–53.

Johnson, Gregory R., ed. *Kant on Swedenborg: Dreams of a Spirit-Seer and Other Writings*. Translated by Gregory R. Johnson and Glenn Alexander Magee. West Chester, PA: Swedenborg Foundation Publishers, 2002.

Kant, Immanuel. *Critique of Pure Reason*. Translated by Norman Kemp Smith. New York: St. Martin's Press, 1965.

———. "*Dreams of a Spirit-Seer.*" In *Kant on Swedenborg: Dreams of a Spirit-Seer and Other Writings*, edited by Gregory R. Johnson, translated by Gregory R. Johnson and Glenn Alexander Magee, 5–66. West Chester, PA: Swedenborg Foundation Publishers, 2002.

———. *Religion within the Boundaries of Mere Reason, and Other Writings*. Edited and translated by Allen Wood and George di Giovanni. Cambridge Texts in the History of Philosophy. Cambridge: Cambridge University Press, 1998.

Kantorowicz, Ernst. *The King's Two Bodies: A Study in Mediaeval Political Thought*. Princeton, NJ: Princeton University Press, 1957.

Kany, Roland. *Augustins Trinitätsdenken: Bilanz, Kritik und Weiterführung der modernen Forschung zu "De trinitate."* Tübingen: Mohr Siebeck, 2007.

———. "Typen und Tendenzen der De Trinitate-Forschung seit Ferdinand Christian Baur." In *Gott und sein Bild: Augustins "De Trinitate" im Spiegel gegenwärtiger Forschung*, edited by Johannes Brachtendorf, 13–28. Paderborn: Ferdinand Schöningh, 2000.

Kern, Walter, S.J. "Dialektik und Trinität in der Religionsphilosophie Hegels: Ein Beitrag zur Diskussion mit L. Oeing-Hanhoff." *Zeitschrift für katholische Theologie* 102 (1980): 129–55.

———. "Schöpfung bei Hegel." *Theologische Quartalschrift* 162 (1982): 131–46.

———. "Das Verhältnis von Erkenntnis und Liebe als philosophisches Grundproblem bei Hegel und Thomas von Aquin." *Scholastik* 34 (1959): 394–427.

Koslowski, Peter. "Hegel—'der Philosoph der Trinität?' Zur Kontroverse um seine Trinitätslehre." *Theologische Quartalschrift* 162 (1982): 105–31.

Kuhn, Evan F. "The Johannine Logic of Augustine's Trinity: A Dogmatic Sketch." *Theological Studies* 68 (2007): 572–94.

Küng, Hans. *The Incarnation of God: An Introduction to Hegel's Theological Thought as Prolegomena to a Future Christology.* Translated by J. R. Stevenson. New York: Crossroad, 1987.

La Bonnardiere, Anne-Marie. *Recherches de Chronologie Augustinienne.* Paris: Études augustiniennes, 1965.

Lakebrink, Bernhard. "Hegel und Augustin vor dem Rätsel der Geschichte." In *Studien zur Metaphysik Hegels*, 163–81. Freiburg: Verlag Rombach, 1969.

Lakeland, Paul. *The Politics of Salvation: The Hegelian Idea of the State.* Albany, NY: SUNY Press, 1984.

Lauer, Quentin. "Hegel on the Identity of Content in Religion and Philosophy." In *Essays in Hegelian Dialectic*, 153–68. New York: Fordham University Press, 1977.

———. "Hegel's Critique of Kant's Theology." In *God Knowable and Unknowable*, edited by Robert J. Roth, S.J., 85–105. New York: Fordham University Press, 1973.

Léonard, Andre. *La foi chez Hegel.* Paris: Desclée, 1970.

Lessing, G. *Theological Writings.* Translated by H. Chadwick. Stanford, CA: Stanford University Press, 1957.

Levinas, Emmanuel. *Totality and Infinity: An Essay on Exteriority.* Translated by Alphonso Lingis. Pittsburgh: Duquesne University Press, 1969.

Lewis, Thomas. *Freedom and Tradition in Hegel.* Notre Dame, IN: University of Notre Dame Press, 2005.

———. *Religion, Modernity, and Politics in Hegel.* Oxford: Oxford University Press, 2011.

Lienhard, Marc. *L'évangile et l'église chez Luther.* Paris: Éditions du Cerf, 1989.

Lorenz, R. "*Fruitio Dei* bei Augustin." *Zeitschrift für Kirchengeschichte* 63 (1950–51): 75–132.

Löwith, Karl. *From Hegel to Nietzsche: The Revolution in Nineteenth Century Thought.* Translated by D. E. Green. New York: Doubleday, 1967.

———. "Hegels Aufhebung der christlichen Religion." *Hegel Studien*, Supplement 1 (1964): 193–236.

Markus, Robert. "Augustine on Magic: A Neglected Semiotic Theory." *Revue des études augustiniennes* 40 (1994): 375–88.

———. *The End of Ancient Christianity.* Cambridge: Cambridge University Press, 1990.

———. *Saeculum: History and Society in the Theology of St. Augustine.* Cambridge: Cambridge University Press, 1988.

———. *Signs and Meanings: World and Text in Ancient Christianity.* Liverpool: Liverpool University Press, 1996.

———. "St. Augustine on Signs." *Phronesis* 2, no. 1 (1957): 60–83.

Marrevee, William H. *The Ascension of Christ in the Works of St. Augustine.* Ottawa: University of Ottawa Press, 1967.

Marrou, H. I. *Education in Antiquity.* Translated by George Lamb. Madison: University of Wisconsin Press, 1956.

Mathewes, Charles. *The Republic of Grace: Augustinian Thoughts for Dark Times.* Grand Rapids, MI: Eerdmans, 2010.

Mayer, C., O.S.A. "'Attende Stephanum conservum tuum' (Serm. 317,2,3): Sinn und Wert der Märtyerverehrung nach den Stephanuspredigten Augustins." In Fructus Centesimus: *Mélanges offerts à Gerard J. M. Bartelink à l'occasion de son soixante-cinqième anniversaire*, edited by A. A. R. Bastiaensen, A. Hilhorst, and C. H. Kneepkens, Instrumenta Patristica 19, 217–37. Dordrecht: Kluwer Academic, 1989.

———. *Die Zeichen in der geistigen Entwicklung und in der Theologie des jungen Augustinus.* Würzburg: Augustinus-Verlag, 1969.

McCarthy, Michael C., S.J. "An Ecclesiology of Groaning: Augustine, the Psalms, and the Making of the Church." *Theological Studies* 66, no. 1 (2005): 23–48.

McGrath, Sean J. "Boehme, Hegel, Schelling, and the Hermetic Theology of Evil." *Philosophy & Theology* 18, no. 2 (2006): 257–86.

Meconi, David V., S.J. *The One Christ: St. Augustine's Theology of Deification.* Washington, DC: Catholic University of America Press, 2013.

Meijering, E. P. *Augustine: "De Fide et Symbolo": Introduction, Translation, Commentary.* Amsterdam: J. C. Gieben, 1987.

Merklinger, Philip M. *Philosophy, Theology, and Hegel's Berlin Philosophy of Religion, 1821–1827.* Albany, NY: SUNY Press, 1993.

Milbank, John A. "Divine Triads: Augustine and the Indo-European Soul." *Modern Theology* 14 (1997): 451–74.

Min, Anselm K. "Hegel's Absolute: Transcendent or Immanent?" *Journal of Religion* 56, no. 1 (1976): 61–87.

———. "The Trinity and the Incarnation: Hegel and Classical Approaches." *Journal of Religion* 66, no. 2 (1986): 173–93.

Morrison, Karl. *The Mimetic Tradition of Reform in the West.* Princeton: Princeton University Press, 1982.

Mostert, Walter. "Hinweise zu Luthers Lehre vom Heiligen Geist." In *Der Heilige Geist im Verständnis Luthers und der lutherischen Theologie*, edited by Joachim Heubach and Sibrand Siegert, 15–45. Erlangen: Martin-Luther-Verlag, 1990.

Norton, Robert E. *The Beautiful Soul: Aesthetic Morality in the Eighteenth Century.* Ithaca, NY: Cornell University Press, 1995.

Novatian. *The Trinity.* In *The Trinity, The Spectacles, Jewish Foods, In Praise of Purity, Letters*, translated by Russell J. DeSimone, Fathers of the Church 67, 23–114. Washington, DC: Catholic University of America Press, 1974.

O'Connell, R. J. *The Origin of the Soul in St. Augustine's Later Works.* New York: Fordham University Press, 1987.

O'Donovan, Oliver. *The Problem of Self-Love in St. Augustine.* New Haven: Yale University Press, 1980.

———. "'Usus' and 'Fruitio' in Augustine, *De Doctrina Christiana* I." *Journal of Theological Studies* 33 (1982): 361–97.

Oeing-Hanhoff, Ludger. "Hegels Trinitätslehre: Zur Aufgabe ihrer Kritik und Rezeption." *Theologie und Philosophie* 52 (1977): 378–407.

Olson, Alan M. *Hegel and the Spirit: Philosophy as Pneumatology.* Princeton, NJ: Princeton University Press, 1992.

O'Regan, Cyril. *Gnostic Return in Modernity.* Albany, NY: SUNY Press, 2001.

———. "Hegel as Roman Catholic Opportunity and Challenge in the Nineteenth Century: The Emblematic Case of Franz Anton Staudenmaier (1800–1856)." Unpublished manuscript, 1995.

———. "Hegelian Philosophy of Religion and Eckhartian Mysticism." In *New Perspectives on Hegel's Philosophy of Religion*, edited by David Kolb, 109–29. Albany, NY: SUNY Press, 1992.

———. "Hegel's Retrieval of Philo: Constitution of a Christian Heretic." *Studia Philonica Annual* 20 (2008): 101–27.

———. *The Heterodox Hegel.* Albany, NY: SUNY Press, 1994.

———. "The Religious and Theological Relevance of the French Revolution." In *Hegel and the Modern World*, edited by Ardis B. Collins, 29–52. Albany, NY: SUNY Press, 1995.

Ormiston, Alice. *Love and Politics: Re-interpreting Hegel.* Albany, NY: SUNY Press, 2004.

Ozment, Steven E. *Homo Spiritualis: A Comparative Study of the Anthropology of Johannes Tauler, Jean Gerson and Martin Luther (1509–16) in the Context of Their Theological Thought.* Leiden: Brill, 1969.

Pelikan, Jaroslav. "*Canonica Regula*: The Trinitarian Hermeneutics of Augustine." *Proceedings of the PMR* 12–13 (1987–88): 17–29.

Pocock, J. G. A. *The Machiavellian Moment: Florentine Political Thought and the Atlantic Republican Tradition*. Princeton, NJ: Princeton University Press, 1975.

Poppi, A. M. *Lo Spirito Santo e l'unità de corpo mistico in S. Agostino*. Rome: Editrice "Miscellanea Francescana," 1955.

Powell, Samuel M. *The Trinity in German Thought*. Cambridge: Cambridge University Press, 2001.

Prien, Hans-Jürgen. "Grundgedanken der Ekklesiologie beim jungen Luther." *Archiv für Reformationsgeschichte* 76 (1985): 96–119.

Puškarić, Djuro. "La chiesa e il mistero trinitario nella predicazione di S. Agostino." *Augustinianum* 19 (1979): 487–506.

Rahner, Karl. *The Trinity*. Translated by Joseph Donceel. 1970. New York: Crossroad, 2003.

Ratzinger, Joseph. "The Holy Spirit as *Communio*: Concerning the Relationship of Pneumatology and Spirituality in Augustine." Translated by Peter Casarella, *Communio* 25 (1998): 324–39.

Reeves, Majorie. *The Influence of Prophecy on the Later Middle Ages: A Study in Joachimism*. Oxford: Clarendon Press, 1969.

———. *Joachim de Fiore and the Prophetic Future*. New York: Harper & Row, 1977.

Ricoeur, Paul. "Evil, a Challenge to Philosophy and Theology." *Journal of the American Academy of Religion* 53, no. 4 (1985): 631–48.

———. "Freedom in the Light of Hope." In *Essays on Biblical Interpretation*, edited by Lewis S. Mudge, 155–81. Philadelphia: Fortress, 1980.

Ringleben, Joachim. *Hegels Theorie der Sünde: Die subjektivitäts-logische Konstruktion eines theologischen Begriffs*. Berlin: De Gruyter, 1977.

Rist, John. *Augustine: Ancient Thought Baptized*. Cambridge: Cambridge University Press, 1994.

Rüfner, Vinzenz. "Die zentrale Bedeutung der Liebe für das Werden des Hegelschen Systems." In *Erkenntnis und Verantwortung: Festschrift für Theodor Litt*, edited by Josef Derbolav and Friedhelm Nicolin, 346–55. Düsseldorf: Pädagogischer Verlag Schwann, 1960.

Schindler, Alfred. *Wort und Analogie in Augustins Trinitätslehre*. Hermeneutische Untersuchungen zur Theologie 4. Tübingen: Mohr, 1965.

Schlitt, Dale M., O.M.I. *Divine Subjectivity: Understanding Hegel's Philosophy of Religion*. Scranton, PA: University of Scranton Press, 1990.

———. *Hegel's Trinitarian Claim: A Critical Reflection*. Leiden: Brill, 1984.
———. "The Whole Truth: Hegel's Reconceptualization of Trinity." *The Owl of Minerva* 15, no. 2 (1984): 169–81.
Schmaus, Michael. *Die psychologische Trinitätslehre des heiligen Augustinus*. 1927. Münster: Aschendorff, 1967.
Schmidt, Erik. *Hegels System der Theologie*. Berlin: De Gruyter, 1974.
Schultz, Werner. "Die Bedeutung der Idee der Liebe für Hegels Philosophie." *Zeitschrift für deutsche Kulturphilosophie* 9 (1943): 217–38.
———. "Die Transformierung der *theologia crucis* bei Hegel und Schleiermacher." In *Theologie und Wirklichkeit: Ausgewählte Aufsätze von Werner Schultz, aus Anlass seines 75. Geburtstages mit einem Geleitwort*, edited by Hans-Georg Pust, 76–103. Kiel: Lutherische Verlagsgesellschaft, 1969.
Smith, Andrew. *Porphyry's Place in the Neoplatonic Tradition: A Study in Post-Plotinian Neoplatonism*. The Hague: Martinus Nijhoff, 1974.
Smith, John E. "Hegel's Reinterpretation of the Doctrine of Spirit and the Religious Community." In *Hegel and the Philosophy of Religion: The Wofford Symposium*, edited by Darrel E. Christensen, 155–75. The Hague: Martinus Nijhoff, 1970.
Smith, John H. *Dialogues between Faith and Reason: The Death and Return of God in Modern German Thought*. Ithaca, NY: Cornell University Press, 2011.
———. "Hegel: *Logos* as Spirit (*Geist*)." In *Dialogues between Faith and Reason*, 95–119.
———. *The Spirit and Its Letter: Traces of Rhetoric in Hegel's Philosophy of* Bildung. Ithaca, NY: Cornell University Press, 1988.
Souche-Dagues, Denise. "Thinking *Logos* in Hegelianism." *Philosophical Forum* 31, nos. 3–4 (Fall 2000): 216–32.
Splett, Jörg. *Die Trinitätslehre G. W. F. Hegels*. Symposion 20. Freiburg: Verlag Karl Alber, 1965.
Stanciu, Diana. "Augustine's (Neo)Platonic Soul and Anti-Pelagian Spirit." *Studia Patristica* 61 (2013): 63–73.
Staudenmaier, Franz Anton. *Darstellung und Kritik des Hegelschen Systems: Aus dem Standpunkte der christlichen Philosophie*. Mainz: F. Kupferberg, 1844.
———. *Die Philosophie des Christentums, oder Metaphysik der Heiligen Schrift als Lehre von den göttlichen Ideen und ihre Entwicklung in Natur, Geist, und Geschichte*. 1840. Frankfurt: Minerva, 1966.

———. *Pragmatismus der Geistesgaben; oder, Das Wirken des göttlichen Geistes in Menschen und in der Menschheit*. 1835. Frankfurt: Minerva, 1975.

———. *Zum religiösen Frieden der Zukunft, mit Rücksicht auf die religiöspolitische Aufgabe der Gegenwart*. 1846–51. Frankfurt: Minerva, 1967.

Stepelevich, Lawrence S. "Hegel and Roman Catholicism." *Journal of the American Academy of Religion* 60, no. 4 (Winter 1992): 673–91.

———. "Hegel and the Lutheran Eucharist." *Heythrop Journal* 27, no. 3 (1986): 262–74.

Strauss, G. *Schriftgebrauch, Schriftauslegung und Schriftbeweis bei Augustin*. Tübingen: J. C. B. Mohr, 1959.

Straw, Carole. "Martyrdom." In *Augustine through the Ages: An Encyclopedia*, edited by A. Fitzgerald, 538–42. Grand Rapids, MI: Eerdmans, 1999.

Studer, Basil. *The Grace of Christ and the Grace of God in Augustine of Hippo: Christocentrism or Theocentrism?* Translated by M. J. O'Connell. Collegeville, MN: Liturgical Press, 1997.

———. "'Sacramentum et exemplum' chez Saint Augustin." In *Dominus Salvator: Studien zur Christologie und Exegese der Kirchenväter*, Studia Anselmiana 107, 141–212. Rome: Edizioni Abbazia S. Paolo, 1992.

———. "La teologia trinitaria in Agostino d'Ippona: Continuita della tradizione occidentale?" In *Cristianesimo e specificita regionali nel mediterraneo Latino (sec. IV–VI)*, Studia Ephemerides Augustinianum 46, 161–77. Rome: Augustinianum, 1994.

———. "Zur Pneumatologie des Augustinus von Hippo (*De trinitate* 15, 17, 27–27, 50)." *Augustinianum* 35 (1995): 568–83.

Sweeney, Leo. "Augustine and Gregory of Nyssa: Is the Triune God Infinite in Being?" In *Augustine: Presbyter Factus Sum*, edited by Joseph Lienhard, Earl Muller, and Roland Teske, 497–516. New York: Peter Lang, 1993.

———. "Divine Attributes in *De doctrina Christiana*: Why Does Augustine Not List 'Infinity'?" In De doctrina christiana: *A Classic of Western Culture*, edited by Duane Arnold and Pamela Bright, 195–204. Notre Dame, IN: University of Notre Dame Press, 1995.

Taylor, Charles. *Hegel*. Cambridge: Cambridge University Press, 1975.

———. *Hegel and Modern Society*. Cambridge: Cambridge University Press, 1979.

———. *Sources of the Self: The Making of the Modern Identity*. Cambridge, MA: Harvard University Press, 1989.

Tertullian. *Tertullian's Treatise against Praxeas*. Edited, translated, and with a commentary by Ernest Evans. London: SPCK, 1948.

TeSelle, Eugene. *Augustine the Theologian*. London: Burns & Oates, 1970.

Teske, R. "Love of Neighbor in St. Augustine." In *Atti, Congresso internazionale su S. Agostino nel XVI centenario della conversione, Roma, 15–20 settembre 1986*, 3 vols., 3:81–102. Rome: Institutum Patristicum Augustinianum, 1987.

———. "St. Augustine and the Vision of God." In *Augustine: Mystic and Mystagogue*, edited by Frederick Van Fleteren, Joseph Schnaubelt, and Joseph Reino, 287–308. New York: Peter Lang, 1994.

Theunissen, Michael. *Hegels Lehre vom absoluten Geist als theologisch-politischer Traktat*. Berlin: De Gruyter, 1970.

Ulrich, Ferdinand. "*Gnosis* und *Agape*: Ein Beitrag zum Verhältnis von Philosophie und Religion bei Hegel." *Kairos* 15 (1973): 280–310.

Ulrich, Jörg. *Die Anfänge der Abendlandischen Rezeption des Nizänums*. Berlin: De Gruyter, 1994.

Van Bavel, Tarcisius J. "The Double Face of Love in St. Augustine: The Daring Inversion 'Love Is God.'" In *Atti, Congresso internazionale su S. Agostino nel XVI centenario della conversione, Roma, 15–20 settembre 1986*, 3 vols., 3:69–80. Rome: Institutum Patristicum Augustinianum, 1987.

———. "God in between Affirmation and Negation according to Augustine." In *Augustine: Presbyter Factus Sum*, edited by Joseph Lienhard, Earl Muller, and Roland Teske, Collectanea Augustiniana 2, 73–97. New York: Peter Lang, 1993.

———. "'No One Ever Hated His Own Flesh': Eph. 5:29 in Augustine." *Augustiniana* 45 (1995): 45–93.

———. *Recherches sur la christologie de saint Augustin: L'humain et le divin dans le Christ d'après saint Augustin*. Paradosis 19. Fribourg: Éditions universitaires, 1954.

Van der Meer, F. *Augustine the Bishop: Religion and Society at the Dawn of the Middle Ages*. Translated by Brian Battershaw and G. R. Lamb. New York: Harper & Row, 1965.

Van Fleteren, F. "Per Speculum et in Aenigmate: I Corinthians 13:12 in the Writings of St. Augustine." *Augustinian Studies* 23 (1992): 69–102.

Vannier, Marie-Anne. *'Creatio,' 'conversio,' 'formatio,' chez S. Augustin*. Fribourg: Éditions universitaires, 1991.

Van Reyn, Geert. "Divine Inspiration in Virgil's *Aeneid* and Augustine's Christian Alternative in *Confessions*." *Studia Patristica* 61 (2013): 15–30.

Verhees, Jacques. "Die Bedeutung des Geistes Gottes im Leben des Menschen nach Augustinus frühester Pneumatologie (bis 391)." *Zeitschrift für Kirchengeschichte* 88, nos. 2–3 (1977): 161–89.

———. *God in Beweging: Een onderzoek naar de Pneumatologie van Augustinus*. Wageningen: H. Veenman & Zoonan N.V., 1968.

———. "Heiliger Geist und Gemeinschaft bei Augustinus von Hippo: Biographische und kirchengeschichtliche Hintergründe des Themas." *Revue des études augustiniennes* 23 (1977): 245–64.

———. "Heiliger Geist und Inkarnation in der Theologie des Augustinus von Hippo." *Revue des études augustiniennes* 22 (1976): 234–53.

Von Harnack, Adolf. *History of Dogma*. 7 vols. New York: Dover Publications, 1961.

Wagner, Falk. "Die Aufhebung der religiösen Vorstellung in den philosophischen Begriff." *Neue Zeitschrift für systematische Theologie und Religionsphilosophie* 10 (1968): 44–88.

———. *Der Gedanke der Persönlichkeit Gottes bei Fichte und Hegel*. Gütersloh: Mohn, 1971.

Wallmann, Johannes. "Geisterfahrung und Kirche im frühen Pietismus." In *Charisma und Institution*, edited by Trutz Rendtorff, 132–44. Gütersloh: Gütersloher Verlagshaus Gerd Mohn, 1985.

Wendte, Martin. *Gottmenschliche Einheit bei Hegel: Eine logische und theologische Untersuchung*. Berlin: De Gruyter, 2007.

———. "Lamentation between Contradiction and Obedience: Hegel and Barth as Diametrically Opposed Brothers in the Spirit of Modernity." In *Evoking Lament: A Theological Discussion*, edited by Eva Harasta and Brian Brock, 77–98. London: T&T Clark, 2009.

Westphal, Merold. "Hegel and the Reformation." In *History and System: Hegel's Philosophy of History; Proceedings of the 1982 Sessions of the Hegel Society of America*, edited by Robert L. Perkins, 73–99. Albany, NY: SUNY Press, 1984.

White, Hayden. *Metahistory: The Historical Imagination in Nineteenth-Century Europe*. Baltimore: Johns Hopkins University Press, 1972.

Wilken, Robert L. "Is Pentecost a Peer of Easter? Scripture, Liturgy, and the Proprium of the Holy Spirit." In *Trinity, Time, and the Church: A Response to the Theology of Robert Jenson*, edited by Colin Gunton, 158–77. Grand Rapids, MI: Eerdmans, 2000.

Williams, A. N. "Contemplation: Knowledge of God in Augustine's *De Trinitate.*" In *Knowing the Triune God: The Work of the Spirit in the Practices of the Church*, edited by James J. Buckley and David S. Yeago, 121–46. Grand Rapids, MI: Eerdmans, 2001.

Williams, Rowan D. "'Good for Nothing'? Augustine on Creation." *Augustinian Studies* 25 (1994): 9–24.

———. "Language, Reality and Desire in Augustine's *De doctrina.*" *Literature and Theology* 3 (1989): 138–50.

———. "The Paradoxes of Self-Knowledge in the *De trinitate.*" In *Augustine: Presbyter Factus Sum*, edited by Joseph Lienhard, Earl Muller, and Roland Teske, 121–34. New York: Peter Lang, 1993.

———. "Politics and the Soul: A Reading of the *City of God.*" *Milltown Studies* 19–20 (1987): 55–72.

———. "*Sapientia* and the Trinity: Reflections on *De trinitate.*" In *Collectanea Augustiniana: Mélanges T. J. van Bavel*, edited by B. Bruning, M. Lamberigts, and J. Van Houtem, 2 vols., Bibliotheca Ephemeridum Theologicarum Lovaniensium 92, 1:317–32. Leuven: Peeters, 1990.

Wilson-Kastner, P. "Grace and Participation in the Divine Life in the Theology of Augustine of Hippo." *Augustinian Studies* 7 (1976): 135–50.

Windelband, Wilhelm. *A History of Philosophy.* Translated by James A. Tufts. 1901. New York: Harper, 1958.

Wolff, Michael. *Das Körper-Seele-Problem: Kommentar zu Hegel, "Enzyklopädie" (1830), §389.* Frankfurt: Vittorio Klostermann, 1992.

Wylleman, A., ed. *Hegel on the Ethical Life, Religion, and Philosophy (1793–1807).* Leuven: Leuven University Press, 1989.

Yerkes, James. *The Christology of Hegel.* Missoula, MT: Scholars Press, 1978. Reprint, Albany, NY: SUNY Press, 1983.

Young, Frances. *Biblical Exegesis and the Formation of Christian Culture.* Cambridge: Cambridge University Press, 1997.

INDEX

actual soul, 197, 198–99
Aesthetics (Hegel), 13, 33
agonic anthropology, 55
animal soul, 196–97
anthropology
  agonic, 55
  Pelagian, 106–7
Apollinarianism, 244
apostles
  baptism by, 147
  love and, 156–57, 337n81
  Pentecost and, 156–59, 337n81
  teaching by, 147
  See also Peter
archaeological narratives, 298–99
Arendt, Hannah, 361n145
Arian subordinationism, 4
Aristotle
  Hegel and, 195–96, 343n68
  on soul, 195
Arndt, Johann, 108
art
  in *Aesthetics*, 33
  Christ in, 33
  God and, 33, 315n39, 316n49
  Holy Spirit relating to, 192–93
  love in, 33, 316n49
ascension, 44–50
Asendorf, Ulrich
  on Lutheran Orthodoxy, 185–86
  on spiritual community, 179, 180, 185–86
astrology, 70
Athanasius, 4

Augustine
  analysis of, 9–12
  Baur on, 4–6, 10–11, 298, 308n10, 308n12
  on birth, 243
  on body, soul, and church, 241–48
  on Christ's birth, 73–74, 76–77
  on Christ's body, 135–37, 151–52
  on Christ's historical life, 19–20
  on church, 145–46, 148–49, 240–48
  on corruption, 242
  on cross, 271
  on devil, 79, 82, 86–88
  on divine goodness, 6
  on Donatists, 250–52, 288–89, 355n67
  on evil, 42–43, 134
  Gangauf on, 10
  on grace, 5–6, 72–74, 75, 106
  Gunton on, 11, 298–99
  Hegel on, 3, 9–11
  on history, 69
  on Holy City, 6
  Idealist interpretation of, 10
  on lament, 222
  language of, 7–8
  Markus on, 290–91
  on martyrdom, 130, 160–69
  on materialism, 246
  on mystery, 264–65, 271
  negative interpretations of, 1–2, 10, 11
  neoscholastics on, 11

Augustine (cont.)
  on original sin, 74–75
  on prayer, 263–364
  on revelation, 222–24
  on sacrament, 136, 260–71, 264–65
  on scripture, 223–24, 259–61, 265–71
  on Sinai, 155–56
  on society and evil, 134
  Trinitarian doctrine of, 1–14, 297–305
  Williams on, 290–91
  on worship, 291–92
  Württemberg Pietism relating to, 105–6
  See also specific works
Augustine's pneumatology
  on conversion of language, 133–50
  on freedom, confidence, and action, 150–69
  Hodgson on, 175–76, 238
  on Pentecost, 93–94, 95–96, 129–50
  on pride, language, and society, 130–33, 147–48
Augustine's rhetorical Christology
  on birth of Word of God, 64, 71–79
  on Christ's baptism, 76–77
  on Christ's death, 79–91
  on creation, 62–65
  on faith, 89–90, 137
  on fall, 62–64, 65–70
  Hegel's logical Christology compared to, 18–20
  immanent Trinity in, 72–74, 137–39
  language distinctions and Word of God, 57–59, 138–40
  linguistic logic in, 59–60
  on love and Word of God, 6, 59–65, 149–50
  on Old Testament, 273–74
  pride, language, and love of God in, 65–71, 133
  on resurrection, 81–82, 84–85, 136–38, 145–47, 242–43, 265–66
  seeking God's image in, 53–56
  Word of God in, 17, 18–20, 53–92
Augustinian confession, 229, 351n181
Augustinianism, 106
Ayres, Lewis, 10
  on body and soul, 256–57
  on Holy Spirit, 256–57

Baader, Franz von, 209
Babel narrative, 129
  language in, 66–67, 147
  Nimrod in, 131
  Pentecost relating to, 133–34, 147
  pride in, 66
  society in, 131
Baker, Kimberly, 359n120
baptism
  by apostles, 147
  birth and, 76–77
  of Christ, 35–39, 76–77
  disciples relating to, 36, 37–38
  immanent Trinity and, 36–37
  kingdom of God relating to, 37–39
  Pentecost relating to, 36, 38
Baur, Ferdinand Christian, 175
  on Augustine, 4–6, 10–11, 298, 308n10, 308n12
  on *De civitate Dei*, 6
  on God, 6–7
  on grace, 6
  on Hegel, 4, 7

on Holy Spirit, 3–6
on language, 7
on love, 6–7
on thought, 5
on Trinitarian doctrine, 3–6
Bengel, Johann Albrecht
  mysticism of, 211–12
  Pietism of, 108
Benz, Ernst, 211–12
birth
  Augustine on, 243
  baptism and, 76–77
  of Christ, 31–32, 73–74, 76–77
  of Holy Spirit, 31–35
  of Word of God, 31–35, 62, 64, 71–79
bodily flesh, 132–33
body
  Ayres on, 256–57
  Christ as head of church and, 189–90, 202–3, 248–60
  church, soul, and, 241–48
  communal, 251–53
  eyes, 252–54
  goodness of, 242
  head and soul imagery, 248–60
  heart, 253
  Holy Spirit, spiritual community, and, 187–203, 349n172
  love relating to, 252–56
  lust and, 247–48
  in marriage, 247–48, 358n113
  in *persona*, 244, 249
  praise and, 247
  resurrection and, 242–43, 254–55
  Rist on, 243, 353n19
  sacrifice and, 292–93
  soul-body imagery, 187–89, 193–203
  transfiguration of, 272–90
  use of, 146–47

Wolff on, 202–3
See also Christ's body; sacramental body
Böhme, Jakob, 87
  Joachimite spiritual community relating to, 184–85
boredom, 267
Brock, Brian, 359nn119–20
brotherly love, 157–58

Cameron, Michael, 260–61, 356n70
Catholicism
  Christological stagnation and, 109–14
  discipline in, 346n126
  freedom in, 112–13
  Hegel's critique of, 111, 127, 175–76, 189–90
  medieval, 111, 177, 191–92
  Pentecost and, 111
  pope in, 191
  society relating to, 112–13
  soul in, 199
  Staudenmaier, Hegel, and pneumatic Catholicism, 98–104, 299–300
Cavadini, John, 60
  on godly doctrine, 64
  on knowledge, 323n70
charity
  Holy Spirit relating to, 287–88
  love and, 153
  martyrdom for, 161
  Word of God and, 80–81
Christ
  in art, 33
  baptism of, 35–39, 76–77
  birth of, 31–32, 73–74, 76–77
  death of, 40–46, 79–91, 249–50
  glorification of, 140–42
  as God, 46–47

Christ (*cont.*)
  as head of body and church, 189–90, 202–3, 248–60
  historical life of, 19–20, 35–44
  Holy Spirit relating to, 72–74
  humanity of, 75, 245–46, 248–49, 254, 262–63
  humility of, 72
  lament of, 274–80
  as mediator, 75–76, 261
  natures of, 75–76
  as sacrament, 135–36
  teaching of, 64, 78
Christian community, 120–21
Christian doctrine, 173–74
Christian freedom, 8, 213, 329n30
Christianity
  during Crusades, 189, 192, 198
  early, 121
  Enlightenment and, 184
  Hegel on, 94–95, 110–14, 302–3
  Joachimite spiritual community and, 211–13
  martyrdom in, 114–15
  Pentecost and, 113–14
  social breakdown relating to, 115
  Staudenmaier relating to, 99–104
Christian mystery, 206–10
Christological stagnation, 109–14
Christ's body
  anointing through, 284–85
  Augustine on, 135–37, 151–52
  church and, 135, 189–92, 202–3, 250–51
  Holy Spirit and, 202, 248–51
  language of, 135–37, 278
  love relating to, 151–52, 278
  mercy and, 284–85
  past and present believers linked through, 280
  search for, 112
  spiritual community relating to, 112, 189–92
church
  Augustine on, 145–46, 148–49, 240–48
  Christ as head of body and, 189–90, 202–3, 248–60
  Christ's body and, 135, 189–92, 202–3, 250–51
  differences in, 232
  hierarchy of, 191–92, 225
  Holy Spirit relating to, 149
  language relating to, 148–49
  love of, 150, 151
  in medieval Catholicism, 191–92
  on resurrection, 135, 145–46
  society and, 101, 103, 112–13
  state and, 109–10, 113, 215, 291
  teaching by, 349n172
  Trinitarian doctrine and, 301–2
  universality of, 145–47, 149
  See also spiritual community
City of God (Augustine), 130, 291–92
claritas, 140–41
cloud imagery, 66
Colossians, 188–89
communal body, 251–53
community
  faith relating to, 89–90
  Holy Spirit and, 95
  humility, language, and, 143–44, 147–48
  love and, 109–11, 114
  See also spiritual community
confession
  Augustinian, 229, 351n181
  judgment and, 117–19

The Phenomenology of Spirit on, 117–19
in *totus Christus*, 295
consciousness
  divine self-, 10–11
  unhappy, 111
conversion, 263
  of language, 133–50
Cook, Daniel, 24
1 Corinthians, 150
corporate imagery, 188–89
corruption, 242
creation
  Augustine's rhetorical Christology on, 62–65
  evil of, 28–29, 62
  freedom of, 29
  goodness of, 6, 29–30, 62–64, 68, 323n66
  of humanity, 74–75
  ideality of, 28, 29
  immanent Trinity and, 27–28
  incarnation and, 28–29
  Lectures on the Philosophy of Religion on, 27–28
  love and, 28, 29
  Staudenmaier on, 101, 102
  of Word of God, 26–31
Croce, Benedetto, 42
cross
  Augustine on, 271
  double negativity of, 40–43
  glory and, 214–15
  Hegel's logical Christology on, 39–44
  immanent Trinity and, 41
  Luther on, 43
  resurrection and, 44–45
  suffering and, 85
Crusades, 189, 192
  soul during, 198

cultus, 227–29

Darstellung und Kritik des Hegelschen Systems (Staudenmaier), 102
death
  of Christ, 40–46, 79–91, 249–50
  devil and, 86–88
  evil and, 42–43
  fall and, 84, 87
  fear of, 162, 274–75, 338n110
  God and, 81–82
  Holy Spirit and, 48–49
  justice and, 82–83
  love and, 40–41
  in martyrdom, 162–63, 165–68, 338n110
  pride relating to, 87–88
  sin relating to, 83–85
  of soul, 84–85, 197–98
  suffering and, 40–44
  See also resurrection
deceit, 145
  praise and, 334n32
De civitate Dei (Augustine), 6, 12
De doctrina Christiana (Augustine), 12
De Genesi adversus Manicheos (Augustine), 65–67
desire, 82
Desmond, William, 221, 228, 309n25
De Trinitate (Augustine), 12, 53–56
deutero-Pauline epistles, 188–89
devil
  Augustine on, 79, 82, 86–88
  death and, 86–88
  fall relating to, 87
  justice relating to, 82
  pride of, 87–88
devotional Pietism, 108

Dickey, Laurence, 164, 185, 211
  on Pietism, 105–9
disciples, 36, 37–38
discipline
  in Catholicism, 346n126
  superstitious, 70
divination, 70
divine becoming, 94
divine goodness, 6
divine justice, 325n122
divine love, 220–22
divine narrative, 63–64
divine self-consciousness, 10–11
Docetists, 245
doctrinal exposition, 349n172
Donatists
  Augustine on, 250–52, 288–89, 355n67
  martyrdom for, 160–61
  Pentecost and, 145–47, 161, 250
double exile, 67
double negativity, 40–43
double resurrection, 84–85
dove
  Holy Spirit as, 143–45
  Pentecost and, 143–45, 161
  sacrifice relating to, 144–45

early Christianity, 121
early pietism, 104
Easter Pasch, 265, 270
Eckhart, Meister
  Baader and, 209
  Hegel and, 209–10
  mysticism and, 209–10
  spiritual community of, 182–87, 346n128
economic Trinity, 21
ecstasy, 277–78
Eden, 65–66

Elements of the Philosophy of Right (Hegel), 14
elitism, 105, 288–89
emerging community, 179
empty tomb, 189, 198
Enarrationes in Psalmos (Augustine), 12–13, 241
Enchiridion (Augustine), 72–73
Encyclopedia of the Philosophical Sciences (Hegel), 13
enemy, love of, 157–58
enjoyment, 229–30
Enlightenment, 2
  Christianity and, 184
  Luther, 183
  Reformation and, 183
equality, 137–38
ethics
  grace and, 107
  Kant on, 107–10
  martyrdom relating to, 123–24
Eucharist, 335n51
  criticism of, 190–91
  different forms and interpretations of, 232
  immanent Trinity and, 234–35
  sacrament and, 174, 227, 229–35, 293
  salvation history and, 233–34
  spiritual community and, 190–92, 231–35
Eucharistic resurrection, 231–35
evil
  Augustine on, 42–43, 134
  of creation, 28–29, 62
  death and, 42–43
  fall and, 30–31, 63–64, 208
  forgiveness and, 116, 119
  Hegel on, 30–31, 116, 208
  humanity as, 30–31, 208

judgment and, 116–17
Kant on, 218
language relating to, 134
love and, 81, 157
in *The Phenomenology of Spirit*, 98, 116–18, 119
society and, 134
external language
freedom from, 60–61
inner word and, 57–61, 65
eyes, 252–54

faith
Augustine's rhetorical Christology on, 89–90, 137
community relating to, 89–90
grace and, 155
in Holy Spirit, 288
in incarnation, 288
love, knowledge, and, 56, 88–90, 255
purgative, 55–56
reason and, 183
resurrection and, 137
salvation and, 89–90
truth relating to, 89
Word of God and, 89–90
fall
Augustine's rhetorical Christology on, 62–64, 65–70
death and, 84, 87
devil relating to, 87
in divine narrative, 63–64
evil and, 30–31, 63–64, 208
human mind and, 58–59
justice relating to, 82
language and, 52–53
pride relating to, 65–71
resurrection relating to, 85–86
society relating to, 130–31
fanaticism, 215–16, 219

fear
of death, 162, 274–75, 338n110
ecstasy and, 277–78
figurative exegesis, 260–61
First Epistle of John, 150–51
flesh, 132–33, 151–52, 333n2
forgiveness
evil and, 116, 119
grace and, 114–26
Hegel on, 114–26
Houlgate on, 318n96
language of, 119–20
in *The Phenomenology of Spirit*, 98, 116, 119–20
spiritual community relating to, 119–20
in totus Christus, 293
freedom
in Catholicism, 112–13
Christian, 8, 213, 329n30
of creation, 29
from external language, 60–61
Hegel's logical Christology on, 29, 49–50
Holy Spirit and, 182–83, 213–14
Judaeo-Christian heritage and, 121–22
in judgment, 320n33
of love, 156–57
Luther on, 182–83
Olson on, 181, 182
Pentecost, confidence, action, and, 150–69
religious, 215–17
soul and, 201–2
spiritual community and, 181–83, 185, 213–14
Staudenmaier on, 99–100
worship relating to, 229

Gangauf, Theodor, 10

Germanic peoples, 200
German Idealism, 11
gift, 72, 283, 288
glorification, of Christ, 140–42
glory
  cross and, 214–15
  Word of God and, 142–43
God
  art and, 33, 315n39, 316n49
  Baur on, 6–7
  Christ as, 46–47
  death and, 81–82
  as good, 323n66
  goodness of, 220–21, 323n66
  incarnation of, 28–29, 32–33, 40, 72
  as infinite, 32–33
  justice of, 81
  knowledge and, 58, 205–6, 209–10
  as love, 33, 220–21
  memory of, 58
  as mystery, 205–7
  personality of, 21–22
  pride, language, and love of, 65–71, 133
  as sacrament, 205–6
  self-manifestation of, 26–27
  teaching of, 36, 64
  as truth, 58, 205–6
godforsakenness, 219–20, 222–23
  lamenting, 274–76
godly doctrine, 64
God's image
  in Augustine's rhetorical Christology, 53–56
  Hegel on, 208–9
  memory and, 57–58
  original sin relating to, 208, 323n70
  Word of God and, 53–56
goodness
  of body, 242
  of creation, 6, 29–30, 62–64, 68, 323n66
  divine, 6
  of God, 220–21, 323n66
  Hegel on, 29–30, 208
  of humanity, 29–30, 208
  self-sacrifice relating to, 29–30
  of soul, 67–68
  truth and, 62
  Word of God as, 72
Good Teacher, 78
Gospels, 37
grace
  Augustine on, 5–6, 72–74, 75, 106
  Baur on, 6
  ethics and, 107
  faith and, 155
  forgiveness and, 114–26
  Hegel on, 114–26, 335n35
  of Holy Spirit, 73–74
  justice and, 325n122
  Kant on, 106–7
  lament and, 274–75
  language as, 77
  love and, 155
  nature, immanent Trinity, and, 281–82
  praise and, 143
  pride relating to, 286
  in Psalms, 274–75
  social and political implications of, 291–92
  Word of God relating to, 72–74, 75, 77
Gregory, Eric, 361n145
grief, 123
groaning, 272, 281–85, 294–95. *See also* lament
Gunton, Colin, 11, 298–99

happiness, 79–80
heart, 253
Hegel, Georg Wilhelm Friedrich
   Aristotle and, 195–96, 343n68
   on Augustine, 3, 9–11
   Baur on, 4, 7
   on Catholicism, 111, 127, 175–76, 189–90
   on Christian community, 120–21
   on Christianity, 94–95, 110–14, 302–3
   on Christ's birth, 31–32
   on Christ's historical life, 19–20, 35–44
   on community of love, 110–11, 114
   Eckhart and, 209–10
   on evil, 30–31, 116, 208
   on fanaticism, 215–16, 219
   on forgiveness, 114–26
   on God's image, 208–9
   on goodness, 29–30, 208
   on grace, 114–26, 335n35
   on history, 69, 90–91
   Hodgson on, 175–76
   on Judaism, 111
   on Kant, 109–10
   on kingdom of God, 110, 112
   on lament, 218–19
   language of, 7–8, 13–14
   on love, 312n1
   on martyrdom, 98, 114–28, 166–67, 332n99, 332n104
   mature philosophy of, 21, 312n1
   on original sin, 208
   on personality, 21–23
   on Protestantism, 182–83
   reading, 8–9
   as religious thinker, 8
   on revelation, 224–25
   on scripture, 224–27
   on soul, 194–99
   The Spirit of Christianity and Its Fate, 9
   Trinitarian doctrine of, 2–3, 6–15, 176, 297–304
   on worship, 227–29, 230, 235
   See also specific works
Hegel and the Spirit (Olson), 176
Hegel's logical Christology
   Augustine's rhetorical Christology compared to, 18–20
   on birth of Word of God, 31–35, 62
   on Christ's baptism, 35–39
   on creation and expression of Word of God, 26–31
   on cross, 39–44
   on freedom, 29, 49–50
   immanent Trinity in, 21–26, 73, 205–6
   Logos of Father and, 21–27
   on resurrection and ascension, 44–50
   Word of God in, 17–20, 21–35
Hegel's pneumatology
   on Catholicism and Christological stagnation, 109–14
   on grace and forgiveness, 114–26
   Olson on, 176, 178
   on Pentecost, 94–95, 96, 111–14
   Staudenmaier, pneumatic Catholicism, and, 98–104, 299–300
   on Württemberg Pietism, sanctification, and political recollectivization, 104–9
heroes, 124–26
history
   Augustine on, 69
   Christ's historical life, 19–20, 35–44
   Hegel on, 69, 90–91

history *(cont.)*
  Joachimite Reformers on, 184
  salvation, 233–34, 284
Hodgson, Peter, 175–76, 238, 309n25
holiness, 100
Holy City, 6
Holy One, 189–90
Holy Spirit
  art relating to, 192–93
  Ayres on, 256–57
  Baur on, 3–6
  birth of, 31–35
  body, spiritual community, and, 187–203, 349n172
  charity relating to, 287–88
  Christ relating to, 72–74
  Christ's body and, 202, 248–51
  church relating to, 149
  communal body and, 251–53
  community and, 95
  death and, 48–49
  as dove, 143–45
  faith in, 288
  freedom and, 182–83, 213–14
  as gift, 72, 283, 288
  goodness, creation, and, 6
  grace of, 73–74
  Gunton on, 11
  humility and, 72
  kingdom of God and, 110
  lament relating to, 283–85
  language relating to, 134–35, 142–43, 148–49
  as love, 24–25, 33–35, 152, 159–60, 203–4
  martyrdom and, 167–69
  narratives of, 1–3
  neglect of, 2
  in New Testament, 143–44
  Olson on, 180
  Pentecost and, 113–14, 148–49, 151–60, 250
  Pietism and, 109
  property of, 287–88
  in Protestantism, 35
  resurrection and, 48–49
  secular life and, 214
  self-manifestation of, 27
  sin against, 286, 360n135
  Spener on, 104
  Staudenmaier on, 98–103
  teaching from, 144
  universality of, 32–33, 46–48, 118–20, 213–15, 321n41, 337n81
  von Harnack on, 1
  water imagery and, 321n49
  witness of, 97, 98, 127, 142–43, 280–81
  Word of God and, 142–43
  Württemberg Pietism and, 109
Homo Spiritualis (Ozment), 182
Honoratus, 274
hope, 265–66
Houlgate, Stephen, 318n96
human development, 178–79, 346n126
human image, 61–62
humanity
  of Christ, 75, 245–46, 248–49, 254, 262–63
  creation of, 74–75
  as evil, 30–31, 208
  goodness of, 29–30, 208
  love for, 249–50, 293–94, 355n62
  Word of God relating to, 245–46
human justice, 325n122
human kinship, 131–32
human mind
  fall and, 58–59

fragmentation of, 58–59
Staudenmaier on, 100
humility
  of Christ, 72
  community, language, and, 143–44, 147–48
  Holy Spirit and, 72
  of incarnation, 74–75
  justice of, 82
  pride and, 83
  Word of God through, 71–72, 78, 80–81, 276

Idealism, 10–11
imagery
  cloud, 66
  corporate, 188–89
  of head and soul, 248–60
  human, 61–62
  marital, 276
  soul-body, 187–89, 193–203
  water, 65–66, 321n49
  word, 57
  of Word of God, 57–58, 61–62, 92
  See also God's image
immanent Trinity
  in Augustine's rhetorical Christology, 72–74, 137–39
  baptism and, 36–37
  creation and, 27–28
  cross and, 41
  equality in, 137–38
  Eucharist and, 234–35
  in Hegel's logical Christology, 21–26, 73, 205–6
  in Joachimite spiritual community, 184
  knowledge of, 289
  language relating to, 137–39
  Logos of Father and, 21–27
  love relating to, 24–26, 203–4, 214–15
  Luther on, 186–87
  martyrdom relating to, 122
  nature, grace, and, 281–82
  personality in, 21–23
  in *The Phenomenology of Spirit*, 23–24
  sacramental body and, 205–6
  Staudenmaier on, 103–4
incarnation
  creation and, 28–29
  faith in, 288
  of God, 28–29, 32–33, 40, 72
  humility of, 74–75
  miracle of, 243–44
  teaching of, 243–44
inclusive Trinity, 21, 317n85
In Johannis evangelium tractatus (Augustine), 12–13
inner word
  external language and, 57–61, 65
  love relating to, 60–61
  Markus on, 60–61
  translation of, 60
  truth of, 57–58

Jaeschke, Walter, 227
Joachimite Reformers, 184
Joachimite spiritual community
  Böhme relating to, 184–85
  Christianity and, 211–13
  divine realization and, 211
  Eckhartian spiritual community and, 182–87, 346n128
  immanent Trinity in, 184
  Lutheranism and, 211–12
  Reformation relating to, 184–85, 211–12
  Württemberg Pietism relating to, 184–85, 211

Job, 348n156
  lament and, 218
Johnson, D. W., 77–78
Jordan, baptism, 35–39
Judaeo-Christian heritage
  freedom and, 121–22
  martyrdom and, 121–22
  in *The Spirit of Christianity and Its Fate*, 94, 110–11
Judaism, 111
judgment
  confession and, 117–19
  evil and, 116–17
  freedom in, 320n33
  knowledge relating to, 323n70
  moral thought and, 116–17
  The Phenomenology of Spirit on, 116–19
  reconciliation and, 119
justice
  death and, 82–83
  devil relating to, 82
  divine, 325n122
  fall relating to, 82
  of God, 81
  grace and, 325n122
  human, 325n122
  of humility, 82
  power of, 79–91
  religion and, 217

Kant, Immanuel, 94
  on ethics, 107–10
  on evil, 218
  on grace, 106–7
  Hegel on, 109–10
  on moral religion, 106–7
  on virtue, 107
  Württemberg Pietism relating to, 106–8
Kany, Roland, 308n10

kingdom of God
  baptism relating to, 37–39
  disciples and, 37–38
  Hegel on, 110, 112
  Holy Spirit and, 110
  The Spirit of Christianity and Its Fate on, 37–38
  Staudenmaier on, 100, 101
  teaching and, 38–39
knowledge
  Cavadini on, 323n70
  God and, 58, 205–6, 209–10
  of immanent Trinity, 289
  judgment relating to, 323n70
  love, faith, and, 56, 88–90, 255
  memory and, 58
  of soul, 289
Kroner, Richard, 312n1

lament
  Augustine on, 222, 272–90
  of Christ, 274–80
  on godforsakenness, 274–76
  grace and, 274–75
  groaning and, 272, 281–85, 294–95
  Hegel on, 218–19
  Holy Spirit relating to, 283–85
  Job and, 218
  marital imagery relating to, 276
  mercy and, 284–86
  praise and, 173–74, 218–31, 272–90
  in Psalms, 273–74, 276, 284–85
  sacramental body and, 218–31, 272–90
  spiritual community and, 218–31
  structural moments of, 218
  totus Christus and, 279–90, 294–95

transformative, 285–86
Wendte on, 218
language
  of Augustine, 7–8
  in Babel narrative, 66–67, 147
  Baur on, 7
  of Christ's body, 135–37, 278
  Christ's glorification relating to, 140–42
  church relating to, 148–49
  in *De Genesi adversus Manicheos*, 66–67
  diversification of, 134, 147–49
  evil relating to, 134
  external language and inner word, 57–61, 65
  fall and, 52–53
  of forgiveness, 119–20
  as grace, 77
  of Hegel, 7–8, 13–14
  Holy Spirit relating to, 134–35, 142–43, 148–49
  human kinship relating to, 131–32
  humility, community, and, 143–44, 147–48
  immanent Trinity relating to, 137–39
  linguistic logic, 59–60
  love and, 149–50
  Pentecost and conversion of, 133–50
  of prayer, 263
  pride, love of God, and, 65–71, 133
  pride, society, and, 130–33, 147–48
  of reconciliation, 141–42
  in scripture, 223–24, 259–60
  signs and, 132
  speaking tongues, 147–51, 250, 251
  spiritualization of, 135–37
  of Staudenmaier, 100–101
  war relating to, 131
  Word of God and distinctions in, 57–59, 138–40
Lectures on the Philosophy of Religion (Hegel), 13
  on creation, 27–28
  on spiritual community, 178, 179
  Staudenmaier on, 103–4
Lessing's ditch, 32
Lewis, Thomas, 309n25
logical pantheism, 101–2
Logos of Father
  Cook on, 24
  in Hegel's logical Christology, 21–27
  immanent Trinity and, 21–27
  in *The Phenomenology of Spirit*, 23–24
love
  apostles and, 156–57, 337n81
  in art, 33, 316n49
  in Augustine's rhetorical Christology, 6, 59–65, 149–50
  Baur on, 6–7
  body relating to, 252–56
  brotherly, 157–58
  charity and, 153
  Christ's body relating to, 151–52, 278
  of church, 150, 151
  community and, 110–11, 114
  creation and, 28, 29
  death and, 40–41
  divine, 220–22
  of enemy, 157–58
  evil and, 81, 157
  faith, knowledge, and, 56, 88–90, 255
  freedom of, 156–57

love (cont.)
  God as, 33, 220–21
  grace and, 155
  Hegel on, 312n1
  Hegel's logic of Christ and, 18
  Holy Spirit as, 24–25, 33–35, 152, 159–60, 203–4
  for humanity, 249–50, 293–94, 355n62
  immanent Trinity relating to, 24–26, 203–4, 214–15
  inner word relating to, 60–61
  language and, 149–50
  in martyrdom, 122–23, 130, 162–66
  of Mary, 33–35
  maternal, 33–35, 316n49
  mercy and, 286–88
  for neighbor, 293–94, 361n145
  orientation of, 60–61
  Ormiston on, 347n138
  Pentecost and, 145, 151–60, 162–69
  persuasion of, 79–91
  pride, language, and, 65–71, 133
  pride and, 88–89
  rest and, 266–68
  spiritual community and, 178, 203–4
  Staudenmaier on, 103–4
  suffering and, 69
  in *totus Christus*, 239–40
  Word of God and, 6, 59–65, 92, 149–50
Love and Politics (Ormiston), 347n138
lust, 247–48
Luther, Martin, 9, 177, 180–81
  on cross, 43
  Enlightenment and, 183
  on freedom, 182–83
  on immanent Trinity, 186–87
Lutheranism, 211–12
Lutheran Orthodoxy
  Asendorf on, 185–86
  emergence of, 184–85
  Olson on, 180–81, 185–86
  Pietism and, 104–6
  soul and, 199–200
  spiritual community relating to, 178–87, 346n128
  on truth, 213
Lutheran reform movements, 108, 184–85

Madonna, 316n49
Manichaeism, 245
marital imagery, 276
Markus, Robert
  on Augustine, 290–91
  on freedom, in judgment, 320n33
  on inner word, 60–61
marriage
  body in, 247–48, 358n113
  marital imagery, 276
martyrdom
  Augustine on, 130, 160–69
  for charity, 161
  in Christianity, 114–15
  death in, 162–63, 165–68, 338n110
  for Donatists, 160–61
  ethics relating to, 123–24
  grief in, 123
  Hegel on, 98, 114–28, 166–67, 332n99, 332n104
  heroes and, 124–26
  Holy Spirit and, 167–69
  immanent Trinity relating to, 122
  Judaeo-Christian heritage and, 121–22
  love in, 122–23, 130, 162–66
  Pentecost relating to, 161–69

of Peter, 161–62, 164–66, 168,
  279–81
reason relating to, 126
reconciliation in, 123
signs relating to, 168–69
of Stephen, 166, 168
Straw on, 163–64, 339n119
totus Christus relating to, 279–81
Mary
  love of, 33–35
  virgin, 72
Mary Magdalene, 85
materialism, 246
maternal love, 33–35, 316n49
mature philosophy, 21, 312n1
McCarthy, Michael, 274
mediator, Christ as, 75–76, 261
medieval Catholicism, 111, 177
  church hierarchy in, 191–92
medieval Germanic peoples, 200
memory
  of God, 58
  God's image and, 57–58
  knowledge and, 58
  remembering, 358n118
mercy
  Christ's body and, 284–85
  lament and, 284–86
  love and, 286–88
  as sacrifice, 292
miracle, 243–44
moaning, 144
modern European state, 177, 188,
  215
  religious freedom and, 215–17
  soul in, 201–3
modernity, 99, 329n30
  social breakdown and, 103
moral religion, 106–7
moral thought, 116–17
Muslims, 332n99

mystery
  Augustine on, 264–65, 271
  Christian, 206–10
  God as, 205–7
  sacramental body and, 205–10
mysticism, 182, 206, 344n93
  of Bengel, 211–12
  Eckhart and, 209–10
  Oetinger and, 211–12

natural soul, 196–99
nature, 281–82
neighbor, 293–94, 361n145
neoscholastics, 11
New Testament, 143–44
Nimrod, 131
Nygren, Anders, 312n1

Oetinger, Friedrich Christoph,
  211–12
Old Testament
  Augustine's rhetorical Christology on, 273–74
  Paul and, 261
Olson, Alan, 105, 108, 309n25
  on freedom, 181, 182
  Hegel and the Spirit, 176
  on Hegel's pneumatology, 176,
    178
  on Holy Spirit, 180
  on Lutheran Orthodoxy, 180–81,
    185–86
  on spiritual community, 179–82,
    185–86
O'Regan, Cyril, 21, 184, 309n25,
  358n118
original sin
  Augustine on, 74–75
  God's image relating to, 208,
    323n70
  Hegel on, 208

Ormiston, Alice, 312n1
  on love, 347n138
Ozment, Steven, 182

pantheism, 101–2
Paul
  Old Testament and, 261
  in Romans, 150
Pauline epistles, 188–89
Pelagian anthropology, 106–7
Pelagianism, 106
Pentecost
  apostles and, 156–59, 337n81
  Augustine's pneumatology on, 93–94, 95–96, 129–50
  Babel narrative relating to, 133–34, 147
  baptism relating to, 36, 38
  Catholicism and, 111
  Christianity and, 113–14
  Christ's glorification and, 140–42
  conversion of language and, 133–50
  Donatists and, 145–47, 161, 250
  dove and, 143–45, 161
  freedom, confidence, and action relating to, 150–69
  Hegel's pneumatology on, 94–95, 96, 111–14
  Holy Spirit and, 113–14, 148–49, 151–60, 250
  love and, 145, 151–60, 162–69
  martyrdom relating to, 161–69
  Peter and, 161–62, 164–66, 168
  preaching of, 157–59
  resurrection and, 136–38, 145–47, 335n51
  Romans 5.5 and, 150, 152, 153, 156, 159
  Sinai and, 155–56
  totus Christus relating to, 282–83
  Verhees on, 155
persona, body and soul in, 244, 249
personality
  of God, 21–22
  Hegel on, 21–23
  in immanent Trinity, 21–23
  Staudenmaier on, 100
Peter, 161–62, 164–66, 168, 279–81
Phenomenology of Spirit, The (Hegel), 13
  on confession, 117–19
  evil in, 98, 116–18, 119
  forgiveness in, 98, 116, 119–20
  immanent Trinity in, 23–24
  on judgment, 116–19
  Logos of Father in, 23–24
  moral thought in, 116–17
Philosophy of Christianity (Staudenmaier), 103
Philosophy of History, The (Hegel), 14, 121, 198, 200
Pia Desideria (Spener), 104
Pietism
  of Bengel, 108
  devotional, 108
  Dickey on, 105–8
  early, 104
  Holy Spirit and, 109
  Lutheran Orthodoxy and, 104–6
  Lutheran reform movements and, 108, 184–85
  during Reformation, 105, 185
  Ritschl on, 105
  social activism and, 108
  Spener on, 104
  spiritual elitism and, 105
  during Thirty Years' War, 108
  of Württemberg, 104–9, 184–85, 211

pneumatic Catholicism, 98–104,
    299–300
political recollectivization, 104–9
pope, 191
power, 69–71
    of justice, 79–91
*Pragmatismus der Geistesgaben,
    Der* (Staudenmaier), 99–100
praise
    Augustine on, 272–90
    body and, 247
    deceit and, 334n32
    grace and, 143
    lament and, 173–74, 218–31,
        272–90
    sacramental body and, 218–31,
        272–90
    spiritual community and, 218–31
    types of, 334n32
prayer, 263–64
preaching, 157–59
pride, 54
    in Babel narrative, 66
    death relating to, 87–88
    in *De Genesi adversus Manicheos*,
        66–67
    of devil, 87–88
    fall relating to, 65–71
    grace relating to, 286
    humility and, 83
    language, love of God, and,
        65–71, 133
    language, society, and, 130–33,
        147–48
    love and, 88–89
    self-destruction and, 68–69
Principle of Autonomy, 183
Principle of Subjectivity, 183
Protestantism
    Hegel on, 182–83
    Holy Spirit in, 35

principles of, 182–83
Protestant reformers, 184
Psalms, 322n65
    grace in, 274–75
    lament in, 273–74, 276, 284–85
purgative faith, 55–56

Rahner, Karl, 11
rain, 65–66
realization
    divine, 211
    of spiritual community, 179
reason
    faith and, 183
    martyrdom relating to, 126
reconciliation
    judgment and, 119
    language of, 141–42
    in martyrdom, 123
Reformation, 35, 177
    Enlightenment and, 183
    Joachimite spiritual community
        relating to, 184–85, 211–12
    Pietism during, 105, 185
religion
    justice and, 217
    moral, 106–7
religious freedom, 215–17
remembering, 358n118
res, 260–61, 356n70
rest, 266–68
resurrection
    ascension and, 44–50
    Augustine's rhetorical Chris-
        tology on, 81–82, 84–85, 136–38,
        145–47, 242–43, 265–66
    body and, 242–43, 254–55
    Christ as God and, 46–47
    Christ's humanity relating to,
        248–49
    church on, 135, 145–46

resurrection (*cont.*)
  cross and, 44–45
  double, 84–85
  Eucharistic, 231–35
  faith and, 137
  fall relating to, 85–86
  Hegel's logical Christology on, 44–50
  Holy Spirit and, 48–49
  Pentecost and, 136–38, 145–47, 335n51
  Rist on, 353n15
  sacrament relating to, 85–86
  sin and, 84–85
  spiritual community and, 190
  touching and, 138
Reuchlin, Christoph, 108
revelation, 184
  Augustine on, 222–24
  Hegel on, 224–25
Rhineland mysticism, 182
Rist, John
  on body and soul, 243, 353n19
  on resurrection, 353n15
Ritschl, Albrecht, 105
Romans 5.5, 150, 152, 153, 156, 159
Romans 8.15, 156

Sabbath, 267–68
sacrament
  Augustine on, 136, 260–71, 264–65
  Christ as, 135–36
  Eucharist and, 174, 227, 229–35, 293
  God as, 205–6
  resurrection relating to, 85–86
  social and political implications of, 290–95
  transfiguration of, 260–71
  worship and, 227–30
sacramental body
  consumption of, 231–35
  defining, 204–5
  immanent Trinity and, 205–6
  lament, praise, and, 218–31, 272–90
  mystery and, 205–10
  social implications of, 292–94
  spiritual community and, 203–35
sacrifice
  body and, 292–93
  dove relating to, 144–45
  mercy as, 292
  self-, 29–30
Saeculum (Markus), 290
salvation
  faith and, 89–90
  history, 233–34, 284
  Word of God relating to, 90
sanctification, 104–9
Schmaus, Michael, 11
Schultz, Werner, 312n1
scientific method, 228
scripture
  Augustine on, 223–24, 259–61, 265–71
  contradictions in, 225–26
  figurative exegesis of, 260–61
  Hegel on, 224–27
  language in, 223–24, 259–60
  for spiritual nourishment, 66
  thought relating to, 226–27
  totus Christus relating to, 259–61
  See also specific scripture
secular life, 214
seeking
  De Trinitate on, 53–56
  happiness, 79–80
  truth, 79–80
self-consciousness, 10–11
self-destruction, 68–69

self-externalism, 195–96, 342n55, 343n63
self-manifestation, 26–27
self-recognition, 206–7
self-sacrifice, 29–30
separatism, 288–89
serpent, 87
signs
    language and, 132
    martyrdom relating to, 168–69
signum, 260–61, 356nn70–71
sin
    death relating to, 83–85
    against Holy Spirit, 286, 360n135
    original, 74–75, 208, 323n70
    resurrection and, 84–85
    Word of God relating to, 83–84
Sinai, 155–56
social activism, 108
social breakdown, 103, 115
society
    Augustine on, 134
    in Babel narrative, 131
    Catholicism relating to, 112–13
    church and, 101, 103, 112–13
    in *City of God*, 130, 291–92
    evil and, 134
    fall relating to, 130–31
    fragmentation of, 103, 115, 130–33
    pride, language, and, 130–33, 147–48
sola fide, 183
soul
    actual, 197, 198–99
    animal, 196–97
    Aristotle on, 195
    Ayres on, 256–57
    body, church, and, 241–48
    -body imagery, 187–89, 193–203
    in Catholicism, 199
    during Crusades, 198
    death of, 84–85, 197–98
    in double exile, 67
    freedom and, 201–2
    for Germanic peoples, 200
    goodness of, 67–68
    head imagery and, 248–60
    Hegel on, 194–99
    immateriality of, 242
    knowledge of, 289
    Lutheran Orthodoxy and, 199–200
    in modern European state, 201–3
    natural, 196–99
    in *persona*, 244, 249
    Rist on, 243, 353n19
    self-externalism and, 195–96
    as substance, 195, 196–97
    telos and, 195–96
    totality of, 198–99
    water imagery for, 65
    Wolff on, 194–95, 202–3
    Word of God and, 244–45
speaking tongues, 147–51, 250, 251
Spener, Philipp Jakob, 104
Spirit of Christianity and Its Fate, The (Hegel), 9, 13, 300
    on Christ's baptism, 35–39
    Judaeo-Christian heritage in, 94, 110–11
    on Kantian ethics, 109–10
    on kingdom of God, 37–38
    on spiritual community, 178–79
spiritual community, 99, 169–70, 174
    Asendorf on, 179, 180, 185–86
    body, Holy Spirit, and, 187–203, 349n172
    Christ's body relating to, 112, 189–92
    doctrinal exposition and, 349n172

spiritual community (*cont.*)
  Eckhartian and Joachimite, 182–87, 346n128
  emerging community, 179
  Eucharist and, 190–92, 231–35
  forgiveness relating to, 119–20
  freedom and, 181–83, 185, 213–14
  human development and, 178–79, 346n126
  lament, praise, and, 218–31
  Lectures on the Philosophy of Religion on, 178, 179
  love and, 178, 203–4
  Lutheran Orthodoxy relating to, 178–87, 346n128
  Olson on, 179–82, 185–86
  realization of, 179
  resurrection and, 190
  sacramental body and, 203–35
  self-recognition in, 206–7
  soul-body imagery in, 187–89, 193–203
  The Spirit of Christianity and Its Fate on, 178–79
  stages of, 179
  Staudenmaier on, 102–3
  subsisting community, 179
  totus Christus compared to, 257–58, 280–81
  universality of, 32–33
spiritual elitism, 105
spiritualization, 135–37
spiritual nourishment, 66, 321n49
springs, 65–66, 321n49
state
  church and, 109–10, 113, 215, 291
  modern European, 177, 188, 201–3, 215–17
Staudenmaier, Franz Anton, 240
  Christianity relating to, 99–104
  on creation, 101, 102
  Darstellung und Kritik des Hegelschen Systems, 102
  on freedom, 99–100
  Hegel, pneumatic Catholicism, and, 98–104, 299–300
  on holiness, 100
  on Holy Spirit, 98–103
  on human mind, 100
  on immanent Trinity, 103–4
  on kingdom of God, 100, 101
  language of, 100–101
  on *Lectures on the Philosophy of Religion*, 103–4
  on logical pantheism, 101–2
  on love, 103–4
  on personality, 100
  Philosophy of Christianity, 103
  Der Pragmatismus der Geistesgaben, 99–100
  on spiritual community, 102–3
  on Word of God, 100
Stephen (martyr), 166, 168
Straw, Carole, 163–64, 339n119
subsisting community, 179
substance, soul as, 195, 196–97
suffering
  cross and, 85
  death and, 40–44
  love and, 69
  silencing, 68–69
superstitious disciplines, 70
Swedenborg, Emanuel, 212

teaching
  by apostles, 147
  of Christ, 64, 78
  by church, 349n172
  of God, 36, 64
  from Gospels, 37
  from Holy Spirit, 144

of incarnation, 243–44
kingdom of God and, 38–39
teleological narratives, 298
telos, 195–96
theocentric Augustinianism, 106
theologia crucis, 43
thinking spirit, 313n4
Thirty Years' War, 108
Thomas Aquinas, 9, 11
thought, 57–58
  Baur on, 5
  moral, 116–17
  scripture relating to, 226–27
  Word of God compared to, 58, 320n27
tongues, 147–51, 250, 251
totus Christus, 174, 221–23
  christological axis of, 258–59
  confession in, 295
  forgiveness in, 293
  lament and, 279–90, 294–95
  love in, 239–40
  martyrdom relating to, 279–81
  Pentecost relating to, 282–83
  scripture relating to, 259–61
  spiritual community compared to, 257–58, 280–81
  Trinitarian axis of, 259
  unity in, 282, 358n113
touching, 138
tower of Babel, 129
transfiguration
  of body, 272–90
  of sacrament, 260–71
  of will, 261–64
transformative lament, 285–86
Trinitarian doctrine
  of Augustine, 1–14, 297–305
  Baur on, 3–6
  church and, 301–2
  of Hegel, 2–3, 6–15, 176, 297–304

  problems in, 8–9
  renaissance of, 297
  See also specific topics
truth
  faith relating to, 89
  God as, 58, 205–6
  goodness and, 62
  of inner word, 57–58
  Lutheran Orthodoxy on, 213
  seeking, 79–80
  Word of God and, 57–58, 63, 320n21
Tyconius, 273–74

Ulrich, Ferdinand, 312n1
unhappy consciousness, 111
universality
  of church, 145–47, 149
  of Holy Spirit, 32–33, 46–48, 118–20, 213–15, 321n41, 337n81
  of spiritual community, 32–33

Verhees, Jacques, 74, 76
  on Pentecost, 155
Virgin Mary, 72, 225, 226
virtue, 107
von Harnack, Adolf, 1

war
  language relating to, 131
  Thirty Years' War, 108
water imagery
  Holy Spirit and, 321n49
  for soul, 65
  springs as, 65–66, 321n49
Wendte, Martin, 218
Western Trinitarian theology, 1–2
will, 261–64
Williams, Rowan, 290–91
Wissenschaft, 98
witness, 97, 98, 127, 142–43, 280–81

Wolff, Michael, 343n68
  on body, 202–3
  on self-externalism, 342n55
  on soul, 194–95, 202–3
word
  imagery, 57
  inner, 57–61, 65
Word of God
  in Augustine's rhetorical Christology, 17, 18–20, 53–92
  birth of, 31–35, 62, 64, 71–79
  charity and, 80–81
  creation and expression of, 26–31
  Enchiridion on, 72–73
  faith and, 89–90
  glory relating to, 142–43
  God's image and, 53–56
  as goodness, 72
  grace relating to, 72–74, 75, 77
  in Hegel's logical Christology, 17–20, 21–35
  Holy Spirit and, 142–43
  in human image, 61–62
  humanity relating to, 245–46
  through humility, 71–72, 78, 80–81, 276
  imagery of, 57–58, 61–62, 92
  immanent Trinity and Logos of Father, 21–27
  language and distinctions in, 57–59, 138–40
  love relating to, 6, 59–65, 92, 149–50
  persuasiveness of, 142
  salvation relating to, 90
  sin relating to, 83–84
  soul and, 244–45
  Staudenmaier on, 100
  thought of God compared to, 58, 320n27
  truth and, 57–58, 63, 320n21
worship
  Augustine on, 291–92
  freedom relating to, 229
  Hegel on, 227–29, 230, 235
  sacrament and, 227–30
Württemberg Pietism
  Augustine relating to, 105–6
  Holy Spirit and, 109
  Joachimite spiritual community relating to, 184–85, 211
  Kant relating to, 106–8
  sanctification, political recollectivization, and, 104–9

Douglas Finn is assistant professor of theology at Boston College.

www.ingramcontent.com/pod-product-compliance
Lightning Source LLC
Chambersburg PA
CBHW052010290426
44112CB00014B/2186